FOURTH·EDITION

International Marketing

RUEL KAHLER
Professor of Marketing
University of Cincinnati

ROLAND L. KRAMER
Former Professor Emeritus
University of Pennsylvania

Published by
S83 **SOUTH-WESTERN PUBLISHING CO.**

CINCINNATI   WEST CHICAGO, ILL.   DALLAS   PELHAM MANOR, N.Y.   PALO ALTO, CALIF.

Preface

INTERNATIONAL MARKETING, fourth edition, presents a managerial view of the marketing process as it applies to international marketing. Several chapters have been added to provide a more complete managerial orientation and no section has escaped at least some updating. The present edition has been divided into four parts.

Part I provides an overview of the international marketing environment and is primarily a consideration of variables that are beyond the control of a marketing manager.

Part II concerns the study of marketing from the viewpoint of the firm. It emphasizes the analysis of marketing opportunity and reviews market entry strategies.

Part III discusses the organization of international marketing within the firm and the development of an appropriate marketing mix. A separate chapter is devoted to import management.

Part IV deals with special issues confronting the international marketer, such as trade promotion, export cooperation, and marketing to centrally planned economies.

Many individuals have aided, guided, criticized, instructed, and prodded in the development of this text. Until his death in 1976 Dr. Roland L. Kramer contributed generously. His previous editions, plus his sage advice, helped guide the new edition through all but the final chapters. Dr. Kramer was an activist in international marketing; he participated in the academic development of the discipline and continued an interest through many professional groups devoted to raising the competence of academicians and practitioners. He was co-founder of the American Society of International Executives.

Earlier editions acknowledged the contributions of numerous executives and associations. To these names should be added many more, especially Raymond Bogart, Bogart International; Stephen Bass, Management Horizons, Inc.; George Hartman, University of Cincinnati; Frank L. Hung, Universal Advertising Co., Ltd., Taipei; Bert McCammon, University of Oklahoma; Felix Turel, United States Department of Commerce; and Chad Wick, Winters National Bank. The University of Michigan provided an initial interest when I served with its Advisory Team to the Republic of China; later, Ronald Dornoff, my department head at the University of Cincinnati, helped make this effort possible. My thanks to all for their help in making this text a reality.

Ruel C. Kahler

Contents

Part 4 Special Issues

Part 1 The Environment of International Marketing

1

Introduction to International Marketing

During recent years numerous American firms have played a sharply increasing role in world trade and investment. One indication of this role change is found in the growth of U.S. exports and imports. In 1974 the United States exported $98.5 billion to other countries and imported $108 billion. In so doing, the U.S. accounted for approximately 12.7 percent of world exports and 13.8 percent of world imports. Thus, the United States is both one of the largest suppliers of goods and services to the rest of the world and at the same time is a very significant customer. This trade is carried out largely through the efforts of private firms operating in the free enterprise system, but trade figures alone do not tell the whole story. U.S. companies have made substantial investments abroad, thereby contributing to the industrial base of many nations and to the investing companies' own sales and profits. By 1973 the book value of American direct foreign investment had reached $101 billion and the sales of majority-owned subsidiaries of U.S. companies were estimated at $291.5 billion. These sales were about three times as large as in 1966 and almost three times the size of American exports.

These data reflect a recent phenomenon in international business — the rapid growth of the multinational company (MNC) which produces and markets in many countries simultaneously. Many U.S. firms have participated in this trend and are now numbered among the world's leading multinational companies. The data also reflect the challenge to American marketers who must develop the marketing and logistical plans which will establish profitable operations in a variety of cultural and political contexts. In many countries American executives increasingly find themselves participating in unfamiliar business systems and catering to customers whose lifestyles are vastly different from their own. Operating in such a diverse environment places a premium on the development of marketing skills required to analyze the needs of these customers and to prepare marketing programs for reaching them effectively. This text seeks to aid the reader in the development of such marketing acumen.

WHAT IS INTERNATIONAL MARKETING?

Consider this statement, "International marketing differs from domestic marketing for one basic reason: it involves doing business with individuals, firms, organizations, and/or government entities in other countries."

True statement? Yes.
Helpful statement? Probably not.
Misleading statement? Probably so.

It is true that marketers throughout the world are concerned with the same general types of problems and activities. Marketing consists of the same broad functions regardless of the part of the world in which it is conducted. All marketers are involved in focusing the firm's resources on the satisfaction of consumers' needs. Marketers ferret out and anticipate the demand for their products, analyze the consumers' needs and motivations to purchase the product, secure physical distribution for the products, design an effective marketing mix, implement the plans, and control marketing activities. Without doubt effective marketing is as vital in international as in domestic business and a refined knowledge of domestic marketing concepts and techniques is invaluable to the international marketer. In fact, one of the major advantages of the multinational firm is that it can transfer its domestic marketing expertise overseas to gain superiority over its competition.

The opening statement is not, however, very helpful in providing guidelines to the individual marketer preparing to market goods overseas. It provides little to aid in the development of a marketing plan. Specifically, the elements that differentiate domestic and international marketing are not clearly set forth and the statement provides no guidelines for the development of international strategy.

Finally, the statement could even mislead by seducing domestic marketers into thinking that there is more similarity between the domestic and foreign markets than is actually present. Although it is possible to use many American marketing concepts and techniques abroad, these domestic marketing methods are not necessarily the most appropriate for every situation. Developing countries, for instance, with their low per capita incomes or meager communication and distribution facilities, are simply not conducive to the use of mass marketing strategies.

Many of the differences between domestic and international marketing are called environmental, meaning that marketers must deal with them but are unable to alter them. People throughout the world do have essentially the same basic needs, such as that for food and shelter, but obviously they do not all seek to satisfy their needs in the same manner. Variations in climate, physical environment, culture, and level of affluence lead to vastly different lifestyles and, consequently, to widely varying product and service requirements. Even a need so basic as that for transportation may be met by a myriad of approaches: shoes, bicycles, ships, donkeys, railroads, automobiles, and airplanes, to name a few. Although the demand for industrial goods is affected more by technical than by cultural factors, environmental factors do force industrial marketers to take different approaches to their overseas customers. Foreign industry may operate under very different cost structures in which labor costs may be low and capital costs high; in such cases buyers will prefer to substitute labor for expensive equipment rather than the reverse as in the U.S. Capital expenditures may be curtailed in order to maximize immediate profits rather than long-run benefits. The lack of adequate maintenance and repair facilities in some countries causes manufacturers to purchase machinery that is less efficient but more sturdy. Sometimes import restrictions, due to a shortage of foreign exchange, cause managers to purchase local supplies and equipment even when these are less efficient than those that could be purchased from abroad.

The marketing manager carefully researches markets to determine similarities and differences in consumer needs. Then the manager formulates an appropriate product policy to service these needs, and in the process takes into account the goals and resources of the firm. As one international student has stated, the marketer must "make what customers need and what we are good at." Since it is hardly practical or profitable for companies to meet all customer needs, the firm must scan the opportunities available to it and determine where it can make its best contribution; that is, determine where it can employ its management, capital, and labor so as to achieve its greatest return. The multinational firm does this on a worldwide basis, employing the firm's most effective resources in whatever country they are located.

International marketing differs from domestic marketing in important respects, especially the fact that marketing opportunities, practices, and constraints differ among the sovereign nations. Nations not only have disparate incomes but they also have different monetary and legal systems and place varying restrictions on the movement of people, goods, and capital. Moreover, they vary in the level of their economic development and in the structure of their economic systems. Cultural variations among the nations provide an intriguing, but difficult, problem for the international marketer. Physical distances and transportation facilities may require the use of logistical systems quite different from their domestic counterparts.

No text can offer its readers a comprehensive treatment of marketing throughout the world markets. It is impossible to present a comparison of all the possible strategies and structures suitable for successful penetration of world markets. We seek, instead, to present a framework useful for the analysis of international marketing problems, to increase an individual's awareness of international marketing opportunities, and to provide information, both conceptual and operational, on the capability of improving marketing effectiveness.

The increased interest in international marketing as an academic discipline has led to a growing body of literature dealing with the topic. Journals have been established, such as the *Journal of International Business Studies*, and existing business journals have devoted increasing space to international marketing. The *Journal of Marketing, Journal of Marketing Research*, and the *Journal of Consumer Research* have evidenced the increased international interests in their coverage of marketing activities. This in turn has resulted in the refinement, but not the standardization, of international marketing terminology. Authors regularly use the same terms to mean slightly different things. So to avoid confusion it is desirable to clarify the meaning of certain basic terms to be used throughout this text.

Definition of Marketing

Marketing is the process by which the demand structure for products and services is anticipated or enlarged and satisfied.[1] This process involves analyzing whether a marketing opportunity exists for the firm, developing suitable products and services to meet this opportunity, securing distribution of the product, designing promotional strategy to persuade potential consumers of the desirability of the offering, and transferring control over the use of the product from vendor to user so the user may enjoy the benefits.

International Marketing

International or *multinational marketing* refers to the marketing of products and services in more than one nation. It may consist of exporting goods from one country to another, or it may refer to a firm that both produces and markets in more than one country without the goods crossing national borders. For example, the Ford Motor Company exports cars from the United States to consumers in other countries. At the same time Ford also manufactures cars in Germany for sale in Germany. Both instances qualify as examples of international or multinational marketing.

The terms international and multinational apply to situations in which companies have a predominantly domestic focus as well as to those in which firms have substantial investments in so many countries that it is difficult to determine the "home country" except by reference to the location of the headquarters office. Most international

---

[1]Adapted from the Marketing Faculty of Ohio State University, "Statement of the Philosophy of Marketing" (May, 1964), p. 2.

marketers represent firms which reside somewhere between these extremes.[2]

International Trade

International or *world trade* refers to the movement of goods across national borders and relates exclusively to exporting and importing. Students of international trade analyze exports and imports and conditions under which such transfers will take place. The academic study of international trade is concerned with trade flows, commercial policy, resource allocation and adjustment, capital movements, balance of payments analysis, and international monetary arrangements.[3]

Comparative Marketing

The comparative approach to the study of international marketing, or *comparative marketing*, focuses on the similarities and differences existing among the marketing systems of various countries. It seeks to identify, classify, and interpret the similarities and differences among the systems used to anticipate demand and market products.[4] Analysis may compare national or sectoral systems either at a particular point in time or over a given period of time. Comparative analyses may be used by management to evaluate the effectiveness of its marketing in several countries. By noting the degree of similarity among countries, executives can determine the relative market potentials and establish more effective controls over the marketing effort.[5] Comparative analysis can be used to estimate the acceptance of a product concept in a developing nation by reference to conditions associated with its acceptance by other nations.[6] Grouping countries, on a basis other than physical proximity, may lead to more appropriate standards for comparison of marketing strategy and efficiency than the comparison of operations in neighboring countries. For example, comparative analysis may indicate more similarity in marketing between Australia and

---

[2]For a different use of the terms, see Donald S. Henley, "Multinational Marketing: Present Position and Future Challenges," in Boris E. Becker and Helmut Becker, *Combined Proceedings, Marketing Education and the Real World and Dynamic Marketing in a Changing World* (Chicago: American Marketing Association, 1973), pp. 41–47.

[3]See Franklin Root, *International Trade and Investment* (Cincinnati: South-Western Publishing Co., 1973) or Charles P. Kindleberger, *International Economics* (Homewood, Ill.: Richard D. Irwin, Inc., 1968).

[4]J. Boddewyn (ed.), "The Comparative Approach," *Comparative Management and Marketing* (Glenview, Ill.: Scott, Foresman and Company, 1969).

[5]See Bertil Liander, Vern Terpstra, Michael Y. Yoshino, and A. A. Sherbini, *Comparative Analysis for International Marketing* (Boston: Allyn and Bacon, Inc., 1967).

[6]Reed Moyer, "International Market Analysis," *Journal of Marketing Research* (November, 1968), pp. 353–360.

Canada than between Australia and Singapore. Management may find Canadian standards of performance a better base for judging marketing efficiency in Australia than regional ones including Singapore and Indonesia.

MARKETING IMPLICATIONS OF THE NATION-STATE

The most distinguishable feature between international and inter-regional marketing is the existence of the national state. Every international marketer must be cognizant of the nation-state, for its laws vitally affect marketing opportunity and operations. Each nation is sovereign with respect to its own internal policies and the manner in which it will deal with other sovereignties. It can pass laws governing the rights and privileges of its citizens and those of other nations residing or doing business within its borders. It can impose taxes and regulations on imported merchandise, bank deposits, investments, or any other activity that citizens of other nations seek to perform within its jurisdiction. It may even refuse to give a company or individual the privilege of doing business. No marketer can ignore the state's sovereign rights, nor can it be assumed that the rights and privileges obtained in the homeland are available overseas. Even large firms or the firms of powerful nations cannot act with impunity, although they may attempt to influence policy.

The sovereign nation not only regulates trade within its borders but also facilitates it by trade promotion. A country also can prohibit its firms from trading with specific nations or prohibit the sale of certain goods (strategic?) to specified countries. Furthermore, a citizen or firm legally can deal with citizens or firms of other nations only to the extent permitted by the respective countries. For example, the United States currently does not permit trade with Cuba and North Korea. An American citizen can legally travel abroad only if the American government issues a passport; but even with a passport, denial of a visa by the foreign host country precludes legal entry and the ability to transact business by personal contact.

Variations in Laws and Policies

The laws and policies relating to the markets of the world are determined by sovereign governments, and the rights that any corporation or person possesses depend upon the treaties and agreements that a country has made with other nations. The various Treaties of Friendship and Commerce negotiated between the United States and a number of foreign nations set out the basic treatments that each will accord to firms of the other nation in the conduct of business affairs.

Monetary Systems

Sovereignty lays the foundation for several other factors that add complexity to international marketing. One of these is the right of a nation to establish its own monetary system. Nearly every nation has its own monetary system, thereby creating problems in pricing, fund allocation, profit remission, etc. When international trade occurs, it is often necessary to deal in two or more currencies in completing the transaction. The trading operation that involves the purchase and sale of the currency of one state with the currency of another is called *foreign exchange*. For example, the number of francs that will be exchanged for one dollar is expressed by the foreign exchange rate U.S. $1 = fr. 2.44.

Variable Internal Standards

Today many governments are committed to policies of full employment and improved standards of living for their people. In such situations more than cold, immediate economic facts may be involved in guiding their commercial and investment policy. Emotion and pride spawn industries not justified by the country's resources or by the local and external markets available under the proposed cost structure (e.g., steel plants). The desire to build a cadre of experienced administrators and to exercise control over the industrial base within its borders leads states to establish work laws requiring the use of nationals in executive positions or laws which restrict the investment of foreigners to that of minority ownership.

National Security Policies

In the case of the more advanced nations, the need to survive in the face of external threats forces them to adopt a national security policy. While often necessary and appropriate, "national security" also is a banner under which many otherwise unjustified trade restrictions are imposed. Such restrictive policies are used not only by nations desiring a closed trade policy, but also by nations formally committed to the development of freer world trade. The contemporary scene demands that political, as well as economic, factors be closely assessed in order to determine the real status of the marketing environment.

Nationalism and Business Policy

Somewhat less obvious is the impact the state has on the outlook of its business people in their relationships with nationals of other countries. Also important, but not readily apparent, is the manner in which nationalism affects business decisions regarding personnel, management practices, business systems, product lines, and executive development. Even aside from the extreme cases of xenophobia, business people may be reluctant to conform to the unfamiliar codes of ethics or business practices that they find abroad, even when it is in their best interests to do so. In order to maintain control, it is common to resist the delegation of authority to foreign employees. However, in today's environment foreign employees are increasingly being appointed to executive positions.

Evolution of the Multinational Firm

The varying orientation of firms toward foreign peoples, ideas, and resources has led to the development of a classification system whereby firms may be designated as *ethnocentric* (home-country oriented), *polycentric* (host-country oriented), or *geocentric* (world oriented).[7] The classification system is useful in analyzing the basic strategy, operations, and evolution of a multinational firm. The interrelationship of the firm's underlying attitudes toward foreigners and its marketing policy is evident, as shown by the following quote:[8]

> [The ethnocentric approach] is concerned with the exploitation of a domestic production base and marketing focus. It is essentially an incremental approach to foreign markets, an attempt to gain marginal business, often on an intermittent basis, through the exportation of standard products.
>
> [Polycentricity] emphasizes differences and similarities between markets, resulting from variations in such factors as income level, socio-cultural systems, and legal framework. . . . More often than not, the view is taken that each market is indeed unique; that few, if any, outsiders can truly understand local conditions; and that local marketing managers should largely be left alone.
>
> [Geocentricity] adds the dimensions of coordination and control to a corporation's global marketing effort. In effect, a multinational (geocentric) marketing manager says, "Yes, there are differences, but we can understand and manage them." Marketing programs are adapted to meet specific marketing needs within the context of an overall corporate strategy.

A firm's early efforts in the international market may bear strong strains of ethnocentricity and are usually characterized by a dominance of home-country personnel, ideas, and strategy. An export policy

---

[7]Howard Perlmutter, "The Tortuous Evolution of the Multinational Corporation," *Columbia Journal of World Business* (January–February, 1969).
[8]Henley, *op. cit.*, p. 42.

based on existing products will likely dominate the marketing approach to foreign markets. Later, if the firm establishes overseas branches or production facilities, a polycentric approach emerges wherein local managers are given a high degree of autonomy. The home-country management is impressed by the uniqueness of the individual markets and therefore does not believe it can effectively control the foreign operation except through financial devices and general policy. Of all the business functions, marketing is especially likely to be decentralized because of the difficulty of interpreting the local market and adapting to the local marketing system and institutions; therefore, the local manager is assumed to be best qualified to determine the appropriate marketing strategy in an area.

At some point, however, it becomes apparent that the polycentric system does not allow the firm to maximize the synergistic benefits of the total company's resources; therefore, management seeks ways in which the various subunits can be more effectively meshed. The geocentric view provides the necessary worldwide orientation, and management seeks to apply a total systems approach. The intent is to find the best solution, regardless of the location and nationality of the units and people.[9] Marketing is also integrated into the overall policy. The geocentric approach is most frequently associated with the larger multinational enterprises and with their more sophisticated control mechanisms.

PLAN OF THE TEXT

The plan of this text is a simple one. It presents an essentially managerial view of the marketing process as it applies to the international field; that is, it presents a framework for aiding the manager in the analysis of international marketing problems and the formulation of marketing policies. Accordingly, the text is divided into four parts: (1) The Environment of International Marketing, (2) Marketing Opportunity Analysis, (3) International Marketing Management, and (4) Special Issues Confronting International Marketers.

Part 1 of the text provides an overview of the environment within which the individual firm must operate. It is primarily a consideration of variables that lie beyond the control of the marketer and to which the company must adjust its policy. In Chapter 2 the reader is first

---

[9]Robinson has pointed to a difficulty in establishing global responsibility and outlook. He notes that "the executives with new global responsibilities possess a set of values and a world perception that is very likely to bias their decision-making. Although they may possess the *willingness* to allocate corporate resources optimally on a global basis, in fact, they are *psychologically* or *legally* incapable of doing so." Richard D. Robinson, *International Business Management: A Guide to Decision Making* (New York: Holt, Rinehart and Winston, Inc., 1973), p. 600.

introduced to the recent trends in world trade and investment. This will provide a perspective on the scope of such activity and the relative positions of the major countries. The chapter also develops the theoretical support for commerce of this type. Chapter 3 presents an orientation to the international marketing position of the United States, showing the contribution of international marketing to the country's well-being. The chapter also describes recent trends in exporting, importing, and multinational operations. An understanding of the position of the United States in the world market provides perspective for viewing the policies and actions of American companies. Because of its impact on marketing, the major facets of the international monetary environment are presented in Chapter 4. This material will facilitate comprehension of the implications foreign exchange has for international trade and marketing.

Part 2 commences the study of international marketing from the perspective of the individual firm. This part begins in Chapter 5 by looking at the various strategies that might be used to tap potential markets abroad. These include exporting; licensing; joint ventures; and overseas branch, production, and turnkey strategies. Knowledge of these alternative strategies and the conditions under which they may be successfully employed is essential for evaluating overseas opportunity. Chapter 6 begins the analysis of foreign markets. Opportunity analysis in this text concentrates on concepts and approaches useful in the international sphere rather than a comprehensive research treatment. The student is assumed to be familiar with the analysis of domestic markets. In Chapters 6 and 7 focus of the analysis is on the economic and cultural foundations of international markets. Chapter 8 discusses regional markets as extensions of national market boundaries. Regional Trading Blocs, such as the European Economic Community (EEC) and various free trade areas and common markets are discussed because of their increased importance in world trade.

Given the existence of a profitable market, Part 3 discusses the organization of international marketing operations within the firm and the development of an appropriate marketing mix. Selected internal organizational structures and distribution systems are examined in Chapters 9, 10, and 11 to determine the conditions under which each is appropriate. Product development and policy is the topic of Chapter 12. The term marketing mix is used in its broad sense to include not only advertising and personal selling, but also pricing and financing. These topics are discussed in Chapters 13, 14, and 15. The final chapters of this section analyze the legal aspect of international marketing and the significant activity of import management.

Several issues have been treated lightly until the reader has grasped the marketing fundamentals. Part 4 presents some of these issues that affect the character, structure, and performance of international marketing. National, state, and private organizations aid in the promotion of international marketing. Their activities are covered in Chapter 18. In Chapter 19 export cooperation policies are discussed. Marketing to centrally planned countries (Chapter 20) is treated separately in this section because it represents unique challenges and opportunities and because the marketing of goods and services to these nations differs in important respects from marketing to the free world.

QUESTIONS

1. How can international marketing be distinguished from purely domestic marketing?
2. How can a marketer be misled by the statement that international marketing differs from domestic marketing only in that it involves marketing in more than one nation?
3. Carefully distinguish the marketing policies likely to be followed by an ethnocentric firm, a polycentric firm, and a geocentric firm.
4. Discuss the implications of sovereignty as a factor peculiar to international marketing.
5. Since a multinational firm operates in more than one country, can it safely avoid the restrictions and laws of the country by using its resources from other countries?
6. How does the multinational firm gain leverage over local competition through its operations in several countries?
7. Does the monetary system of a country really affect the operations of companies whose headquarters is in another country? If so, how?
8. Are marketers from other countries affected by the sovereign rights of the United States, or is the problem only one of restrictions against American firms by their own and foreign nations? Explain your answer.

SUPPLEMENTARY READINGS

Baker, James C., and John K. Ryans, Jr. *Multinational Marketing: Dimensions in Strategy*. Columbus, Ohio: Grid, Inc., 1975.
Carson, David. *International Marketing: A Comparative Systems Approach*. New York: John Wiley & Sons, Inc., 1967. Chapters 1 and 2.
Cateora, Philip R., and John M. Hess. *International Marketing*. Homewood, Ill.: Richard D. Irwin, Inc., 1975. Chapters 1 and 2.
Fayerweather, John. *International Marketing*, 2d ed. Englewood Cliffs, N.J.: Prentice-Hall, Inc., 1970. Chapters 1–3.
Keegan, Warren J. *Multinational Marketing Management*. Englewood Cliffs, N.J.: Prentice-Hall, Inc., 1974. Chapters 1–4.
Miracle, Gordon E., and Gerald S. Albaum. *International Marketing Management*. Homewood, Ill.: Richard D. Irwin, Inc., 1970. Chapter 1.
Robinson, Richard D. *International Business Management: A Guide to Decision Making*. New York: Holt, Rinehart and Winston, Inc., 1973. Chapter 1.
Terpstra, Vern. *International Marketing*. New York: Holt, Rinehart and Winston, Inc., 1972. Chapters 1–4.

2

The Significance and Benefits of International Trade and Investment

The years since World War II have brought many changes in international business. During this time the volume of world trade has increased dramatically and its composition has shifted from commodities to increased emphasis on manufactured goods. The shares of total trade held by individual countries, as well as the volume of imports and exports for each country, also have changed. Of even more significance to marketing is the form of international business. Foreign investment has grown rapidly and sales of foreign subsidiaries are larger than exports for many companies. Concomitant with this growth of investment has been a need to understand the overseas marketing environment, opportunities, and strategies as marketers have become more involved in the development and implementation of marketing strategies within the individual country markets.

This chapter chronicles the changes and trends in international business by showing their quantitative significance. This descriptive material provides a factual base for discussing international trade and investment and the gains derived therefrom. The chapter ends with a discussion of the place of marketing in international business.

Before proceeding it is worth noting that it is difficult to get exact data on world trade and investment; therefore, students are cautioned against placing too much reliance on the exact values of the statistics to be presented. As used in this chapter the data are intended to show trends and gross values. Often the specific data are based on statistics gathered to meet the needs and conditions of individual countries and vary in quality, coverage, and definition.[1] The accuracy will vary both among countries and by type of information due to the systems used for gathering the basic information. While developing nations may

---

[1]For a discussion of the problems and importance of measuring international business, see Stefan H. Robock and Kenneth Simmonds, *International Business and Multinational Enterprises* (Homewood, Ill.: Richard D. Irwin, Inc., 1973), Chapter 3.

have major deficiencies in their statistical programs, this is not universally true, nor can one always rely on data from more advanced countries. Nevertheless, we must use and interpret the available data.

GROWTH OF WORLD TRADE AND COUNTRY MARKET SHARES

World trade expanded rapidly in the period since World War II, but all nations have not shared equally in this growth. Some have increased their volume of trade and yet lost market share. During this period trade has been greatest among the developed nations of the world rather than between developed and lesser developed countries.

Growth of World Trade

There has been a dramatic rise in world trade since 1938, as shown in Table 2-1. During the period 1938–1973, the dollar value of world exports increased from $22.7 billion to $574 billion, or more than twenty-five times, and imports increased from $25.4 billion to $587.4 billion, both of which are spectacular increases. Furthermore, the growth was spread among countries of all three economic types — the advanced market economies (United States, Canada, Western Europe, and Japan), the developing market economies, and the centrally planned or communist economies.

Table 2-1 GROWTH IN WORLD TRADE (Values in Millions of Dollars)

	1938	1948	1958	1968	1973
Exports (FOB)					
World	22,700	57,500	108,600	239,700	574,200
Developed market economies	15,100	36,600	71,400	168,700	407,700
Developing market economies	6,000	17,200	24,900	43,700	108,800
Centrally planned economies	1,600	3,700	12,300	27,300	57,700
Imports (CIF)					
World	25,400	63,500	114,500	252,300	587,400
Developed market economies	17,900	41,200	74,100	179,300	429,700
Developing market economies	5,800	18,600	27,600	45,300	95,800
Centrally planned economies	1,700	3,700	12,800	27,700	61,900

Source: United Nations, *Statistical Yearbook 1974*, Table 148.

In Table 2-2 the export data have been converted to the share of world trade held by the countries grouped into each economic type. The two tables show that exports increased steadily during the postwar period for all three types with the greatest growth occurring in the advanced market economies. They were able to increase their share of world exports from 63.7 percent to 71.0 percent in the 1948–1973 period. Despite the large dollar increase registered by the developing market economies, their market share actually dropped from 29.9 percent in the immediate postwar period to only 19 percent in 1973, reflecting both the unique situation following the war and the changing market and development conditions. The abnormal situation in 1948 is revealed by the fact that the postwar share of world trade held by the developing countries exceeded their prewar share by 3.5 percent. As the industrial countries rebuilt, the share of the developing countries dropped. The low share of the centrally planned economies reflects, additionally, the cold war environment and the restrictive trade policy of both these countries and their possible trading partners.

Table 2-2 SHARES OF WORLD EXPORT MARKET

Year	Developed Market Economies	Developing Market Economies	Centrally Planned Economies
1938	66.5%	26.4%	7.0%
1948	63.7	29.9	6.4
1958	65.7	22.9	11.3
1968	70.4	18.2	11.4
1973	71.0	19.0	10.0

The data in Table 2-1 represent dollar values and, as such, do not take into account the inflation of the period. For example, the unit value index of exports from the world market economies rose from 100 in 1958 to 158 in 1973 (1963 = 100).[2] Thus, the exports of the market economy based on 1958 prices would have been $344 billion instead of $516 billion.

It would seem reasonable that imports should equal exports for the world economy, but note that two different bases are used for evaluation of these transactions. It is customary to value exports on the basis of the price at which they left the country. On the other hand, imports are valued closer to a landed cost. Thus, exports are valued at FOB (the value of the merchandise when placed aboard the vessel or plane). The import valuation includes the costs of insurance and freight in addition to the merchandise cost.

One final comment on the data: they underestimate the value of world trade to the extent that they do not include the trade among China, Mongolia, Democratic People's Republic of Korea, and Democratic Republic of Vietnam as these data were not gathered by the United Nations. World trade has been growing but the major gain has

---

[2]United Nations, *Statistical Yearbook 1974*, Table 150, p. 422.

been made by the developed economies as the increasing proportion of trade was in manufactured goods.

Country Shares of World Exports

Not only does the share of world trade vary for groups of countries, but also for individual nations. Table 2-3 uses United Nations data to show the changing export share for selected countries. Especially note-worthy in this table are the shares of the United States, Federal Republic of Germany, the United Kingdom, and Japan. In 1948 the United States' share of world exports stood at 21.8 percent. This was almost 8.3 percentage points ahead of its 1938 position and reflects the fact that the U.S. had emerged from the war with its production units intact and served as a major supplier to the nations of the world. As Europe and Japan rebuilt and began active marketing abroad, the U.S. share started to decline toward its 1973 level of 12.2 percent. Meanwhile, West Germany and Japan increased their share until they became the second and third most active exporters. These nations are expected to further improve their share in the seventies. The United Kingdom, in contrast, dropped from 12.1 percent of prewar trade to 5.3 percent in 1973.

Table 2-3 EXPORT SHARES OF SELECTED COUNTRIES

	1938	1948	1958	1968	1973
World exports	100.0%	100.0%	100.0%	100.0%	100.0%
United States	13.5	21.8	16.3	14.3	12.2
Canada	3.8	5.4	4.6	5.3	4.4
France	3.9	3.7	5.0	5.3	6.2
West Germany	——	1.4	8.7	10.5	11.9
United Kingdom	12.1	11.5	8.8	6.4	5.3
Japan	4.7	1.2	2.6	5.4	6.6
USSR	1.1	2.3	4.0	4.4	3.7
Other	60.9	52.7	50.0	48.4	49.7

Source: United Nations, *Statistical Yearbook 1974*, Table 148.

Trade Among the Developed and Lesser Developed Nations

Although it is commonplace to think that most of the trade among nations is between developed nations seeking raw materials and underdeveloped countries seeking finished goods, such is not the case. Most of the world trade is carried on among the industrially advanced nations of the world. In 1973 approximately 76 percent of the exports of the developed market nations went to other developed market countries, 4.8 percent to the centrally planned economies, and only 18 percent to the developing market economies. In the same year the developing countries sent 75 percent of their exports to the developed market economies.[3] Market opportunity for both consumer and industrial goods is greatest among the industrial countries where income is high and industrial, cultural, and economic conditions are similar or at least better understood among the participants.

The more affluent nations have both the need and the desire for goods not available through domestic production and have the economic capability to import by virtue of their own production and export capabilities. Food, fuel, and raw materials are the major items of exchange between nonindustrial and industrial nations. In 1973 the OPEC countries provided 42 percent of the exports from developing nations to the developed market economies. Manufactured goods now account for three fourths of the trade among the industrial areas while primary products represent the remainder.

DIRECT FOREIGN INVESTMENT AND MULTINATIONAL ENTERPRISE

Although more tenuous than those on world trade, the data on direct foreign investment are especially interesting to marketers because of the rapid growth in overseas investment since 1950. These data reflect the postwar growth of the multinational enterprise, its subsidiaries, and joint ventures. As such they indicate the shift that has occurred in marketing strategy as firms have turned from exports to the establishment of overseas operations. Marketing systems have had to be designed to meet these new strategies. Internal organization structures have been altered and different channels of distribution used. Furthermore, the sales of foreign subsidiaries have exceeded the export trade of many companies. The sales of U.S. companies' majority-owned foreign subsidiaries in 1973 were $291.5 billion, or about four times as great as U.S. exports of $71.2 billion.[4]

Direct foreign investment, by definition, involves a degree of control over the foreign enterprise that is not present when the firm merely has a minor portfolio investment. Strategy for controlled subsidiaries, although it may be altered in the foreign subsidiary, is at least subject to review and direction by the headquarters unit in order to facilitate global orientation.[5]

---

[3]United Nations, *Statistical Yearbook 1974*, Table 149.

[4]William K. Chung, "Sales By Majority-Owned Foreign Affiliates of U.S. Companies, 1973," *Survey of Current Business* (August, 1975), p. 23.

[5]Direct investment may involve the flow of capital from one country to another. Firms may, however, borrow funds in the local country and use retained earnings to increase the investment. The firm's equity position in a joint venture may reflect the value of technology, equipment, or other transfers. The equity position is assumed to be large enough to exercise some influence or control over policy and practice in the foreign firm.

Estimates of the magnitude of direct foreign investment have shown considerable variation due to the difficulty of obtaining accurate and comparable data and because definitions vary as do accounting and statistical procedures. Tables 2-4 and 2-5, despite these difficulties, clearly indicate the importance of such investments in international business.

Table 2-4 MARKET ECONOMIES: BOOK VALUE OF FOREIGN DIRECT INVESTMENT (Millions of Dollars)

Countries	1967	1971
United States	59,486	86,001
United Kingdom	17,521	24,019
France	6,000	9,540
Federal Republic of Germany	3,015	7,276
Switzerland	4,250	6,760
Canada	3,728	5,930
Japan	1,458	4,480
The Netherlands	2,250	3,580
Sweden	1,514	3,450
Italy	2,110	3,350
Belgium	2,040	3,250
Other	4,860	7,370
Total	108,232	165,006

Source: United Nations, *Multinational Corporations in World Development*, Table 5, p. 139.

Table 2-4 shows United Nations estimates of the book value of foreign direct investment for the years 1967 and 1971. Data are given only for market economies and exclude the centrally controlled economies of Eastern Europe and Asia. In 1971 the total direct foreign investment was approximately $165 billion, over half of which was accounted for by investments of the United States and the United Kingdom.[6] A comparison of the two years indicates, however, that some of the pattern found in world trade is spilling over into direct investment since both the United States and the United Kingdom lost ground in percentage share of the investments. As might be expected, some of this change in share represents investment increases by the Federal Republic of Germany and Japan while minor gains were made by several other developed nations. It is expected that the growth of the German and Japanese economies, together with the devaluations of the dollar in the early seventies, will result in further direct investments by these nations and that many of these investments will occur

---

[6]The OECD governments have declined to accept responsibility for the accuracy of these estimates by the Secretariat.

in the United States. Therefore, direct investments likely will be more evenly spread among the nations and the degree of interdependence among countries will increase. The 1973 book value of U.S. direct foreign investments was approximately $107 billion.

The use of book values in these estimates tends to distort the real market values of these investments mainly because they are historical and understate the values in an inflationary era. The estimates in Table 2-4, however, do appear to be in line with the $140 billion estimate for 1970 made by Robock and Simmonds.[7]

Table 2-5 (on page 21) does not show direct foreign investment, but it does give some clues regarding its importance for individual companies. Leading companies were chosen from an original list of 211 firms in the United Nations study of multinational corporations.[8] Each company on the original list had total sales of over $1 billion in 1971. Data in the table show foreign content as a percentage of sales, assets, and earnings. In examining the table note both the percentages and the absolute values. General Motors' sales to third parties (nonaffiliate firms) outside the home country represented only 19 percent of total sales, yet in dollar value these sales exceeded the total sales of Nestle, which had 98 percent of its sales outside of Switzerland. Foreign content accounts for substantial percentages of earnings and/or employment in many firms, often more than half. The range of markets and production points of the multinational firms are shown by the large number of countries in which the companies have subsidiaries. For example, IBM is represented in 80 countries; British Petroleum in 52; and Royal Dutch Shell in 43.

Management of such complex enterprises calls for high-level professional skills and controls in order to coordinate marketing programs. Companies operating in 30–50 countries and having a substantial percentage of their sales in overseas markets represent the epitomy of the large multinational enterprise. They also are the firms most likely to benefit from the geocentric orientation described in Chapter 1. They have many opportunities to gain from a global orientation and are capable of widely diffusing the knowledge they have gained in other markets.

WHY DO NATIONS TRADE?

Fundamentally, in a market system individuals trade because they expect to profit from the exchange. That is, they expect to be better off as a result of the trading. In this respect, trade occurs for the same reasons among nations as it does among regions within a given country.

---

[7]Stefan H. Robock and Kenneth Simmonds, *International Business and Multinational Enterprises* (Homewood, Ill.: Richard D. Irwin, Inc., 1973), p. 45.

[8]United Nations, *Multinational Corporations in World Development* (New York: United Nations, 1973), pp. 130–137.

Table 2-5 FOREIGN CONTENT OF OPERATIONS AND ASSETS OF SELECTED MANUFACTURING CORPORATIONS, 1971

Company	Nationality	Total Sales (Millions of Dollars)	Foreign Content* as a Percentage of			Number of Subsidiary Countries
			Sales	Earnings	Assets	
General Motors	United States	28,264	19	19	15	21
Standard Oil (N.J.)	United States	18,701	50	52	52	25
Ford Motor Company	United States	16,433	26	NA	40	30
Royal Dutch Shell	The Netherlands United Kingdom	12,734	79	NA	NA	43
IBM	United States	8,274	39	50	27	80
IT&T	United States	7,346	42	35	61	40
British Petroleum	United Kingdom	5,191	88	NA	NA	52
Volkswagen	Federal Republic of Germany	4,967	69	NA	NA	12
Nestle	Switzerland	3,541	98	NA	90	15
British-American Tobacco	United Kingdom	2,262	93	92	82	54
Singer	United States	2,099	37	75	54	30

Source: United Nations, *Multinational Corporations in World Development*, Table 3, pp. 130–137.

*Foreign content percentages refer to years 1967, 1968, 1969, or 1970.

Theory of Comparative Advantage

The theory of comparative advantage is used by economists to explain why international trade occurs and how the gains from trade are distributed.[9] The net gain from international trade results from specialization that capitalizes on differences in the relative abundance of productive resources in the various locales. Differences in climate, natural resources, technology, capital, etc., provide regions with a comparative advantage over other areas in the production and sale of some goods while other regions have a comparative advantage in other goods. Although it is possible that a nation could produce every kind of good and service it requires, it cannot produce each with equal facility. Therefore, it is advantageous for a country to produce and sell those goods in which it is most productive (i.e., has a comparative advantage) and purchase goods of a comparative disadvantage.

NCR Corporation

The United States furnishes some examples of this concept. A high level of technology, a skilled labor force, and access to capital helps explain why the United States exports such products as airplanes and computers. At the same time the country imports bicycles which require relatively less capital, less research and development, and employ lower manufacturing skills. Similarly, the large amount of land

---

[9]The theory of comparative costs is developed more fully in all international trade textbooks. For a lucid explanation see Franklin R. Root, *International Trade And Investment*, 3d ed. (Cincinnati: South-Western Publishing Co., 1973), Chapters 3–6.

favorable for farming, along with capital resources and agricultural technology, allows the U.S. to export agricultural products.

The theory of a comparative advantage shows that through trade countries can obtain both more and different goods than might be available through home production; thus providing an improved standard of living to consumers. This is the major argument favoring free trade among nations. A maximum social product would be available for the whole world if countries produced and traded where they had a comparative advantage when demand conditions warranted such trade.[10]

Theory of Natural Factor Endowments

The simple theory of international trade based on the differences in natural factor endowments has come under increasing criticism. Economists have noted that trade in industrial goods can occur even in the absence of differences in factor endowments. In fact, many of the important comparative advantages of industrial nations are artificial and arise from economies of scale, product differentiation, and technology gaps.[11] Furthermore, the theory does not adequately explain why firms choose to make direct investments rather than trade. This is a significant deficiency because international business has been characterized by greater growth in direct investments than in exports in recent years. Under these circumstances one marketer has stated:

> It is becoming increasingly evident that this traditional approach is entirely inadequate for the 1970s. The theory does not explain real-world trade flows very well, and in concentrating on nation-to-nation flows the theory deals with phenomena that are becoming less significant. In looking at trade from the country's point of view, we have lost sight of the fact that, except in certain special cases, countries do not trade with each other, companies do. . . . Many of these business firms' critical decisions involve decisions on reinvestment of earnings or raising funds in foreign countries, neither of which results in any flow across borders. The decision to export, usually seen as something quite separate from capital flows, is coming to be looked upon as inextricably linked with the decision to invest; to decide to export is a decision *not* to invest in plant, and vice-versa. Contrary to classical theory, such decisions are based more often on demand and competitive considerations than on seeking lowest cost production sites.[12]

[10]Robert M. Stern, "Tariffs and Other Measures of Trade Control: A Survey of Recent Developments," *Journal of Economic Literature*, Vol. XI, No. 3 (September, 1973), p. 857.

[11]Franklin R. Root, *International Trade and Investment*, 3d ed. (Cincinnati: South-Western Publishing Co., 1973), p. 133.

[12]David S. R. Leighton, "The Internationalization of American Business — The Third Industrial Revolution," *Journal of Marketing* (July, 1970), pp. 5 and 6.

Theory of Direct Investment

One explanation of direct investment relies on the theory of industrial organization.[13] In this approach a firm invests abroad when it can earn a higher rate of return abroad than at home, after considering the risks and the costs of operating in a different political and legal environment at some distance from headquarters. To be successful the firm must have some advantage over its competitors in the foreign country that it can transfer from one country to another. Furthermore, this advantage must be one that cannot be readily acquired by the local firms. Direct investment requires "some imperfection in markets for goods or factors, including among the latter technology, or some interference in competition by government or by firms, which separates markets."[14] Kindleberger has itemized four types of monopolistic advantages that produce direct investment:

1. Departures from perfect competition in goods markets, including product differentiation, special marketing skills, retail price maintenance, administered pricing, and so forth.
2. Departures from perfect competition in factor markets, including the existence of patented or unavailable technology, of discrimination in access to capital, of differences in skills of managers organized into firms rather than hired in competitive markets.
3. Internal and external economies of scale, the latter being taken advantage of by vertical integration.
4. Government limitations on output or entry.[15]

This theory of direct investment appears consistent with the product life cycle as expressed in business literature and presented in the following section.

International Product Life Cycle Theory[16]

Figure 2-1 presents a simplified version of the international product life cycle concept. This concept builds on the research of both business and economics scholars and postulates a cycle in which products

---

[13]Charles P. Kindleberger, *American Business Abroad: Six Lectures on Direct Investment* (New Haven and London: Yale University Press, 1969), pp. 1–36. Credit for the origin of the theory is attributed to Stephen H. Hymer, "The International Operation of National Firms: A Study of Direct Investment" (Doctoral dissertation, Cambridge, Mass.: M.I.T., 1960).

[14]*Ibid.*, p. 13.

[15]*Ibid.*, p. 14.

[16]A more extensive coverage of the product life cycle trade model may be found in Raymond Vernon, *Manager in the International Economy* (Englewood Cliffs, N.J.: Prentice-Hall, Inc., 1968), pp. 77–83; and in Louis T. Wells, Jr., (ed.) *The Product Life Cycle and International Trade* (Boston: Graduate School of Business Administration, Harvard University, 1972). The Wells text contains a review of the theoretical contributions to the concept. Several examples in this section are drawn from this text.

are first introduced in high income, advanced nations for use in the local market. Later the products are exported to other advanced countries. Later still, the initiating country loses some of its export market as other advanced nations initiate their own local production. (Some of this production is the result of direct investment by companies of the originating country as they exploit advantages of the types mentioned in the previous section.) Finally, the initiating country loses additional export markets when lesser developed nations begin producing and exporting the product. Some of these last products become imports in the initiating country.

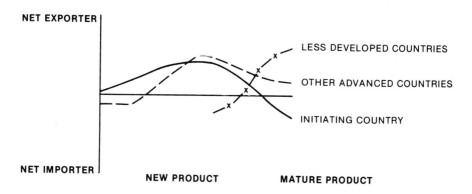

Source: Adapted with modifications from Louis T. Wells, Jr. (ed.) *The Product Life Cycle and International Trade* (Boston: Harvard University Press, 1972).

Figure 2-1 INTERNATIONAL TRADE PRODUCT LIFE CYCLE

In the initial phase of the cycle, manufacturing occurs in a developed country (such as the U.S.) where the innovator is familiar with the needs of the market and senses that a potentially profitable market exists. R&D programs promote product development in the advanced country and the risks of innovation are perceived as being lower. Also, it is advantageous to maintain close contact with the market during the initial stages when it is often necessary to adjust product and marketing programs. For an American firm this means manufacturing in the United States and selling primarily to the domestic market.

Other advanced countries may have needs similar to those of the initiating country. These countries form a potential export market. Later growth of demand in these importing nations may provide sufficient volume to justify local manufacture. Local production is especially likely to occur when the income level and size of the local market are large and when tariffs and transportation costs are high. As production begins abroad, the exports of the initiating nation grow less rapidly, especially as other producing countries begin to export.

The product life cycle theorists hypothesize a third development as the product matures. The mature product uses an already established technology and a lower skilled labor content. Consumers are more apt to be price conscious because the product is no longer a novelty and price competition will likely be prevalent. In this situation the less developed nations may be able to undersell competitors by applying their less skilled labor to the sophisticated machinery already designed to produce the product. Lower production cost will be achieved if the machinery costs do not offset the labor cost advantage.[17] Thus, the less developed nations may become attractive production points and begin exporting the product to more advanced countries. Such products as textiles and electronic components are examples of products reaching this latter phase. In cases where marketing techniques are important to achieving adequate export volume, the exporter is often aligned with a foreign firm having expertise in the developed markets.[18]

The product life cycle concept has been found useful in explaining trade among the nations.[19] In a study of the petrochemical industry Stobaugh found that the theory explained international production and trade patterns during the 1950-1960 period. The United States and West Germany had the largest markets for the intermediate chemicals studied. They also were the first commercial producers of the nine chemicals in the study. For the U.S. producers the large domestic market enabled them to expand rapidly and lower their production costs. After a time lag (during which the individual foreign markets were served by exports of end products) the U.S. began exporting to countries where the market growth had led to the construction of plants using the intermediate chemicals as inputs. Later, as world production and exports of countries other than the U.S. increased, the American exports declined as a share U.S. production but remained high in absolute amounts. Looking to the future Stobaugh saw evidence that nations having low-cost raw materials based on oil and gas supplies would become major exporters of the mature intermediate chemical products. The development plans of the Middle East countries currently reflect this potential.

Seev Hirsch suggested that international competitivness for any one industry is not likely to be constant over time.[20] As the product life cycle concept implies, countries can lose their strong competitive position when industries enter a new phase. The early competitive strength of the U.S. during the 1950s in transistors and some other consumer electronics was quickly dissipated as these products matured. Japan, Hong Kong, Taiwan, and other countries entered the

---

[17]Vernon, *op. cit.*, p. 81.
[18]Jose R. de la Torre, Jr., "Marketing Factors in Manufactured Exports from Developing Countries," in Wells, *op. cit.*, pp. 227–256.
[19]The following examples are drawn from Wells, *op. cit.*
[20]*Ibid.*, pp. 39–50.

market and began exporting to the U.S. not only because of their lower labor costs, but also because the mature product required relatively less engineering and managerial skill.

THE INCREASING ROLE OF MULTINATIONAL ENTERPRISE

Much of the trade literature is concerned with the movement of goods on the assumption that factors of production such as labor, management, technology, natural resources, and capital are relatively immobile between nations due either to natural or political restrictions; yet data earlier in the chapter (Table 2-4) also show the growth of international production under the control of multinational firms implying at least some mobility of capital and management.

Some of the shift from international trade to foreign production reflects the rapid growth of markets abroad such as that of the European Economic Community and Japan. In order to develop a market position or to retain an existing market share in these countries, American companies have acquired or established production facilities abroad. The growth of these markets has been a major inducement for expansion by foreign companies not only because it provides enlarged sales, but also because the potential warrants economically efficient scales of operation. As markets grow, the large-scale effort of the firm permits the use of management and marketing techniques that have been tested and found successful at home.

Restrictions placed on the importation of goods and national economic development planning have given additional impetus to the rise of multinational firms. The existence of tariff and nontariff barriers means that a firm must often establish production units within a country or region in order to compete effectively with local firms. Regional trading blocs, such as the European Economic Community (EEC), the Central American Common Market, etc., have widened the market for local firms by removing many of the restrictions among the nations within the bloc, thereby making possible efficient scales of operations for local producers. Since no tariff is applied to trade within the bloc but is applied to outsiders, trade may actually be diverted from the more efficient producers outside the bloc. For example, an American firm might have been the low-cost producer of certain machinery sold in West Germany prior to the formation of EEC. Following formation of the Common Market, the German industry might be served by French firms that face no tariff barriers. The American firm, though still the most efficient, would have to overcome price resistance from the higher landed cost resulting from the tariff. In this instance a possible response of the outsider is to establish production and marketing capabilities inside the Common Market. This strategy will preserve the firm's position by avoiding the tariff applied to producers outside the bloc.

Table 2-6 TYPICAL INVESTMENT — EXPORT RELATIONSHIPS OF 53 COMPANIES

Situation	Canada	Latin America	Europe Including United Kingdom	Other Areas — Developed	Other Areas — Less Developed	Total	Percent
1. Foreign governments reduced exports from the United States by tariffs, exchange restrictions, quotas, internal taxes, or other restrictions; thus requiring investment to preserve or develop a market.	15	41	29	27	20	132	22
2. The exports were being reduced by the rise of local or third-country competitors in the foreign markets; the only access to the market was through local production.	18	31	31	26	17	123	20
3. Exports of a product opened the market for sales at a volume requiring greater investment in the United States or abroad, and the decision was made to invest abroad to meet the expanded demand.	12	12	24	10	8	66	11
4. Exports of one type of product opened investment opportunities in other products of the line not formerly exported.	8	9	13	7	7	44	7

Table 2-6 continued

Situation	Canada	Latin America	Europe Including United Kingdom	Other Areas		Total	Percent
				Developed	Less Developed		
5. Investment in one line opened export opportunities for a finished product not previously exported.	10	10	13	11	7	51	9
6. Investment occurred in a market which could not be supplied by exports because a distinct local design, product, packaging or service was necessary, thus opening up export opportunities in parts and materials for these finished products.	11	9	14	9	4	47	8
7. Former exports were displaced by the investment but new and different exports were induced: materials, parts, components, finished items through and outside the affiliate.	21	23	23	22	18	107	18
8. Exports were displaced without a significant expansion of other exports.	4	8	9	6	5	32	5
	99	143	156	118	86	602	100

Source: Jack N. Behrman, *Direct Manufacturing Investment, Exports, and the Balance of Payments* (New York: National Foreign Trade Council, Inc., 1968), p. 20.

Table 2-6, on pages 28–29, presents some of the reasons given by 53 companies for their foreign investments. It reflects the complex relationship between exports and direct foreign investment as perceived by these firms. In the original study export-investment situations were outlined and companies were asked to indicate which situation was most typical for their investment in each region.[21] Several factors are evident in the results:

1. The role of market size is indicated by the number of investments in each region. The study showed that *developed* regions accounted for most of the investments by the respondent firms: 373 of 602 decisions related to Canada, Europe, or other developed areas.
2. The effect of trade restrictions on investment is represented in the response to situation 1 in Table 2-7. Twenty-two percent of the decisions were said to be influenced by governmental restrictions on imports.
3. In only 20 percent of the cases was the impetus to investment the result of an improved ability of local or third-country competition.
4. Respondents to this study indicated that in only 5 percent of the cases were exports displaced without a significant expansion of other exports. In other words, foreign investment displaced exports in very few instances without resulting in the increased import of other products of components.

Other studies tend to corroborate these results and reaffirm that market size is the major incentive for direct foreign investment.[22]

Adverse reaction on a major scale to the growth of multinational companies is of relatively recent origin. However, multinational firms are currently under attack in many parts of the world, especially among the lesser developed nations. The Andes Pact nations have sought to secure gradual replacement of foreign ownership; Mexico controls foreign ownership; and several nations including Chile and Peru have nationalized foreign firms. Even advanced nations such as Canada and the United States are concerned over the potential or actual percentage of their industry coming under foreign control. The United States government has controlled the foreign investment by U.S. firms in order to improve the balance of payments, and U.S. labor has become concerned about the effect that overseas production will have on employment. More recently, foreign investments in the United States have been under attack as protectionists have sought to retain U.S. control over its industries. Multinational oil, mining, food, and

---

[21]Jack N. Behrman, *Direct Manufacturing Investment, Exports, and the Balance of Payments* (New York: National Foreign Trade Council, Inc., 1968), p. 20.

[22]A. E. Scaperlanda and L. J. Mauer, "The Determinants of U.S. Direct Investment in the E.E.C.," *American Economic Review*, Vol. LIX (September, 1969), p. 566. Also, Robert B. Leftwich, "Foreign Direct Investments in the United States, 1962–71," *Survey of Current Business* (February, 1973), p. 35.

communications firms have been investigated to determine their impact on economies and governments.

The power of multinational firms relative to host-country governments, the influence of the firms on employment and development policy, their ability to circumvent governmental policy through access to foreign capital, and their attempts to influence internal politics are among the frequently mentioned concerns of host nations.[23]

The recency of multinational growth and the lack of data, together with differences among countries in the desire for economic development versus control of resources, makes it difficult to evaluate the merit of the arguments regarding the exact influence of the multinational firms. Various national governments and international groups currently (1975) are investigating the status and influence of multinational firms. The outcome of these investigations is likely to lead to policy measures aimed at strengthening national control over the activities of the firms within a country's boundaries.

International marketers need to be flexible in their use of various strategies for market entry to meet specific situations. The multinational firm employs several strategies in its approach. Emphasis shifts regarding the desirability of exporting, licensing, joint ventures, or the establishment of subsidiaries. For example, in 1973 the Arab countries established plans to reduce foreign ownership and control over the production and marketing of crude oil, even though foreign investment had been encouraged earlier and had played a significant role in the development of some of these countries.

The basis for much shifting strategies is evident from the comment by Ray McDonald, president of Burroughs Corporation, who noted changes in underlying conditions when he said, "In the Fifties the basic reason for overseas production was foreign restrictions on U.S. exports. In the Sixties the basic reason was cost."[24] Conditions have since changed again with the removal of some trade barriers and the rise in wage levels abroad, especially in Europe. In 1973 the dollar devaluations and the revaluations of the Japanese yen and German deutsche mark altered investment plans so that more Europeans and Japanese were considering the establishment of production units within the United States. From such a base they anticipated being in a stronger position to market goods in the large American market. These changed conditions also tended to make American products less expensive and U.S. exports increased. Thus, American initiative shifted to recognize increased potential of exports due to the devaluation and consequent effective lowering of overseas prices.

---

[23]The term "host nation" refers to the foreign country where production or marketing facilities are located or operative in contrast to the "home country" where company headquarters are located.

[24]Quoted in Sanford Rose, "Multinational Corporations in a Tough New World," *Fortune Magazine* (August, 1973), p. 52.

NATIONAL GAINS FROM TRADE

Nations gain from international trade and investment in many ways. The most obvious one is that the variety of goods available in a country is increased. Often it is either impossible or not economically feasible to produce certain goods within a country even though the demand for them may be great. Tropical fruits are an oft-cited example. Although the U.S. might produce tropical fruits in greenhouses, it is more economical to import them. Importation results in availability at a lower cost which, in turn, presents the possibility of more widespread consumption.

The increased variety of goods available through trade enhances the standard of living within a country. It provides new consumption experiences plus the possibility of buying products that more closely meet the requirements of varying lifestyles. International trade opens the world market to producers of these goods, thereby allowing more efficient and profitable production than would be possible with only local sales.

Sometimes natural resources, or derived products, cannot be developed within the nation. Scarce resources such as tin, copper, and other basic commodities must be extracted where they are found. These commodities are essential for industrial production and the only source of supply may be through trade. If the commodities are not imported, production of goods using these materials must obviously cease. Japan and the United Kingdom are good examples of countries that depend on such trade to keep their industrial plants in operation. The significance of imports is obvious where the country lacks a strong resource base but similar conditions exist even in more endowed nations. The production of many items in the United States, for example, depends on the importation of critical raw materials and energy supplies.[25]

The quantity of goods available for consumption also can increase through trade. A nation, by concentrating production on the items having the greatest comparative advantage, can trade a portion of this output for goods that have a comparative disadvantage at home. The importation of goods that are produced more efficiently abroad results in a greater variety and quantity of goods on the local market than if resources were applied to the production of goods where the country does not have a comparative advantage.

Wider markets available through international trade lead to possible expansion of plant size. If such expansion results in scale economies, there is a good possibility that the benefits of lower cost will be available to either, or both, the domestic and foreign consumers. The presence and the degree of domestic competition will determine

---

[25]See Chapter 3.

whether and how much of the savings will be passed on to consumers. This lower cost may further broaden the domestic market and make luxury products available to lower income segments.

Even when the foreign market is serviced by producing abroad, there are advantages for domestic consumers and producers since both gain from the transfer of products and technology among countries. Usually Americans think basically of selling technology abroad but America also imports technology. Think of such technological imports as radial tires, improved X-ray film, double-bladed razors, compact prefabricated construction elevators, and disc brakes. Moreover, foreign markets have been found to ease the difficulty of introducing new drug products through the Food and Drug Administration procedures.[26]

While imports sometimes are viewed as competing with domestic products, it must be recognized that imports of goods, services, and capital are necessary to provide foreigners with the means of payment for domestically produced exports. Without imports a country merely sends away its resources and products without receiving usable products in return.

GAINS FOR THE INDIVIDUAL FIRM

The value of international marketing to individual producers, financial institutions, merchants, carriers, and other businesses is not difficult to understand. They are interested in foreign trade or investment because of the direct and indirect profits derived from it. Producers not only expect a profit on the commodities sold abroad but they also see foreign markets as a basis for expanding production beyond the limits set by the domestic market. Exports enable many industries to keep their labor and capital employed more fully and continuously, to expand their plants more rapidly than domestic commerce would warrant, to realize the lower costs of operating at a more efficient size, or to distribute sales more widely so the adverse effects of local or national business recessions are minimized.

Production and marketing abroad basically are geared toward expanding markets for the firm's products, but as we have seen, they may be only attempts to maintain existing markets by producing behind trade barriers. Early penetration of the foreign market may have as its goal the preempting of the market before local competition becomes established or rivals from another country secure a foothold.

Some international marketing activity takes place because a firm's customers have moved abroad. It may be necessary to establish branches or subsidiaries in the foreign nation to continue to serve

---

[26]Bro Utall, "A Return Flow of Technology From Abroad," *Fortune Magazine* (August, 1973), p. 63.

these customers. Advertising agencies, banks, and marketing research agencies are examples of such expansion.

While many manufacturing industries in the United States historically have not been highly dependent on foreign markets, the significance of these foreign markets is growing. Despite this growth, it is possible to underestimate the effect of the foreign market on a firm's profits. A company may have only ten percent of its output in foreign trade; yet the loss of that ten percent may cause a much greater percentage loss in profits because of its effect on efficiency and overhead allocation. Some foreign sales may be made at higher profit margins than the sale of identical products in a highly competitive home market. Also, the establishment of foreign subsidiaries can expand exports of the domestic plant through the sale of both components and finished goods needed to offer a complete line of goods.

The worldwide location of production and marketing capacity provides opportunity for increased profits. An integrated logistic system can capitalize on the advantages of production and marketing in specific localities. Reduced transportation costs may result from overseas production. Advantages of scale may be achieved by concentrating production in one location and exporting to other countries.

There are other indirect methods by which profits are increased. The profits of the total company may be increased by the method of transfer pricing used when products or services are sold by one company unit to another.[27] The subsidiary may pay royalties based on its production or sale of patented products or a charge may be levied for management services from headquarters. Considered to be payment for needed services to improve the subsidiary's operation, these services also represent a technology export.

INTERNATIONAL MARKETING

It is apparent that there are multiple avenues for gain through international operations. Many of these would remain inert if it were not for marketing. It is too frequently assumed that the products of an industry having a comparative cost advantage will flow automatically to foreign markets. Actually the size of the flow depends both upon the ability of the industry to produce and upon marketing. Unless foreign markets can be developed, neither exports nor foreign investment will occur. Many exportable products will be legally excluded by potential importing countries in order to satisfy domestic employment and development policies. The foreign demand, even for necessities, may be at a minimum because of low purchasing power. However, the foreign

---

[27]The British Monopolies Commission is reported to have estimated that one international firm made $60 million from the sale of two products in Britain in seven years, sending $47.5 million back to the parent company through the transfer price, and only $7.5 million as profit. See "A Pricing Headache at Hoffman-Le Roche," *Business Week* (May 12, 1973), p. 62.

demand for many products is subject to stimulation by effective marketing and trade promotion, and one of the strengths of the American business system has been its marketing effectiveness.

QUESTIONS

1. How does a country gain from international trade?
2. Compare a policy of national self-sufficiency with a policy of international marketing from the standpoint of the economic welfare of a country.
3. What country currently is the world's leading exporter? Importer? Where can a researcher find this information?
4. "Most of the world's trade is between underdeveloped countries producing raw materials and advanced nations selling manufactured products." Comment on the validity of this statement.
5. "The share of world exports of individual countries has changed since the end of World War II." Is this statement true or false? Why?
6. Why does the text stress the significance of direct foreign investment in recent periods? How does this affect marketers?
7. International trade is advantageous to both buyers and sellers according to the theory of comparative advantage. Do you agree?
8. What significance do you see in the international trade product life cycle?
9. "Overseas investment merely replaces exports and causes employees to lose jobs." Do you agree? Why or why not?

SUPPLEMENTARY READINGS

Boddewyn, Jean. *Comparative Management and Marketing*. Glenview, Ill.: Scott, Foresman and Co., 1969.
Blough, Roy. *International Business: Environment and Adaptation*. New York: McGraw-Hill Book Company, 1966. Chapters 1–3.
Bureau of International Commerce, United States Department of Commerce, *The Multinational Corporation, Studies on U.S. Foreign Investment*, (Washington: Government Printing Office, March, 1972).
Fayerweather, John. *International Marketing*, 2d ed. Englewood Cliffs, N.J.: Prentice-Hall, Inc., 1970. Chapters 1–3.
Kindleberger, Charles P. *International Economics*, 5th ed. Homewood, Ill.: Richard D. Irwin, Inc., 1973. Chapters 1–5.
Miracle, Gordon E., and Gerald S. Albaum. *International Marketing Management*. Homewood, Ill.: Richard D. Irwin, Inc., 1970. Chapters 2 and 3.
Robock, Stefan H., and Kenneth Simmonds. *International Business and Multinational Enterprises*. Homewood, Ill.: Richard D. Irwin, Inc., 1973. Chapters 2 and 3.
Root, Franklin. *International Trade and Investment*. Cincinnati: South-Western Publishing Co., 1973. Chapters 1–5.
Salera, Virgil. *Multinational Business*. Boston: Houghton Mifflin Company, 1969. Chapters 1 and 2.
Terpstra, Vern. *International Marketing*. New York: Holt, Rinehart and Winston, Inc., 1972. Chapters 1 and 2.
United Nations, *Statistical Yearbook*.
Wells, Louis T. *The Product Life Cycle and International Trade*. Cambridge: Harvard University Press, 1972.

3

The International Marketing Position of the United States

The preceding chapter was devoted to an analysis of world marketing. It portrayed the trends and dramatic growth in both international trade and direct foreign investment. The theory of comparative advantage and the theory of direct investment were reviewed to determine the basis for these activities. Furthermore, the kinds of advantages obtained through trade and investment were seen to be significant to the nation and to the firm.

In the present chapter the focus specifically shifts to the United States, a leading world marketer. The significance of this perspective is that it permits us to view American international marketing relative to the general trends indicated earlier. We also can see the importance of international marketing in the context of a nation that traditionally has relied heavily upon its domestic production for the major part of its product requirements, a nation which has placed far less reliance on world markets for acquiring resources and selling its production than many industrial and developing nations.

In this chapter we show the contribution of international marketing to the overall well-being of the United States. The salient features of export and import trends are identified along with American multinational operations. The chapter contains a brief overview of the reasons for increased interest in international marketing by U.S. firms and concludes with a review of America's international marketing position in 1976. The material in this chapter will aid in understanding the relationship between international marketing and U.S. well-being and policy.

Before turning to a discussion of the unique position held by the United States, it should be noted that the importance of world marketing varies considerably among the nations. Most nations rely on foreign trade for at least some consumer goods as well as raw materials of all sorts, but the degree of dependence on foreign supply and markets varies from insignificance to critical dependence. The United

States is more self-sufficient than most; yet a review of world trade clearly indicates that national self-sufficiency is not a viable policy for nations aspiring to high levels of economic development and consumer affluence. Not even the United States can rely on domestic production for all of its goods and services and even if it were possible to produce all goods domestically, it might not make sense economically. The previous chapter indicated that a higher standard of living may be attained by trading those goods and services for which the nation has a comparative advantage for those in which it has a comparative disadvantage. These facets of our national welfare become evident in an analysis of the United States' international marketing position.

DEPENDENCE ON FOREIGN MARKETS AND RESOURCES

The U.S. is fortunate in not being as dependent on foreign sources of supply as are many other nations, including those of Western Europe and Japan. Within the boundaries of the United States there is a wide range of natural resources and climatic conditions that enable it to be more self-sufficient. In 1974 the U.S. had a population of 212 million people with a per capita disposable income of $4,623, and personal consumption expenditures of $4,139 per capita. The U.S. labor supply is educated and skilled. Business is characterized by a high degree of managerial skill and energy, the application of advanced technology, and effective communication and transportation services. Heavy capital outlays have complemented these resources and led to the development of mass production and marketing. This combination of resources has made possible the development of industries capable of providing a wide range of goods and services to the American people and to the foreign markets.

Import Dependence

The U.S. is both an industrial and an agricultural nation — the range of its manufacturing industries, indeed, is constantly widening, but at the same time the nation is also a substantial producer of farm, mineral, and marine products.

Despite its impressive list of resources and the wide variety of American-made products, the United States imports many products. In 1974 the country imported approximately $100 billion of goods and services.[1] While some of these imports could have been produced within the U.S., it was not profitable to do so. In fact some of the 1974 imports were critical minerals not available from domestic sources.

---

[1]U.S. Department of Commerce, "United States Foreign Trade Annual, 1968-1974," *Overseas Business Report 75–22* (April, 1975), p. 10.

For example, we get 100 percent of our diamonds and chromium from abroad. Some imports could have been produced within the U.S., but only at higher costs than purchasing them from abroad, thus prices to consumers would have risen to meet the higher costs. Finally, some imports such as sports cars, perfumes, and television sets add zest to our lifestyles by increasing the variety of goods and entertainment available. These products meet the requirements of specific market segments not adequately served by domestic output. In 1970 fifteen percent of our passenger cars and thirty percent of our radios and TVs were imported. Interesting too is the fact that most of our favorite hot beverages are imported — coffee, tea, and cocoa. From these examples it is apparent that both our industrial structure and our consumption patterns would be noticeably altered if we were denied access to foreign sources of supply.

Export Dependence

Nations are dependent on foreign markets not only as sources of supply, but also as outlets for domestically produced goods and as investment opportunities that permit firms to capitalize on their knowledge and skills by exporting product, process, and management technology.

As in the case of imports, American industries are not as dependent upon foreign markets as those of many other nations. Because the nation is relatively self-sufficient (compared to other developed countries) in its home market and because of the very large domestic market potential, American firms have found it possible to support efficient-sized operations based on the domestic market.

Export sales, however, have been an important factor in the profitability of certain American industries and firms. U.S. Department of Commerce data covering the period from 1960 to 1968 indicate that a number of U.S. industries have regularly exported in excess of 15 percent of their output — for a few of these the percentage is much higher.[2] In Chapter 2, Table 2-5, some of the large U.S. multinational firms were shown to have up to 50 percent of their sales and up to 75 percent of their earnings from exporting and overseas production.

Except for that portion of their output which is returned to the U.S., overseas production by American firms is wholly dependent on foreign markets. Some of these markets are now growing more rapidly than the U.S. market, especially in product areas approaching high levels of saturation at home. Even when these markets cannot be tapped by exporting goods and services, they represent a potential for

---

[2]U.S. Bureau of the Census, *Statistical Abstract of the United States, 1971* (Washington: U.S. Government Printing Office, 1971), Table 1246, p. 776.

exporting technology through the strategies of licensing, joint venture, and turnkey operations.[3]

QUANTITATIVE IMPORTANCE OF U.S. INTERNATIONAL TRADE

The United States is the world's leading exporter and importer of merchandise. Out of a total world export trade (including the centrally planned economies) in 1973 of $574 billion, the United States accounted for $70.2 billion, or 12.3 percent, followed by West Germany with 11.9 percent, and Japan with 6.6 percent.[4]

As the world's leading import nation, the United States in 1973 imported $68.7 billion or 11.7 percent of world imports of $587.4 billion. Germany followed with $55.5 billion, or 9.4 percent, France with 6.3 percent, the United Kingdom with 6.6 percent, and Japan with 6.5 percent.[5]

Value of U.S. Exports and Imports

The quantitative history of American exports and imports is portrayed in Table 3-1. The data show a marked continuous increase in both exports and imports during the present century except during the worldwide depression of the 1930s. Merchandise exports underwent sharp increases in the World War II and postwar periods. Since the end of World War II the United States has been able to maintain and increase total exports until they reached $97.9 billion in 1974. Imports followed a similar pattern, but rose rapidly in the early 1970s until they exceeded exports in 1971 and 1972, thereby producing a deficit in the merchandise balance.[6] The year 1973, however, saw a resurgence of exports due to world supply and demand conditions for agricultural products and because of the dollar devaluations which made U.S. products more competitive in the world market.[7] By 1974 imports again exceeded exports, but in a dramatic reversal the U.S. had a trade surplus in 1975 partly due to a high level of agricultural exports and reduced imports.[8] Exports and imports were affected by the reduced level of industrial activity in the U.S. and Europe as economic recovery was slow.

---

[3]Turnkey operations involve contracts to establish functionally operating plants in other countries. See Chapter 5 for details.

[4]*United Nations Statistical Yearbook, 1974*, Table 148, pp. 406–413.

[5]*Ibid.*

[6]U.S. Bureau of the Census, *Highlights of Exports and Imports*, Report FT990 (Washington: U.S. Government Printing Office, 1974), Tables E-1, p. 37, and I-1, p. 79.

[7]"Basic Developments in U.S. Balance of Payments," *Federal Reserve Bulletin* (April, 1974), p. 239.

[8]*Federal Reserve Bulletin* (March, 1976), p. A58.

Changes in price levels, of course, can conceal the actual volume changes in foreign trade. The sixties and early seventies were periods of inflation; thus, the quantity of exports and imports increased less than their total dollar value. The unit value index of U.S. exports increased from 101.4 (1967 = 100) in 1968 to 175.5 in 1974. The quantity index for the same years moved from 108.2 to 179.5. During the same period the export value index rose from 109.7 to 315 reflecting the increases in both unit value and quantity.[9]

Table 3-1   MERCHANDISE EXPORTS AND IMPORTS OF THE U.S. (In Millions of Dollars)

Yearly Average	Total Exports	Total Imports	Imports as a Percentage of Exports
1901–1910	1,616	1,159	71.7
1911–1915	2,371	1,712	72.2
1915–1920*	6,521	3,358	51.5
1921–1925	4,397	3,450	78.5
1926–1930	4,777	4,033	84.4
1931–1935	2,025	1,713	84.6
1936–1940	3,220	2,482	77.1
1941–1945	10,051	3,514	35.0
1946–1950	11,829	6,659	56.3
1951–1955	15,333	10,831	70.7
1956–1960	19,204	13,650	71.5
1961–1965	24,007	17,656	73.5
1966–1970	36,013	32,293	89.7
1971	44,130	45,563	103.2
1972	49,778	55,583	111.7
1973	71,314	69,121	96.9
1974	97,907	100,972	103.1

Sources: U.S. Bureau of the Census, *Statistical Abstract of the United States*, annual editions (Washington: U.S. Government Printing Office); U.S. Department of Commerce, *United States Foreign Trade Annual 1968–1974* (Washington: U.S. Government Printing Office); U.S. Bureau of the Census, *Highlights of the U.S. Export and Import Trade*, Report FT990, December, 1973 (Washington: U.S. Government Printing Office, 1974).
*July 1, 1915–December 31, 1920.

Gross National Product and International Marketing

Efforts to measure the importance of international marketing to the total economy of a country lead to a comparison of international trade and some macro-indicator of output. One common comparison is

---

[9]U.S. Department of Commerce, *United States Foreign Trade Annual 1968–1974, Overseas Business Report*, OBR 75-22, p. 4.

that between exports and gross national product. Since 1929 U.S. exports have generally ranged from 3 to 6.8 percent of GNP. In 1973 exports were $71.3 billion or 5.5 percent of GNP. Many countries of the world have much higher ratios — a fact which may help to account for their more pronounced interest in foreign trade and the support their governments are willing to give to promote trade. The small percentage of GNP accounted for by U.S. exports, however, understates the importance of that trade for many individual companies.[10]

Exports As a Share of Domestic Production

The Department of Commerce periodically publishes compilations revealing the relation of exports to production for a number of individual commodities. The data show wide variations among the commodity groups. For example, in 1971 the compilations showed that for certain minerals, such as molybdenum and phosphate, our domestic exports represented about 47 percent of domestic output. Some 60 percent of civilian aircraft production was exported along with 27 percent of the domestic output of sewing machines and parts. The airplane exports reflect the technological position of the American airplane industry. On the other hand, only 4 percent of the domestic production of passenger cars and chassis and 18 percent of household television receivers were exported. The large American car meets a limited market abroad while the U.S. actually imports many TVs. Clearly the export function is of more importance for certain industries than for others. These data reflect only exports from the U.S. and do not indicate the sales of foreign subsidiaries, joint ventures, or other strategies other than exporting. For some companies these overseas production strategies for tapping foreign markets are much more significant than exporting.[11]

Imports As a Percentage of New Supply

One measure of the significance of imports is to compare the value of imports for specific products to the domestic production plus imports for that commodity. Imports plus domestic production represent the "new supply" for the item, i.e., the increased amount available in the domestic market. Since domestic production does not exist for some products, the percentage of imports to "new supply" of these items is 100 percent. As might be expected, this is true for such agricultural products as coffee, cocoa beans, copra, and sisal. Also, sources

---

[10] See Chapter 2, Table 2-5.
[11] U.S. Bureau of the Census, *U.S. Commodity Exports and Imports as Related to Output, 1971 and 1970* (Washington: U.S. Government Printing Office, 1974).

using minerals such as diamonds and chromium rely totally on imports, while 61 percent of the mercury and 97 percent of our manganese ores come from abroad, along with 68 percent of our newsprint. Among manufactured products 49 percent of the sewing machines, 30 percent of the radio and television sets, and 15 percent of passenger cars and chassis are imported.[12]

High percentages indicate heavy reliance on imports as a source of supply; yet even low percentages of critical items may be extremely important in maintaining output and employment in specific industries and companies. The imports, when priced lower than domestic goods, also create pressures to lessen the rate of inflation and to expand the variety of goods available to meet the needs of specific market segments.

As consumers and industrial buyers, we have become acutely aware of the value of imports. Significant impact has been made on the American lifestyle by the importation of automobiles, motorcycles, television sets, bicycles, and sewing machines. They have provided both new and differentiated products as well as lower-cost products.

The Port of New York Authority

The Arab embargo in 1973–1974 and the energy crisis focused attention on the critical nature of certain imports. Whereas earlier the attention in trade negotiations was focused on obtaining easy access to

---

[12]*Ibid.*

markets for exports, Treasury Secretary George Schultz told the Congressional Joint Economic Committee that "more emphasis is needed with respect to *restrictions on the supply* of internationally traded commodities, alongside the traditional emphasis on access to markets." He added, "We need a 'least-favored-nation' concept of some kind on supply. . . . If there are to be some restrictions on supply they should apply as a trading rule to everybody."[13] While these words may have been provoked by the selective use of the embargo for political ends, they nevertheless reflect increasing concern over our ability to compete for foreign resources. This aspect of international marketing may become even more important as the demand for fuels and minerals grows. Some fuels and metals may already be in short supply.[14] Already over half of the U.S. supply of six basic metals (aluminum, chromium, manganese, tin, nickel, and zinc) is now imported.[15] The prognosis is for increased reliance on imports to support our expanding industrial structure.

Exports and Imports by Commodity Group

Figure 3-1 (page 44) provides an overall view of U.S. international trade by commodity groups for the year 1974. One striking feature is the importance of manufactured products. If the two categories "Other Manufactured Goods" and "Machinery and Transportation Equipment" are combined, they account for 56.3 percent of American exports. Interestingly, these same two categories represented 51.7 percent of imports. The two-way flow, however, represents the marketing of dissimilar items within the same broad classification. Some of these are different items such as automobiles, aircraft parts, or furniture, or they are different styles and brands in the same category. Automobiles are both exported and imported, but Fords and Cadillacs meet the requirements of different market segments than do Datsuns and Volkswagens. International marketing thus provides for a better fit between need and product.

Agricultural commodities represented a smaller percentage of both imports and exports than nonagricultural commodities. But the agricultural trade represents a higher percentage in 1973 and 1974 relative to previous years. The year 1973 was a period of food shortage in many parts of the world due to poor harvests and demand for high protein foods. This was the year in which heavy grain shipments were made to the USSR, India, Japan, People's Republic of China, and Korea. Prices of agricultural exports rose 50 percent and volume rose by 25 percent

---

[13]"U.S. May Focus More on Access to Supply in International Trade Talks," *The Wall Street Journal*, February 11, 1974, p. 4.

[14]Cf. the September and October 1972 issues of *Fortune* for "Our Finite Riches," a discussion of energy and metals problems.

[15]Richard J. Levine, "America's Dependence on Imported Metals Seen Leading to a New Crisis," *The Wall Street Journal*, December 26, 1973, p. 1.

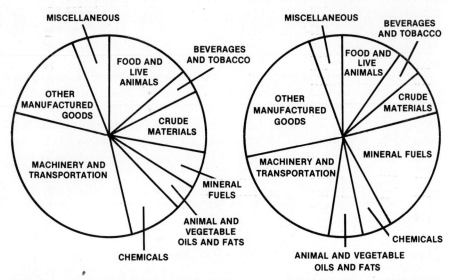

EXPORTS

MISCELLANEOUS
FOOD AND LIVE ANIMALS
BEVERAGES AND TOBACCO
OTHER MANUFACTURED GOODS
CRUDE MATERIALS
MACHINERY AND TRANSPORTATION
MINERAL FUELS
ANIMAL AND VEGETABLE OILS AND FATS
CHEMICALS

IMPORTS

MISCELLANEOUS
BEVERAGES AND TOBACCO
FOOD AND LIVE ANIMALS
OTHER MANUFACTURED GOODS
CRUDE MATERIALS
MINERAL FUELS
MACHINERY AND TRANSPORTATION
CHEMICALS
ANIMAL AND VEGETABLE OILS AND FATS

Source: Adapted from U.S Department of Commerce, *United States Foreign Trade Annual, Overseas Business Report*, OBR 75-22 (April, 1975).

Figure 3-1 U.S. EXPORTS AND IMPORTS OF DOMESTIC MERCHANDISE BY COMMODITY GROUP IN 1974

during the year.[16] Many of these food shortages and shipments continued in 1974 and 1975.

The import data for mineral fuels reflect the combined impact of the Arab embargo and increased prices. In 1972 fuels accounted for only 8.6 percent of imports, but by 1974 that share had grown to 25.1 percent despite governmental and private attempts to reduce our dependence on imported fuels. The dollar value of petroleum imports alone grew from $4.3 billion in 1972 to $24 billion in 1974 reflecting both price increases and increased dependence on imported oil.

MARKETS FOR U.S. PRODUCTS AND SOURCES OF SUPPLY

Having seen in a general way the trends of U.S. trade and its composition, it is useful to locate the markets for these products. Where are these products sold and how important are the individual markets? At the same time many of these countries also supply goods to the U.S. An overview of both these markets and sources of supply is shown in Figure 3-2. Growth in the dollar value of trade to all areas is revealed by the comparison of 1967 and 1974 data.

---

[16]"Recent Developments in the U.S. Balance of Payments," *Federal Reserve Bulletin* (April, 1974), p. 239.

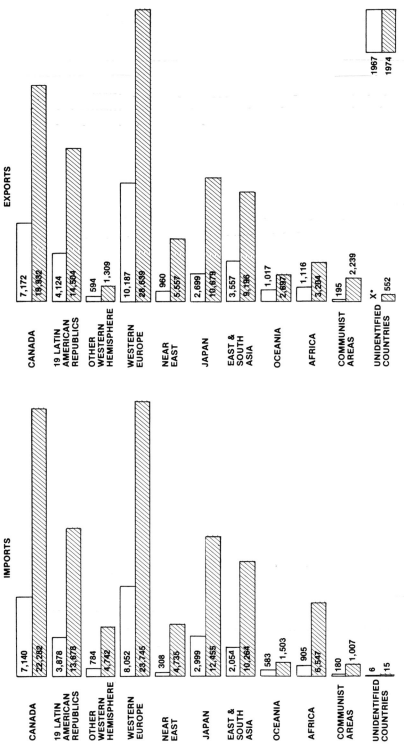

Source: U.S. Department of Commerce, *United States Foreign Trade Annual 1967–1973*, *Overseas Business Report*, OBR 74-06 (April, 1974), Table 10, p. 18, and *United States Foreign Trade Annual 1968–1974*, OBR 75-22, p. 18.

X* Not applicable.

Figure 3-2 U.S. EXPORTS AND IMPORTS BY GEOGRAPHIC AREA IN 1967 AND 1974 (Values in Millions of Dollars)

EXPORTS

Area	1967	1974
CANADA	7,172	19,932
19 LATIN AMERICAN REPUBLICS	4,124	14,504
OTHER WESTERN HEMISPHERE	594	1,309
WESTERN EUROPE	10,187	28,639
NEAR EAST	960	5,557
JAPAN	2,699	10,679
EAST & SOUTH ASIA	3,557	9,196
OCEANIA	1,017	2,697
AFRICA	1,116	3,204
COMMUNIST AREAS	195	2,239
UNIDENTIFIED COUNTRIES	X*	552

IMPORTS

Area	1967	1974
CANADA	7,140	22,282
19 LATIN AMERICAN REPUBLICS	3,878	13,678
OTHER WESTERN HEMISPHERE	784	4,742
WESTERN EUROPE	8,052	23,745
NEAR EAST	308	4,735
JAPAN	2,999	12,455
EAST & SOUTH ASIA	2,054	10,264
OCEANIA	583	1,503
AFRICA	905	6,547
COMMUNIST AREAS	180	1,007
UNIDENTIFIED COUNTRIES	6	15

Canada is America's largest single international market and supplier. This is not too surprising when Canada's relative affluence, industrial development, and proximity are considered. The mobility and frequent border crossings of both Canadians and Americans along with overlapping broadcast and print media facilitate cultural exchange. Similar industrial and agricultural conditions also tend toward parallel needs. In 1974 the U.S. supplied 67 percent of Canada's imports, while 66 percent of Canada's exports went to the U.S.[17] In 1974 U.S. exports to Canada were valued at $19.9 billion.

Western Europe absorbed $28.6 billion of U.S. exports and provided $23.7 billion of imports. One would expect fairly high exchanges with Europe based upon earlier findings that much of international trade occurs among advanced countries. The years since World War II have brought remarkable recovery to the Europeans who now represent both an important market and a source of competition.

Both imports and exports from Japan quadrupled in value between 1967 and 1974 and Japan became our second largest market. Imports from the Near East increased dramatically to $4.7 billion in 1974 due to rising oil prices. Taken as groups, the 19 Latin American republics and the East and South Asia markets each represent significant markets which account for $13.7 billion and $10.3 billion respectively.

While these data point to the significance of markets for all U.S. exports, the relative importance of the countries as buyers or sellers of specific products may be quite different. A market that takes only a small portion of U.S. exports may, nevertheless, be a major market for a specific product because that product meets a specific need. For example, the potential for oil drilling or mining equipment may not conform to the general pattern of trade among nations, but rather depends on the existence of an oil field or mine in a country.

DIRECT FOREIGN INVESTMENT

Export and import data do not completely reflect a nation's marketing posture when investments have been made in foreign production facilities. The sales of U.S. foreign subsidiaries are not considered as U.S. exports. Some estimates of the sales made by these subsidiary operations show them as much as four or five times greater than exports.[18] In 1973 the sales of majority-owned foreign affiliates of U.S. companies were estimated at $291.5 billion while exports were $71 billion.[19] Obviously these subsidiaries represent an alternate strategy

[17]*United States Foreign Trade Annual, 1968–1974*, p. 19.
[18]"U.S. Global Firms' Output Tops Our Exports 5-1," *Journal of Commerce* (April 18, 1973), p. 2.
[19]William K. Chung, "Sales by Majority-Owned Foreign Affiliates of U.S. Companies, 1973," *Survey of Current Business* (August, 1975), p. 23.

for tapping the potential of the foreign markets and become significant sources of revenue for individual companies. Names such as Ford, General Motors, Singer, and Procter and Gamble are associated with their overseas operations as much or more than with their exporting.

American firms are widely represented in the world. Investment statistics indicate participation in most of the free world. In fact, direct investment by U.S. companies may well approximate one half of the total worldwide direct investment.[20] Even though European nations early recognized and capitalized on investment opportunities in other nations, U.S. direct investments have dominated the scene since World War II. These foreign investments are large in dollar terms, but they represent only a minor portion of total private investment by American firms in all markets combined including the United States. These foreign investments have been extremely significant in maintaining market position abroad where trade barriers preclude exports and in securing a position in growing markets. Also, American firms have invested abroad because in the past these investments have promised higher returns than those available in the highly competitive U.S. markets. In 1973 the direct foreign investment of American firms approximated $107 billion, or more than double the 1965 investment of $49 billion. Rapid growth in investment has occurred in petroleum and manufacturing as these two industries account for $66 billion of the total.

The location of direct investments is not necessarily coincidental with its marketing impact because subsidiaries sell in several markets when it is profitable to do so, including the U.S. However, the geographic spread does indicate where American firms have found it profitable to invest. Approximately 26 percent of U.S. direct foreign investment was made in Canada. Percentages for other areas were: United Kingdom, 10.4 percent; the expanded European Economic Community (including the United Kingdom), 29 percent; and Latin America, 13.8 percent.

Foreign investments also flow the other way. The U.S., as the largest market in the world, also attracts investments from abroad as well as imports. Many foreign companies have been operating in the U.S. for so long that they are often considered U.S. firms, such as Nestle (Nestle Alimentana, Switzerland), Shell Oil (Royal Dutch Shell, The Netherlands), and Lever Brothers (Unilever Group, United Kingdom and The Netherlands). Foreign direct investment in the United States at $17.7 billion in 1973 is small compared to the U.S. investment abroad and compared to the U.S. economy.[21] For individual companies, however, the strategy can produce dramatic results. For example,

---

[20]In 1966 the U.S. direct investment was $54.5 billion, or 60 percent of the global total of $89.6 billion. S. Stanley Katz, *The Multinational Corporation: Studies on U.S. Foreign Investment* (Washington: U.S. Government Printing Office, March, 1972), p. 8.

[21]Robert B. Leftwich, "Foreign Direct Investment in the United States in 1973," *Survey of Current Business*, Vol. 54 (August, 1974), p. 7.

Matsushita Electric Industrial Company of Japan consolidated its position in the U.S. television and radio market and surpassed such competitors as Sony and Hitachi by purchasing the Motorola color TV facilities.[22]

WHY THE INCREASED U.S. INTEREST IN INTERNATIONAL MARKETING?

For longer than it has been a nation the United States has been involved in foreign trade; yet only recently has international business and marketing become prominent in the U.S. Lately the federal government has more actively supported foreign trade and, increasingly, private entrepreneurs are expanding into the international market. Some specific reasons may be given for this increased awareness.

The major reason for considering export operations or direct investment has been the dramatic growth of foreign markets. Industrial recovery in the postwar era and emphasis abroad on economic development and increased incomes have created a substantial potential for American goods and services. Furthermore, the enlarged markets provide an opportunity to employ American mass marketing skills, especially as regional groupings (e.g., The European Economic Community) expand marketing opportunities beyond the borders of the country where a factory might be located. The formation of free trade areas and common markets facilitates trade within the member countries, but maintains trade barriers against outsiders. Thus, American interests are attracted to the larger and more affluent markets, but they quickly find that new strategies are needed for marketing. Some approached the problem by locating production units within the market and marketing through these subsidiaries to the enlarged market.

The United States market, at the same time, was becoming increasingly competitive and growing at a slower rate than some foreign markets. For products with relatively high levels of saturation at home, it appeared more profitable to investigate expansion abroad. Higher profit rates abroad with lesser marketing effort could bring substantial results in markets where product saturation was low and competition sometimes less severe.

Additionally the U.S. government became concerned over a declining balance of trade (and finally a deficit). Expanded trade was one route to improving the balance of payments situation; therefore, government began a more concentrated international trade promotion program and actively sought to involve companies that previously

---

[22]"Why Matsushita Bought Motorola TV," *Business Week* (March 16, 1975), pp. 30–31.

were not exporting. Foreign aid programs created additional opportunities for marketing abroad when grants were tied to purchases from the U.S. Changing monetary relations through devaluations and currency floats also changed trading opportunities. The dollar devaluations tended to make U.S. goods more competitive when it lowered their prices in local currency.

Increased tourist travel, military service abroad, and business travel brought Americans into increased contact with foreign cultures, thereby stimulating interest in foreign products and providing an awareness of marketing opportunities abroad. Courses in international business and marketing contributed to this awareness by clarifying the opportunities, challenges, and methods of international commerce. In this sense foreign markets, even though unique, were less strange.

AMERICA'S BICENTENNIAL POSITION

By 1976 the international market had changed from that of the post-World War II era and the 1960s. Many of the recovery trends had run their course in Europe. Worldwide recession and inflation shifted the economic balance among countries, and political developments changed marketing prospects in East-West trade as well as in individual countries such as Chile and Argentina. Some multinational firms were suspect in lesser developed countries for various reasons including the disclosures of commercial bribery and grain inspection scandals. These and other factors were causing companies to reappraise their marketing strategy. Nor was the effect only on American firms since European and Japanese companies faced the same international market and needed adaptation to their special circumstances. Some of the European reassessment involved consideration of marketing and production in the U.S. through direct investment.

Important among the many factors leading to changed marketing strategies were the continued strength and structure of the U.S. economy, the effects of dollar devaluation and other currency realignments, supply shortages, and political developments here and abroad.

The American economy and political system has been able to weather the strains of the deepest recession since the 1930s. In relative terms the U.S. remains strong as the world's largest national market and as a major marketer and investor abroad. A large agricultural base provides much needed grains to the world market and contributes to a favorable trade balance. U.S. rates of inflation in the middle seventies are high relative to the immediate past, but are lower than in other industrial countries, and dollar devaluations have lowered prices in foreign currencies. Thus, American goods again became bargains. Inflation abroad also brought about a realignment of wage rates so that European and Japanese firms no longer have as great a labor advantage and in some instances foreign productivity has not matched that in the U.S.[23]

In Europe conditions promoted consideration of overseas investment even by European companies which were traditionally reliant on exports. In early 1976 Volkswagen decided to begin assembly operations in the United States and Volvo was already building a plant in Virginia. Nestle had purchased Stouffer's and acquired control of Libby, McNeil and Libby. BASF, the West Germany chemical giant, had invested $700 million in the U.S.[24] Other British, Swiss, and French companies were active in acquiring U.S. firms and facilities. What conditions prompted the large growth in U.S. investments by these firms? What is their effect on U.S. markets and marketers?

Economic instability, unemployment, and inflation replaced the rapid European and Japanese growth pattern of the 1960s. In Europe population growth rates declined and consumer markets became less expansive. Public sector expenditures absorbed a large portion of GNP. In addition, the European entrepreneur faced an array of business restrictions and labor woes. Technological innovations and modern management methods were likely to be less an expansion factor than in the sixties as attention turned to unemployment problems rather than labor saving.[25] These conditions, together with the large U.S. market, American trade barriers, and the ability to cut labor and transportation costs, prompted some Europeans to place more emphasis on direct investment in the U.S. rather than on exporting as a marketing strategy.

Direct foreign investment in the U.S. approximately tripled between 1965 and 1975 reaching an estimated $25 billion.[26] Those investments were made as market entry strategies or to expand or maintain market share. The recent growth of these investments has made many Americans wary of foreign control, which led the U.S. Congress to pass the Foreign Investment Study Act of 1974 to gain more information regarding the phenomenon. In some instances, (e.g., Copperweld), the foreign investment was actively resisted. Meanwhile, however state trade missions continued to seek such "reverse investment." One mission reported talking to 50 European companies to encourage them to invest in Ohio.[27] Thus, the marketing and investment strategy of Europeans was being both resisted and assisted. Meanwhile, American

---

[23]In West Germany unit labor costs in manufacturing rose 17.4 percent (in terms of U.S. dollars) from 1970–1975, while the increase in the U.S. was only 6.4 percent. "More Foreign Investors Are Beating a Path to America," *U.S. News & World Report* (April 26, 1976), p. 66.

[24]*Ibid.*

[25]"Business: Europe's 'Sick Man'," *U.S. News & World Report* (April 12, 1976), p. 78.

[26]"More Foreign Investors Are Beating A Path To America," *loc. cit.*

[27]*Ohio/World Trade News* (April, 1976), p. 1.

firms continued their own direct investments abroad. In 1974 these private U.S. direct investments abroad amounted to $7.5 billion.[28]

The effective penetration of U.S. markets by foreign exporters has encountered resistance from American producers in particular industries. Manufacturers of nonrubber shoes, for example, sought higher duties and/or import quotas when imports reached 287.7 million pairs valued at $1.1 billion in 1975.[29] The International Trade Commission found that imports were a substantial cause of serious injury to the American shoe industry but did not agree on a proper remedy. Later President Ford rejected the imposition of higher tariffs and quotas and opted for trade-adjustment assistance to workers and manufacturers to help them adjust to the new competitive situation. Shoe retailers claimed that higher duties would have added $1 billion dollars to the consumers' annual shoe bill.[30]

The shoe case represents only one of a number of U.S. industries asking for relief from foreign competition. In a case involving specialty steels the International Trade Commission recommended the imposition of import quotas. Stainless steel flatware, gloves, mushrooms, tobacco wrappers, and industrial fasteners have also sought protection under the Trade Act of 1974.

Thus, on balance, the United States continues its active role as a major exporter and direct investor. In addition the American market remains a major attraction to foreign exporters and importers. Unemployment in the U.S., the size of foreign exports and investment together with their effect on particular groups, and claims of foreign government subsidiaries have, however, increased the pressures within the country to resist freer international trade. Officially, though, the American policy is committed to freer access to markets and supplies and continued support for multinational companies. That official policy is not clear, but it is evident in the statement of Will E. Leonard, Chairman of the International Trade Commission:

> Is the Trade Act a veneer of free trade platitudes over a hard core of home market protection? Probably not, but the final verdict is still out.[31]

While we ponder these remarks, America's overseas competitors continue to improve their products and marketing know-how. The distinct advantage held by American marketers in the past several years has given way to sophisticated competition from European and Japanese multinational companies and from increasingly effective export

---

[28]*Federal Reserve Bulletin* (March, 1976), p. A58.
[29]"Ford Rejects Nonrubber-Shoe Import Curbs," *The Wall Street Journal*, April 19, 1976, p. 1.
[30]*Ibid.*
[31]"The Protectionist Pressures Build Up," *Business Week* (February 23, 1976), pp. 32–34.

operations, some of which are supported by governmental legislation and financing.[32]

QUESTIONS

1. Discuss the relative dependence of the United States and Japan upon international trade and investment.
2. What country is currently the world's leading exporter? Importer?
3. What changes have occurred recently in the geographical distribution of U.S. exports?
4. What were U.S. exports and imports in the most recent year for which you are able to obtain data?
5. In terms of their imports from the United States, what countries are the United States' best customers?
6. How is it possible for the United States to both export and import certain types of goods, such as automobiles and electrical machinery?
7. What reasons can you give for the importance of Canada and Western Europe as sources of U.S. imports?
8. What has caused some American firms to shift from exports to direct investment in certain countries?
9. Does the shift from exporting to investment abroad affect the marketing techniques that a firm might employ?
10. Why do European and Japanese firms invest in production and marketing facilities in the U.S.?

SUPPLEMENTARY READINGS

International Monetary Fund. *International Financial Statistics*. Washington: International Monetary Fund, monthly.
Root, Franklin R. *International Trade and Investment*, 3d ed. Cincinnati: South-Western Publishing Co., 1973. Chapters 15, 19, 20, and 24.
Statistical Yearbook. New York: United Nations, annual.
Survey of Current Business. Washington: Government Printing Office, monthly.
U.S. Bureau of the Census. *Guide to Foreign Trade Statistics*. Washington: Government Printing Office, 1975).
_____. *Highlights of the U.S. Export and Import Trade*. Report FT990. Washington: Government Printing Office, monthly.
_____. *U.S. Exports — Schedule B Commodity by Country*. FT410. Washington: Government Printing Office, monthly.
_____. *Statistical Abstract of the United States*. Washington: Government Printing Office, annual.
U.S. Dept. of Commerce. *Historical Statistics of the United States: Colonial Times to 1957*. Washington: Government Printing Office, 1960.

---

[32]For a discussion of American export promotion programs see Chapter 18.

4

The International Monetary Environment for Marketing

Money exerts considerable influence on the marketing process; indeed, modern marketing would be impossible without money as a means of exchange and a standard of value. Therefore, we turn our attention in this chapter to viewing the monetary system and exchange rates as they affect marketers. The world monetary environment and the relationships that exist among various national currencies have the potential for facilitating, or retarding, trade expansion and economic development. The need for understanding the monetary environment has become even more apparent after 1971 when the dollar was devalued, the Bretton Woods system collapsed, and a system of floating exchange rates was evolved.

In this chapter we concentrate on those aspects of the monetary environment that most directly affect international marketers. No effort will be made to survey the entire monetary situation, nor are we concerned with the field of foreign exchange from the viewpoints of foreign exchange bankers, brokers and dealers, speculators, and others whose activities are influenced by foreign exchange operations. For those viewpoints complete texts are available on international finance.[1] Banking facilities and sources of funds for marketing will be discussed in Chapter 15.

International marketers think primarily in terms of their own currency. American sellers, regardless of whether they quote prices in terms of the dollar or a foreign currency, expect eventually to receive U.S. dollars for their merchandise. Similarly the British marketers expect to receive pounds, the French expect francs, and the Mexicans expect pesos. Likewise, an American importer may agree to pay a price

---

[1]For example, see David K. Eiteman and Arthur I. Stonehill, *Multinational Business Finance* (Reading: Addison-Wesley Publishing Company, 1973); J. Fred Weston and Bart W. Sorge, *International Managerial Finance*, (Homewood, Ill.: Richard D. Irwin, Inc., 1972); or Lee C. Nehrt, *International Finance for Multinational Business*, 2d ed. (Scranton, Pa.: Intext Educational Publishers, 1972).

quoted in pounds, francs, or pesos, but the American is interested in the dollar cost. Thus, the prevailing foreign exchange rates — the price of one currency in terms of another — are of direct concern to marketers. The rate of exchange affects the price foreign buyers must pay for the product in terms of their own currency.

THE INTERNATIONAL MONETARY SYSTEM

Each sovereign nation has reserved to itself the right to establish its own national currency. Within that country, buying and selling normally are carried out through the use of the national currency. Since each unit of the national currency is of equal value, the money serves as a convenient basis for exchange. A problem arises, however, when someone in one country wishes to buy a product in another. Not only must the price of the product itself be established, but also the rate at which one currency will be valued in terms of another. What is the dollar price of a franc or guilder? The system used for foreign exchange determines that price. But before investigating the nature and effect of foreign exchange, a brief review of world monetary developments is in order.

Pre-World War II

From about 1870 to the beginning of World War I the major trading nations operated on the international gold standard under which each nation defined its monetary unit in terms of a weight of gold and stood ready to convert its money into gold when requested. Under this system the various national currencies were related to each other by the gold content of their monetary unit. But wartime economic disruptions and the creation of nongold money to finance the war, plus the postwar reconstruction, doomed the classic gold standard. When only the U.S. maintained convertibility, the gold standard was finished and was replaced by a gold exchange standard. Under the new gold exchange standard, countries revalued their money in terms of gold, but they also counted sterling and U.S. dollars as part of their gold reserves.[2] Thus, the rigid tie between a nation's gold stock and its domestic money supply was loosened by the existence of reserve currencies. The currency was backed by gold plus dollars and sterling.

The world-wide depression of the 1930s and massive flows of speculative capital collapsed this gold exchange system. Both Great Britain and the United States stopped convertibility and in 1933 the U.S. devalued the dollar by raising the price of gold from $20.67 to $35 per ounce.[3] Nations faced with severe political and economic problems

---

[2]Virgil Salera, *Multinational Business* (Boston: Houghton Mifflin Company, 1969), pp. 312–313.

[3]Franklin R. Root, *International Trade and Investment* (Cincinnati: South-Western Publishing Co., 1973), pp. 455–456.

sought to restore employment, to expand exports, and to reduce imports by a series of monetary and fiscal moves. These included competitive devaluations of their currencies, tight foreign exchange control, and import restrictions. They hoped, in a sense, to solve their employment problems by exporting them to other nations.

Mindful of these past events the representatives of the Allied nations met during World War II to establish a postwar international monetary system that would be more conducive to trade and would facilitate reconstruction. At Bretton Woods in 1944 they devised the new set of rules. The International Monetary Fund (IMF) was established to relieve exchange shortages and to provide some measure of control over the values of exchanges and variations in such values. The representatives sought a system of relatively stable exchange rates. They did this through a system of fixed or pegged rates. They also provided for consultation among nations on foreign exchange problems, and established a means for helping members who were having temporary balance of payments problems.

Purposes of the IMF

The specific purposes for which the International Monetary Fund was established are:

1. To promote international monetary cooperation through a permanent institution which provides the machinery for consultation and collaboration on international monetary problems.
2. To facilitate the expansion and balanced growth of international trade. This trade expansion contributes to high levels of employment and real income and to the development of the productive resources of all members.
3. To promote exchange stability, to maintain orderly exchange arrangements among members, and to avoid competitive exchange depreciation.
4. To assist in establishing a multilateral system of payments to facilitate trade between members and to assist in the elimination of foreign exchange restrictions which hamper the growth of world trade.
5. To give confidence to members by making the Fund's resources available to them under adequate safeguards, thus providing them with opportunity to correct maladjustments in their balance of payments without resorting to measures destructive of national or international prosperity.
6. To give confidence to IMF members by making the Fund's resources available under proper safeguards to help members correct maladjustments in their balance of payments.[4]

---

[4]A country's balance of payments is a statistical record of its economic transactions between domestic and foreign residents.

In order to accomplish these objectives, each member of the Fund was to establish an initial par value for its monetary unit. This was to be expressed in terms of gold or United States dollars. Then members were obligated to keep the rate of exchange from rising or falling more than one percent of the par value, thereby stabilizing the exchange rate. Financial short-term aid was available to members, within the limits of the Fund rules, to help maintain these exchange rates during periods when the member country was having temporary balance of payments problems. In the event of more basic long-run problems it was assumed that occasional changes in the par value might be necessary. If the country changed the par value of a currency ten percent or more from the original parity, IMF approval was required. Failure to do so might mean that the country would be denied use of the Fund's resources. Several changes, such as the British devaluations of 1949 and 1969, occurred under this provision.

Postwar and Recent Developments

During the post-World War II period, the American dollar achieved widespread use as a reserve currency. Many countries preferred to hold dollars as a reserve and trusted in the stability of the dollar. In the 1960s, however, concern developed over the persistent balance of payments deficit of the U.S., which placed stress on the dollar since Americans were investing abroad and imports were increasing faster than exports.[5] Under a floating exchange system the value of the dollar would have declined relative to some other major currencies, but the U.S. felt it could not devalue the dollar under the IMF rules without drastic effects on other countries because the dollar was a reserve currency. The American government sought to correct the deficit by intervening in the foreign exchange market.[6] But these efforts were not sufficient to correct the deficit. Finally, on August 15, 1971, President Nixon suspended the gold convertibility of the dollar and imposed a temporary ten percent surcharge on dutiable imports.[7] The Bretton Woods Agreement was dead. The major foreign currencies were allowed to float and the market (including intervention by central banks) indicated higher values for some currencies relative to the dollar.

In December 1971 the Smithsonian Agreement was reached, under which IMF member countries were permitted to allow exchange rates to vary as much as 2.25 percent from their par. In the Agreement the U.S. agreed to a dollar devaluation of approximately 8.5 percent by raising the price of gold to $38 per ounce.[8] However, these rates could

---

[5] See Chapter 3, Table 3-1, p. 44
[6] Root, *op. cit.*, pp. 472–476.
[7] *Federal Reserve Bulletin* (March, 1972), p. 228.
[8] *Ibid.*, p. 229.

not be maintained and in early 1973 a further official dollar devaluation of ten percent was made. But even this devaluation, plus continued intervention by foreign authorities, failed to stem a speculative flow of capital.[9] Several important currencies were allowed to float as countries ceased holding rates within stated margins against the dollar. This float resulted in fluctuating exchange rates and the dollar declined further in value. The dollar rate stabilized in 1973 when the U.S. achieved a trade surplus, and rose strongly following the oil crisis because the U.S. was expected to be affected less than other industrialized nations. The energy crisis and other factors led to a situation where monetary reform had not yet been achieved by the middle of 1976. Meanwhile the business community learned to cope with the fluctuating rates despite the earlier exclamations of preference for fixed rates.

THE NEW YORK FOREIGN EXCHANGE MARKET

The New York foreign exchange market has evolved to meet the needs international traders and investors have for a mechanism to convert funds from one currency to another. Unlike the stock exchanges or the commodity exchanges, the foreign exchange market does not have a central meeting place, hours, or rules. It is, however, a mechanism for bringing together buyers and sellers of foreign exchange and establishing foreign rates.

A Federal Reserve Bank study of the market described it as:[10]

> The New York foreign exchange market may be broadly described as a three-tiered market. First are the transactions between the banks and their commercial customers who are the ultimate users and suppliers of foreign exchange. Second, there are the transactions among the banks that "make the market"; dealings in this domestic interbank market are conducted through foreign exchange brokers and are supplemented, from time to time, by transactions by the Federal Reserve Bank of New York on behalf of the United States Treasury and the Federal Reserve System as well as on behalf of foreign monetary authorities. The third tier consists of transactions between New York banks and banks abroad. These are also occasionally supplemented by Federal Reserve transactions either through the market or directly with or through foreign central banks. All three segments of the market are of course closely related.

The banks provide a service to their customers by converting foreign exchange into dollars and vice versa. In a single day they will both purchase foreign exchange from some customers and sell it to others. In order to meet the needs of their customers, the larger banks

---

[9] *Federal Reserve Bulletin* (April, 1974), pp. 236–237.
[10] Alan R. Holmes and Francis H. Schott, *The New York Foreign Exchange Market* (New York: Federal Reserve Bank of New York, 1965), p. 12.

maintain deposits in branches or commercial banks abroad while smaller and inland banks work through these banks on a correspondent basis. The bank quotes rates at which it will buy or sell foreign exchange. The rates will differ among the currencies, thereby establishing the price of one currency in terms of another — the exchange rate. Several exchange rates on December 8, 1975, appear in Table 4-1.

Table 4-1 FOREIGN EXCHANGE RATES*

Country	Currency	Exchange Rate (in Dollars)
Australia	dollar	1.2590
Brazil	cruzeiro	.1140
Britain	pound	2.0243
30 day futures		2.0154
90 day futures		2.0011
180 day futures		1.9810
Canada	dollar	.9888
Colombia	peso	.033
France	franc	.2249
Hong Kong	dollar	.1990
Iran	rial	.0153
Italy	lira	.001468
Japan	yen	.003261
30 day futures		.003252
90 day futures		.003250
180 day futures		.003249
Mexico	peso	.08006
Netherlands	guilder	.3725
Switzerland	franc	.3818
Venezuela	bolivar	.2340
West Germany	mark	.3817
30 day futures		.3825
90 day futures		.3842
180 day futures		.3872

Source: Bankers Trust Company of New York in *The Wall Street Journal*, December 9, 1975.

*Selling prices for bank transfers in the U.S. for payment abroad in U.S. dollars on December 8, 1975.

A distinction is to be drawn between "spot" and "future" exchange. When an importer purchases *spot exchange*, actual delivery is taken of a definite amount of foreign exchange at the time of purchase and the rate then being quoted is paid for the particular bill of exchange. When a *future exchange* contract is purchased, the purchaser agrees to buy a given amount of exchange on a fixed date in the future at the rate specified in the future contract. This future rate may be higher or lower than the spot rate. The direction and extent of the deviation from the spot rate is largely governed by two factors: (1) the supply and the demand for delivery of a given currency at a future time, and (2) the speculative opinion of the market concerning the future course of the rate of exchange. Figure 4-1 is an illustration of how the futures contract works and one use of it by a U.S. manufacturer.

HOW THE FORWARD CURRENCY MARKET WORKS

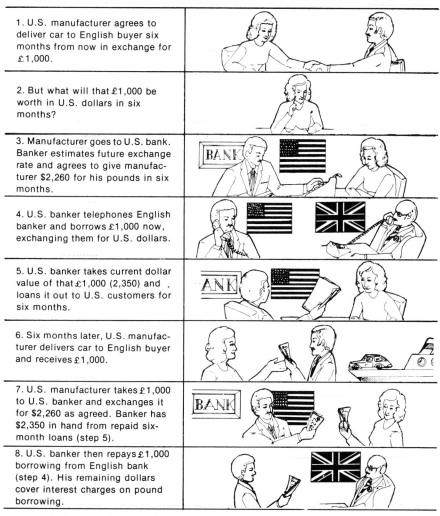

1. U.S. manufacturer agrees to deliver car to English buyer six months from now in exchange for £1,000.	
2. But what will that £1,000 be worth in U.S. dollars in six months?	
3. Manufacturer goes to U.S. bank. Banker estimates future exchange rate and agrees to give manufacturer $2,260 for his pounds in six months.	
4. U.S. banker telephones English banker and borrows £1,000 now, exchanging them for U.S. dollars.	
5. U.S. banker takes current dollar value of that £1,000 (2,350) and loans it out to U.S. customers for six months.	
6. Six months later, U.S. manufacturer delivers car to English buyer and receives £1,000.	
7. U.S. manufacturer takes £1,000 to U.S. banker and exchanges it for $2,260 as agreed. Banker has $2,350 in hand from repaid six-month loans (step 5).	
8. U.S. banker then repays £1,000 borrowing from English bank (step 4). His remaining dollars cover interest charges on pound borrowing.	

Source: Forbes (April 15, 1974), p. 33.

Figure 4-1 HOW THE FORWARD CURRENCY MARKET WORKS

FACTORS AFFECTING EXCHANGE RATE FLUCTUATIONS

Free or uncontrolled exchange rates fluctuate almost continuously, for they are constantly subject to a variety of influences. If countries were still on the gold standard, the fluctuations would be limited by the cost of shipping gold from one country to another, but between these limits constant fluctuations could occur. In the absence of the gold standard, gold embargoes, currency inflation, or similar abnormal disturbing factors, the fluctuations in the exchange rate are caused basically by the supply of and the demand for the currencies being exchanged.

A maze of merchandise and other business transactions is constantly conducted between the United States and foreign countries. These transactions influence the supply of and the demand for foreign exchange.

The transactions comprising the credit items (in-payments) of the U.S. balance of payments tend to increase American holdings of foreign exchange and/or to reduce foreign holdings of dollar exchange; the debit items (out-payments) have, of course, the reverse effect.

The principal items that normally constitute the supply of foreign exchange in the United States are American exports, American stocks and bonds sold to investors abroad, foreign capital movements to the United States, interest and dividend payments on foreign securities held in the United States, foreign securities resold to foreigners, and payments due Americans for shipping, insurance, and other services. All of these items require remittances to this country and therefore result in a demand for dollars or a large volume of claims against foreign currencies.

The principal items constituting the demand for foreign exchange are merchandise imports into the United States, foreign stocks and bonds sold in the United States, American securities bought back from foreigners, interest and dividends on American securities held abroad, United States tourist expenditures abroad, and payments to foreigners for services.

Foreign exchange rates, however, are not always dominated by these normal forces of supply and demand. A number of other factors may cause people to lose confidence in a currency and lead to a decline in its value. Loss of confidence may result from governmental instability, large public debts, high rates of inflation, major industrial or banking failures, etc. At times speculative trading may also contribute to exchange fluctuations even though speculators usually have a stabilizing effect. However, if a preponderance of them believe the currency is overvalued, they may all be trying to sell at the same time.

Exchange rates are normally also influenced by the money market in the United States and foreign countries, because interest rates influence the flow of funds and, consequently, the supply of and demand for foreign exchange. Rising interest rates in the United States normally attract foreign bank funds to this country and bring home American bank balances held abroad. The effect is to depress exchange rates. Declining interest rates in the United States tend to reverse this flow of bank funds and to raise exchange rates. Similarly, a rise in money rates in a foreign money market normally tends to draw foreign bank funds held in the United States and available American bank balances to the foreign market, while a decline in money rates abroad tends to cause a reverse flow of bank funds.

It does not follow that every fluctuation in the money market will promptly be reflected in foreign exchange rates. In the absence of exchange control or restriction plans, however, changing money rates frequently do cause fluctuations in foreign exchange.

EFFECT OF EXCHANGE FLUCTUATIONS ON PRICE QUOTATIONS OR INTERNATIONAL TRADE PROFITS

When a seller quotes an export price for a product or receives an offer in terms of foreign currency, there is concern with the exchange rate fluctuations that may occur before the seller receives payment. Even when quoting prices in terms of the foreign currency, the exporter knows how many American dollars are to be received. However, a customer will pay in pounds sterling, deutsche marks, francs, pesos, or some other acceptable foreign currency, and therefore the amount received in terms of dollars will depend upon the rate of exchange. When the price is quoted in the foreign currency, the exporter accepts the risk of exchange fluctuation. Unless steps are taken to protect expected profits, a decline in exchange rates may reduce them or even convert them into a loss.

Exporter's Means of Protection

An American exporter can obtain protection against exchange losses by quoting a price in terms of American dollars, thereby shifting the exchange risk to the foreign importer. In that case, unless the importer seeks protection, an unfavorable change in the exchange rate may cause the importer to pay a higher price (on the basis of his/her own currency) than had been anticipated.

When quoting prices in a foreign currency, the American exporter may deliberately accept an exchange risk if it is believed that exchange fluctuations will be slight, or if it is believed that the rate will be more favorable later. Then the exporter is speculating on merchandise export transaction, for the amount of profit will not be known until the payment has been converted to U.S. dollars. The American exporter may be more inclined to accept this risk if exchange rates have recently been quite stable and if a product carries a wide price margin. Although the exchange risk may be taken into account in quoting export prices, such action could raise the price and thereby limit sales.

Agreed-Upon Exchange Rate. When exchange rates fluctuate within a comparatively narrow range, the exporter may be able to induce the foreign importer to agree upon a fixed or guaranteed rate of exchange, but arrangements such as these may be unobtainable at the very time the exporter is most anxious to protect profits. When the exchange risk is greatest because of wide fluctuations, the exporter who quotes foreign currency prices may find that the only safeguard is in the open exchange market, where foreign currency bills for future delivery are bought and sold.

Hedging. When an exporter makes a sale, foreign currency may be sold for future delivery. When a draft from the foreign customer is received, the exporter will present it to a banker and receive payment on the basis of the agreed-upon rate. Thus, the exporter has, in effect, taken advantage of a fixed rate of exchange.

A business person may hedge or protect export profits in a large measure by selling futures contracts, if there is a futures market for the foreign currency.[11] To illustrate the hedging process, assume that an exporter in the United States sells equipment worth $10,020 to a Japanese importer and payment is to be made in 60 days. The quotation is made in yen, at a rate of $.00334 or 3,000,000 yen. In order to hedge, the exporter sells a futures contract to deliver this number of yen. Assume that the price for the futures contract is at or near the January 1 spot rate of $.00334 per yen. Thirty days are allowed for the transfer of documents between the United States and Japan.

As will be seen in the following illustration, this is an ideal transaction, since the dates, rates, and amounts fit exactly. They rarely, if ever, fit so nicely in everyday business.

Merchandise Transaction	*Futures Transaction*
Jan. 1 Sells equipment for 3,000,000 yen. At $.00334 per yen this equals $10,020.00	Sells 90-day contract for 3,000,000 yen at $.00334, or $10,020.00.
Apr. 1 Receives payment of 3,000,000 yen worth $.0034, or $10,200.00.	Buys spot yen to cover at $.0034, $10,200.00.
Profit due to exchange, $180.00.	Loss on futures contract, $180.000.

---

[11]There are only a few currencies for which a futures market exists, such as U.S. dollars, British pounds, Japanese yen, and German deutsche marks.

When a sale is made, the exporter who expects to receive foreign currency at some future date may sell an equivalent amount of foreign currency for delivery in the future at the time the foreign currency is expected to be received by the exporter. If the exchange rate declines, the exporter will receive fewer American dollars on the merchandise transaction than anticipated, but will be able to cover or buy back at a reduced rate the foreign currency that had been sold for future delivery. The profit derived from this future exchange transaction will approximately balance the reduced number of dollars the exporter is paid for the merchandise. In effect a fixed rate of exchange will again have surfaced for the exporter.

The sale of futures contracts often affords real protection to the exporter, but it does not always eliminate the exchange risk entirely because the exporter may be unable to close the export sales contract and sell the futures contract at exactly the same moment. In the meantime the exporter bears the exchange risk. The futures and spot markets may not fluctuate in the same amount, so the transactions exactly offset each other. Bankers also have at times withdrawn from future exchange operations in some currencies, so hedging may not be possible in a currency. Hedging through the use of futures contracts implies that there is such a market. If the sale is to a small country, or one with few international dealings, there may be no futures market for the currency.

Importer's Means of Protection

American importers, when buying foreign merchandise in terms of foreign currencies, are faced with a possible loss of profit resulting from unfavorable exchange fluctuations. The American importer, knowing that a given amount of foreign currency will have to be delivered at a future date, may purchase spot exchange when ordering imported merchandise. This will eliminate the danger of a rise in the exchange on the importing country, but in doing so the exporter ties up funds until the merchandise is received. When purchasing imports in terms of a foreign currency for which there is a market for futures exchange, the American importer may hedge import transactions by purchasing a futures exchange contract. Thus, the importer is assured that when the time comes for payment, the necessary foreign currency will be available at a price determined when the future contract was purchased.

Indirect Risks

The most complete safeguard against unfavorable exchange fluctuations is, of course, enjoyed by American marketers when payment is to be made in United States dollars, but even then they have an interest in exchange fluctuations. Fluctuations following the closing of the sales contract may be so unfavorable that the foreign customer may refuse to accept delivery, or, having accepted the goods, may be unable or unwilling to meet the financial obligation. Thus, the exchange rate fluctuations may increase the exporter's credit and commercial risks.[12]

The American importer who has purchased foreign goods in terms of United States dollars also may have an indirect interest in exchange rate fluctuations because losses resulting from exchange fluctuations may induce the foreign seller to delay shipment or fail to make delivery of the ordered merchandise. Although the American importer will not make payment and therefore will not suffer a direct loss from exchange rate fluctuations, business is disrupted and, if any of the ordered items have been resold in advance of their receipt, the importer cannot deliver.

Influence of Price Levels

If price levels could be promptly readjusted as exchange rates depreciate and a so-called international purchasing power parity[13] could be maintained, the depreciated exchange would have little effect upon merchandise exports and imports. Such a prompt readjustment, however, rarely occurs.

Exchange rates can depreciate very substantially, even though the general commodity price level within a country does not change. If the foreign currency depreciated relative to the dollar while U.S. prices remained stable, exports from the United States would be handicapped. American prices, quoted on the basis of the current depreciated exchange rate with a view to obtaining the number of dollars normally expected, would appear high to the foreign importer in comparison with the general level of the domestic prices prevailing in the other country and higher than the import prices that were formerly paid.

If the American exporter quotes prices in line with the domestic price level of the foreign country, or if price offers from abroad are accepted on that basis, then the exporter would receive fewer dollars than before the exchange rates depreciated. Imports received from the foreign country would be encouraged because the American importer could temporarily purchase merchandise at prices that, in terms of United States dollars, would be attractive. The resulting decline of exports and increase of imports would eventually tend to readjust the

---

[12]See Chapter 15.

[13]International purchasing power parity is a theory by which inconvertible currencies can be related. If at the beginning of a period the exchange rates of Countries A and B had been at par, that is 1 to 1, then an increase in the price level of A of 150 percent, while an increase in the price level of B was 100 percent, would reflect a relationship of 1.5 of Country A's currency to 1.0 of Country B's, etc.

exchange rates because there would be an increasing demand for the foreign currency and a declining demand for the dollar.

The exchange situation also is complicated by inflationary conditions. When inflation occurs within a country, the prices of its products increase and, even if the exchange rate does not change, exporters find sales more difficult. The increased cost of imported items leads foreign buyers to other countries. Thus, the exporter whose products are price-sensitive faces either a declining market or the need to cut the export price and receive a lower profit. Antidumping laws in many countries might make the latter policy unlawful.[14]

Consumers and industries in the country with the inflated currency would find, however, that the rise in internal prices has made importing more attractive. Lower prices abroad, relative to the higher domestic prices, may lead to increased use of foreign sources of supply.

The inflation thus affects not only the market for domestic and foreign goods and services, but also the demand and supply for the currencies of the various countries. In a fluctuating, or floating, exchange system this should change the rate of exchange to partially compensate for the shift to the use of foreign suppliers. In a managed currency system, as under the IMF, inflation may result in a reduction of exports and an increase in imports in the inflationary country. If this persists, it would pressure the country to consider a change in par value, i.e., pressure to formally devalue the currency. By devaluing the currency the monetary managers want to make exports cheaper; therefore, hopefully, the exports will expand and imports, now more expensive, will be reduced. During 1973 and 1974 the devalued dollar appeared to be having these effects.

FOREIGN EXCHANGE CONTROL

In today's world nations are reluctant to have the value of their currency determined solely by the normal supply and demand for it in order to facilitate trade and investment. Monetary authorities intervene in the foreign exchange market either to stabilize the value of the currency in accordance with arrangements under the International Monetary Fund or because of other trade and national goals. Furthermore, governments can restrict the amount of exchange that is available for trade and investment and thus indirectly influence exchange rates. Any governmental measures affecting the volume of exports and imports influence exchange rates. A country may restrict the importation of certain goods in conformance with its economic development program in order to conserve foreign exchange for projects with a higher priority. Furthermore, protective tariff rates, import quotas, license requirements, export subsidies, governmental price control, and trade agreements all imply a certain amount of exchange control.

---

[14]See Chapter 16.

Direct Government Intervention

When countries suspended the gold standard in the 1930s they often took direct action to change or stabilize exchange rates, thereby altering the market potentials. Currencies were devalued in order to increase exports, stabilization funds were used to buy and sell foreign currencies in the open market, gold exports were controlled, and blocked accounts were used to overcome exchange rate depreciation problems. Even in the post-Smithsonian Agreement period of the seventies the floating exchange rates have been affected by governmental purchases and sales of currencies to maintain rates within limits.

Foreign Exchange Restrictions

Although the direct intervention methods referred to have influenced many exchange rates, they do not fully serve the needs of countries with a continuous shortage of foreign exchange. To supplement the direct measures many countries adopted a number of *exchange restrictions*. Beginning in the early thirties the number of countries with restrictions has increased so that most countries have employed them from time to time. Developing countries especially have found restrictions necessary to secure compliance with their development plans.

An exchange restriction plan implies that the government of a nation restricts the uses to which the available supply of exchange shall be put. Foreign exchange may be allocated specifically for the payment of import bills, interest on foreign loans, and/or other specific purposes. Sometimes the restrictions prevent the use of exchange for trade with a given (unfriendly) country. In the latter case the purpose may be political, but the basic reason for most exchange restrictions is the shortage of foreign exchange sufficient to meet freely all of the requirements of international marketing and finance. More specifically, exchange restrictions are designed:

1. To provide the exchange necessary for the financing of essential imports and to discourage specific imports that are considered to be luxuries or that may be available from local producers.
2. To allocate or limit exchange for the servicing of external debts and investments.
3. To prevent the flight of capital.
4. To limit speculation.
5. To encourage lagging exports.
6. To encourage tourist travel.

In addition to these objectives, all of which are primarily related to a shortage of exchange, exchange restrictions also constitute a method of influencing or determining foreign exchange rates. When a government limits and prescribes the uses of all or most of the available exchange, it fixes the nation's official exchange rates. The exchange rate fixing power of some governments is further enhanced by import quotas, licensing plans, and other foreign trade control measures. This ability of a government to manipulate the rate of its exchange can thus become an important instrument in the foreign commercial and even political policy of a country.

Administration of Exchange Restrictions

Exchange restrictions are administered through a designated bank, exchange control commission, or other agency. Exporters in such countries are required to receive payment in foreign currency and turn over to the exchange restriction authority all or such portion of their exchange as the current regulations require at an official buying rate. Importers and others requiring foreign exchange then purchase it, so far as the restrictions permit, at an official selling rate.

In some countries there is also a free exchange market in which exchange derived from certain exports or from other authorized services may be obtained, usually at higher cost to the buyer. Thus, in a single country there may be one or more pegged exchange rates for official exchange and also a free market rate. This is known as a system of *multiple exchange rates*. Multiple exchange rates are most likely to be used by developing countries when a nation faces a shortage of foreign exchange.

Thus, in 1949 when Argentina announced depreciated exchange rates varying from 17 to 30.5 percent, the scale of exchange rates was established as illustrated in Table 4-2.

Table 4-2 ARGENTINA'S SCALE OF EXCHANGE RATES — 1949

Class of Exchange	Pesos per United States Dollar	
	Buying	Selling
Basic	3.3582	6.0857
Preferential A	4.8321	3.7313
Preferential B	5.7286	5.3714
Special	7.1964	——
Free	9.0000	9.0000

Marketers are interested in these rates since their imported product would cost the Argentine consumers more pesos under the special rate rather than the basic rate. Multiple rates are established to inhibit the importation of specific products. The least favorable rates are set for luxury goods such as automobiles, especially if these are also produced locally. As the economy develops the items might be shifted from one category to another. In the Argentine case the basic buying rates applied to meats, wheat, corn, linseed oil, and seed. The free rate applied to officially approved transactions such as tourists, services, and the transfer of profits.

Other types of exchange restriction systems of interest to marketers include those in which a country requires that a license be obtained in order to import certain products. These import licenses are allocated by the exchange control authority in accordance with priorities set by the government. Countries also have levied import surcharges and have provided export subsidies to local producers. They have required that importers pay an advance deposit for desired exchange, thereby tying up the importer's capital and increasing the cost of importing. In addition, various measures have been used to affect capital movements. For example, the United States maintained an Interest Equalization Tax and instituted a program of voluntary restraints on lending and investing abroad. This later program was superceded by a mandatory program in 1968 and was retained until 1974.

Effects of Exchange Restrictions

Exchange restrictions, although intended to accomplish the internal objectives of the country enforcing them, have necessarily affected the international trading of the other trading nations throughout the entire world. As they are imposed primarily because certain countries are faced with a shortage of foreign exchange, international trading as a whole has not always been curtailed. But it is clear that exchange restrictions have:

1. Affected the importation of some classes of goods more adversely than others, the essential character of imports being considered in the allocation of exchange.
2. Affected the trade of some exporting countries more seriously than that of others.
3. Tended, particularly in connection with certain international agreements, to channelize trade bilaterally.
4. Been used by some countries for bargaining purposes.
5. Been utilized by some countries for the purpose of subsidizing particular exports.
6. Influenced domestic prices in some countries so as to handicap exports.
7. Complicated the routine work of importers and exporters.

Exchange restriction measures, however, also have certain desirable features under conditions of serious and more than seasonal or strictly temporary exchange shortage. Exchange restrictions have:

1. Stabilized exchange rates for both importers and exporters.
2. Aided various needy countries in obtaining a larger supply of the commodities considered most necessary by their governments.

3. Enabled debtor nations to safeguard their currency, control exchange rates in the national interest, protect their domestic economy to some extent against unfavorable commodity price changes, regulate interest and other financial payments, and otherwise protect themselves against threatening disturbances.

In general it is clear that marketing opportunities and efforts for specific firms have been altered as a result of governmental intervention in the exchange process. No marketing program is complete until it has taken into account the potential effect of anticipated changes in governmental policies and rates of exchange.

David Carson, a student of international marketing, has said, "Foreign exchange or political developments may often outweigh strictly marketing considerations in tipping management's judgments regarding certain market decisions. Unfortunately, professional literature in marketing has not adequately reflected these broader managerial considerations."[15]

Floating exchange rates probably have not inhibited trade to the degree expected by the proponents of fixed rates. They have, however, altered the conditions under which international marketing occurs. Businesses have adjusted and become better managers of foreign exchange. The larger multinational firms and commercial banks are improving their information systems for monitoring the foreign exchange market and forecasting foreign exchange rates.

QUESTIONS

1. Define foreign exchange rate. What is its significance for international marketers?
2. How does the New York foreign exchange market facilitate international trading for a firm in Cincinnati, Ohio?
3. How does the exchange rate affect the price a buyer pays for an imported item?
4. How did the exchange rates set under the Bretton Woods agreement differ from those under a freely floating exchange?
5. What effect would you expect a devaluation of the United States dollar to have on United States exports and imports?
6. What is the current exchange rate between U.S. currency and those of England, France, West Germany, and Japan?
7. If everything else remained unchanged, what effect would you expect increased exports to have on the value of a currency?
8. How can an American exporter obtain protection from exchange losses when the foreign customer is expected to make payment in sixty days?
9. Why might an American importer prefer to pay for purchases in U.S. dollars? In foreign currency?

---

[15]David Carson, "Present State of the Art of Comparative Marketing," in Thomas V. Greer, *1973 Combined Proceedings* (Chicago: American Marketing Association, 1974), pp. 67–70.

10. Define hedging. How may an exporter hedge a transaction for which foreign currency is to be received? How may an American importer hedge a transaction for which foreign currency is to be paid?

SUPPLEMENTARY READINGS

Eiteman, David K., and Arthur I. Stonehill. *Multinational Business Finance*. Reading, Pa.: Addison-Wesley Publishing Company, 1973. Chapters 2, 11.

Federal Reserve Bank of New York. *The New York Foreign Exchange Market*. New York: Federal Reserve Bank of New York, 1965.

Federal Reserve Bulletin. Washington, D.C.: U.S. Government Printing Office, monthly.

International Monetary Fund. *Annual Report*. Washington, D.C.: International Monetary Fund.

_____ . *International Financial Statistics*, monthly.

Nehrt, Lee Charles. *International Finance for Multinational Business*. 2d ed. Scranton: International Textbook Company, 1972.

Salera, Virgil. *Multinational Business*. Boston: Houghton Mifflin Company, 1969. Chapters 19, 21–25.

Weston, J. Fred, and Bart W. Sorge. *International Managerial Finance*. Homewood, Ill.: Richard D. Irwin, Inc., 1972. Chapter 5.

Part 2 Marketing Opportunity Analysis

2

5

Entering the World Market

A variety of strategies are used in tapping world markets. Some companies merely respond to orders from abroad without undertaking any promotional effort. Others sell to U.S. merchants who export the products and thus the producer avoids actual involvement in the export process. U.S. firms frequently use some form of independent middleman to reach their overseas markets or may even rely on the marketing departments of other producers who already have contact abroad. Some companies employ licensing and/or joint ventures to gain many of the benefits of exporting. Still others, with even greater commitment, establish marketing and production subsidiaries abroad.

Table 5-1 (page 74) summarizes the major strategies available for entering world markets. Larger companies will tend to employ them selectively, using only certain ones to gain access to markets where other strategies would not be effective or may even be prohibited. Thus, the company might actually prefer exporting, but high tariffs or import quotas might force them to utilize licensing or joint ventures. The General Electric Company, for example, derives about $1 billion of its revenues from its European markets with a combination of exporting, licensing, and sales by its European operations such as the 53 percent owned GE Espanola in Spain or its 80 percent owned Cogenel in Italy.[1]

Some of the basic strategies that will be considered in this chapter have already been mentioned or implied in previous chapters. In this chapter we focus on the details of each strategy: how each differs from its alternatives, why and when it is employed, and its implications for marketing management. Developing the knowledge of the entry strategies will prove helpful in understanding the nuances of the marketing policy and administration material covered in later chapters.

---

[1]"Multinationals: GE's New Assault on European Markets," *Business Week* (July 27, 1974), p. 33.

Table 5-1   FOREIGN MARKET ENTRY STRATEGIES

Term	Definition
Exporting	Marketing goods in one country that were produced in another.
Foreign licensing	Method of foreign operation whereby a firm in one country agrees to permit a company in another country to use the manufacturing, processing, trademark, know-how, or some other skill provided by the licensor.
Joint venture	An enterprise in which two or more investors share ownership and control over property rights and operations.
Wholly-owned subsidiary	Company completely owned by the parent firm.
Turnkey	The contractor agrees to provide the buyer with a complete operating plant in the foreign country. The contractor agrees to design and build the physical plant and to train local personnel in its management and operation.
Management contracts	Contracts involving the sale of management services for operation of the overseas facility.

THE STIMULI FOR ENTERING THE WORLD MARKET

The opportunity to enhance profits remains the major goal for firms entering international marketing. Even if other considerations are involved, the firm's executives are seldom willing to commit themselves to foreign marketing unless a satisfactory return can be obtained on their investments. The specific factors that give rise to potential profits from international operations include the desire to utilize unused capacity, a chance to offset seasonal fluctuations in sales, declining margins on goods sold in the domestic market due to market saturation and/or competitive activity, a chance to make wider applications of research and development findings, a desire to keep pace with competitors who have begun marketing internationally, the need to continue servicing customers who now have plants overseas, or even to capitalize on opportunities perceived during travel to foreign countries. Also, the impetus for international operations can come from the export promotion activities of government, such as trade fairs, export expansion programs, and methods of aiding in the financing of export sales or insuring overseas investments.

A number of companies have been prodded into investigating foreign marketing opportunities when they received an unsolicited order from abroad. While the unsolicited order has been a positive factor for many companies, others, unfortunately, overlook the opportunity because they perceive the translations, documentation, shipment, and financing problems as too great for the return on that specific order — thus passing up long-run opportunities.

A study of small and medium-sized manufacturers in Tennessee indicated that while both exporters and nonexporters were often exposed to similar stimuli, such as unsolicited orders, they differed noticeably in their perceptions of the gains and costs of exporting.[2] Those who decided to export had higher profit and lower risk perceptions than did the nonexporters. Nonexporters perceived the cost of exporting to be higher than did the exporters for such items as communications, executive time, packaging, insurance, clerical, and shipping. Apparently the perceptions of executives differed materially between exporters and nonexporters on these key evaluative factors regarding the potential profitability of foreign markets even though some of these perceptions did not reflect the actual situations. The high cost estimates may reflect the inexperience with exporting. Frequently both cost and profit potential are unknown until the company institutes a formal investigation or begins exporting. Actual experience may alleviate some initial fears.

A PHILOSOPHY FOR MARKETING ABROAD — THE BASIC OUTLINE OF STRATEGY

Even if the decision is finally made to enter into the international market, the firm still requires a solid commitment by its executives to be effective. Foreign buyers, just as domestic buyers, expect continuous availability of product and service. If a company cannot provide these basic conditions, the foreign customer must seek alternative sources of supply. Thus, regardless of whether the decision is to export or to establish overseas production and marketing, the U.S. firm cannot expect sustainable international sales and profits unless it is committed to international markets as a long-run endeavor. Some of the strategies presented provide foreign customers such assurance that a commitment has been made.

A number of years ago Stanley C. Allyn, then Chairman of the Board of the National Cash Register Company, a leading multinational company, presented his company's view of foreign operations:

> Every company which has been engaged in foreign trade for any length of time has, of necessity, developed a certain philosophy of doing business abroad. It has been hammered out on the anvil of experience, shaped by disappointment as well as success, tailored to meet

---

[2]Claude L. Simpson, Jr., and Duane Kujawa, "The Export Decision Process: An Empirical Inquiry," *Journal of International Business Studies* (Spring, 1974), pp. 107–117.

a myriad of fast-changing situations around the world. . . . For whatever value it may be to others, I should like to discuss nine principles of overseas operation which we have found effective over a long period of time. . .:

1. When we go into any foreign country, we go in for keeps.
2. We believe in staffing our overseas operations with nationals of the countries concerned.
3. We consistently invest part of our profits in the countries where those profits are earned.
4. We do not treat overseas employees as stepchildren. We treat them exactly as we treat our people at home.
5. We try to give the foreign market the product which the market wants . . . not the product which we think the market ought to have.
6. We have learned that . . . for us at least . . . service or maintenance of the product comes ahead of sales.
7. We believe in company operation overseas instead of general agencies.
8. We believe in firsthand contacts with our foreign markets, and that means we are constantly traveling.
9. Finally, we are extremely careful to respect the customs, traditions, religions, and sensitivities of foreign people.[3]

These philosophic concepts provide evidence that NCR recognizes the basic need for commitment — the need to "go in for keeps." They further provide a sound base for the selection and implementation of effective strategy. Several of the points warrant additional analysis in view of the increased significance of international marketing and environmental changes in the intervening years.

Need for Executive Interest

Whether a firm goes into international marketing to stay, or merely as a temporary expedient, depends entirely on executive attitude. Those who are in charge of international operations often complain that top executive backing is not provided for the international marketing effort, or that a drastic change has occurred in support when executives change or retire.

Fortunately the increased significance of foreign operations for many firms has meant the promotion of executives who are familiar with the requirements of international marketing and business.[4] Thus, W. S. Anderson, current Chairman of the Board at NCR, formerly headed National Cash Register Co. (Japan) Ltd. The growing significance of the international operations and the combined impact of

---

[3]Stanley C. Allyn, Address to 1958 National Foreign Trade Convention.
[4]See Chapter 2 for the table showing the importance of international activities of selected firms.

nationalism, foreign currencies, politics, servicing, and other foreign problems has placed a premium on the ability to understand the foreign markets. Company executives need an international perspective, especially when sometimes 60 percent of the profits come from overseas operations or when half of a company's employees are foreign.[5]

Despite the increased awareness of overseas operations, executives still may not give sufficient and continuous support. One reason is that the sheer size of the domestic market may lead companies to ignore foreign opportunities. In addition, the domestic market requirements may take precedence and executives may withdraw from foreign markets as the domestic business grows or is in periods of temporary shortage. Thus, in the commodity crunch of 1973 several companies cut back on foreign deliveries to meet the needs of domestic buyers. International divisions find it difficult to reestablish themselves in these countries where supplies have been cut because they lost their image of dependability. The pressure from domestic buyers and the relatively larger domestic organization, however, frequently make it difficult for them to carry the day in the boardroom.

Staffing Overseas Operations

A challenge to American marketing today is to find capable people for staffing overseas operations. Traditionally American companies have preferred to place "their own people" in charge of foreign operations. This ethnocentric view was partly due to the lack of competent management personnel in the countries in which the company operated; to the belief that only their own personnel could properly represent the company overseas; and to a general suspicion of "foreigners" in responsible positions within U.S. companies. More recently these views have given way to more rational behavior. Now the companies largely utilize nationals from the country in which they operate.

Staffing overseas operations largely with nationals from the respective countries makes good business sense when capable people are available who can interpret the culture, traditions, and nuances of the foreign market. They may also be acquainted with important business and government officers. In the years since World War II, an increasing supply of excellent executive talent has become available. Educational gains, development plans, and exposure to modern business methods have materially improved the supply of executive talent in lesser developed nations, while international competition has sharpened the skills of executives in both advanced and advancing nations.

In developing countries the company may have little choice. These countries often require the use of nationals to further their own plans

---

[5]"Gillette Sharpens Its Multinationalism," *Business Week* (July 6, 1974), p. 41.

of development. Strong feelings of nationalism lead to laws aimed at assuring an indigenous executive pool. These may require the employment of local personnel in executive and operating positions.

For marketing especially, the employment of local personnel is desirable since marketing is the firm's primary contact with the population. Indeed, it is the only contact for much of the population. Being able to anticipate the requirements of the market and to provide effective communication are skills at least as necessary as knowledge of modern marketing techniques.

American multinational companies employ relatively few Americans abroad, though these may be in key executive positions. IBM claims it could bring almost all its U.S. personnel back to the States in one 747 airplane.[6] In the past, some American executives have passed up opportunities to work abroad because they perceived it as removing them from the mainstream of promotional opportunity. This is less true now because of the importance of multinational operations, but another factor is at work as companies are making more effective use of foreign nationals and are integrating them into the executive organization.

Product Adaptation

The company's product is crucial to its success in international marketing. American manufacturers have been criticized for attempting to push their products abroad without due consideration for the differences in environment, tastes, and use-patterns in the foreign markets. There often are good reasons for selling essentially the same product as in the domestic market.[7] These include cost savings from producing for the combined domestic and overseas markets. Also, the product may be purchased abroad precisely because it is an American product or in the belief that American products in that category are technologically superior. Only too often, however, the criticism is valid. Companies may not be aware of preferences in the markets or they may have too much faith in their ability to overcome these preference differences by selling and advertising.

One study reported that such respected names as Campbell's Soup, General Foods, General Mills, The Ford Motor Company, and Philip Morris were among companies suffering from problems of customer acceptance for specific products due to poor adaptation during the 1960s.[8] These were not extreme cases of selling raingear in northern

---

[6]"New Era for the Multinationals," *Business Week* (July 6, 1974), p. 74.
[7]See Chapter 12.
[8]David Ricks, Marilyn Y. C. Fu, and Jeffrey S. Arpan, *International Business Blunders* (Columbus, Ohio: Grid, Inc., 1974), pp. 16–20.

Chile where it seldom rains or offering bacon slicers to Israel or to Arab countries. They represent cases of inadequate adaptation by firms that are known for their sophisticated U.S. marketing.

Contact With Foreign Markets

Modern communications have greatly facilitated contact with foreign operations. Telephone, teletype, radio, and satellites have made rapid contact possible and have improved our ability to convey ideas. They have not, however, proved to be perfect substitutes for face-to-face contact and on-the-scene perception. Executives still find considerable travel to be essential for understanding. Executives visit overseas areas to familiarize themselves with markets, production, personnel, and finance conditions. As Stanley Allyn said, "You can read reams of reports and statistics and still not know the most important element in any situation . . . which is simply people . . . , the people in your own organization and the people who are your customers. That is why our executives travel thousands of miles a year in visits overseas."[9] The regular visits of executives to their foreign operations indicates this is still a fact of international marketing.

In international business today the traffic is two-way. Not only do Americans travel abroad, but foreign executives, representatives, dealers, and production and service personnel frequently are brought to the U.S. where they become more familiar with the company and its traditions, facilities, policies, and personnel to increase the understanding each has of the other's viewpoints, problems, and policies.

ENTRY STRATEGIES

A well-conceived and supported plan for overseas operations is essential for successful penetration of world markets. Without an entry strategy the firm's efforts remain uncoordinated and executives are unable to develop consistently effective marketing programs. This is not to say that a firm is bound to a single strategy for entering international markets. Conditions vary so greatly among the several world markets that a single method of operation may not be feasible, but the entry strategy should be suited to the specific marketing environment. The firm's strategies should provide the firm with its best chance to service each individual market and still meet its own company-wide objectives. Consideration of several strategy alternatives and criteria for evaluating them will be discussed at this point.

----

[9]Allyn, *op. cit.*

Exporting

The most traditional entry to international markets is through exporting. Throughout the commercial history of the world people have traded goods produced in one country for those produced in another, thereby gaining some of the advantages of geographic specialization — a wider variety of goods at a lower cost than if they were produced at home. Spices, pottery, arms, furs, and manufactures became more accessible as exporters plied their trades. This was the process of international trade as envisioned and implemented by the great traders of Phoenicia, Rome, and Britain. It is the process characterized in the classical theories of international trade and it still is the most important entry strategy for many companies.

Under the export concept Cincinnati Milacron, an American firm, might manufacture machine tools in Cincinnati, Ohio, and sell them in Canada, Europe, or Asia. Exporting also occurs when the English subsidiary of the Ford Motor Company sells its products in the U.S. or in Africa, but in this latter case it is a British export. An American firm can utilize an export strategy to promote overseas sales of its domestic product, or it might export from subsidiary operations abroad. However, exporting usually refers to the process of selling domestically produced goods abroad.

National governments often favor the export strategy because it emphasizes domestic production and employment and aids the country in its balance of payments problems. Indeed, governments frequently provide considerable aid to potential exporters. The United States government, for example, provides data and embassy aid in assessing specific markets, locating distributors for the product, and insuring against commercial and political risks arising from export transactions.[10]

Why Export?

Private companies may favor exporting either as an initial entry strategy or as the most effective means of continuous servicing. Numerous American firms began by exporting, but now operate their own production and marketing operations abroad. They tested the market by exporting and then employed other strategies to hold or expand it.

Not only manufacturers are interested in exporting but also some large integrated retailers. Sears, Roebuck and Company, which operates its own stores in South America and Spain, recently established catalog agencies in Japan through an agreement with the Seibu Group, a conglomerate of retail department stores and supermarkets.

---

[10]Chapter 18 discusses in fuller detail the promotional activities of government.

Japanese customers order the items, the order is transmitted to the U.S. via satellite, and the goods are shipped.[11]

Nancy Palmer Agency

Exporting is an attractive initial strategy because it involves less risk and provides more flexibility than some other approaches. The company may already have sufficient capacity to produce for the foreign market. Thus, no additional production facilities are needed, and the additional volume may even help the domestic plant operate at a more efficient level. The investment in assessing marketing opportunities may be minimal and will likely be aided by the use of middlemen, trade fairs, secondary data, and personal visits by executives. Promotional expenses will vary with the product and market, but these would be needed even under alternative strategies. Indeed, if production facilities are established abroad (rather than exporting), there may be a need for substantial promotional expenditures to achieve the basic volume required to profitably operate the new facilities.

The U.S. Small Business Administration points out that exporting takes advantage of the operating leverage from domestic operations where fixed costs may already have been covered. Exporting presents a minimal exposure to the political and other risks of the foreign

---

[11]"Sears Sets Catalog Bow in Japan," *Merchandising Week* (January 1, 1973), p. 64.

environment, and it helps the firm gain experience for further expansion abroad through other strategies.[12]

An exporting firm can easily (relatively) shift from exporting to another strategy if increased volume warrants the additional risk, or if profit opportunities are found to be greater through production abroad. The firm also can withdraw from an unsuccessful marketing attempt with less exposure to investment loss. In the event of failure in the foreign market, the primary losses are those of market development expenditures, inventory losses, and credit expense.

A firm is said to be involved in *casual exporting* when it merely reacts to orders that come its way. The unsolicited order might come from abroad or from the purchaser's representative in the producer's country. It might also come from an export merchant who perceives an opportunity for profitable resale. Such approaches to exporting may result in additional sales with a minimum of effort, but usually active export promotion is needed to establish sufficient volume to make exporting really profitable. This requires considerably more planning and market cultivation. Active exporting means the firm develops a program for aggressively seeking export orders. The firm can use independent middlemen to help develop these plans and to aid in marketing in the overseas markets. For example, one plumbing fixture manufacturer contracts with an independent company that specializes in exporting to act as an export department. Whirlpool Corporation uses a Sony trading company to export its major appliance cookwares products to Japan.[13] If more volume is expected, a company may establish its own export organization to tap the foreign potential.[14]

Dollar devaluations, market growth abroad, and the relaxation of trade barriers have made it profitable for American firms to export again after a period of reliance on direct investment. Demand from the Middle East for American goods increased in 1973 as oil prices rose. Currency alignments involving both dollar devaluation and revaluation of the yen made American goods cheaper in Japan during the same period, and crop shortages in many parts of the world resulted in large U.S. exports of grain and other commodities.

Export strategies sometimes are combined effectively with other approaches. As discussed in Chapter 3, some 25 percent of U.S. exports were made to subsidiary operations of U.S. firms. Products of foreign subsidiaries may be designed to include U.S. components. Furthermore, the subsidiaries may gain since the integration of the foreign and domestic units can assure supply, coordinate production, and reduce cost. In a similar manner foreign exports (U.S. imports) are fit into American production and marketing operations.

---

[12]*Export Marketing for Smaller Firms* (3d ed; Washington, D.C.: U.S. Small Business Administration, 1971), pp. 3–4.

[13]"Interest Heightens on Exports of U.S. Products for Japan Sales," *Merchandising Week* (November 12, 1973), p. 3.

[14]See Chapter 9.

Export Barriers

Exporting is not always feasible or desirable, even when a firm has a product suited to the needs of consumers in other countries. A company may not be able to export because of the relatively high costs of domestic production and marketing abroad, or because of trade barriers in the foreign market. The cost structure of a firm may be so high that it cannot effectively compete in foreign markets. This high cost may be due to many factors. Competing producers located abroad may have access to lower cost raw materials, components, and labor. Foreign producers may also have higher levels of productivity, lower transportation costs, or a well-established market position. In instances such as these, the off-shore producer may be effectively excluded from the market so long as exporting is relied upon as the primary strategy. The off-shore producer may, however, be able to compete by moving at least part of an operation abroad to a location with lower costs. The long transportation routes and attendant inventory problems also may be reduced by this approach.

Tariffs. Even very efficient producers marketing products in high demand may be excluded from markets by artificial barriers designed to protect local producers or to furnish the government with revenue. The most obvious of such barriers are the *tariffs* established by individual countries or by common markets. The tariff is a tax levied on goods entering the market. It may be a *specific tariff* assessed per unit of the import, or an *ad valorem* based on the value of the imports. It might even be a combination of the two. Regardless of the type, the effect of the tariff is to make imported items more expensive and to reduce their ability to compete with local products. Substantial progress has been made recently in reducing tariffs. The General Agreement on Tariffs and Trade (GATT) has provided a forum for negotiating multilateral tariff reductions among the member nations. Despite these negotiating efforts, however, many tariffs still exist and much effort is still required to lower these barriers.

Nontariff Barriers. Nations and companies have begun to seek reductions in other barriers that may be even more significant in their effect on world trade. These so-called nontariff barriers are common. Their effects are extremely difficult to evaluate and, as might be expected, their diversity makes it difficult to negotiate reductions, though strong efforts are now being made to incorporate these matters into GATT trade negotiations among nations.

The import *quota* is a prevalent nontariff barrier encountered by exporters. It places a limit on the amount of a commodity that is permitted to enter the country. The quota may be an absolute limit placed on imports so that all imports stop when the quota is filled, or it may be combined with tariffs so that a limited amount enters the country duty-free with a higher rate on further imports. *Boycotts* have been employed by governments to exclude the goods of companies from countries with whom they have a political difference. For example, Coca-Cola and Ford were boycotted by Arabs because of their operations in Israel. *Exchange* barriers exist in numerous forms. Importers may not be able to get exchange to pay for their purchases, they may have to pay a premium for foreign exchange used to import luxury items, or they may have to make deposits of local currency long before the goods arrive and the foreign exchange is required.[15] Even more insidious are the myriad of administrative and legal barriers involving customs procedures and delays, health and safety regulations, antidumping regulations, subsidies paid to local producers, governmental procurement regulations, and an array of taxes.

The Committee on Trade in Industrial Products catalogued some 800 separate nontariff barriers in 1967 as it began its work in preparation for GATT negotiations.[16] Nontariff barriers concern not only the U.S., but also other trading countries. The EEC Commission recognized the significance of such barriers even among the members of the European Economic Community.[17]

Most of the major trading nations, including the U.S., employ a variety of measures similar to those described. Exporters who hope to penetrate these markets must cope with these barriers. Even though effort is made to reduce their significance, there is no hope that they will disappear. It is small wonder, then, that firms also seek strategies other than exporting as a means for carrying on international business.

Foreign Operations

Strategies other than exporting may provide the firm with greater sales and profit opportunities. They may also be more acceptable to governments and customers abroad.

Foreign operations is the term used to embrace many forms of business conducted in foreign countries by enterprises of different nationalities. From the point of view of the United States, the term means the operation of businesses in foreign countries by American companies.

The industrial nations of Western Europe were among the first to engage in what is now known as foreign operations. History has recorded how such European firms built railroads, canals, public utilities, and factories. American companies did not conduct foreign operations until some time later. In fact, it was not until almost the

---

[15]See Chapter 17.

[16]"Reduced Trade Barriers Aim As Negotiators Meet to Plan Worldwide Talks," *Commerce Today* (October 15, 1973), p. 9.

[17]"EEC Commission Attacks Non-Tariff Barriers," *Business International* (October 12, 1973), p. 335.

twentieth century that American companies began such activity. Among the earliest of America's foreign operations were meat packers, petroleum companies, mining companies, and a few enterprising manufacturers. Among the early manufacturers was H. J. Heinz, whose first foreign operation was the establishment of a pickle factory in Scotland in 1867.

Why Foreign Operations? Since World War II, American firms have shown increased interest in foreign operations. The world has become smaller as transportation and communication methods improved. Also, the recovery of Europe and Japan from the effects of war reestablished these markets. Along with the increased demand, their recovery also meant increased competition for American producers from European and Japanese companies who had very modern production and marketing facilities. The technical knowledge and research activities in the U.S. have been found readily applicable to foreign markets and operations. Common markets have been established to promote free trade within regions, and to make available wide markets to the country members. These, and other developments, have created conditions whereby firms must consider the possibility of foreign operations when they evaluate the foreign market.

More specifically, the following factors have prodded firms into the establishment of production and marketing facilities abroad:

1. The creation of a substantial market potential due to the new affluence of markets such as Europe and Japan. To these must be added the recent income increases in the Middle East as a result of substantial rises in the price of oil. A large potential volume makes local investment attractive where smaller markets previously were served by exporting.
2. An increasing spirit of nationalism among countries has led to demands for the development of local firms and greater national returns from the development of natural resources. The establishment of a foreign operation affords the host country a sense of permanency and more clearly identifies the foreign firm with national interests. Moreover, nationalism may be expressed in terms of incentives to the investment of foreign capital for joint ventures with local entrepreneurs. Such investment increases the value added to a country's raw materials and provides an experience base and qualified personnel for further expansion.
3. Improved financial resources have made possible foreign operations, whereas previously firms needed to conserve resources.
4. Trade restrictions instituted by the importing country may make foreign operations the only means for maintaining or expanding a market that has been developed for the company's products.
5. The development of common markets and free trade areas throughout the globe has meant that nonmembers were at a disadvantage in servicing the needs of any member countries. The large influx of American firms to the European continent in the 1960s was partly prompted by a desire to get behind the EEC tariff wall and

establish operations so that goods could be marketed to the Community's countries without the tariff disadvantage.

Foreign Licensing. Licensing is a method of foreign operation whereby a firm in one country (the licensor) agrees to permit a company in another country (the licensee) to use the manufacturing, processing, trademark, know-how, technical assistance, merchandising knowledge, or some other skill provided by the licensor.

Licensing may cover any number of processes, rights, or skills. It may be applied to patents, copyrights, and trademarks permitting the licensee to use these valuable property rights. It also may refer to technical processes and marketing or management techniques. In a very real sense licensing is the exporting of knowledge and valuable property rights.

U.S. companies are interested in foreign licensing because it is a source of additional earnings with a few financial risks and a low cost in executive time. It can give the firm a marketing advantage in meeting the needs of foreign customers, overcoming trade barriers, building goodwill on which further market advances may be based, or protecting patents and trademarks by having the licensee use them and keep them effective (if use is required by the law of the country). Reciprocal licensing agreements between companies allow a licensor to gain from the research activities of the foreign country. This reciprocal knowledge transfer can be very valuable, especially as research and development capability grow abroad.

Licensing allows a company to penetrate a foreign market with a minimum investment. At least licensing may avoid the large expenditure of capital and the assignment of key personnel that would be needed to establish a subsidiary or joint venture. The licensee may already be established in the market or be able to provide the capital to set up operations. Presumably (though one should investigate to be certain) the licensee knows the market and can provide capable administrative and technical personnel. Licensing can provide a quick entry to foreign markets when the licensee is experienced in the line.

There are drawbacks to the licensing strategy, not the least of which is the possibility of establishing a potentially strong competitor if the license agreement is not carefully drawn. Furthermore, a firm may find that it has contracted away very valuable rights. The plight of one U.S. manufacturer has been described:

> A U.S. manufacturer of a technical line of products granted an English firm a license to manufacture and sell its products as well as the exclusive right to sublicense its know-how to all other countries of the world. At the time, the U.S. firm had no particular plans for expanding overseas and the exclusive worldwide sublicense right seemed to provide for a continuing stream of royalty income that required no additional investment on the firm's part. But within a few years, applications and opportunities for the firm's product line were

found in many markets throughout the world. The U.S. firm was frustrated by its inability to take advantage of direct involvement due to the exclusive sublicense right granted to its English licensee. Substantial long-range business prospects and profits became closed to the manufacturer due to its earlier hasty decision.[18]

Even in a less extreme case a company may find that its licensee is not actively producing and marketing the product. The license may even be used by the licensee to keep potential competition from the licensor out of the market while the licensee actively promotes another product. Licensors try to protect themselves from this by contract provisions that stipulate minimum production requirements, termination dates and procedures, and sometimes minimum royalty payments.

Marketers using licensing agreements should carefully consider the difficulty of controling the licensee's operations. The agreement may provide for quality inspections and audits, but the licensor has little ability to control day to day operations and market development. Furthermore, U.S. firms should be aware of possible violations of U.S. or foreign antitrust laws when they attempt to control the licensee or to restrict the scope of operations.

Licensing may provide the firm with a relatively small profit compared to that available if the company itself manufactured and/or sold abroad. The royalty payment can mean immediate returns, but the company relies on its licensee for market development. If the licensee is effective, the gains can be substantial, but when the licensee does not perform, royalties remain small.

Royalty payments are the primary financial return to the licensor. The level of such payments (the royalty rate) will depend heavily on the value of the rights that are exchanged, the bargaining power of each party, and normal rates paid by other licensees. Some additional benefit may be derived when licenses are granted to foreign subsidiaries and thus may become a means of profit repatriation through the royalty payment. Property rights such as trademarks and patents can be protected in the licensing agreement only in accordance with country laws and international conventions.

In general, the licensing agreement stipulates the responsibilities of each party, the rights transferred, markets to be served, and control provisions and payments. Protective clauses relate to maintenance of property rights, protection against disclosure of information, and arbitration or litigation procedures. Termination clauses state the length of the contract and circumstances under which either party may end the relationship.

Franchising is one form of licensing that has received wide attention in consumer goods. Such American firms as McDonald's, Kentucky Fried Chicken, Dairy Queen, Tastee Freeze, Holiday Inn, and others have expanded rapidly by franchising. Their proven systems of

---

[18]David Ricks, Marilyn Y. C. Fu, Jeffrey S. Arpan, *op. cit.*, pp. 39–40.

operation have been effective in many countries. Kentucky Fried Chicken had 113 outlets in the United Kingdom in 1972 and 102 outlets in Japan by late 1973.[19]

Licensing has been important in reaching the Eastern European countries. It is one of the few avenues available for U.S. firms to penetrate in these markets. The Eastern European countries have been interested in obtaining technology and know-how by licensing to develop their industrial plant. Some U.S. Defense Department officials have even complained that the Soviets are acquiring important technological know-how (that has military implications) under commercial agreements.[20] But not all Eastern European licenses are for high technology items. For example, Pepsi Cola sells its concentrates to Russia where the Russians bottle the soft drink for their market.[21]

Ownership Strategies

Acquiring or developing production and marketing facilities abroad is a market entry strategy that has been widely employed in recent years to penetrate trade barriers. Increased use of this strategy resulted partly from the larger potential of the expanding foreign markets, partly from the advantages of integrated operations in the global firm, and partly from the potentially less costly operation abroad. But the increased investment required by this strategy involves the firm in a heavy commitment to international marketing, and exposes the firm to greater risk of loss of assets. It may, however, be the most profitable strategy under specified conditions. The degree of ownership may range anywhere from a minor investment to 100 percent ownership, and may be acquired by purchasing an interest in an existing foreign firm or by developing a new entity.

Degree of Ownership and Control. When the firm makes a *portfolio investment*, it takes a minority interest and participates in the gains of the foreign venture by receiving dividends or interest payments. Usually under these circumstances the investing company exerts little influence on policy formation. A more common situation in recent years occurred when the company invested to acquire a sufficiently large ownership share to exercise control over foreign production, financial, and marketing policy. This has been described as direct foreign investment.[22] It may result in a wholly-owned subsidiary where 100 percent of the ownership is held by the parent company or

---

[19]Charles L. Vaughan, "International Franchising," *The Cornel H. R. A.* (February, 1974), pp. 108–109.

[20]"Detente: A Trade Giveaway?" *Business Week* (January 12, 1974), pp. 64–66.

[21]"To Russia with Pepsi," *Fortune Magazine* (August, 1974), pp. 191–193.

[22]See Chapter 2.

in some form of joint venture with one or more foreign firms as investors. In the joint venture both ownership and control are shared. Often the partner in the joint venture is a company in the host country. The participation by the American investor may result in a majority, minority, or equal ownership position, although American multinationals generally have preferred wholly-owned subsidiaries or at least majority control. Restrictions by host governments have led to a reconsideration of this position, especially as some countries limit alien ownership in specific industries.

No set formula exists for determining the percentage of ownership which is ideal for all companies and situations. In addition to the political restrictions above, there are tax considerations and antitrust problems. Also, the desire of management for control or its past inability to work with foreigners may lead a management to believe that control is possible only through a substantial equity position. This usually implies an assumption that contractual rights cannot or will not be enforced by the host government.[23]

Wholly-Owned Subsidiaries. Proponents of complete ownership appear to equate ownership with control and to insist that complete control is necessary to most effectively meet the corporate objectives. Once the objectives have been chosen, total control permits rapid implementation of policy and eliminates conflict of interest with other management groups. Conflicts may still exist, however, between the firm and goals of the host country or the interests of employees, local consumers or other groups. Total control enables the multinational firm to employ its assets on a worldwide base and thereby increase the firm's efficiency. Such strategies are not always beneficial to the country in which the plant is located. The interests of host governments may be tied to the production of the specific plants within their boundaries. Thus, the host government may, itself, curtail management's freedom by restricting local borrowing, profit repatriation, pricing, and employment practices. Despite such weakening of control, wholly-owned subsidiaries still provide advantages in minimizing ownership conflicts and continue to be preferred by many firms. By value, more than 90 percent of U.S. foreign investments are made without joint-venture partners.[24]

High technology companies, such as IBM, whose products are in high demand are able to exert considerable leverage to maintain 100 percent ownership, but in the automobile industry even General

---

[23]Richard D. Robinson, *International Business Management* (New York: Holt, Rinehart & Winston, Inc., 1973), pp. 345–366. Robinson has noted 5 factors that are relevant to the ownership decision: competitive position, availability of acceptable associates, legal constraints, control requirements, and benefit/cost relationships.

[24]David K. Eiteman and Arthur Stonehill, *International Business Finance* (Reading, Pa.: Addison-Wesley Publishing Company, 1973), p. 246.

Motors has shifted from a "100 percent or nothing" policy to a joint venture with Isuzu in Japan.[25] Some observers believe it will be increasingly difficult to maintain a policy of 100 percent ownership. For example, executives of international firms are aware that they may be forced to relinquish some ownership and control in the Andean Common Market where free trade benefits are available to enterprises which are 51 percent owned by local investors.

> In order to enjoy the advantages of the enlarged (Andean) market, foreign enterprises will have to become at last 'mixed' enterprises. Mixed enterprises may have up to 49 percent foreign ownership. To enjoy the free trade benefits under the Andean agreement, existing companies must sign an agreement with their host countries to 'fade out', by selling equity interest to local investors within a period of 15 years so that the foreign ownership drops to no more than 49 percent. (This period is 20 years for Bolivia and Equador.)[26]

The above policy also applies to trademarks, patents, licenses, and royalties. It restricts foreign companies from applying any geographical marketing area restrictions within the Andean Common Market.

Joint Ventures. A joint venture is an enterprise in which two or more firms or investors share ownership and control over operations and property rights. The investors may share patents, trademarks, or control over manufacturing and/or marketing. A major factor in the growth of joint ventures has been, as noted previously, the attitude of host governments and their desire to avoid the domination of their industry by foreigners. The joint venture also tends to develop local technology and managerial capability more rapidly than either wholly-owned subsidiaries or licensing.

Partners for the joint venture may be local private firms or governmental units and enterprises. In some instances the partner will be another foreign enterprise. The joint venture with local partners provides a means of gaining entry to markets where local participation is required. In fact, the local partner may make entry more feasible and rapid even when there is no legal requirement for local participation. The local firm may have access to channels of distribution and may already be established as a quality producer of allied products. Local partners can provide the firm with physical facilities, a labor pool, and contacts with local officials and businesses, while the foreign firm may contribute capital, technology, know-how and managerial talent. An example of a joint venture operating within the U.S. is Dow Badische

---

[25]"New Strategies for a World Auto Market," *Business Week* (December 24, 1973), p. 39.

[26]"Colombia in the Andean Group," *Colombia Today*, Vol. 8, No. 2 (1973). New York: Colombia Information Service.

Company, a 50/50 joint venture between the American Dow Chemical Company and BASF, the world's largest chemical company, based in West Germany. The venture is to produce nylon, polyesters, dyestuffs and other chemicals. BASF also operates in the United States through a subsidiary, BASF Wyandotte. Some concept of the scope of these operations is provided by the plans of BASF to invest over $400 million in North America by 1979.[27] Armco Steel Company, an American firm, has successfully operated through minority participation in several foreign steel companies.[28]

Joint ventures which are made with state enterprises and governmental agencies have become somewhat more common as host governments seek to maintain control over basic industries. Probably the best known example of such a venture is Aramco, a combination of oil companies and the Saudi Arabian government. Although U.S. companies have resisted governmental partners in the past, there is some evidence that companies are now taking a more flexible view.

The joint venture does have some potential disadvantages. As in any case where control is shared, there may be different points of view regarding company policy and practices. In international joint ventures this possibility becomes even more likely than in domestic operations. The foreign partner represents a different culture in which the business system may be quite dissimilar. Marketing may not have played a major role in development up to this point and therefore the foreign partner may not believe that expenditures should be made for advertising, expansion of the sales force, or marketing research. Even if a foreign partner believes in the efficiency of marketing, there may be disagreement on the appropriate distribution of these expenditures by media or advertising themes, thus blocking the development of an effective marketing program. As in the case of oil companies, governments may increase their share of ownership and control. Conflicts can arise from a myriad of sources including dividend policy, expansion programs, pricing policies, and the relative contributions of the partners to successful operation.

Other Strategies

The above categories do not represent the only alternatives available to American firms. Two such remaining strategies should be mentioned because of their current use.

Turnkey. In the *international turnkey operation* a supplier agrees to provide an operating facility to the buyer. Under this system the seller

---

[27]"A New World for the Chemical Giants," *Business Week* (September 7, 1974), pp. 52–58.

[28]John Fayerweather, *International Business Management* (New York: McGraw-Hill Book Co., 1969), p. 160.

typically contracts to design and build the physical facilities and to train local personnel in the system for operation. The idea is to provide an operating plant with trained personnel and management. This approach usually is associated with large-scale plants requiring technology that is not available in the local market. It fits the development aspirations and plans of countries such as the USSR, the People's Republic of China, India, and Turkey by speeding up the development process. It has been applied to the building of steel mills, fertilizer, and chemical plants.

Management Contracts. *Management contracts* involve the sale of management services and may be used in connection with turnkey operations when the contractor agrees to operate the plant until local management is ready to take over. The management contract is also a vital part of some franchises and has even resulted in a few instances where facilities have been expropriated, but the management was retained to operate the enterprise under contract.

FLEXIBLE MARKET ENTRY STRATEGY: THE AUTOMOBILE INDUSTRY EXAMPLE

The automobile industry clearly shows the desirability of employing multiple strategies. In 1973 U.S. manufacturers exported approximately $6 billion worth of automobile and other road vehicles and parts.[29] Yet, both General Motors and Ford have operated manufacturing facilities abroad since 1926 and 1911 respectively.[30] Both have preferred wholly-owned subsidiaries, but Chrysler continued to serve its overseas markets by exporting until the late fifties. Now all have major operations in Europe, Australia, and South America. In Japan, Chrysler has a 15 percent interest in Mitsubishi Motors and General Motors has a 34 percent interest in Isuzu, while Ford is said to be attempting to set up a sales company in Japan.

The Basic Transportation Vehicle developed by GM is produced within the Andean Common Market (in Ecuador) by Aymesa, which was the local distributor for Bedford trucks (produced by GM in England). In Surinam the BTV is produced by one local company and marketed by another; yet in the Philippines, Portugal, and Malaysia the BTV is produced by GM plants.[31]

Thus, exporting, licensing, joint ventures, and wholly-owned subsidiaries are each used wherever they are deemed appropriate.

[29]U.S. Department of Commerce, *Highlights of Exports and Imports* (December, 1973), Table E-6, p. 58.

[30]The following industry description depends heavily on "New Strategies for a World Auto Market," *Business Week* (December 24, 1973), pp. 38–47.

[31]*Business Latin America* (November 28, 1973), pp. 300–381.

QUESTIONS

1. Why would a U.S. company consider marketing abroad with all the unknown factors that exist in the overseas markets and given the large United States market?
2. Why do some companies exploit the overseas markets following an unsolicited order from abroad while others ignore the potential from foreign marketing?
3. Is Stanley Allyn's philosophy acceptable today?
4. What reaction would you expect from company executives when the company expanded into foreign markets but now finds that the domestic market would absorb the entire capacity of the firm? How would overseas buyers interpret this action?
5. Why have American companies recently utilized a larger number of nationals from the overseas markets in their international marketing?
6. Why is exporting often the initial market entry strategy for a firm that has no previous experience with international marketing?
7. What is a nontariff barrier to international trade? What forms do such barriers take?
8. What difference does it make whether an item is subject to an ad valorum or specific duty?
9. What advantages and hazards do you perceive for the company that decides to expand overseas by licensing foreign manufacturers to produce and sell its products?
10. Does a company have complete control over its subsidiaries if they are wholly-owned?
11. How can joint ventures be useful for expansion into international markets? What potential problems do you see in this approach?
12. When might a company employ several different entry strategies in its foreign market penetration?

SUPPLEMENTARY READINGS

Ball, George W. (ed). *Global Companies: The Political Economy of World Business*. Englewood Cliffs, N.J.: Prentice-Hall, Inc., 1975.

International Marketing Institute. *Export Marketing for Smaller Firms*, 2d ed. Washington, D.C.: Small Business Administration, 1966.

Norbury, Paul, and Geoffrey Bownas (eds.). *Business in Japan*. New York: John Wiley & Sons, Inc., 1974. Chapters 7-9.

Robinson, Richard D. *International Business Management*. New York: Holt, Rinehart and Winston, Inc., 1973. Chapters 1, 8.

Robock, Stefan H., and Kenneth Simmonds. *International Business and Multinational Enterprises*. Homewood, Ill.: Richard D. Irwin, Inc., 1973. Chapter 17.

Root, Franklin R. *Strategic Planning for Export Marketing*. Scranton, Pa.: International Textbook Company, 1966.

Terpstra, Vern. *International Marketing*. New York: Holt, Rinehart and Winston, Inc., 1972. Chapter 10.

6

Analysis of Foreign Markets

The decision to market products and services internationally generally requires that the firm make a major commitment of resources to such activity. Before making such a commitment, careful analysis is needed to reduce entry risks and to improve profit possibilities. Resources applied to the international markets will not be available for other opportunities arising in domestic markets. Furthermore, competitive pressures, government regulations, and market development needs work against short-term commitments. Although some companies may limit their international activity to filling occasional orders from foreign customers, or may use foreign markets to dispose of temporary surpluses, many firms have committed themselves to establishing and maintaining market share through substantial investment in plants, organization, and promotion. In order to successfully export and produce abroad, continuous marketing effort is essential.

Figure 6-1 graphically portrays the major environmental influences that need to be considered in making the market entry decision.

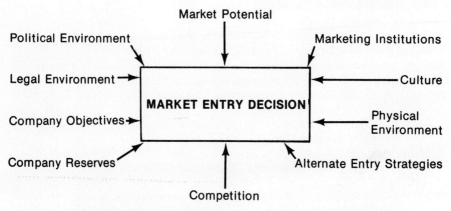

Figure 6-1 ENVIRONMENTAL AND POLICY FORCES AFFECTING THE MARKETING ENTRY DECISION

If executives are to make this important decision on the basis of fact rather than hunch, they need to establish procedures for selecting the most profitable countries for entry and for determining the operating conditions once entry occurs. Information is needed on all the environmental forces bearing on effective marketing but a major problem is the development of a data base. Information sources must be identified which provide insight for evaluating the political, economic, social, and marketing environment in order to determine market potential, forecast sales, and project profits. Somehow the facts and opinions that form the basis for intelligent judgment must be obtained. That is the objective of market analysis.

The specific information inputs for analysis are established by the executive decision process. They include all of the normal inputs for analysis of a comparable domestic decision plus environmental and company data to judge factors specific to the foreign market. Since the data requirements differ among executives and market situations, this chapter concentrates on basic concepts, sources, and approaches. These can be adapted to fit specific models appropriate for specific products, markets, and available information. Companies that market a small volume through independent middlemen take fewer risks and may require far less information and less elaborate analysis than those contemplating overseas operations through direct investment. The decision to license, enter a joint venture, or establish production abroad entails more risk; therefore, a more complete understanding of the market situation is needed.

This chapter introduces the concept of market analysis, reviews the process for screening countries to determine whether a marketing opportunity exists, develops the information base for developing a marketing strategy, presents sources of information on foreign markets, and relates the marketing information system to the requirements for comparative analysis.

MARKET ANALYSIS — A TWO-PHASE APPROACH

Market analysis begins with the initial decision to investigate foreign marketing opportunities. This decision, grounded in the firm's objectives and goals, sets in motion a series of investigations and choices that culminate in a decision to commit resources to the foreign market or to withhold these resources. A broad outline of this process appears in Figure 6-2 (see page 96).

Although both are part of the overall evaluation, the analysis may be viewed in two phases. First, the countries of the world are subjected to a selection process for determining those countries which show promise for successful marketing. This is called "determining foreign market opportunities." Second, a very few countries with the greatest potential are analyzed in detail to determine the feasibility of alternate entry strategies and the marketing program needed. This phase is the "development of the marketing program." The process involves desk research using published secondary sources of information as well as surveys, interviews, and personal contacts. Much of the information needed for initial screening is available through government sources, libraries, and other local sources.

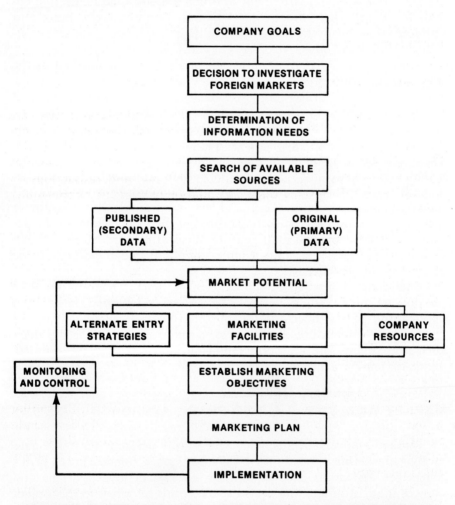

Figure 6-2 MARKET ANALYSIS — THE FEASIBILITY OF MARKET ENTRY

As Figure 6-2 indicates, the analyst first needs to know the company's objectives in considering the foreign market. Does the company contemplate further expansion, foreign manufacturing, or extended use of domestic manufacturing facilities? The company objectives, together with a knowledge of the information that is relevant to the decision process, leads to a search of available information sources. The resulting data are then used to rank the marketing opportunities based on potential return. Those countries that show promise are evaluated against feasible entry strategies and company resources that will be available. A marketing plan is developed and its feasibility is assessed. When the company is interested in only one market, the entire analysis may be focused on it. However, such concentration may overlook profitable alternative strategies in reaching regional markets; consequently, the following section is premised on a need to screen several markets.

The Screening Process

When initially screening potential country markets, executives are interested in thorough coverage without a great deal of depth. The objective is to isolate the best potential markets for further study. In this screening the analyst is interested primarily in market size, market trends, competitors and their policies, pricing, and restrictions on market entry.[1] Essentially the determination of marketing opportunity entails a series of steps.[2]

(1) The analyst determines the basic needs served by the product and the characteristics of the potential customer. Often the needs are similar to those served in the home market. Coca-Cola, Pepsi Cola, and other soft drinks are representative of this group. But sometimes a product may serve different functions abroad such as the refrigerator without a freezer that serves only as temporary storage between frequent shopping trips or that becomes a status symbol in lesser developed countries. At this stage the analyst must also be aware that the basic "use system" may differ in the foreign market so that, for example, highly automated washing machines may not be necessary when the buyer has employees within the household to perform such tasks. For industrial goods the needs and use conditions may be quite similar around the world, yet even here differing wage rates, physical conditions, and maintenance programs affect the buyer's needs. Under conditions of rising incomes or industrial development the needs of potential buyers may be changing rapidly.

Potential consumers may be identified by age, income, tastes, style and quality preferences, and lifestyles. Industrial customers are characterized by the type of product produced, the production processes,

---

[1] See Johan Aucamp, "Marketing Research As an Aid to Increase Exports," in Edward M. Mazze (ed), *1975 Combined Proceedings* (Chicago: American Marketing Association, 1975), pp. 298–301.

[2] Adapted from F. T. Haner, *Multinational Management* (Columbus: Charles E. Merrill Publishing Company, 1973), p. 24.

technology levels, cost structures, etc.[3] Thus, producers facing a cost squeeze as a result of high wage rates are a better market for automated machinery than those where labor is abundant and cheap.

(2) The manner in which these needs currently are being met must be established. The analyst can consult published government and trade data to determine whether the basic product is available in the market from local sources or imports from the U.S. or other countries. The published data, discussions with informed people, and primary research also can establish the degree to which present products meet the market's requirements. An essential concept is to find out whether the company's own product and/or marketing strategy have advantages from the consumer's viewpoint over existing products. Without some superiority in product or marketing, it is increasingly difficult to establish the product overseas in the face of both local and import competition.

(3) Market indicators are selected to reflect the market potential for the product. For consumer goods these might include population, market growth, income per capita or others that have been earlier established as being correlated with purchases of the product. Industrial goods indicators include the sales of industries using a process, number of companies, employment in an industry, transportation costs, planned government projects, etc. It is essential that these indicators be (1) correlated with market potential and (2) readily available.

General economic indicators are widely available from the U.S. and foreign governments and from international sources such as the United Nations or the International Monetary Fund. Trade data may be gleaned from trade associations and trade journals. Published sources may provide composite indicators. For example, *Business International* publishes a series of indicators including one of market size which measures the relative size of each national market as a percentage of a regional market (e.g., Europe). It is based on an average of nine underlying indicators. A market intensity composite measures the degree of concentrated purchasing power based on various per capita and ownership levels. These and underlying indicators are available annually in the company's publications.[4]

(4) Market potential is estimated from the chosen indicators. Single factor indices (based on one indicator) or multiple factor indices may be used for this purpose. Multiple regression or other analytic techniques may help establish the relationship between the indicator and market potential.

---

[3]*Export Marketing for Smaller Firms* (3d ed.; Washington: Small Business Administration, 1971), pp. 20, 21.

[4]For details see, "Latest Indicators for 76 World Markets," *Business Europe*, 1976 Reprint Edition.

(5) Eliminate countries which do not meet the company's minimum requirements for market potential, economic growth, political risk, and available labor or natural resources.

(6) Rank the remaining countries by potential.

(7) Check for geographical clusters that would facilitate expansion. In this part of the analysis the company is interested in determining the best base for regional market penetration. Hungary or Finland might provide access to Eastern European markets. Similarly, England or West Germany could be the base for penetration of the European Economic Community or Brazil could be a compatible environment for marketing to the other Latin American Free Trade Area countries.

(8) Eliminate countries where trade or investment barriers prohibit profitable market entry. These barriers would include tariffs, quotas, currency regulations, investment restrictions, or other laws establishing operating conditions that are not acceptable to the firm.

(9) Select the most suitable countries for further analysis, the development of entry strategy, and the formulation of a marketing plan. Generally the firm will want to select relatively few countries for initial entry. A successful penetration of these will facilitate expansion later.

An Illustrative Experience

Sometimes this initial screening is accomplished by using an outside research organization. The experience of an American manufacturer of wrapping equipment illustrates such an approach.[5] The company employed a United Kingdom research agency to determine whether the product could profitably be sold in Europe. The United Kingdom research agency conducted a desk research of published data to provide the company with information from each country on the following:

1. Number of machines in use.
2. Suppliers of machines.
3. Annual replacement of machines.
4. Exports/imports of machines.
5. Price structure of machines.

The published research was augmented with a small number of interviews. As a result of the screening the firm isolated two countries where there was a large market and satisfaction with existing suppliers was low. Further research then was conducted in more depth on these two countries.

In this example the screening relied on secondary or published information but interviews were used to supplement the data. Use of the

---

[5]Aucamp, *op. cit.*

outside research organization enabled the U.S. manufacturer to gain the benefit of their research competence and local knowledge. Also, the researchers' proximity to the markets studied enabled the firm to carry out a minor amount of primary research at a relatively low cost.

DEVELOPMENT OF THE MARKETING STRATEGY

When it has been established that a potential market exists, attention is concentrated on the development of a marketing plan to capitalize on that potential. The emphasis shifts to an analysis of the factors that affect the individual company's ability to reach the market potential. Development of the marketing plan, however, requires more detailed information on customer needs and buying habits, available channels of distribution, promotional media, and pricing to shape the company's proposed strategy. Figure 6-2, on page 96, shows that the market potential must be assessed against the alternative entry strategies, marketing facilities, and company resources in order to establish the plan.

The Marketing Plan

The marketing plan is a program showing the company's strategy within the foreign market. Such a plan should be market oriented to reflect customer needs and market conditions. Figure 6-3 illustrates the steps involved in the formulation and implementation of such a marketing plan. The plan should include:

1. An analysis of market conditions including demand analysis, competitive analysis, and the basic consumer purchase motivation and buying behavior patterns of the relevant market segments.
2. A statement of marketing objectives showing what is to be accomplished within the time frame covered by the plan. It includes a definition of the market segments the firm desires to tap.
3. A marketing strategy that defines the marketing mix to be used in reaching the marketing objectives. It includes product policy, channels of distribution, pricing, promotional strategy, organizational needs, and marketing research support.
4. Estimated operating results that are developed on the basis of proposed strategy including sales forecasts, expense budgeting, cash flow, and estimated profits. The plan should provide a method for monitoring the implementation of the program to facilitate supervision and control. (These are included under "initiating operations" and "feedback" in Figure 6-3.)
5. An estimate of the company resources that will be required to implement the plan. Such resources include manpower, financing, materials, and management.

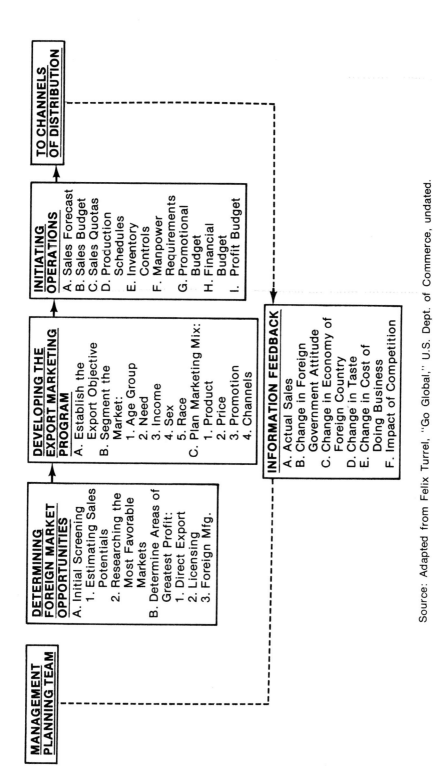

MANAGEMENT PLANNING TEAM

DETERMINING FOREIGN MARKET OPPORTUNITIES

A. Initial Screening
 1. Estimating Sales Potentials
 2. Researching the Most Favorable Markets
B. Determine Areas of Greatest Profit:
 1. Direct Export
 2. Licensing
 3. Foreign Mfg.

DEVELOPING THE EXPORT MARKETING PROGRAM

A. Establish the Export Objective
B. Segment the Market:
 1. Age Group
 2. Need
 3. Income
 4. Sex
 5. Race
C. Plan Marketing Mix:
 1. Product
 2. Price
 3. Promotion
 4. Channels

INITIATING OPERATIONS

A. Sales Forecast
B. Sales Budget
C. Sales Quotas
D. Production Schedules
E. Inventory Controls
F. Manpower Requirements
G. Promotional Budget
H. Financial Budget
I. Profit Budget

TO CHANNELS OF DISTRIBUTION

INFORMATION FEEDBACK

A. Actual Sales
B. Change in Foreign Government Attitude
C. Change in Economy of Foreign Country
D. Change in Taste
E. Change in Cost of Doing Business
F. Impact of Competition

Source: Adapted from Felix Turrel, "Go Global," U.S. Dept. of Commerce, undated.

Figure 6-3 PLANNING A SUCCESSFUL EXPORT MARKETING PROGRAM

The Informational Base For Planning

The information base for formulation of such a plan is outlined in Table 6-1. The specific items to be included are illustrative rather than comprehensive; however, they do provide insight regarding the kinds of information required for the strategy decision. Information sources for such data are treated later in this chapter. More detailed discussion of the components of the marketing mix is found in Part 3 of this text.

Demand analysis establishes the size of the market and its major characteristics. Economic characteristics relate to market potential, market growth, and the stage of market and economic development. Behavioral analysis bears on the customer's purchase motivation, buying habits, and cultural and social influences on the purchase decision.

Table 6-1   THE INFORMATIONAL BASE FOR THE MARKETING PLAN

Area and Type of Analysis	Information Required
Demand Analysis	
Economic	Market potential, market growth, stage of development, and income and expenditure patterns.
Behavioral	Purchase motivation, buying behavior, cultural and social influences, and attitude.
Industry	Technology, product cycle, product saturation, and new products.
Competition Analysis	Industry structure, competitor identification, marketing policy, competitors' strengths and weaknesses, company and product advantages and weaknesses, costs, and discretionary margins.
Marketing Environment	Available channels of distribution, promotional facilities, research facilities, transportation alternatives and costs, and pricing.
Market Entry Conditions	Tariffs, quotas and other nontariff barriers, investment restrictions, availability of foreign exchange, legal environment, and trade promotion.
Political Environment	Governmental structure and stability, direction and control of business, and policy and/or attitude toward foreign firms.
Company Resources	Manpower, financial, materials and equipment, and management.

Industry analysis provides information on the state of technology and product developments at home and abroad that may affect product offerings. The competitive analysis seeks to determine a firm's position within the industry and the types and degree of competition in the local market. Thus, demand analysis indicates market size. Competitive and industry analyses indicate the degree and manner by which the potential is currently being or may be tapped.

The marketing environment analysis describes the marketing infrastructure. Important facets of this environment include the retailing and wholesaling institutions that are available for distributing the product; the modes of transportation and freight costs, packaging and storage facilities; and the available media and manpower for advertising, sales promotion, publicity, and personal selling. Facilitating institutions for product and marketing research may also be identified. Closely allied to the marketing environment is an analysis of the various trade and investment barriers that restrict specific marketing approaches and the trade promotion activities of government that are designed to increase foreign investment.

The political environment forms a special area of analysis due to the significant role played by government in economic affairs. In many foreign countries government plays a more active role than in the United States. It not only sets the rules for the game, but exercises influence on the direction of business activity through its planning procedures and by direct ownership participation in the formation of state enterprises. Marketers are concerned about the political structure of a country and the stability of governments in order to assess future potential and risks. The structure and philosophy of existing governments and political opposition provide insight regarding governmental attitude and policy toward business and especially toward foreign firms. Political analysis, however, is difficult because of the need to overcome the unconscious reference to one's own preferences and value systems.[6]

Even though a market potential exists and the marketing and political infrastructure is favorable, marketing strategy choice can be restricted by the available company resources. An ideal market entry might be through the establishment of a wholly-owned subsidiary for both production and marketing within the foreign market, but this approach requires access to funds and an organizational capacity to provide skilled management and technical personnel from within or outside the firm. Lacking such resources, or being unwilling to commit them, the company might chose another strategy rather than give up. The timing of a series of moves could be crucial as the firm plans its overseas expansion in order to take advantage of current limitations while seeking broader objectives in the long run.

---

[6]This problem is present in cultural analysis in general and is discussed in the next chapter.

SOURCES OF MARKET INFORMATION

Successful planning of marketing strategy relies on accurate information. Marketing research provides the manager with the information needed to make marketing decisions.

At first the task of gathering information on foreign markets appears formidable since there are more than one hundred countries whose markets could provide additional profits to the firm. Each of these is similar in some respects to others, yet each retains some distinctive features. Probably the lack of knowledge regarding sources of international marketing data has detered some substantial, but unknown, number of potential international marketers.

Fortunately a wide variety of information sources is becoming available to meet the needs of expanding trade and investment. Many of these sources are accessible to the potential exporter or investor through public and university libraries, from the U.S. government, from international publications, and from local trade and business associations. Information has increased along with the growth of international business and its importance to individual companies, countries, and the world. For most countries basic economic data are available as well as much information on marketing systems and consumption. This is especially true for the industrial nations that represent the major market for U.S. goods and services. There also are considerable data available on the developing nations, but these may be less detailed and sometimes less reliable. However, a little ingenuity and considerable effort often turn up far more information than was originally thought to be available.

General References to Information Sources

Several published guides are available to help the analyst find specific sources of information on foregin markets. For example, U.S. reference works include the *Encyclopedia of Business Information Sources*[7] which provides references to 1,600 subject areas and 500 geographic categories. Referenced sources include yearbooks, specialized encyclopedias, indexes, trade associations, periodicals, and price sources. The *Guide to Foreign Trade Statistics*[8] from the Bureau of the Census is useful for understanding the content and arrangement of data concerning U.S. exports and imports. *A Compendium of Sources: International Trade Statistics*[9] issued by GATT (General Agreement on Tariffs and Trade) is a bibliography of international publications

---

[7]*Encyclopedia of Business Information Sources* (Detroit: Gale Research Company, 1971).

[8]Bureau of the Census, *Guide to Foreign Trade Statistics* (Washington: U.S. Government Printing Office).

[9]*A Compendium of Sources: International Trade Statistics* (Geneva: The General Agreement on Tariffs and Trade).

containing statistics and a catalog of statistics collected by international organizations. The *Foreign Commerce Handbook*[10] from the Chamber of Commerce of the United States references the functions and services of the U.S. Government, intergovernmental organizations, and private organizations concerned with foreign commerce. A list of data and information sources is arranged by subject headings and the handbook also contains a bibliography of reference works, books, pamphlets, and periodicals dealing with foreign trade and marketing.

The *International Executive*,[11] a quarterly publication, reviews and indexes current books and articles significant to international marketing, financing, organization, and control. *Export Marketing for Smaller Firms*[12] from the Small Business Administration is a manual for smaller firms that seek foreign sales. It outlines the steps needed for assessing these foreign markets and contains a bibliography of information sources on international statistics, data on foreign markets, and material related to the mechanics of exporting.

A Classification of Information Sources

The sources of information that provide data on foreign markets and international marketing can be grouped into three categories: governmental sources, private sources, and primary research. Some of the information from these sources is free, or nominal in cost, while other services are available only upon payment of a fee. Some of the published data, especially from governmental sources, is easily accessible in local libraries, but ingenuity may also reveal corporate subscribers such as banks or suppliers that are willing to make their copies available as a service to their customers.

A simple classification of sources is useful as a guide to be sure no major source has been overlooked. One such grouping would divide the sources as follows:

Governmental sources

U.S. government
Foreign governments
International and regional organizations

Private sources

General reference publications
Trade and business associations
Trade journals
Service industries

---

[10]*Foreign Commerce Handbook* (Washington: Chamber of Commerce of the United States).

[11]*The International Executive* (Hastings-on-Hudson: Foundation for the Advancement of International Business Administration, quarterly).

[12]Small Business Administration, *Export Marketing for Smaller Firms*, (3d ed.; Washington: U.S. Government Printing Office, 1971).

Suppliers and customers
Syndicated services
Consultants and research agencies

Primary research

Personal visits
Trade fairs and trade missions
Surveys and product studies
Market testing

Any list of information sources touches on only a few of the total that are available; furthermore, such a list soon becomes outdated. No attempt has been made to provide a comprehensive list in this chapter, although the chapter appendix beginning on page 110 presents a sampling of the types of publications available from the United States government. The reader is encouraged to use leads from these publications and other sources to find the specific data required for analysis.

The sources previously listed make data available in several forms. The U.S. and foreign governments, together with such international and regional organizations as the United Nations and the Organization for Economic Cooperation and Development (OECD), provide a wealth of information in published form. To carry out their responsibilities such governmental and other organizations develop economic data on their sphere of influence such as data on population, income, consumption patterns, exports and imports, balance of trade, economic trends, and government projects. In addition, they make studies that provide insight on social trends, lifestyles, health, regulations, etc. *The Monthly Catalog of United States Government Publications* indexes the publications of all branches of the government. The *United Nations Documents Index* provides a similar function for UN data.

Some of the private sources listed publish information on international business in general (Rundts), specific industries (The Economic Intelligence Unit), specific functions (*Financial Times*), or geographic areas (*Business Asia*). Market studies for specific products such as small computers or health care products are available for a fee. Consultants and marketing research agencies perform market studies tailored to meet the needs of their clients. These latter agencies may be American-based with branches or research capability in selected markets,[13] or in the major markets there may be local agencies to perform this service. *Bradford's Directory of Marketing Research Agencies and Management Consultants in the United States and the World* is a list of these organizations.

A personal visit to the countries under consideration gives executives an opportunity to learn more about the market and to get a feel for marketing there. Also, the visit makes it possible to fill gaps in the

---

[13]For example, Burke Marketing Research, a U.S. based firm, has access to the major world markets through ten branches in Europe, South America, and Japan.

information from published studies. It can help to establish relationships with trade representatives and with government agencies. The visit can facilitate the selection of distributors by providing first-hand knowledge of their facilities and policies. In this respect it can help to avoid some problems that become more obvious in the local setting. For example, one American firm entered preliminary negotiations for representation of its product line in the Far East. A personal visit would have quickly revealed that its correspondent had no facilities, no sales organization, and had contacts in only one of the markets concerned.

Personal visits can be made in conjunction with participation in international trade fairs such as those held regularly at Canton, Leipzig, Hanover, Milan, and Zagreb. Some of these fairs offer goods from a wide range of industries while others specialize in a single industry. A potential exporter can join a U.S. trade mission or exhibit at U.S. trade centers in foreign countries. The fairs, exhibits, and trade missions present an opportunity to meet with people who already show an interest in the kinds of products the firm produces.

When a major investment is to be made in production or marketing, the company should consider the possibility of product and market testing. Such a procedure is commonly used in the U.S. and often in Europe. It enables the company to evaluate product acceptability and the effectiveness of the proposed marketing mix.

COMPARATIVE MARKETING ANALYSIS AND THE INTERNATIONAL MARKETING INFORMATION SYSTEMS

Foreign market studies are needed to locate markets for a firm's products and to measure the potential of such markets. These studies provide information for the initial entry decision, but market analysis should not be considered a "one shot" approach. When the firm markets internationally there is need for a system to continuously monitor environmental changes and the company's performance. Furthermore, the firm can capitalize on its experience in other markets if comparative data are available. Figure 6-3 shows this need by providing for feedback of information to evaluate performance.

Many of the elements to be monitored are the same as those monitored for domestic marketing. Studies of sales results in relation to market potential are indicative of the firm's marketing effectiveness. The environment is continually checked for changes in consumer tastes, competitors' strategy, and technological development. Product studies and market testing evaluate the acceptability of new products and of changes in design, size, color, price, and packaging. Sales results, attitude change, and readership studies analyze advertising, sales promotion, and personal selling.

The firm's marketing information system keeps its marketers continuously aware of conditions in foreign markets to determine when basic strategy should be altered, promotion or prices changed, or the product modified. The system will include continuous monitoring of some facets of the environment and operations and periodic studies of others. Such an information system will receive input from internal reports and personal contacts as well as published data. The system should be capable of detecting changes in basic economic conditions such as gross national product, income levels and sources, economic development plans, and industry trends. It also should provide early warning of changes in consumer tastes, lifestyles, and shopping patterns along with social and political changes that impair or enhance the marketing effect.

The basic functions of corporate headquarters in the multinational firm are planning, control, and evaluating foreign operations.[14] Headquarters has access to a wealth of experience from its operations in other countries or other periods of time that can be vital to intelligent planning. Comparative analysis of these data aid corporate headquarters in setting goals and preparing for market entry. Grouping countries and gathering information on success and failure helps to extrapolate from present markets to similar ones being considered for entry. In searching out foreign markets many researchers and exporters look for a degree of similarity between the foreign market and that at home.[15] Comparative analysis facilitates the identification of countries that possess common characteristics relevant to the marketing process. Furthermore, global marketing strategy relies on the ability to segment markets so that similar decisions can be applied to groups of countries or to similar types of customs in different countries.

Country data can be subjected to cluster analysis to form relatively similar groups based on cultural, religious, socioeconomic, political characteristics, and similar marketing networks.[16] Similar customer segments may be found across country groups such as the buyers of blue jeans or of high-priced automobiles. However, before such an international segmentation model can be developed for planning, three conditions must exist: (1) a methodology must be developed to group countries, (2) the grouping must be relevant to marketing decisions, and (3) data describing the country characteristics must be available at low cost.[17] This last is the function of a firm's international marketing information system. If the relevant information is available, comparative analysis can provide the multinational firm with leverage over its competitors in the transfer of experience. Additionally,

---

[14]Bertil Liander, Vern Terpstra, Michael Y. Yoshino, and A. A. Sherbini, *Comparative Analysis for International Marketing* (Boston: Allyn & Bacon, Inc., 1967). The study was sponsored by the Marketing Science Institute.

[15]Eugene D. Jaffe, *Grouping: A Study for International Marketing* (New York: AMACOM, Division of American Management Associations, 1974), p. 3.

[16]S. Prakesh Sethi, "Comparative Cluster Analysis for World Markets," *Journal of Marketing Research* (August, 1971), pp. 348–354; Charles Ramond, *The Art of Using Science in Marketing* (New York: Harper & Row Publishers, Inc., 1974), pp. 213–237.

[17]Jaffe, *op. cit.*, p. 5.

comparative analysis facilitates control by helping to establish appropriate standards for judging the effectiveness with which the marketing plan is implemented. Comparisons can be drawn between countries having similar characteristics rather than the more common comparison of countries within a geographic marketing region.

QUESTIONS

1. What objectives are served by each of the two phases of market analysis when a company intends to enter world markets?
2. Describe the screening process for selecting countries with high potential for a firm's products.
3. How do market indicators aid in selecting countries with high market potential for a company's products?
4. What are the essential elements of the marketing plan? How does the plan affect an analyst's gathering of information on foreign markets?
5. What are the three major components of demand analysis? Why is it necessary to investigate each?
6. Why might the analysis of the political environment not be prominent in domestic analysis, yet be significant when investigating foreign markets?
7. Comment on the statement that "there is a dearth of published material on foreign markets."
8. Why is the U.S. government a major supplier of information to U.S. firms on foreign markets and marketing?
9. Why would a multinational firm be interested in comparative market analysis? Where would it get the information for such an analysis?
10. Select a product and a country to which you would like to export it. What sources of information are available to provide the necessary data to determine whether it is a viable market?
11. Prepare an analysis of the marketing opportunity for a specific product (e.g., hospital beds) in a specific country.

SUPPLEMENTARY READINGS

Export Marketing for Smaller Firms, 3d ed. Washington: Small Business Administration, 1971.

Haner, F. T. *Multinational Management*. Columbus, Ohio: Charles E. Merrill Publishing Company, 1973.

Jaffee, Eugene D. *Grouping: A Study for International Marketing*. New York: AMACOM, Division of American Management Association, 1974.

Kracmar, John Z. *Marketing Research in Developing Countries*. New York: Praeger Publishers, Inc., 1971.

Ramond, Charles. *The Art of Using Science in Marketing*. New York: Harper & Row Publishers, Inc., 1974.

Robinson, Richard D. *International Business Management*. New York: Holt, Rinehart & Winston, Inc., 1973.

Robock, Stefan H., and Kenneth Simmonds. *International Business and Multinational Enterprises*. Homewood, Ill. Richard D. Irwin, Inc., 1973.

Root, Franklin R. *Strategic Planning for Export Marketing*. Scranton, Pa.: International Textbook Co., 1966. Chapters 2 and 3.

Stuart, Robert Douglass. *Penetrating the International Market*. New York: American Management Association, 1965. Chapters I, III, and IV.

APPENDIX

U.S. Government Publications Providing Information For Researching Foreign Markets

Bureau of the Census, *Foreign Trade Report FT 410 U.S. Exports Commodity by Country* (monthly). A statistical record of the shipments of merchandise from the U.S. to foreign countries showing both quantities and dollar value to individual countries.

U.S. Department of Commerce

International Economic Indicators and Competitive Trends (quarterly). Basic economic data on the U.S. and seven other industrial countries.

Index to Foreign Market Reports. An index of some 200 reports received monthly from the U.S. Foreign Service. Classifies market information by SIC code, product, topic, and country.

Market Share Reports (annual). U.S. participation in foreign markets in latest five-year period. Separate reports on 82 import markets comparing U.S. performance in 880 manufactured products with eight other principal suppliers.

Overseas Business Reports. Basic background data showing pertinent marketing factors and economic/commercial profiles of countries.

Global Market Surveys. Market studies on target industries identified by the Department of Commerce, the U.S. Foreign Service, and American business as having export potential.

Commerce America (bi-weekly). Formerly *Commerce Today*. Reports news of domestic and international commerce, including developments affecting U.S. markets, market prospects, calendar of trade promotions, and a listing of licensing, sales, and construction opportunities.

Special Reports. The East-West Trade Bureau issues special reports on the markets for specific products in Eastern Europe and China. Special reports also are issued on specific markets of interest. For example, *The Near East Market* reported on marketing opportunities, business climate, and business customs for twelve Near East countries in 1974 to meet the needs of business firms interested in that expanding market.

In addition to its regularly published sources, the Department of Commerce and the U.S. Foreign Service provide assistance in locating distributors, provide descriptive data on specific foreign firms (*World Traders Data Reports*), and aid the business person in establishing contacts on personal visits to the country. (these activities are further described in Chapter 18.)

Other U.S. Government Agencies

The U.S. Department of State. *Background Notes* give profiles of individual countries. The U.S. Foreign Service cooperates in the development of business opportunities through the commercial attaches in U.S. embassies abroad.

The U.S. Department of Agriculture appraises the agricultural trade showing the outlook for trade, the world agricultural situation, and individual country reports.

CHAPTER **7**

Culture and Marketing

Chapter 6 developed certain concepts and indicators which determine whether a firm can profitably market its products within a foreign country. Cultural factors such as family and government were largely ignored in that discussion, although markets consist of people who are influenced by social norms. As members of society, consumers' responses to marketing efforts reflect the traditions, customs, and mores of their society. Furthermore, what seems appropriate to the members of one society may not be so to members of another. People adapt to their unique environments by developing different solutions to the problems of everyday consumption and production. The solutions generated within this consumption process are generally considered a major aspect of the society's culture.

WHAT IS CULTURE?

The term *culture* has many meanings. In this chapter, the term is used to describe a society's design for living. Here culture refers to "the sum total of learned behavior traits which are manifest and shared by the members of a society."[1]

Culture provides the members of a society with a means to comfortably interact with their environment and each other. People think and act according to the norms of the culture in which they have been reared. Values and beliefs adopted from the family, reference, and social groups provide individuals with a sense of security and help them function in the society.

Culture, as defined in this chapter, emphasizes that our values and beliefs are learned, passed on from generation to generation, purposeful, and not static. These concepts are important to marketers in their efforts to provide for the wants of consumers. If consumption problems are to be solved efficiently, world marketers must, at a minimum, come to understand the culture in the markets they intend to serve and the constraints imposed by those societies. Culture affects all areas of marketing: product design and acceptance, communication

[1]E. Adamson Hoebel, "The Nature of Culture," in *Man, Culture and Society*, edited by Harry L. Shapiro (Oxford: Oxford University Press, Inc., 1971), p. 208.

methods, the role of family members in the purchasing process, relations with distributors, and even physical distribution.

Characteristics of Culture

Some of the basic characteristics that underlie all cultures are indicated in the following quotation:

> First, *culture is learned*, it is not present at birth but must be acquired. Second, *culture is passed from one generation to another*. Inculcation involves not only the passing on of techniques and knowledge but also the disciplining of the child's animal instincts and impulses in order to adjust him to social life. Third, *culture is social by nature* and consists of groups of habits formed in relationship with others. In effect, culture prescribes the manner of social interaction. Fourth, *group habits, to an extent, are conceptionalized as ideal norms of behavior*. Most people show an acute awareness of their own cultural norms. Fifth, *culture always satisfies some basic or secondary need*. Its elements are tested, habitual techniques for gratifying human impulses in man's interaction with the external world. Any product of culture that is not gratifying tends to be changed over time. Sixth, *culture tends to adjust to the geographic environment by borrowing from the social environment of neighboring peoples*. It also tends to adjust to the biological and psychological demands of the people composing the culture. Seventh, *elements of a culture tend to form a consistent and integrated whole*.[2] [Italics added]

These characteristics indicate that a society's culture is very complex, purposeful, and slow in changing, and that this change partly results from borrowing from another culture. For the international market, this suggests a need for research and openmindedness in order to understand the cultural nuances; a need to recognize that cultural patterns reflect a specific society's adjustment to its environment; and finally that cultural factors, though eventually changing, are likely to be environmental factors to which the marketer must adjust the immediate marketing program. To gain such insight, the various dimensions of culture are presented. These major dimensions become key factors in analyzing the cultural context within which the firm operates in its overseas market.

Dimensions of Culture

Students of culture have evolved several classifications to gain a better understanding of its key components or dimensions. One such classification appears in Figure 7-1. These cultural dimensions remind marketers of the critical elements that affect the marketing plan. The concept of culture is both complex and pervasive; this is evident from

---

[2]C. Glenn Walters, *Consumer Behavior: Theory and Practice* (Homewood, Ill.: Richard D. Irwin, Inc., 1974), p. 323.

the dimensions shown. The chart indicates essentially two major dimensions of culture: the material shown as technology and economics and the abstract shown as social institutions, ideas, aesthetics, and language. Abstract elements include values, attitudes, ideas, personality types, and constructs such as religion. The material elements of culture are the artifacts of society and include products of all types from computers, to automobiles, hair tonic, and housing.[3] Both the material and abstract components of culture are of vital interest to the international marketer since the consumer reacts in the marketplace to the entire complex of culture rather than to one single overpowering element. Although any one of the dimensions may be more important than others in a given purchase situation, and thus critical to the analysis of behavior, that element is still only one part of the total situation and may account for less than half of the variance in behavior.[4]

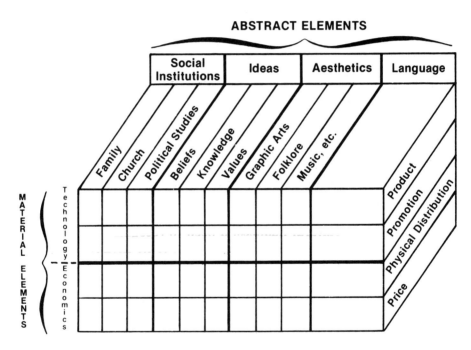

Figure 7-1 INTERACTION OF THE MARKETING MIX AND THE DIMENSIONS OF CULTURE

The matrix portrays the major dimensions of culture and the interaction of the various dimensions with the marketing mix. Although

[3]James F. Engel, David T. Kollat, and Roger D. Blackwell, *Consumer Behavior* (2d ed.; New York: Holt, Rinehart and Winston, Inc., 1973), p. 72.
[4]Rom J. Markim, *Consumer Behavior: A Cognitive Orientation* (New York: Macmillan Publishing Co., Inc., 1974), p. 465.

marketing itself is part of a society's culture, here it is treated separately because of the interest in the marketing management process. The matrix indicates that decisions regarding any of the four elements of the marketing mix — product, promotion, physical distribution, and pricing — are all influenced by both the material and abstract dimensions of culture. The matrix further suggests the presence of interrelations among the material and abstract components. The international marketer must consider both the individual components and their interaction in the design of an appropriate marketing mix for specific countries or market segments.

Direction of Relationships

One feature of the matrix should be noted: the flow of influence among the dimensions and between them and marketing is not unidirectional. On the one hand marketers need to recognize the restrictions that culture imposes on the marketing process. Products that are introduced should be acceptable to the existing culture; similarly, the promotional program should take into account the cultural imperatives and proscriptions. However, marketing also plays an important role in changing the existing cultural patterns. It acts as a change agent and, with the family, church, government, and other social institutions, it affects the beliefs, attitudes, and values of consumers. Multinational marketing is an important medium of intercultural interaction bringing to one country the marketing and technical know-how and lifestyles from other areas and cultures. It serves to transform attitudes, lifestyles, and business customs and has been significant in changing both consumption and production in underdeveloped and developing countries.[5] Because of its influence, the marketer should understand how the company's marketing program dovetails with the existing culture. The marketers should also understand the effect the marketing program may have on other elements of the culture, including the existing religious and political power structures and consumer attitudes. Marketing programs that run counter to existing values and beliefs are likely to encounter resistance, but those that can recognize and build upon existing cultural values improve their chances for success.

Subcultures

One other significant concept that is important to the marketer is not apparent in the matrix: no culture is monolithic. Each contains within the dominant culture one or more *subcultures*. Subcultures

---

[5]These concepts are developed by Hans B. Thorelli in "The Multinational Corporation as a Change Agent," *The Southern Journal of Business* (July, 1966), pp. 1–9.

include teenagers, ethnic groups within a society, urban or rural societies, and scientific or religious groups. Although the behavioral patterns of these groups reflect many norms of the dominant culture, they deviate significantly when the norms are not compatible with those of the subculture.[6] For example, although different nationality groups within a country may be in sympathy with the dominant culture, they may still reflect the ideas and values of their heritage in eating, housing, and social behavior.

Subcultures are interesting to the marketer for two reasons. One, they often form the basis for distinct market segments. As such, these subcultures may represent market potential for a specific product in spite of the dominant norms (e.g., rock music among the young in cultures long associated with the classics). Or these market segments may be reached through advertising media that cater to their special interests (international or scientific publications). A second reason why subcultures are of interest lies in their function as *contracultures*. Since they do not share all the values of the dominant group, they can act as change agents within their own culture. They, accordingly, could represent ascending or descending value systems — at least they may provide some index of the direction of change within a country. Subcultures may serve as significant aids or barriers to the introduction of foreign ideas and products.

The urban subculture within a nation illustrates the value of subcultural analysis for the marketer. In many nations the urban population represents the major marketing opportunity for the multinational firm. Major cities contain a substantial percentage of the total population. The urban population usually includes much of the industrial wealth of the nation, has a higher per capita income, and is the segment most closely associated with foreign products and ideas. Urbanites often represent the major market for consumer manufactured products that are not endemic to the culture. The urban sector frequently has greater exposure to products via the mass media of television, magazines, radio, and personal contact. In some countries the urban society is heavily represented by the national capitol which controls both commercial and diplomatic contacts abroad. The industrialization process, plus the alienation from the rural family heritage, often leads to relaxation of the customs and traditions of forebears. The extended family loses its influence and the nuclear family is more prominent in the consumption decisions. The city is the center of manufacturing and the core market for industrial goods. Corporations replace family enterprises and traditional festivals are no longer celebrated. Even such customs as the long break from work at mid-day give way to the discipline of the industrial society. The relative

---

[6]Peter D. Bennett and Harold H. Kasserjian, *Consumer Behavior, Foundations of Marketing Series* (Englewood Cliffs, N.J.: Prentice Hall, Inc., 1972), p. 124.

affluence of the city dweller enables the expenditure of increasing percentages of the family budget on nonessentials that permit a different lifestyle from the traditional.

The impact of urbanization may create a market that differs in degree, if not in kind, from that of the rural society. Although increasing affluence may, in time, create more similarity between urban and rural cultures, most societies maintain sufficient differences so that the residents of each are not entirely satisfied with the lifestyle of the other. Marketers then must adapt to significant market segments.

SOURCES OF CROSS-CULTURAL INFORMATION

Although cultural analysis relies heavily on approaches developed by cultural anthropologists, international marketers actually have a variety of sources and methods available for extending their knowledge of specific cultures. Many concentrate on cultural elements that directly affect international business. Cultural knowledge may be gained from documentary sources, from personal contacts with the culture or persons intimately acquainted with it, or from formal research. The international marketer often must use all three general sources. These sources are discussed in the following sections.

Documentary Sources

Documentary reports include numerous publications from the fields of anthropology, sociology, history, and political science, as well as the publications of news services. Reports also emanate from the firm's own subsidiary operations as special reports or as regular operating documents.

Texts and journals in the fields of anthropology and sociology are replete with studies of specific cultures which help marketers understand various cultures. Some marketers have educational and experience backgrounds that sensitize them to cultural elements that are important to the introduction of their product within the culture. Other marketers, knowing their geographical expansion plans, may adapt to the specific culture through an educational program. Often, however, the manager refers to specific data relating to the environment for buyer behavior and business customs rather than an analysis of the total culture. The marketer seeks information on receptivity to change, trading customs, etc.

The number of both published and internal sources of information has increased in recent years as American firms have become more involved in international business. Coverage of special issues involving aspects of culture pertinent to the marketing effort are found in general publications such as *The Wall Street Journal* and *Business Week*, in U.S. government publications, and in foreign publications in both

English and other languages. Banks and other service organizations provide information for their clients in periodic reports which indicate changes in the political, legal, and economic climate. Some publications sponsored by government information offices, such as *Colombia Today*, *Free China Weekly*, and the *British Record* are available in many public libraries or by request.

A major problem for the marketer is the establishment of a monitoring system to audit the profusion of information that is available, especially when the company markets a wide line of products in many different countries. The reliability of the information must be assessed. Since some aspects of culture are changing more rapidly than in previous times, there is danger that information may not be current. For this reason many marketers rely heavily upon current periodicals and commercial services. Also, the decision-making process in the firm often means that the time available for gaining cultural insights and monitoring information is limited. The ability to monitor many sources is especially difficult when staff assistance is minimal.

Sometimes documentary studies are the only source of information available to the marketer, due to time and money constraints or because the marketer is not permitted the personal contact or formal research. More often they supplement other sources. For example, the author of a study of Soviet consumers concentrating on the rural Europeans, the Asian minorities, and the frontier settlers rather than the inhabitants of Moscow commented:

> Although the author has made trips to the U.S.S.R. and conducted research there, and had valuable assistance from the Soviet Embassy in Washington, D.C., the methodology, to a considerable extent, consists of a careful analysis and synthesis of Russian-origin literature. Admittedly not ideal, this methodology is nevertheless standard practice among scholars interested in the Soviet Union in every academic discipline.[7]

Personal Contact

For many executives a preferred source of information is personal contact. The marketer either personally visits the country and/or makes contact with knowledgeable people. The significance of these personal contacts is evident in a recent study of information sources used to scan the international scene. Human sources accounted for 67% of all important external information reported by executives,[8]

---

[7]Thomas V. Greer, "Cross-Cultural Consideration in Consumer Behavior: The Case of the Consumer in the Soviet Union," *Proceedings of the Third Annual Conference of the Association for Consumer Research*, M. Venkatesan, ed. (Chicago: Center for Continuing Education, University of Chicago, 1972), pp. 830–838.

[8]Warren J. Keegan, "Multinational Scanning: A Study of the Information Sources Utilized by Headquarters Executives in Multinational Companies," *Administration Science Quarterly* (September, 1974), p. 413.

thereby corroborating previous research indicating the preference for personal sources. Prominent among these human sources are corporate executives in the multinational firm's subsidiaries and affiliates, service organization staffs (banks, advertising agencies, etc.), and other business firms. Personal contact also is made with consumers, distributors, and government representatives.

A personal visit to the potential market provides marketers with an opportunity to check information from other sources and to see how the consumer's needs are presently met. The executive gains first-hand knowledge of how the proposed product will fit into the consumers' use system. Furthermore, the marketer develops personal relationships with distributors and other key personnel and gains a better insight regarding their customary modes of operation. The marketer obtains factual knowledge through personal perception and gains a "feel" for the interpretation of information from other sources.

Executives may seek the experience of knowledgeable people at trade meetings and seminars where "experts" relate their views of the significant aspects of the foreign cultures. One recent conference was addressed by U.S. government representatives acquainted with the Near East, by the representatives of Near Eastern governments and executives of companies experienced in marketing to the Near East nations.[9] Speakers and club members at World Trade meetings often relate their experiences in foreign cultures — especially in the areas of political, legal, and market developments.

Primary Research

Primary research on foreign culture often is necessary to secure information directly pertaining to the firm's marketing program. This research can use several approaches.

One research approach is *intensive field studies* where the researcher is located within the culture. Data are obtained through observation, participation in on-going activities, or by administering various tests. Some of these studies are exploratory without explicit research designs, while others are structured descriptive studies utilizing survey techniques. Professional journals often report such studies; for example, the *Journal of Marketing* has reported studies on marketing in Spain, Brazil, Peru, Nigeria, and several other countries. Often these studies rely heavily on the insight of the individual observer. Research performed by the company's subsidiaries may also be of this type.

Content analysis can be employed to determine the values, norms of behavior, and other elements of a culture by examining the verbal

---

[9]"Exporting and Investment with the Major Oil-Producing Countries of the Near East," Seminar at Miami University, September 10, 1975.

materials produced by the culture.[10] The researcher analyses the content of newspapers, magazines, TV, advertising, or other verbal expressions of the culture. In this type of analysis, the researcher does not need to physically enter the culture to perform the analysis. For example, Zaltman and Burger report that researchers from an advertising agency analyzed unstructured interviews that had been recorded on tape in order to prepare an advertising campaign in Central America. The analysis enabled them to identify several specific mores and to develop appropriate advertising appeals.[11]

Several techniques can be used to gain cultural insights directly related to marketing problems. One study of Sao Paulo, Brazil, used the *survey* technique to examine the shopping and consumption patterns of individuals in various social classes.[12] The study employed a stratified random sampling procedure and personal interviews to investigate differences among the social classes in the types of stores frequented, sources of information used, use of installment financing, mode of transportation, and the importance of store services. The general hypothesis was that differences existed between the shopping patterns of individuals in the different social classes. The study revealed these differences and demonstrated that social class can be used for market segmentation in industrializing economies. The Sao Paulo market was found to be a diversified society with distinct shopping characteristics.

In another survey the *case method* was used to study the transferability of advertising. Top marketing and advertising executives in thirty companies, with representatives of their advertising agencies, were interviewed to determine how much the companies used their U.S. advertisements in other countries and to find the economic, cultural, and media criteria that were used in making the decision. The results indicated that economic criteria were more widely used than cultural or media criteria. However, the study provided insight regarding the ability to transfer advertising approaches from one country to another.[13]

CROSS-CULTURAL ANALYSIS

A wide variety of data-gathering techniques may be used to obtain information on relevant cultural characteristics. The few examples above can be supplemented by other frequently utilized research

---

[10]Engel, Kollat, and Blackwell, *op. cit.*, p. 80.

[11]Gerald Zaltman and Philip C. Burger, *Marketing Research: Fundamentals and Dynamics* (Hinsdale, Ill.: The Dryden Press, 1975), p. 150.

[12]William H. Cunningham, Russell M. Moore, and Isabella C. M. Cunningham, "Urban Markets in Industrializing Countries: The Sao Paulo Experience," *Journal of Marketing* (April, 1974), pp. 2–12.

[13]S. Watson Dunn, "The Case Study Approach in Cross-Cultural Research," *Journal of Marketing Research* (February, 1966), pp. 26–31.

concepts from domestic marketing and social science research. However, a major problem still exists in determining how the information can be structured for analysis. In the next section three approaches are briefly described for evaluating the cultural impact on product introductions through cross-cultural analysis.

An Outline for Research. Engel, Kollat, and Blackwell have presented a partial outline of research questions that could be asked in a cross-cultural analysis.[14] This outline is reproduced in Figure 7-2. The outline questions, first, the need for the product by members of the culture and proceeds to investigate purchasing behavior. Item three questions whether there are existing beliefs and values that will affect acceptance of the product and if any potential conflicts with these values can be resolved. If the product is acceptable, the research seeks to determine who influences the purchase and how the decision is made. Five and six deal with cultural impacts on communication methods, themes, and techniques for introduction, and with the marketing institutions that are appropriate and available. The analysis investigates the cultural environment within which the need exists and the beliefs, values, and institutions that will characterize the marketing effort. The questions can be expanded to account for the specifics of the product, industry, and market.

Analysis of Basic Values. Sommers and Kernan investigated the reasons for product acceptance in the domestic market and failure abroad on the premise that "individuals within a culture generally rely on basic hard-core values for all types of decisions — those dealing with consumption as well as others."[15] Their research relied on six categories of value orientation previously developed by Parsons and Lipset. Cultural patterns were distinguished by the degree to which people: (1) are egalitarian or elitest; (2) are prone to stress accomplishment or inherited attributes; (3) expect material or nonmaterial rewards; (4) evaluate individuals or products in terms of objective norms or subjective standards; (5) focus on the whole or the distinctiveness of the parts; and (6) are oriented toward personal or group rewards. Four countries were scaled on these variables to see how cultural variations would affect both product and promotion. Cultural values were found to determine the position of sanctioned products in a market. Dominant value orientations of the cultures provided clues for development of both product and promotional strategy.

A Theory of Buyer Behavior. Sheth and Sethi have provided a tentative cross-cultural model to aid in the analysis of buyer behavior (see

---

[14]Engel, Kollat, and Blackwell, *op. cit.*, p. 80.

[15]Montrose Sommers and Jerome Kernan, "Why Products Flourish Here, Fizzle There," *Columbia Journal of World Business* (March/April, 1967), pp. 89–97.

(1) **Determine relevant motivations on the culture:**
What needs are fulfilled with this product in the minds of members of the culture? How are these needs presently fulfilled? Do members of this culture readily recognize these needs?

(2) **Determine characteristic behavior patterns:**
What patterns are characteristic of a purchasing behavior? What forms of labor exist within the family structure? How frequently are products of this type purchased? What size packages are normally purchased? Do any of these characteristic behaviors conflict with behavior expected for this product? How strongly ingrained are the behavior patterns that conflict with those needed for distribution of this product?

(3) **Determine what broad cultural values are relevant to this product:**
Are there strong values about work, morality, religion, family relations, and so on, that relate to this product? Does this product connote attributes that are in conflict with these cultural values? Can conflicts with values be avoided by changing the product? Are there positive values in this culture with which the product might be identified?

(4) **Determine characteristic forms of decision making:**
Do members of the culture display a studied approach to decisions concerning innovations or an impulsive approach? What is the form of the decision process? Upon what information or sources do members of the culture rely? Do members of the culture tend to be rigid or flexible in the acceptance of new ideas? What criteria do they use in evaluating alternatives?

(5) **Evaluate promotion methods appropriate to the culture:**
What role does advertising play in the culture? What themes, words, or illustrations are taboo? What language problems exist in present markets that cannot be translated into this culture? What types of salesmen are accepted by members of the culture? Are such salesmen available?

(6) **Determine appropriate institutions for this product in the minds of the consumer:**
What types of retailers and intermediary institutions are available? What services do these institutions offer that are expected by the consumer? What alternatives are available for obtaining services needed for the product but not offered by existing institutions? How are various types of retailers regarded by consumers? Will changes in the distribution structure be readily accepted?

Source: From CONSUMER BEHAVIOR, Second Edition by James F. Engel, David T. Kollat and Roger D. Blackwell. Copyright © 1968, 1973 by Holt, Rinehart and Winston, Inc. Reprinted by permission of Holt, Rinehart and Winston.

Figure 7-2. Outline of Cross-Cultural Analysis of Consumer Behavior

Figure 7-3).[16] A central construct in their theory is the culture's propensity to change. This measures the receptivity of a culture in seeking alternatives to present consumption. The propensity to change is determined by (1) the cultural lifestyle (activities, interests, and opinions with respect to those cultural universals that are salient to consumption), (2) generalized opinion leadership (role of a select group of individuals or institutions to lead in search for change and improvement), and (3) communication about the innovation from commercial, central (public), or social (friends, relatives) sources.

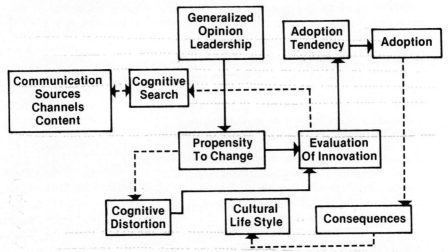

Source: Adapted from Jagdish Sheth and S. Prakash Sethi, "Theory of Cross-Cultural Buyer Behavior," in *Foundations of Consumer and Industrial Buying Behavior*, edited by Arch Woodside, Jagdish Sheth, and Peter Bennett (New York: American Elsivier Company, 1977).

Figure 7-3 CROSS-CULTURAL MODEL: ANALYSIS OF BUYER BEHAVIOR

When propensity to change is high and innovation is favorably evaluated, there is a tendency to adopt. Several factors such as per capita income, marketing institutions, and the value of time have been identified as influencing this tendency to adopt. Also, the customers may search for support of their adoption decision by consulting communication sources and the generalized opinion leadership. A strong adoption tendency may lead to trial and permanent adoption unless impeded by unpredictable factors such as political instability, recession, government controls, etc. If permanent adoption occurs, it will have impact on both the propensity to change and on evaluation of the innovation.

---

[16]Adapted from Jagdish Sheth and S. Prakash Sethi, "Theory of Cross-Cultural Buyer Behavior," in *Foundations of Consumer and Industrial Buying Behavior*, edited by Arch Woodside, Jagdish Sheth, and Peter Bennett (New York: American Elsivier Company, 1977).

The authors' presentation of the model is enriched by more detail than presented here; the original source should be consulted for these details. The value of this model lies in the organization of cultural constructs for analysis of critical elements. The theory is a first attempt to integrate research from anthropology and diffusion theory and apply it to cross-cultural buyer behavior.

Some Cautions on Cross-Cultural Analysis

Marketers of products abroad may recognize that cultural variations are significant. They may be quite willing to invest time and money to determine the importance of the critical cultural factors that affect marketing strategy; but before accepting the research results they should be critical of biases in the analysis and of the need for cultural competence as distinguished from cultural knowledge. A third warning relates to the rapidity of change.

The Self-Reference Criterion. Many of the items in the earlier sections of this chapter may seem obvious, but marketers should be aware of one problem: we are all products of our own culture and may interpret other cultures from our own perspective. We operate without a conscious reference to our own cultural norms, but when operating abroad we can no longer rely on those norms. Careful analysis is required to avoid unintentionally violating the norms of other cultures where we want to sell our goods and services. James Lee believes that the self-reference criterion (SRC) — the unconscious reference to one's own cultural values — is the root cause of most international business problems overseas.[17] He suggests a four-step process to minimize the effect of our own value systems upon the analysis of a product's potential in another country. These are:

1. List the American (or Western) traits, economics, values, needs, or habits that are fundamental to the success of the product here in the United States.
2. List the related traits, economics, values, needs or habits in the proposed market culture and compare them with those in Step 1.
3. The SRC can then be seen to account for the differences between Steps 1 and 2.
4. These differences, if they are significant, serve as the warning signal that the product should be modified or discarded, or that the product should be designed to fit the market needs listed in Step 2.[18]

---

[17]James A. Lee, "Cultural Analysis in Overseas Operations," *Harvard Business Review* (March–April, 1966), p. 106.
[18]*Ibid.*, p. 110.

Cultural Competence. In the marketer's own society there is security in knowing the attitudes and value systems of its members (although even at home the marketer's knowledge may be less perfect than assumed). However, contact with the foreign market is more remote; indeed, the marketer may never have had the need or opportunity to contact its members either socially or in a business transaction prior to the firm's market entry. Knowledge of the foreign culture may well be minimal; nevertheless, the marketer has no alternative but to work with customers as whole individuals, considering any cultural influences that affect their attitude toward the firm and its offering.

Furuhashi and Evarts, commenting on the requirements of international business management, state that unless proper emphasis is given to cultural competence, performance in the technical and managerial areas of marketing cannot be effective. They recognize that international executives need proper motivation, technical knowledge, and managerial competence (just as the domestic marketer), but *add* that the international business person also must have cultural competence. This cultural competence can be a determining factor in the effective application of technical know-how and managerial skills.[19] They conclude that cultural competence includes more than mere factual knowledge of the cultural differences. It also requires:

1. Sensitivity to cultural differences.
2. Cultural empathy, or the ability to understand the inner logic and coherence of other ways of life, and the restraint not to judge them as bad because they are different from one's own ways.
3. Ability to withstand the initial cultural shock or sum of sudden jolts that awaits the unwary American abroad.
4. Ability to cope with and adapt to foreign environment without "going native."[20]

Studies of blunders made by international firms underscore the need for cultural sensitivity in the design of multinational organization and programs.[21] Blunders reflecting the difficulty of cultural assessment and adaptation include many involving advertising, product adaptation, and marketing mix. Some of these have become well-known, such as the translation of the General Motors' slogan, "Body by Fisher" into the Flemish language as "Corpse by Fisher,"; Campbell Soup's problem of establishing condensed soup in the British market where ready-to-eat soups were prevalent; and Phillip Morris' difficulty

---

[19]Hugh Furuhashi and Harry F. Evarts, "Educating Men for International Marketing," *Journal of Marketing* (January, 1967), p. 53.

[20]*Ibid.* In their article the authors acknowledge building on the concepts presented by Harlan Cleveland, Gerald J. Mangone, and John Clark Adams in *The Overseas Americans* (New York: McGraw-Hill Book Company, 1960).

[21]David Ricks, Marilyn Y. C. Fu, and Jeffrey S. Arpan, *International Business Blunders* (Columbus, Oh.: Grid, Inc., 1974).

in persuading Canadians to accept its American blend rather than the straight Virginia tobacco common to the Canadian market.[22]

Cultural Change. Although cultural change is relatively slow, marketers should be aware of the speed at which changes occur in many societies. In Africa, for example, it has been said that:

> New trends are suggesting future growth potentials for both consumer and industrial products on this continent where nearly everyone used to go to sleep at dusk and arise at dawn. But with all-night radio and some television, African society is becoming more nocturnal.
>
> Other traditional customs also are changing — marriage, burial, tribal and family relationships, number of children, and the role of women. Africa is a continent comprised of many nations, races, religions, and subcultures, but such changes as the role of women, literary, and educational levels also affect marketing opportunities.[23]

The Africans are not unique with respect to cultural change. Rapid change is occurring in the Middle East, South America, Asia, and the United States. Change is occurring more rapidly as contacts among the nations increase and communication and trade facilitate the innovation of new concepts. Marketers gain as they recognize and adapt to this situation. The multinational firm, recognizing its function as a change agent, needs not only to adapt, but also to make plans for change and to anticipate the problems and strategy requirements of introducing new products and methods into a society.

CULTURAL SIMILARITIES AND MARKETING STANDARDIZATION

The previous sections have argued for careful adaptation to foreign cultures; but before leaving the study of culture and marketing we should recognize that there are powerful pressures for the standardization of marketing in a world which many view as becoming more homogeneous as a result of economic development and better communications. If there are cultural similarities as well as differences among the markets several questions might be asked: Is it profitable for a firm to employ the same promotional strategy, the same pricing practices, the same product, and the same channels of distribution to more than one market? Or would the firm benefit from varying its strategy in each of the separate markets where its products are distributed? If some variation among countries is desirable, should the firm change certain policies (e.g., pricing and advertising) while maintaining others (e.g., product) in all markets? These are among the difficult

---

[22]*Ibid.*, pp. 11–28.
[23]Robert J. Small, "New Trends in Africa Hint at New Markets," *Marketing News* (September 1, 1974), p. 4.

strategy decisions required of international marketing managers that involve cultural assessments.

If standardization of marketing policy can be accomplished, there are important benefits to be gained from cost savings and efficient market penetration. However, if the markets differ significantly, a policy of standardization or the application of domestic policy (which is the same thing) can lead to disaster. The issue often revolves around the cultural similarities and differences extant in the market. Those marketers who propose a high degree of standardization of marketing policy rely on the similarity of basic human wants and behaviors. Others, however, willing to admit that basic wants may be similar, point to the different manner in which societies have chosen to solve their problems. One group says that all humans share certain wants such as shelter, food, a better life for their children, etc. The second group says that although that is correct, the types of housing, food, education, and desirable vocations for their children are very different in the various societies. Chinese food may be very nutritious and eaten in Western countries, but it is not the expected normal food for the population in their everyday living.

It might be well to study the arguments for and against standardization of marketing effort to see more clearly the issues and pressures faced by the international marketing manager. In the discussion, however, it must be remembered that all variations and degrees of standardization may be found in actual practice. We have seen that the ethnocentric firm, believing in the superiority of its own culture and policy, tends to favor standardization. The polycentric firm, in contrast, favors the policy of extreme non-standardization, while the geocentric firm adopts a middle ground, seeking to effectively transfer the knowledge it has gained from operations in several countries.

A recent study of 27 large multinational firms in the food, soft drink, soap-detergent-toiletries, and cosmetic industries confirmed that there was a tendency among these firms toward standardization of marketing programs in their European and United States operations. The authors noted that the tendency occurred despite "all the arguments that consumer goods marketing needs local custom tailoring and in view of the many failures of U.S. companies that have dared to transfer American marketing strategies abroad."[24] A high degree of standardization was found in product characteristics, brand names, packaging, basic advertising messages, and in the roles of the salesforce and middlemen. Some of the elements show much higher degrees of standardization than others. The reasons for this will become apparent in later chapters when marketing management is discussed.[25]

---

[24]Ralph Z. Sorenson and Ulrich E. Wiechmann, "How Multinationals View Marketing Standardization," *Harvard Business Review* (May–June, 1975), pp. 38–54.

[25]See Chapters 9 to 17.

Why do firms attempt standardization? Among the benefits that are ascribed to such a policy are the following:[26]

1. Economies resulting from standardization of product design, packaging, and promotional materials.
2. Achieving consistency in relations with customers. There are heavy cross-border flows of tourists and advertising that permit customers to make comparisons with the products, prices, and services available in their home markets.
3. Improved planning and control.
4. The exploitation of good ideas when they have a universal appeal.

Potentially, the concept of standardization provides an opportunity for the firm to develop a consistent image among its customers on a worldwide or regional base. It can bring cost savings through more intensive usage of product and package design and advertising production costs. Advertising may be able to capitalize on effective appeals in several markets as illustrated by the now famous "Put a Tiger in Your Tank" campaign by Esso where the product met similar needs in its markets.

Despite the advantages of standardization, there are a number of limitations to the process. Among the factors that limit the firm's ability to employ similar programs in its several markets are: differences in market conditions, marketing institutions, industry conditions, and legal restrictions. The market itself differs not only by physical and economic conditions, but also cultural differences — in the customs and traditions, in the values and attitudes that are present, and in the social institutions that have evolved. The opportunities for standardization of the marketing effort are constrained by cultural differences in the markets.

QUESTIONS

1. What is culture?
2. Why should a marketer be concerned with an analysis of foreign cultures?
3. What are the major dimensions of culture? Are markets concerned only with the material elements of culture?
4. Do marketers merely adjust to existing culture or does marketing act as a change agent?
5. Why are subcultures important to marketers? Can you list several important subcultures for specific products?
6. What are the major sources of cultural information used by international marketers?
7. How does the self-reference criterion concept help marketers develop their marketing programs?

---

[26]Robert D. Buzzell, "Can You Standardize Multinational Marketing?" *Harvard Business Review* (November–December, 1968), pp. 102–113.

8. "Cultural competence requires only the study of foreign cultures to learn their characteristics." Discuss.
9. How can cultural similarities and differences affect the marketing programs of multinational firms?
10. Cultural variations are important considerations in the development of marketing plans. Since cultural variations are widespread, how do you account for the employment of similar strategies in more than one country?

SUPPLEMENTARY READINGS

Gelfand, M. Richard. "French Canada as a Minority Market," in Ronald C. Curhan, *1974 Combined Proceedings*. Chicago, Ill.: American Marketing Association, 1975, pp. 680–682.

Goldstucker, Jac L. "The Influence of Culture on Channels of Distribution," in Robert L. King, *Marketing and the New Science of Planning*. Chicago, Ill.: American Marketing Association, 1968, pp. 468–473.

Heston, Alan W. "Some Socio-Cultural Facets of Marketing and Diffusion of Change in India," in Robert L. King, *Marketing and the New Science of Planning*. Chicago, Ill.: American Marketing Association, 1968, pp. 500–503.

Hansz, James E., and James D. Goodnow. "A Multivariate Classification of Overseas Country Environments," in Boris W. Becker and Helmut Becker, *Combined Proceedings of 1972 Spring and Fall Conferences*. Chicago, Ill.: American Marketing Association, pp. 191–198.

Kroeber, A. L., and Talcott Parsons. "The Concepts of Culture and of Social System," *American Sociological Review* (October, 1958), pp. 582, 583.

Lee, James A. "Cultural Analysis in Overseas Operations." *Harvard Business Review* (March–April, 1966), pp. 106–114.

Woodside, Arch, Jagdish Sheth, and Peter Bennett, ed. *Foundations of Consumer and Industrial Buying Behavior*. New York: American Elsivier Company, 1977.

8

Regional Market Integration

Despite rising feelings of nationalism in the 1960s and early 70s, the world also was characterized by a quite different phenomenon — economic integration. The success of the European Economic Community together with the needs for rapid economic development and a limited ability to secure worldwide free trade led to the fostering of regional development programs. Regionalism, in this context, took several forms depending on the countries' immediate problems — sometimes integration meant only the cooperation of countries on certain specific projects such as the Indus Water Treaty to develop the water resources of the Indus River Basin for the benefit of both India and Pakistan. In other circumstances free trade areas and common markets were formed to facilitate trade and the use of capital and labor. Regardless of the specific approach, individual countries subordinated national positions in the hope of economic or political gain and altered patterns of trade among themselves and the outside world.

Although such integration was not unknown in prior times, the post-World War II period saw a major surge of integration efforts. The formation of groups such as the European Economic Community (EEC), the European Free Trade Association (EFTA), the Latin American Free Trade Area (LAFTA), and the Andean Common Market (AnCom) has forced many marketers to change their strategies if they wish to continue selling in these markets. Furthermore, the integration of these national markets has caused changes in both the production and marketing structures within the member countries themselves.

Some of the integration efforts of the postwar era have achieved considerable success, although not always reaching the high goals established by those who sponsored them. The European Economic Community is an example of such — achieving considerable economic gain for its members, but not yet gaining the level of political union anticipated by some of its principal architects. Other groups formed on less conducive foundations have moved more slowly or erratically, often for periods with little or no apparent progress. The Latin American Free Trade Area illustrates this group. A third classification might consist of those that have been formed and later were dissolved, such as the West Indian Federation. It is apparent that good intentions and the formation of a regional organization are not enough to assure success. Underlying economic, political, and social factors must be favorable and the business and governmental institutions of the countries must adapt if the integration is to become a fact and its goals achieved. Marketers dealing with these countries must be alert to determine the effects of regional groups on their own markets and companies.

This chapter defines the concept of a regional market and several types and degrees of integration. The question of why countries form these trade blocs, and the effects of these blocs, are discussed along with the strategic and tactical marketing implications of such blocs both for marketers operating within the group and for those outside sellers trying to penetrate the market. A final section describes some of the existing blocs.

FORMS OF REGIONAL MARKET INTEGRATION

In this chapter a regional market is defined as a multinational market in which the independent countries have decided on some degree of economic integration to enable goods and services to flow more freely among the countries.

A basic rationale for the development of these regional markets is that the resources of a region can be used more effectively when applied to larger market areas than merely to the national market. This is accomplished by removing trade barriers among the member nations to facilitate intraregional trade and to strengthen the members' market position in dealing with outsiders. The most efficient business firms can more effectively compete in all member countries, yet tariff and other barriers may be maintained against outsiders. Various degrees of economic integration have been used. Some groups reflect only a desire to facilitate the flow of goods and services among the members by the removal of artificial restraints such as tariffs. Others define the trading relationships between member and nonmember countries by removing barriers among members and establishing common tariff barriers against outsiders. Still others seek even more complete integration by permitting free flows of capital and labor among member countries and by harmonizing transportation and monetary relations.

Figure 8-1 portrays the major forms of regional trade blocs extant at present. This figure shows five major forms and indicates that in general, higher forms of integration include the essential characteristics of the lesser forms. This does not mean that common markets or economic unions can only develop after experiencing a period of operation as free trade areas, nor does it mean that the more complicated forms will necessarily evolve. It does indicate, however, that these free trade areas and customs unions can provide an experience base for further development. Thus, the European Free Trade Association did not progress beyond the free trade area concept. In contrast, Benelux started as a customs union between Luxembourg and Belgium in 1921, and was joined by the Netherlands in 1948, and is now also part of the EEC, a common market that is progressing toward an economic union.

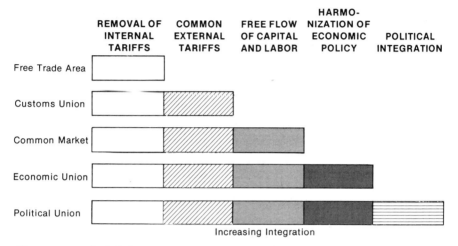

Figure 8-1 FORMS OF ECONOMIC INTEGRATION IN REGIONAL MARKETS

Free Trade Areas

A free trade area consists of a group of countries that have removed artificial barriers to trade within the group. Most commonly this means that tariff and quota barriers have been removed from trade among the members of the free trade association. That is, goods and services move freely among member nations without being subject to tariffs, etc. In some forms, such as the European Free Trade Association, barriers are removed only on certain goods such as industrial products, but free trade could apply to all products when there is full free trade among member countries in goods and services. Each of the member countries maintains its own tariff schedule and quotas with respect to nonmember countries.

The European Free Trade Association, formed in 1960 by countries that were not willing to associate with the European Common Market, probably is the best-known example of a free trade area. Composed of the United Kingdom, Austria, Denmark, Norway, Portugal, Sweden, and Switzerland, the EFTA was more loosely integrated than the European Common Market and placed fewer demands on its members. In

1973, however, Britain, Denmark, and Ireland became members of the more inclusive EEC.[1]

Organizational looseness causes certain problems for the free trade associations and their members. The variation in tariff schedules, for example, means that rules must be established for goods to qualify for movement within the area without the payment of duty, otherwise outsiders would export to the country with the lowest tariff and then transship to other member countries free of further duty. The free trade associations usually meet this problem by requiring certificates of origin to indicate where the products were produced. A stipulated percentage of the value of a product must come from production within the free trade area in order to claim duty-free movement.

Customs Unions

Customs unions, like free trade areas, seek to eliminate tariff and quota restrictions on intraunion trade. In addition, the countries comprising the union agree on a common tariff schedule that will apply to all nonmember countries desiring to trade with the members. Benelux is probably the best-known example of the customs union. The three member countries agreed to abolish duties on trade among themselves and adopted a common external tariff even prior to their entry into the EEC. The conversion of the Caribbean Free Trade Association to a customs union is a lesser-known example.

Common Markets

Common markets are the next higher level of economic integration. As Figure 8-1 indicates, a common market is characterized not only by the removal of internal tariffs and the existence of a common external tariff, but it also features the free movement of capital and labor. Thus, goods, services, and the factors of production are to move freely within the common market. In practice there may be some limitation to this movement despite the theoretical concept, especially when depressed economic conditions lead to unemployment among a country's nationals while workers from abroad retain their jobs.

Although the EEC is the most outstanding and best known of the common markets, it is not alone. Its success has led to the formation of others, including the Central American nations of Guatemala, El Salvador, Honduras, Costa Rica, and Nicaragua which formed the Central American Common Market in 1961. Also, in 1967 the Andean Common Market was formed within LAFTA by Chile, Colombia, Ecuador, Peru, and Bolvia.

---

[1]The remaining members maintain the EFTA organization and agreed to a free trade area with the EEC.

Economic Union

An *economic union* requires that member countries harmonize their economic policies, especially monetary and fiscal policy. To some observers this means the harmonizing of taxes, interest rates, transportation, agricultural policy, and regulation of capital markets. Many of these are logical extensions of the customs union and common market concepts, but they are more difficult to effect than such quantitatively oriented concepts as tariffs and quotas. They involve submission of a country to supranational authorities in policy areas traditionally reserved for national action. Through some of its community-wide institutions the EEC is the most advanced toward economic union of the common markets currently extant.

Political Union

A *political union* is most difficult to place on a scale of regional integration. As some of the proponents of a united Europe might visualize, the economic union would eventually evolve as a base for the political unification of Western Europe. This is the case illustrated in Figure 8-1. In a sense, some political integration already exists within the EEC on a limited scale through the European Commission, Council of Ministers, Assembly, and Court of Justice. The difficulties of achieving concerted political action imply, however, that further integration may be slow and, necessarily, preceded by a greater degree of economic and social integration. National sentiment still is strong within the European Economic Community member countries.

Before leaving the notion of political integration it is well to remind ourselves that some moderate degree of political harmonization occurs even in bilateral treaties among nations when they decide on very limited trade concessions and agree to treaties of friendship, commerce, and navigation.

EFFECTS OF REGIONAL INTEGRATION

It is desirable that the potential effects of the formation of regional markets be understood if we are to assess accurately the opportunities and difficulties these multinational markets present. The development of a regional market can be a major environmental change both for companies located within the market area and for those outsiders selling to the area. Marketing opportunities change for both groups, growing for some companies and declining for others. More efficient companies within the region can penetrate markets that formerly were protected by national tariffs. Companies from nonmember nations may lose if they are replaced by member companies that no longer face national barriers. They may gain, however, if the integration results in market growth and increased potential demand. Companies must reassess their preintegration marketing strategies to facilitate market entry or to expand an existing market share. Firms located within the area probably will face a more highly competitive situation when they are exposed to competition formerly discouraged by national trade barriers.

Trade Creation and Diversion

Trade creation occurs when the removal of protective tariffs leads a country to substitute lower cost foreign goods for the higher cost domestic product. For example, Table 8-1 assumes that France and Italy both produced refrigerators prior to their entry into the EEC. In France, if there was no tariff, prices would be as in Column A. Italy is shown to be a lower cost producer but if France levied a 20 percent tariff on refrigerators, prices would be those in Column B, and Italy would be at a price disadvantage. The establishment of a common external tariff when Italy and France combine in a common market leads to the prices in Column C. Under these conditions French consumers might substitute Italian refrigerators for the French-made ones. Thus, French consumers would gain from lower prices and the French resources could be shifted to a more productive use. Trade creation, then, occurs when inefficient production within the union is displaced by imports from one of its more efficient members.[2]

Table 8-1 ILLUSTRATION OF TRADE CREATION AND DIVERSION

	A No Tariff	B French Tariff 20%	C Common Market Tariff 20%
Price of:			
French refrigerator in France	400 fr.	400 fr.	400 fr.
Italian refrigerator in France	360	432	360
American refrigerator in France	320	384	384

However, formation of the regional market affects nonmembers as well as members. In the preceding example removal of the French tariff led to imports from Italy. The common external tariff of the customs union might also affect nonmember trade. Suppose that at a price of 384 francs, U.S. producers had been supplying the French

[2]Mordechai E. Kreinen, *Trade Relations of the EEC: An Empirical Investigation*, Praeger Special Studies in International Economies and Development (New York: Praeger Publishers, 1974), p. 20.

market even with the French tariff. Formation of the Common Market might have caused French purchases to shift to a relatively higher-cost producer within the market (Italy) because of the tariff removal among members. When imports from nonmembers are shifted to relatively less efficient producers within the market, trade diversion is said to have occurred. Thus, nonmembers may be excluded from a market even if they are more efficient than member countries on comparable goods.

The trade creation (rather than diversion) effects of a customs union tend to be enhanced when these factors are present: (1) the share of world trade held by the customs union is large so there is a good probability that low-cost producers are located within the union; (2) the economies of the members are competitive so there is a chance for production specialization and enhanced trade among the countries; and (3) the preunion tariffs of the individual countries were high.[3] A low common external tariff also leads to less diversion.

Dynamic Effects of Growth

Probably even more important than trade creation are the dynamic effects of customs unions in economic growth. These include economies of scale, increased competition, and a stimulus to investment.[4] Wider markets are available to the firms of member countries when they are no longer handicapped by the individual country's tariffs. These enlarged markets enable some firms to increase plant size to more efficient levels, especially when industries require large-scale operation for efficiency. The enlarged markets may have little consequence if technology permits efficient operation at the size required to serve only a single national market, or where existing firms already achieve efficiency by selling in the world market. Thus, scale economies may be particularly important to developing countries whose national markets are too small for efficient operation. However, the larger regional markets also attract foreign companies that are more familiar with mass distribution techniques, thereby limiting the growth of local firms.

An important potential dynamic effect of regional markets is the possibility for increasing competition and the resultant increase in efficiency, lower prices, increased product variety, and the breaking of traditional business methods. There is no guarantee that regional integration will result in increased competition as cartel-like arrangements *could* result. However, the interpenetration of markets as a result of trade barrier reductions should increase rivalry.[5] Such

[3]Franklin R. Root, *International Trade and Investment* (Cincinnati: South-Western Publishing Co., 1973), pp. 390–399.
[4]Charles P. Kindleberger, *International Economies* (5th ed.; Homewood, Ill.: Richard D. Irwin, Inc., 1973), p. 179.
[5]Cartels are discussed in Chapter 19.

competition can result in lower costs to consumers, more aggressive marketing by firms, and a larger number of products for sale. The market structure resulting from the integration should be more efficient since local firms can no longer rely on the protection afforded by national tariffs and nontariff barriers. These firms are exposed to competition from a number of sources. Some of the increased rivalry will come from more efficient firms in member countries, but the market growth may also attract the attention of firms located outside the region. Growth of the regional market can create marketing opportunities for increased exports by nonmembers to offset the potential trade diversion in certain industries. Competition may improve efficiency by forcing the use of the most efficient plants to serve the total market and by forcing more aggressive pricing plus heightened competition in product development, services, and promotional effort.

Increased investment within the market is a potential benefit to the region. Member-country firms may increase their investment to better serve the larger and more competitive market or outsiders may increase their investments to get behind the tariff wall in order to compete on more equal footing with the local firms. Indeed, American firms viewing the EEC during the 1960s sought to retain their export market by investing in production and marketing facilities in Europe.[6] Marketing strategies shifted from exporting to licensing, joint ventures, and direct investment in subsidiaries. Thus, investment in Europe increased both from European and American sources. Some of the latter may even have represented funds diverted from the U.S., Asia, or other areas as firms sought to retain or improve their positions in the large and growing European market.

Some common-market arrangements, such as that of the Central American Common Market (CACM), strive to achieve economic complementarity and increased trade by allocating industries among the member countries. Without an effort of this kind the countries may all produce similar products and therefore have little reason to trade. Complementarity provisions, however, raise the question of which country is going to operate which industries and the allocation process itself becomes an additional strain on group unity.

Enlarged markets and increased income in a region may also bring about additional investments in infrastructure. These increased expenditures for transportation, education, power, and communications facilitate marketing by lowering costs of physical distribution, reducing physical loss, providing better communication facilities and improving skills in the labor pool. They often represent export opportunities for companies in both member and nonmember countries.

Political and social reasons, as well as economic, have been factors in regional integration. And some integration has been defensive in the sense of protecting member countries from political foes. Thus, the

---

[6]See Chapter 3, page 47.

United States was interested in aiding the development of a strong Western European sense of unity as a defense against the USSR. Similarly, the Council for Mutual Economic Assistance (COMECON), formed in 1949 to coordinate economic activity and development among Eastern European nations, may have received impetus as a counter to the Marshall Plan.

More importantly, however, political integration and economic integration often are complementary. But since economic integration seemed more feasible, it received the initial emphasis in integrating the Western European nations and political integration was expected to follow.[7]

IMPLICATIONS OF REGIONAL INTEGRATION FOR INTERNATIONAL MARKETING

It is difficult to establish the precise effects of successful market integration as these vary both among the regions and by product classifications. A detailed analysis, then, would require specific studies of each market association — its scope, administration, and degree of integration as it affects each product. That would be beyond the scope of this chapter.[8] In general, however, we can summarize several possible effects.

1. Successful integration that leads to an increased growth for the region provides opportunities to penetrate a larger market. The previous national markets may have been too small to permit efficient operation, or even to provide enough potential sales to interest a company. The regional market provides opportunity both for mass production and also for mass marketing.
2. Growth in income within the region can lead to increased exports for both member and nonmember countries. Often the increased income leads to increased imports by the region in order to meet its industrial requirements and to satisfy the demand for a variety of consumer goods.
3. The amount of trade diversion will differ among the various product lines, but it is potentially large for agricultural products when the regional markets seek to protect local producers. Manufacturers that produce differentiated products in high demand are not likely to be as subject to diversion as those producing simple and undifferentiated goods.
4. Trade creation and diversion possibilities may lead international businesses to invest in production and marketing facilities within the region in order to get behind the tariff wall and to minimize nontariff barriers. Such facilities may also serve as supply points

---

[7]Finn B. Jensen and Ingo Walter, *The Common Market: Economic Integration in Europe* (Philadelphia: J.B. Lippincott Company, 1965), p. 242.

[8]See Kreinen, *op. cit.*, for a study of the trade effect of the EEC.

for marketing products to other regions as well as to other countries within the region.

5. Increased competition within the region makes marketing more difficult, but international firms often are able to capitalize on their effective marketing organizations. Thus, they should have an advantage in the more competitive market.

6. The desire to increase competition among its members in order to achieve efficiency sometimes leads to changed antitrust policy and new standards of fair competition may be imposed.[9] In this manner traditional business customs and organizations may be upset and more aggressive marketing may result.

7. In some instances local industries may be favored to improve the regional community's position relative to outsiders. Thus, in the EEC governments sought to develop or maintain high technology industries such as computers and aircraft. Governments may foster mergers among the region's firms in critical industries and governmental aid may subsidize these industries.

From a marketing viewpoint regional integration means wider markets with the potential for encouraging competition, providing for a more extensive range of mass marketing techniques, increasing the variety of goods available to consumers, lowering prices, and shifting marketing strategy to take advantage of local production.

THE UNCOMMON MARKET

Although an expanded market and reduced trade barriers may facilitate marketing and increase the range of products available within the region, it would be a mistake to assume too high a degree of homogeneity within the region. Several factors lead to the conclusion that from a marketing standpoint common markets are not common in their demand characteristics or in important cultural aspects. Even at the economic level, trade barriers may be reduced under integration but they still exist. Figure 8-2 illustrates some of the nontariff barriers that remained in the EEC in 1973. This study by *Business International* tabulates seven different kinds of nontariff barriers to trade that still existed among the EEC members.

Perhaps even more important are the market differences that remain among the countries because of their individual cultures. Although cultural barriers may be diminishing as a result of increased trade and improved communications, they still are important for many product categories. Traditional preferences for food, as an example, remain strong in many countries. Language problems continue to impede advertising, labelling, and personal selling. Religious differences and the different levels of economic development act as deterrents to product flow between the EEC and its associate members.

---

[9]See Chapter 16 for EEC antitrust policy.

I. Technical Standards:
   A. German law prohibits importing of fuel with a high lead content (blocks the imports of French and Italian cars).
   B. Technical equipment entering France must go through massive red tape and examination by the Ministry of Science and Industrial Development.
   C. Strict German standards for packaging will inhibit imports of packaged foods and beverages after 1/1/74.
   D. The UK requires a costly "Air Worthiness" certificate for all aircraft.
   E. Belgian law labels "pure wool" as 97% wool; this restricts French wool, which is 85% wool.
   F. Italian standards on milk production require a health certificate of inspection at the time of milking and pasteurization, necessitating Italian customs' inspection at plants in other countries (costly to Bavarian milk dealers).
   G. French cheese standards do not permit importing of cheese produced from milk powder (protects market against some Dutch exports). The French also require health certification for honey and tinned fish.

II. Licenses
   A. Ireland requires licenses for imports of egg albumen and tobacco.
   B. Italy requires licenses for imports of vinegar, cork, silk, umbrellas.
   C. Germany requires licenses for worsted yarn and vinegar.
   D. Belgium/Luxembourg require licenses for petroleum and chemical imports.
   E. France requires licenses for petroleum and electronic components.

III. Restrictive Sales Practices and Administrative Obstacles.
   A. French insurance rates place a special burden on the vehicles from other countries.
   B. French auto manufacturers limit the amount of their cars that dealers in EEC countries may sell, which artifically keeps prices higher.
   C. French repair shops, often directly controlled by the manufacturers, will sometimes delay their obtaining of spare parts for foreign makes to create an obstacle to their use.

IV. Charges on Imports
   A. Italy and France levy huge taxes on grain-based spirits.
   B. Imports of wine into France must pay a special "wine-transport fee."

V. State Aids Which Divert Trade
   A. Germany gives assistance to the industry that regenerates waste oil by an equalization levy on regenerated oil im ports.
   B. France subsidizes the clock and leather industries through a quasi-fiscal charge levied on imports.
   C. Italy taxes chemical pulp and paper imports to subsidize its own newspaper industry.

VI. State-trading
   A. France has a state monopoly on phosphates that has sole selling rights.
   B. Germany has an import monopoly on ethyl alcohol.
   C. Italy and France have state monopolies on matches and alcholic beverages.

VII. Government (National) Procurement Policies
   A. All European governments have commitments to purchase domestically.
   B. Germany limits use of architects on its projects to German nationals, even if the contract is with another country.
   C. The Netherlands allows state industries a first call on resources, even if they have been reserved by another government.
   D. Italy gives out its construction bids secretively and selectively without Communitywide announcement.
   E. The French Electrical Company deals solely with French producers, allowing them to recoup research and development overheads.

Source: *Business International*, October 12, 1973, p. 335.

Figure 8-2 NONTARIFF BARRIERS IN THE EEC

Politics also plays its part in market segmentation as national leaders seek to maintain their country's identity and power position.

While the term "common market" seems literally to cry out for a standardized approach to marketing within that region, the above caveats are a strong indication that most common markets have not achieved the degree of homogeneity required for complete standardization. Indeed, even in the United States companies expect to find regional differences in consumption between the North and South, industrialized East and rural Midwest, etc. We should expect even greater differences among countries. One team of researchers satirically commented that early attempts to standardize marketing in the EEC failed when marketers expected that with falling tariffs "the European consumer would come alive, and he was to have had the politeness of a Frenchman, the calmness of an Italian, the sense of humor of a German, the puritanism of the Danes, the sense of organization of the Belgian, the liveliness of a Dutchman, an Englishman's flair for cuisine, the soberness of an Irishman, and the frivolity of the Luxembourg people."[10] Clearly, this is not the case and marketers have a continuing need to treat market differences by applying the concepts of market segmentation and adapting strategy consistent with each segment's requirements even when the segments form parts of a legally defined common market.

On the other hand, the existence of similar market segments in several countries may permit the establishment of similar basic strategies for reaching them even when specific tactics or languages may need to be varied. For example, the teenage market for some products has shown many similarities in product demand (jeans) among the nations.

REPRESENTATIVE MARKET GROUPINGS

The number and composition of economic and political groupings change as countries decide their advantage lies in belonging to or separating from established markets. Nevertheless, important groups have remained. In this last section of the chapter essential characteristics of market groups that have implications for international marketing by American companies are reviewed.

Europe

Europe currently divides itself into several regional groups. Most notable are the European Economic Community, the European Free

---

[10]Etienne Cracco and Guy Robert, "The Uncommon Common Market," in Ronald C. Curham, *1974 Combined Proceedings* (Chicago: American Marketing Association, 1975), p. 661.

Trade area, and the Eastern European nations brought together under the Council for Mutual Economic Assistance (CMEA or COMECON). Each of these is briefly described.

European Economic Community As previously indicated in this chapter, the European Economic Community (EEC) is the most successful of the postwar integration efforts. From a marketing viewpoint, it is useful to consider this market in some detail to perceive its structure and its effect on international markets.

Despite the strong nationalistic sentiments that were expressed in two World Wars and the 1930s, some European leaders recognized a need for both economic and political collaboration. Following World War II, their efforts also were supported by the United States. However, the EEC did not suddenly spring into being without a number of antecedents as a base for the formation of the regional group.[11] Benelux was one of these. Also, the European Coal and Steel Community included all six of the original EEC members and provided experience in regional cooperation. Further, the Organization for European Cooperation (OEEC) was established in 1948 to allocate aid under the Marshall Plan and one of its agencies, the European Payments Union, aided in the restoration of convertibility to European currencies.

Finally, in 1955 at a conference in Messina, a plan for a European Common Market was presented. Further negotiations led to the signing of the Rome Treaty in 1957 and the official beginning on January 1, 1958. The aim was to promote economic growth and stability by aligning the economic policies of the member nations — Belgium, The Netherlands, Luxembourg, Germany, France, and Italy.[12] In 1973 these six were joined by the United Kingdom, Ireland, and Denmark.

The EEC sought free trade in industrial goods among its members by providing for the gradual reduction of tariff barriers. A common external tariff was to be assessed against imports from nonmembers and labor and capital were to move freely among the member countries. By 1962 the Community also began to evolve a basic policy on agriculture. Since then the Community has sought to harmonize transportation and monetary relations and to form a common antitrust policy.

The Community is governed by four basic institutions. The *Commission* is the executive group which has the main administrative authority and also helps formulate policy. Commission members have the responsibility for operating in the interest of the Community as a whole. The *Council of Ministers* is the policy-making unit and is comprised of one representative from each of the member countries. The

---

[11]Virgil Salera, *Multinational Business* (Boston: Houghton Mifflin Company, 1969), p. 179.

[12]Emile Benoit, *Europe at Sixes and Sevens* (New York: Columbia University Press, 1961), p. 4.

Council acts on proposals from the Commission and the Council members represent their respective national governments. The *Court of Justice* rules on disputes regarding the Treaty and can take cases initiated by individuals and private business, as well as governments. The *European Parliament* does not pass laws, but does have the power to remove the Commission.

Although we normally refer to the EEC by mentioning only the member nations, such referral greatly understates the significance of the Community. The Community may be viewed as a much larger association of members, associate members, and countries with whom preferential agreements have been negotiated. Presumably it is this expanded group that achieves benefits from the association. In addition to the trade advantages for the nine members, there are additional privileges extended to former colonies and to European and African nations that have associated with the EEC but are not yet able or willing to assume full membership. The remaining EFTA members, after the United Kingdom and Denmark joined the EEC, have an agreement to form a free trade area with the Community. Some nations benefit from a system of general preferences accorded to developing nations.

The full members (9) of this Community represent a population of 258 million people with a gross domestic product of $1,158 billion. It is the largest importing market in the world and its members and associates constitute both industrialized and developing nations that affect trade among both developed and developing nations.

European Free Trade Association. The EFTA originally was formed as a reaction to the EEC, but has been less successful than its counterpart. The reduced EFTA (minus the United Kingdom and Denmark) represents Austria, Iceland, Norway, Portugal, Sweden, Switzerland, and Finland with a population approximating 40 million people. Some of these nations, such as Sweden, Switzerland, and Norway, have high per capita incomes and represent important trading relations with the U.S. and the rest of the world. These nations have elected to maintain their free trade area with its less binding political and economic integration rather than joining the EEC.

Council for Mutual Assistance (COMECON). This regional grouping represents the Eastern European nations of the USSR, Czechoslovakia, East Germany, Hungary, Poland, Romania, and Cuba. Finland is an associate member. COMECON is neither a free trade area nor a customs union. Its members do not share a common commercial policy; rather, the members work out strategies on an ad hoc basis and many of the trade negotiations are carried out by the individual members.[13] COMECON has, however, recently sought direct negotiations with the

---

[13]"Little More Than a Name," *The Economist* (March 2, 1974), p. 59.

EEC as the Soviet Union abandoned its hostility to the community.[14] Some of the Eastern European nations such as Poland, Hungary, and Czechoslovakia depend heavily on foreign trade and have desired direct trade relations with the EEC.

Latin America

The Americas represent a diverse group of economies. Some are relatively developed, such as Brazil and Mexico, while others are yet to emerge from their basic agricultural and traditional economies.

Latin American Free Trade Area. The largest regional grouping in the Americas is LAFTA — the Latin American Free Trade Association. LAFTA was established in 1960 when seven countries signed the Treaty of Montevideo.[15] They were joined shortly by Colombia and Ecuador and, in 1967, by Bolivia and Venezuela. The objectives of this association included enlarged trading areas, improved living standards, coordination of development, and the establishment of a common market.[16] The desire for economic development led to regional economic integration, but LAFTA has faced serious problems due to differences in the economic structure of its members and a lack of political support for LAFTA.

Within LAFTA, six countries — Colombia, Peru, Chile, Boliva, Ecuador, and Venezuela — form the Andean Common Market (AnCom). The objectives of this regional grouping are an economic development policy in which all member countries share the benefits, regional integration, and a common policy toward foreign commerce and investment.[17] One of the significant developments of this group for foreign investors and marketers is "Decision 24." This decision contains a rule that grants free trade benefits to enterprises that are 51 percent owned by local investors. In order to gain the advantages of the Andean market, existing foreign enterprises must sign an agreement to sell equity interest to local investors within 15 years. This decision also applies to trademarks, patents, licenses, and royalties.[18] It poses a strategic problem for foreign enterprises that are established in these countries as they decide whether to continue serving the national market or whether they should regionalize. Serving the regional market involves the marketing costs of reaching the expanded market

---

[14]"Their Solidarity Isn't So Good," *The Economist* (August 11, 1973), pp. 35–36 and "The Mood Relaxes As Russia and Europe Join the Danes," *The Economist* (October 20, 1973), p. 83.

[15]Argentina, Brazil, Chile, Mexico, Paraguay, Peru, and Uruguay.

[16]Thomas Gannan (ed.), *Doing Business in Latin America* (American Management Association, p. 46.

[17]"Colombia in the Andean Group," *Colombia Today*, Vol. viii, No. 2, 1973.

[18]*Ibid.*

plus the changes in ownership structure required by Decision 24. These costs, in addition to uncertainty regarding the market's stability, make the marketing decision difficult for foreign investors.[19] AnCom also has served to prod LAFTA into considering the development requirements of the smaller countries.

Central American Common Market (CACM). The Central American Common Market countries of Honduras, El Salvador, Nicaragua, Guatemala, and Costa Rica began integration efforts shortly after World War II. These were largely agricultural nations with low per capita incomes and rapid population growth. They sought, through integration, to achieve more rapid economic development and to gain the benefits of industrial specialization and to provide for integration of monetary policy. During the 1960s intraregional trade increased, but the countries did not all gain equally. Further, the Convention on Integrated Industries had concluded that the regional market was too small to support several firms in some industries. These pressures led to considerable dissatisfaction among the members and culminated in 1969–1971 when Honduras suspended its participation in the common market. Thus, after an auspicious beginning the future of CACM became less secure.

Caribbean Community. The Caribbean Free Trade Association (Carifta) represented an economic integration effort by several Commonwealth Caribbean countries. In 1968 Jamaica, Trinidad, Tobago, and Montserrat formed Carifta to promote the expansion and diversification of trade within the region, to assure fair competition and to encourage economic development. Carifta was seen as the first step toward more complete integration and, indeed, in 1972 the Caribbean Community was formed with the objectives of establishing a common market to strengthen trade among the member States, to expand and integrate economic activities among the members, and to achieving greater economic independence in dealing with outsiders.[20]

Other Regional Markets

The regional concept has expanded beyond Europe and Latin America to include groupings in Africa, the Middle East, and in

---

[19]See Edward Verl Fielding, "Some Strategic Ownership Considerations for Foreign Investors in the Andean Pact Region," Working Paper, Alfred P. Sloan School of Management, Massachusetts Institute of Technology, for a study of the strategy implications of AnCom for U.S. investors.

[20]The formation and development of the Caribbean Community is chronicled by Frank Paul LeVeness in "Caribbean Integration: The Formation of Carifta and the Caribbean Community," *Research Series No. 2, Papers in Government and Politics* (New York: St. John's University, 1974).

Southeast Asia. A detailed discussion of each is beyond the scope of this text, but their existence creates significant impact on specific markets that might attract the attention of American marketers. The membership and scope of these organizations change from time to time; therefore marketers should be wary of reliance on historical data as a base for the formulation of marketing strategy.

QUESTIONS

1. Define the various forms of regional integration discussed in this chapter.
2. How does a "free trade area" differ from a "common market"?
3. Can an American market the same product and apply a standard form of marketing within an entire common market such as the EEC? Why or why not?
4. What effect does the formation of a common market have on marketers within the market?
5. How might the formation of an integrated regional market affect marketers from nonmember countries?
6. What is meant by trade creation and trade diversion? Of what significance are these to marketers?
7. Why might the dynamic effects of growth be more significant than the trade creation effects of a customs union?
8. How do the EEC, LAFTA, and COMECON differ in their approaches to economic integration?
9. Would you classify the EEC as a common market, an economic union, or a political union? Why?
10. How do you account for the large number of regional integration blocs in the world today?

SUPPLEMENTARY READINGS

Baker, James C., and John K. Ryans, Jr. *Multinational Marketing*. Columbus, Ohio: Grid, Inc., 1975. Chapter 27.

Cateora, Phillip R. and John M. Hess. *International Marketing*, 3rd ed. Homewood, Ill.: Richard D. Irwin, Inc. Chapter 9.

Duerr, Michael. *The Expanded EEC and U.S. Business*. New York: The Conference Board, Inc., 1974.

European Community Information Service. "Basic Statistics of the Community," (annual). Washington, D.C.

European Community Information Service. "European Community," (monthly). Washington, D.C.

Fielding, Edward Verl. "Some Strategic Ownership Considerations for Foreign Investors in the Andean Pact Region," Working Paper, Alfred P. Sloan School of Management, Massachusetts Institute of Technology.

Grzybowski, Kazimerz. "COMECON," in Robert Starr, *East-West Business Transactions*. New York: Praeger Publishers, 1974. Chapter 6.

Jensen, Finn B. and Ingo Walter. *The Common Market: Economic Integration in Europe*. Philadelphia: J.B. Lippincott Company, 1965.

Kindleberger, Charles P. *International Economics*, 5th ed. Homewood, Ill.: Richard D. Irwin, Inc., 1973. Chapter 11.

Kreinen, Mordechai E. *Trade Relations of the EEC: An Empirical Investigation*. New York: Praeger Publishers, 1974.

LeVeness, Frank Paul. "Caribbean Integration: The Formation of Carifta and the Caribbean Community," *Research Series No. 2, Papers in Government and Politics*. New York: St. John's University, 1974.

Root, Franklin R. *International Trade and Investment*, 3d ed. Cincinnati: South-Western Publishing Co., 1973. Chapter 16.

Salera, Virgil. *Multinational Business*. Boston: Houghton-Mifflin Company, 1969. Chapter 14.

Part 3 International Marketing Management

3

CHAPTER 9

The Organization and Administration of International Marketing

The expansion of international operations has resulted in changed organizational structures for many businesses. In a relatively short time some companies have experienced initial exposure to foreign markets through exporting and have further penetrated these markets by licensing company technology or establishing overseas production units. A few of these companies have become worldwide corporations, viewing the home market as only one of many such markets throughout the world. This development of foreign markets has activated forces that lead to modified or new organizational forms more appropriate to the enlarged scope of operations. Multinational companies need an organizational structure and administration which facilitate knowledge of worldwide marketing opportunities and environments. The corporation seeks economies of scale and global logistics while still providing the incentive for local initiative and adaptation. Moreover, the structure must provide the flexibility necessary for adaptation to increasingly competitive markets. This structure is important for international marketing because it establishes the organizational environment within which marketing strategy is formulated and implemented.

ORGANIZATIONAL ADAPTATION

Ideally, the administration of international marketing would be fully integrated into the total operations of the firm. Management would be as aware of developments in India as in Indiana. Unfortunately this ideal organization is extremely difficult to attain. The difficulty of adaptation and the typical responses of firms were highlighted in a study by Booz, Allen, and Hamilton, Inc.

> In the majority of cases, organization difficulties emanate from appending the international business to the domestic business instead

of integrating the two parts into a world business. Typically, the organization structure just evolves rather than being carefully planned. For example, most businesses tend to be organized along a product or functional line. Where the foreign business is added, it is usually geographically oriented at the first two organizational levels. If the basic organization rationale of the business is either product or functional, an immediate organizational divergence results. This creates problems starting with the chief executive, who must supervise and coordinate a geographical international organization with a product or functional domestic organization. Also, the transfer of know-how and technical competence is more difficult between these two diverse organizational entities and so catalyzes other problems. . .

The major international management problem is orientation — getting the top management team to think, act and operate in terms of a single integrated world business instead of a domestic business with an international arm. . . .[1]

When export volume is small a company can employ outside firms to organize and implement the export trade; however, as export volume expands, an export department may be established within the firm to make a more concerted marketing impact. Further expansion of exports and additional involvement by means of licensing and overseas production often result in the establishment of an international division or international headquarters company to coordinate the international marketing program. Attempts to secure a global outlook for the firm have increased; each market is judged on its merits and opportunities are developed wherever it is economically desirable and politically feasible. To facilitate this viewpoint, several basic organizational forms have been used: area or geographic structures; worldwide product structures; and grid systems to link products, areas, and functions.

This description of evolving structure is simplistic in at least two major ways: (1) Not all organizations necessarily evolve through this process. Some companies may initiate international involvement by means of licensing, joint ventures, or foreign production and may have established an international division to implement the program. (2) The organizational structure of a firm is the net result of many additional influences including the past history of the company and the business philosophy of its management; the number, diversity, and technological requirements of the product line; the expected sales volume; the formation of common markets; and the political, legal, and cultural environment of both the host and home countries.

Selected organizational prototypes are discussed in the following sections. Although this text is concerned with the global approach to marketing, understanding can be furthered by first studying the

---

[1]Booz, Allen, and Hamilton, Inc., *The Emerging World Enterprise*, pp. 14–15. Copyright by Booz, Allen, and Hamilton, Inc., quoted by permission.

approaches used by firms still dominated by exports. The managerial rather than legal implications of organization are emphasized in this chapter.

EXPORT AND IMPORT ORGANIZATION

Export activity may be generated by the firm's own export department or by independent middlemen who act in lieu of such a department. One such middleman is represented by the Export Management Company.[2]

Export Management Company (EMC)

Many small and medium-sized manufacturers have turned to Export Management Companies as a method of organizing their export trade. These companies perform an extensive array of services that permit the manufacturer to expand into world markets without establishing its own export department. They further reduce the risks of entering foreign markets. The Export Management Company, in effect, acts as the manufacturer's export department and often provides services that would not be economical for an individual manufacturer. The EMC is able to provide the services because it represents several manufacturers of non-competing, but allied, products and can spread its costs over the entire line.

Services provided by the EMC for the manufacturers it represents include: researching the overseas market; appointing overseas distributors; traveling to support the marketing effort; preparing advertising and sales literature; preparing export documents; and overseeing shipping, financing, and insurance requirements. The EMC may also help establish local production under license when conditions warrant. The basic reasons for using the EMC are the international marketing and finance expertise of the firm, its distribution contacts abroad, and its ability to implement programs beyond the capability of manufacturers with low export volumes.

EMCs commonly either are paid a commission or they purchase products at a discount. In either case the international marketing cost for the producer is a variable cost since payment occurs only after the sale and is directly tied to sales volume. The traditional payment is a commission and the EMC acts as the manufacturer's exclusive overseas representative. Correspondence and contracts are negotiated in the name of the manufacturer. Under this system the manufacturer invoices the customer directly and handles all the financing that is

---

[2]The Export Management Company is also known as a Combination Export Manager (CEM).

needed.[3] Most EMCs today, however, place orders with the manufacturer after receiving an order from customers. The EMC pays for the item and invoices the customer. The margin obtained covers credit costs, commissions to overseas representatives, overhead, and profit.

There are certain disadvantages in using the EMC. Extensive, rather than intensive, market coverage may result in insufficient marketing effort within a country for a specific product. If the number of products carried by the EMC are few, and if they are related lines, the EMC may be able to provide support for each; but many export firms are naturally anxious to add new lines to secure added income from the existing organization. Also, the EMC usually works with established rather than new technology products. It serves the overseas customer by offering a relatively complete line of products so the customer can deal with a single supply source.

The EMC is discussed here rather than under channels of distribution because of the close relationship between the EMC and the manufacturer, and the strong reliance placed on the EMC to perform the export functions. This relationship is most useful to the manufacturer who is new to international marketing with either an untested or low volume of export. Despite this close relationship, if the EMC develops a substantial export volume and the manufacturer develops expertise in exporting, the EMC may be replaced by an export department within the producer's organization.

Built-in Export Departments

A relatively simple method of organizing the export activities of a firm is to distribute the work on a functional basis among personnel currently performing those activities for the domestic market. Such a plan, called *built-in*, requires one additional person, the export manager, to coordinate international efforts and insure that the proper balance of attention is devoted to overseas markets. The export manager is the only person solely involved in international marketing. Although the built-in concept recognizes special international managerial functions, these typically are restricted to documentary and procedural matters such as letters of credit, export controls, customs clearance, international shipping, marine insurance, etc.[4] The primary responsibility for the performance of marketing functions remains with the firm's functional executives.

---

[3]U.S. Department of Commerce, "The EMC — Your Export Department," Brochure dated April, 1972, p. 6. Also, "Export Marketing for Smaller Firms," 3d ed., Small Business Administration, Washington, D.C., Superintendent of Documents (December, 1971), pp. 77–82.

[4]E. J. Kolde, *The Multinational Company* (Lexington, Mass.: Lexington Books, D. C. Heath and Company, 1974), pp. 103–104.

Export sales may be supervised by the firm's domestic sales manager in cooperation with the export manager, or they may be solely the responsibility of the export manager. The firm's treasurer handles all of the financial arrangements and the credit manager devotes some of his time to foreign credits. The regular domestic departments are responsible for the actual document preparation, packing, shipping, advertising, and other functions.

The flexibility, economy, and simplicity of this plan derive from its use of existing facilities, but performance is not always efficient. The export manager is responsible for instilling an interest in, and an enthusiasm for marketing the firm's products abroad, but he lacks line authority to fully implement a plan. The degree of tact and persuasion possessed by the manager determines the extent to which cooperation will be obtained.

The difficulties of managing in such an organization become apparent. The export manager must suggest to capable, experienced fellow officers in the company precisely which changes should be made in product or procedure to meet the needs of the overseas market. The credit manager may be asked to be more liberal in granting terms to overseas customers. The traffic manager, who may have developed the methods of packing merchandise for safety and economy in domestic trade, is advised to alter procedures to assure safe overseas shipment. Production methods which have been fully standardized may have to be altered to provide a different assortment for foreign customers.

A major problem with the built-in plan is that the functional executives of the company see the large domestic operation of prime importance and, therefore, may not pay sufficient attention to export requirements. Also, the export manager may have only marginal influence on the development of the company's total marketing strategy. The plan is primarily used by companies selling a standardized product or raw material and utilizing intermediaries, such as trading companies, to set and implement marketing plans in the export markets.[5]

Import departments of the built-in type are rare. Among manufacturers imports are usually the responsibility of the purchasing division and under the control of the purchasing agent. The built-in concept is feasible for large retailing establishments that import for their own account. In such cases an import manager coordinates the import functions of the merchandise departments. Foreign offices and agents, supervised by the import manager, assist buyers on the foreign market trips, maintain records of imports, handle and expedite the orders, and work with customs or customhouse brokers to clear the merchandise. However, the prime purchasing responsibility remains with the merchandise department buyers.

---

[5]*Ibid.*

Separate Foreign Trade Departments

When the international sales volume of a company increases but is primarily represented by exports, the firm may find it economical to establish a separate export department. This is especially true when the company establishes its own overseas contacts rather than using domestic intermediaries. Such a unit overcomes some of the limitations of the built-in concept since the separate department performs the essential functions of the export process. One example of such an organization is depicted in Figure 9-1. This department is organized functionally under the control of an export manager.

The export manager supervises all foreign sales. The manager selects and trains the sales personnel who work through distributors abroad. The manager also selects the distributors and makes periodic visits abroad to supervise the marketing effort. Moreover, the department, in cooperation with the corporate advertising manager, processes and implements the promotional plans in export markets. Orders are filled, packed, and shipped by the export shipper from inventories held expressly for exports. The department maintains its own system for processing orders, maintaining records, and billing overseas customers. However, credit is controlled by a special committee consisting of the export manager, assistant export manager, treasurer, general manager, and the export auditor.

The major advantage of the separate export department is the employment of specialists whose primary responsibility is to the export market. Policies and operations are best adapted to the diverse requirements of the separate country markets. However, the gain may be illusory; the export department is still dependent on product divisions to supply some of its needs. In functionally-organized companies the department may still be subordinate to marketing (or to purchasing, if it is an import department). Often the domestic market still dominates corporate policy. In times of product scarcity the domestic market is given priority. Since the export manager typically does not have a major and direct input in the formulation of corporate policy, export markets may not receive sufficient products or promotion. In any case, since the primary responsibility is for exports the manager may not have the skills or interest to develop overseas production or other alternative market development strategies.

THE INTERNATIONAL DIVISION

Increased sales in foreign markets, licensing, participation in joint ventures, and/or the establishment of overseas production complicate the administration of international business and increase its significance within the firm. A multi-pronged strategy for tapping overseas markets frequently results in the view that (1) the responsibility for

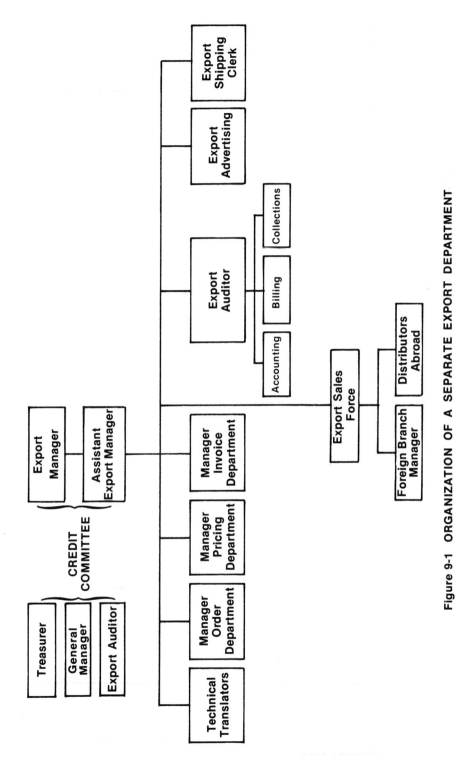

Figure 9-1 ORGANIZATION OF A SEPARATE EXPORT DEPARTMENT

international activities should be separated from domestic to concentrate the expertise in dealing with foreign markets and (2) the international unit should have direct access to top management. Such a philosophy leads to the establishment of an international division (see Figures 9-2 and 9-3).

Structure of the Division

The international division typically is headed by a vice-president who reports directly to the company's chief executive officer, and thus has direct contact with those responsible for the formation of corporate policy. The division, if large, may contain in-house staff support in marketing, research, production, etc., or, the division may rely on worldwide functional support from corporate headquarters.

Figures 9-2 and 9-3 show international divisions grafted onto functional and product corporate organizations. In Figure 9-2 the marketing, finance, and other functional executives are responsible to the domestic market but are expected to support the international division.

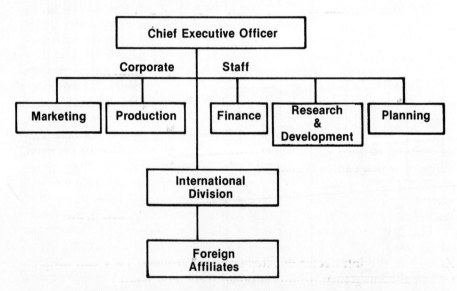

Figure 9-2 INTERNATIONAL DIVISION IN A FUNCTIONAL ORGANIZATION

Figure 9-3 illustrates that product divisions are responsible for domestic operations. In each diagram the international division is responsible for the development of international markets, yet the division must rely on the cooperation and support of domestic executives. The foreign affiliates in the diagrams may be licensees, branch offices, joint ventures, or foreign subsidiaries.

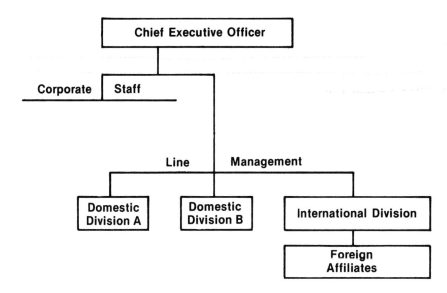

Figure 9-3 **INTERNATIONAL DIVISION IN A PRODUCT ORGANIZATION**

The international division, itself, may be organized according to geographical or product lines. A geographical organization delegates to regional managers the responsibility for all operations within a given area. Thus a manager's responsibility might include all the affiliates and operations in Europe, the Middle East, or Latin America. This geographic pattern emphasizes regional differences in the corporation's service area. It is appropriate when the company markets a narrow or relatively homogeneous product line where there are pronounced cultural, legal, or other differences among the regions. The geographic pattern permits decentralization of authority to regional affiliates which can be organized as profit centers.[6] On the other hand, product organization within the division tends to be implemented when the company markets diverse, high technology products so that specialized product knowledge is important to the marketing plan.

The international division structure provides several advantages for the firm.[7] It brings together executives who are aware of and experienced in the intricacies of international business. They can achieve technical competence in international trade and learn the differences in markets, business customs, legal requirements, taxes, etc., that are present in their area of operation. The division allows international decisions to be based on company-wide considerations to determine which assets can best be employed overseas. The international markets can be more objectively assessed to determine which products

[6]William A. Dymsza, *Multinational Business Strategy* (New York: McGraw-Hill Book Company, 1972), p. 23.

[7]*Organizing for Worldwide Operations* (New York: Business International, 1965), pp. 11–24.

should be marketed, what brands and trademarks should be exploited in the world markets, and what is the most effective market entry strategy. The concentration of foreign activities within the division permits a degree of coordination that has the potential to increase the total international performance beyond that achieved by independent subsidiaries.

The degree of influence on corporate policy achieved by the international division varies considerably among companies. When the division is new and its activities are a small percentage of the company's total business, the international vice-president may exert little influence; however, this situation will change as the division grows and increases its importance to the company. At first the international division may operate with relatively little headquarter's control and without close relationship to the domestic divisions. Similarly, when first formed, the divisional headquarters may have little effect on the previously independent foreign subsidiaries. The ability to coordinate and control subsidiary activities may increase as the division executives gather experience. Coordination through centralization, however, may be difficult for marketing when local conditions vary widely.[8]

Despite the advantages claimed for the international division structure, it appears to have several inherent weaknesses. The international division remains dependent on the domestic divisions. Products manufactured abroad are similar to domestic products and are dependent on technical development and design in the domestic market. Communications linkages with the domestic product or functional departments are strained as each strives to meet primary responsibilities. Internal political stress may culminate in an unwillingness of domestic units to provide products to the foreign market when shortages exist. Also, the prices at which goods are transferred to the international division profit center can be distorted.[9] Probably one of the most significant defects of the split between domestic and international activities lies in the inability of the firm to fully capitalize on the executive and technical expertise that is spread throughout the organization.

Regional Management Centers *decentralization*

A number of approaches have been used to increase the effectiveness of the international division. One, the formation of regional management centers makes the international operations more responsive to local needs by decentralizing some decisions to a regional office.

---

[8]See John M. Stopford and Louis T. Wells, Jr., *Managing the Multinational Enterprise* (New York: Basic Books, Inc., 1972), pp. 15–25, for a discussion of the evolution of the international division.

[9]Transfer pricing is discussed in Chapter 14.

The regional center coordinates the activities of national affiliates that previously reported directly to division headquarters. In this manner regional policies can be coordinated and some administrative efficiencies can be gained.

This approach is illustrated by experiences in Europe during the 1960s. At that time a number of U.S. firms established regional headquarters. Some of these headquarters were developed to coordinate efforts within the emerging European Economic Community (EEC) or the European Free Trade Association (EFTA); a few, however, including Standard Oil of New Jersey and Union Carbide, saw potential gain in regarding Europe as a whole.[10] Several benefits were derived from the establishment of such regional centers. The center permitted some "policy decentralization while at the same time raising some issues up to the regional level which had previously been settled at the national level."[11] This unification of European operations at the regional level provided an opportunity to shift production and marketing to take advantage of the EEC and EFTA agreements. Some shifting of production did occur, but the attempt was not always successful.[12] Moreover markets were not always susceptible to centralization as nationalism, cultural barriers, and communications barriers continued to exist despite the Common Market. The regional management center did, however, provide an opportunity to integrate the activities of previously independent marketing subsidiaries that had been established on a national basis to serve only that country's markets. Although most commonly employed for consumer goods, the center concept was also used for industrial goods. Univac applied the regional concept to Scandanavia to pool resources, save cost and time in shipping, and secure better use of specialized technical and marketing teams in selling to the government market.[13]

The regional headquarters speeds information to the parent company. It provides close control over marketing and enables the firm to adapt more quickly to local situations (without a regional center, all major decisions must be referred to corporate headquarters). Close relations can be maintained with subsidiaries, distributors, and customers. Furthermore, decentralization of control to the regional office can provide economies in purchasing, warehousing, and other routines.[14]

A disadvantage of the regional plan is that it can be expensive to establish, especially when product specialists provide the technical

[10] "U.S. Business in the New Europe," *Business Week* (May 7, 1966), p. 100.

[11] Jack N. Behrman, *Some Patterns in the Rise of the Multinational Enterprise* (Chapel Hill, N.C.: Graduate School of Business Administration, University of North Carolina, 1969), p. 65.

[12] "A Giant Multinational Finds Unified Activities Aren't Easy to Set Up," *The Wall Street Journal*, February 20, 1974, p. 1.

[13] "Organizing for Scandanavian Operations: The Univac Case," *Business International* (March 29, 1974), p. 101.

[14] Richard T. Bickers, *Marketing in Europe* (London: Gower Press Limited, 1971), p. 33.

expertise. Expenses rise due to the duplication of staff between head-quarters of the region.

Deciding where to locate the regional headquarters is a significant problem. In general, the site chosen should be centrally located, with good communication facilities and adequate office space. The location should provide easy access to banking facilities, to a supply of trained personnel, and major markets and customers. The headquarters city should be an attractive home for the executives and their families, and it should provide a hospitable atmosphere for the headquarters unit and its personnel.[15]

The regional concept implies some decentralization of authority to regional managers so they can adapt company policy to their specific area; at the same time, centralization of authority is involved in coor-dinating the activities of previously independent country subsidiaries. Although the regions are coordinated by the parent company head-quarters through budgets, planning sessions, frequent communication, and executive visits, the regional organization places great emphasis on capable executive manpower. Plans for developing management ca-pability and molding the overseas executives into an effective manage-ment team are crucial to the success of the regional concept. Decisions must also be made regarding the specific marketing activities that can best profit from decentralization.

The International Headquarters Company   *Subsidiary*

The international division can be organized as a separate corpora-tion. The international vice-president of the parent company becomes the president of the headquarters subsidiary. The subsidiary has its own board of directors, interlocking with the parent corporation. This structure has been utilized by companies such as Coca-Cola, Interna-tional Business Machines, Pepsico and Upjohn. Often the subsidiary emphasizes its function and the parent-subsidiary relationship by in-cluding the parent company in its name such as the IBM World Trade Corporation or Coca-Cola Export Corporation.

The entire foreign operations of the company, including produc-tion, may be supervised by the international headquarters company. Such a subsidiary is delegated the responsibility for planning and key operational decisions.[16] The separate corporation becomes a profit center; it is billed for products and services furnished by the parent at agreed upon transfer prices and makes its profit from the spread be-tween its costs and sales revenue. Executives of the headquarters com-pany usually possess greater authority and responsibility than under the previously discussed plans. The subsidiary, itself, may be organ-ized on a functional, geographic, or product base.

---

[15]*Ibid.*, p. 35.
[16]Dymsza, *op. cit.*, p. 26.

The subsidiary may provide tax advantages for the parent when the income tax of foreign countries calculates the tax on the total sales or profit of the company, regardless of where its operations occur. When the subsidiary qualifies as a Western Hemisphere Trade Corporation or a Domestic International Sales Corporation there are gains under U.S. tax law. [17] To qualify as a Western Hemisphere Trade Corporation, the subsidiary must be an American Corporation transacting all its business in the Western Hemisphere and ninety-five percent of its income must be derived from sources outside the United States.

WORLDWIDE ORGANIZATION MODELS

The limitation of the international division in providing a worldwide perspective for planning and operations has caused many firms to abandon the international division and seek alternative structures.[18] Among the evolving structures was the worldwide product division in which the product executives were given responsibility for production and marketing of the division's products throughout the world. A second alternative established geographically based structures providing an area executive with responsibility for a given region in the world market. These structures try to avoid the split between international and domestic operations found in the international division. There is a centralization of worldwide responsibility in the chief executive's office and operational responsibility is assigned to product divisions or area managers. The purpose of worldwide organization models is to force executives to assume their roles in a global perspective that treats each subdivision on the merits of its potential and results.

Worldwide Product Structures

Figure 9-4 illustrates the prototype worldwide product structure in which emphasis is placed on product rather than area. The manager of each product division is responsible for all marketing, production, and planning for the division's products. The product division becomes a profit center and each manager is held accountable for results, although each receives technical, legal, research, and financial support from corporate headquarters to supplement the division's own staff. In turn, the divisions provide management, technical, and marketing assistance to foreign affiliates.

A product structure has several advantages.[19] It emphasizes product rather than area differences and sets the stage for worldwide

---

[17]See *DISC, A Handbook for Exporters* (Washington: U.S. Department of the Treasury, January, 1972).

[18]Stopford and Wells, *op. cit.*, p. 25.

[19]These advantages are based on the findings of Arvind Phatak. For a more complete listing see Arvind V. Phatak, *Managing Multinational Corporations* (New York: Praeger Publishers, Inc., 1974), pp. 181–184.

product planning. New products are readily added and a product's progress through the product cycle is monitored so the firm can adjust its marketing mix. Customers receive help from technically knowledgeable personnel and each major product group receives the emphasis warranted by its market and profit position.

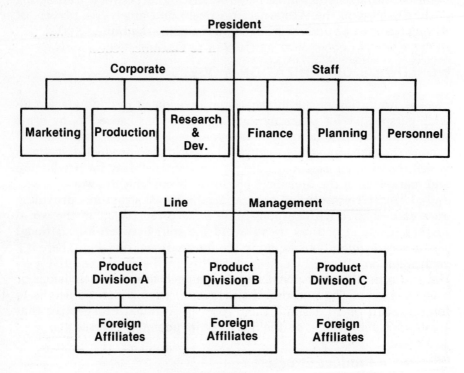

Figure 9-4 **WORLDWIDE PRODUCT STRUCTURE**

Like other organizational forms, the worldwide product structure has its weaknesses. Problems of communication and coordination exist among the product divisions. The product executive must be well-rounded. The product structure requires knowledge and skills in general management and international expertise in addition to product-related knowledge. However, corporate officers promoted from the product divisions may lack the broader experience in dealing with the company's total line. Furthermore, when each product group has its own staff there is considerable duplication within the corporation, resulting in high staff costs.

The product organization tends to be adopted when the company produces and markets a highly diversified line of products requiring different technologies to produce and different marketing strategies and channels for their sale. Often, however, products may be grouped when the technology, use, and marketing conditions are similar.

Worldwide Geographic Structures

The worldwide geographic structure emphasizes area rather than product differences. Such an organizational prototype is shown in Figure 9-5. The area managers are responsible for all operations within their geographic region. Companies using the geographic structure typically produce a wide variety of products that can be marketed through similar or common channels of distribution to similar end-users. Their products need adaptation to customer requirements, and marketing rather than production is the critical variable.[20]

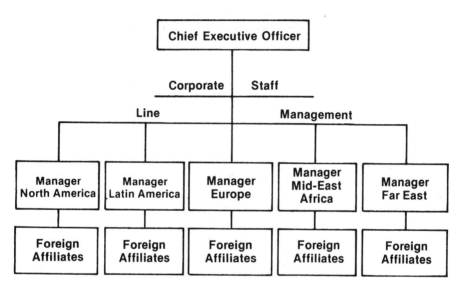

Figure 9-5 WORLDWIDE GEOGRAPHIC STRUCTURE

Consumer package-goods companies often possess these characteristics. Food processors, for example, frequently sell a wide line of products whose consumption is affected by tradition and by cultural variations in the marketplace. Some product adjustment may be needed, but the major difference among countries may be the marketing mix employed. Where product differences exist, they may reflect only minor adjustments in formulation or processing.

Unilever, Nestle's, International Flavors and Fragrances, and Corn Products (CPC) with their broad consumer product lines are examples of companies that have used the worldwide geographic pattern. However, the pure geographic pattern tends to be ineffective when the product line is highly technical because of difficulties in securing sales

---

[20]*Ibid.*, p. 177.

and technical personnel who are well-trained in all lines. Also, it is difficult to achieve a balanced sales effort on the total line.

Hybrid Structures

Companies have responded in several ways to the difficulties expressed under the "pure" forms previously described. Some have established a *management board* or executive committee to provide the chief executive with a nucleus of key product and functional executives to exercise strategic planning on a worldwide scale.[21] Thus, strategic planning and control are centralized in the headquarters committee. Other firms have experimented with *grid structures* that attempt to link product, area, and functional knowledge in a structure of overlapping authority.[22] In this form the general manager is responsible for organizational balance. Others, such as Sperry Rand, have established *umbrella companies* to secure regional cooperation.[23] In this system, individual country subsidiaries are replaced by an umbrella company responsible for the coordination of cash management, corporate image efforts, administrative services, and transportation. Product divisions remain responsible for divisional profits within the country, but work through the umbrella subsidiary. Thus, product expertise is obtained and there is less duplication of administrative services.[24] The precise nature and form of these hybrids is not yet fixed as companies continue to experiment.

QUESTIONS

1. Define a built-in export department and evaluate its strengths and its weaknesses.
2. Assume a company produces a narrow line of industrial goods, but has little experience in exporting. What alternative structural forms might you suggest to organize their export effort?
3. Compare the functions and operation of the built-in export department and the separate export department.
4. Evaluate the strengths and weaknesses of the export management company.
5. Explain the worldwide or global concept and its implications for organizing international marketing.
6. Comment on the reasons for establishing an international headquarters company.
7. What are the advantages of an international division? Its weaknesses?

---

[21]Gilbert H. Clee and Alfred di Scipio, "Creating a World Enterprise," *Harvard Business Review* (November–December, 1959).
[22]See Warren J. Keegan, *Multinational Marketing Management* (Englewood Cliffs, N.J.: Prentice-Hall, Inc., 1974), pp. 480–483.
[23]Stopford and Wells, *op. cit.*, p. 43.
[24]Keegan, *op. cit.*, p. 484.

8. What reasons can you give for the establishment of a worldwide product structure?
9. How have the worldwide structures attempted to overcome deficiencies in the international division?
10. Evaluate the use of worldwide product or geographic structures for (a) a large food processor and (b) a diversified producer of chemicals and machine tools.

SUPPLEMENTARY READINGS

Brooke, Michael Z., and H. Lee Remmers. *The Multinational Company in Europe*. Ann Arbor: The University of Michigan Press, 1972.

Business International. *Organizing for European Operations*. Geneva: Business International, S.A., 1967.

Dymsza, William A. *Multinational Business Strategy*. New York: McGraw-Hill Book Company, 1972. Chapter 2.

Kolde, E.J. *The Multinational Company*. Lexington, Mass.: Lexington Books, D.C. Heath and Company, 1974. Chapters 7, 8, and 9.

Phatak, Arvind V. *Managing Multinational Corporations*. New York: Praeger Publishers, 1974. Chapter 7.

Stopford, John M., and Louis T. Wells, Jr. *Managing the Multinational Enterprise*. New York: Basic Books, Inc., 1972.

Wiechmann, Ulrich E. *Marketing Management in Multinational Firms*. New York: Praeger Publishers, 1976.

10

International Marketing Channels

International marketing organization refers to those administrative relationships necessary for internal administration of the firm and to the extensive external organization required to contact customers. Every firm faces a problem of providing a linkage between its internal organization and the market. The institutional structure that supplies this linkage is known as the channel of distribution or the marketing channel. The marketing channel is defined by the American Marketing Association as "the structure of intracompany organization units, and extracompany agents and dealers, wholesale and retail, through which a commodity, product, or service is marketed."[1]

Chapter 10 investigates the channels available to the international marketer for the distribution of products and services. The major concepts of the marketing channel and some of the alternatives that are available will be reviewed. This chapter describes the types of intermediaries that may be found in the producer's home country and those found abroad, including a discussion of marketing through distributors. Distribution systems within developing nations and Western Europe are compared in a final section.

MARKETING CHANNEL CONCEPTS

The relationship between the internal organization of the business firm and the marketing channel is a close one. Chapter 9 included the Export Management Company (an independent intermediary) in the discussion of the internal organization to illustrate the close tie between the producing and distributing organizations. Marketing managers need to integrate the channel members into their marketing plans for successful market development. The behavior of the channel intermediaries — and consequently, the effectiveness of marketing — is dependent on recognition of capabilities and upon the methods used

---

[1]*Marketing Definitions: A Glossary of Marketing Terms* (Chicago: American Marketing Association, 1960), p. 10.

to provide incentive for cooperation. If any marketing channel is to meet and reconcile the goals of each participant, the activities of the entire channel must be coordinated. This leadership and coordination are the tasks of the channel captain. Especially in international marketing, "the market" should not be considered as the next link in the channel, but rather the final consumer and any intermediate markets should be considered. International channels of distribution must further consider the problem of marketing *between* countries as well as *within* countries.

Marketing channel decisions are important for several reasons: (1) they determine how and where the product will be made available; (2) the choice of a channel structure is closely interrelated with the other variables in the marketing mix such as pricing, advertising, display, packaging, inventory, etc; and (3) the development of effective international channels requires time and funds to organize and support a co-ordinated market approach.

Before channel decisions are made, the markets must be analyzed to determine who buys the product, how it is purchased, under what conditions the purchase is made, and the strengths and weaknesses of the present channels used by the trade. The decisions involve specifying the number and location of distribution units and selecting the specific distributors to include in the channel. In addition to these decisions, it is necessary to provide incentives and control to insure that the channel performs as planned.

Channel Flows

The international marketing channel provides the services needed to make a product available when it is demanded and in quantities desired by the customer. It makes possible shipment and storage of the physical product and arranges to transfer control of the product to the potential user, either by sale or by leasing. The channel provides any necessary service after the sale is transacted. These concepts are illustrated in Figure 10-1 which shows the marketing flows that must exist between the producer and the user of the product or service.[2] Orders flow from the user, through any intermediaries, and on to the producer; payment is made in reverse order. The physical product moves from producer to user and is accompanied by transactions that transfer control to the user. Communication in the form of promotional efforts by means of the sales force and advertising is directed toward the user; a reverse communication flows back through research

---

[2]See George Fisk, *Marketing Systems: An Introductory Analysis* (New York: Harper & Row Publishers, 1967), Chapters 4–12, or Ben M. Enis, *Marketing Principles* (Pacific Palisades: Goodyear Publishing Company, Inc., 1974), p. 88, for a discussion of these flows.

to provide information for planning as well as feedback concerning the effectiveness of the marketing program.

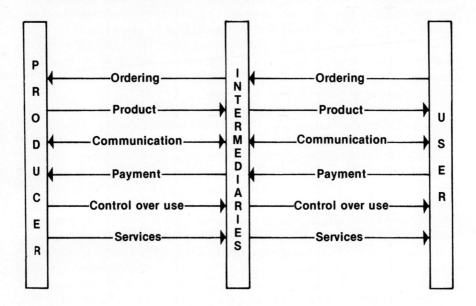

Figure 10-1 MARKETING FLOWS IN THE CHANNEL

Channel Variations

A number of channel options are available to the international marketer. Some of those are illustrated in Figure 10-2. The firm may use its domestic or subsidiary sales force to contact customers, or it may use any of a wide variety of intermediaries in the home country or abroad to facilitate the sale. The company can employ agents to represent it overseas or it may market through a trading company or another producer (allied company).

Figure 10-2 represents only a few of the channels found in international marketing. Various types of agent and merchant intermediaries will be discussed later. The chart does illustrate, however, that similar types of intermediaries exist in both the home country and abroad. Also, some international transactions are initiated by buyers rather than sellers. These buyers contact sellers directly or make contact by means of intermediaries.

The choice of a channel is a complex decision in which marketers pursue several goals. Since representation is needed in all the company's target markets, a channel must provide the geographic and industry coverage desired. Usually the firm seeks institutions that can provide continuous coverage and service but sometimes brokers or

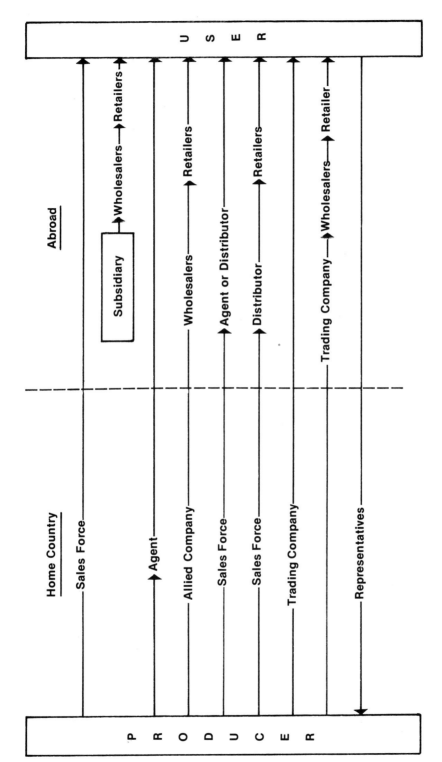

Figure 10-2 SELECTED INTERNATIONAL MARKETING CHANNELS

other agents are needed to bring buyers and sellers together for a single transaction. Sellers and buyers seek channel members who can provide the types and quality of services needed at a reasonable cost. Durable goods producers need a channel that can provide aggressive marketing with adequate display, demonstration, and repair service. Agricultural marketers may require transportation and storage in addition to help in finding and negotiating with prospective buyers. In addition, marketers seek varying degrees of control over marketing policy. Control may be best exercised by direct channels using company sales personnel; however, varying degrees of control can be exerted in other channels.

The choice of an appropriate channel is affected by factors other than these policy objectives. First, channel choice is dependent on the *characteristics of the product* marketed. Physically perishable products (or fashion merchandise) tend to be distributed by direct contact between producers and retailers. Similarly, high value-high technology products require direct contact to explain the product's qualities, to fit it into a production or consumption system, and to make necessary modifications. On the other hand, staple, frequently purchased products with low value and low perishability usually are sold through intermediaries. Secondly, the *market characteristics* can lead to channel variation. A marketer might use a company sales force to contact the dense major urban markets but employ agents and distributors in outlying areas. Thirdly, even the *characteristics of the producer* affect the decision. An ideal channel might be acquired through direct selling, but if a producer is small, financially weak, and has a narrow product line, direct selling may be too costly.

The final channel choice inevitably involves reconciling all of these factors and rests on a knowledge of the alternatives that are present in the company's specific situation. However, a general knowledge of the trading institutions of international marketing is a prerequisite to successful marketing. The following sections describe some of these institutions to indicate how and when they are useful.

RESIDENT BUYERS IN THE HOME MARKET

Many export shipments are derived from sales to buyers for overseas companies located in the home country. For the U.S. producer these are essentially domestic sales with delivery either abroad or in the U.S., although these sales may require special handling because of their export nature. Resident buyers in the home market represent either private or governmental interests abroad. Large American and foreign-owned companies abroad frequently have a resident buyer or an office in the United States to purchase supplies and equipment from American sources. Thus, Petro-Peru maintains a buying office in Houston, Texas while the government of Israel Ministry of Defense has an office in New York. Some resident buyers purchase for American companies that have contracted overseas for construction of pipelines, desalinization plants, or other projects; for example, Morrison-Knudsen International Co., Inc., orders from Boise, Idaho.

Because of the extensive foreign operations of American firms, a sizable share of United States exports results from orders placed in this country by such firms. American oil, mining, manufacturing, or construction companies place orders for equipment through the headquarters organization in this country for delivery abroad.

Foreign countries whose governments are committed to state trading also conduct trade through purchasing and sales missions located in the U.S. For example, the USSR purchases some American products through Amtorg Trading Corporation — a New York corporation. Other foreign governments also have established purchasing missions in the U.S. to make military purchases and facilitate purchases made under some foreign aid programs.

INTERNATIONAL MARKETING INTERMEDIARIES

Some international marketing intermediaries are located in the home market and function for domestic and foreign buyers and sellers. Others are located abroad and perform similar functions. These intermediaries are generally divided into the following categories:

1. Export and/or import commission houses.
2. Export and/or import merchants.
3. Manufacturer's export agents.
4. Export and import brokers.
5. Export houses or trading companies.
6. Allied companies.

These market intermediaries may be broadly distinguished by their characteristics of operation as follows:

1. The commission house acts in the interest of the buyers, receiving a purchasing commission from the buyer.
2. Merchants act in their own interests. They buy, accept the risks of ownership, and sell. Their income is derived from a profit on the sale.
3. Manufacturers' export agents act for producers or manufacturers and receive a sales commission from their principal.
4. Brokers represent either buyers or sellers and usually trade in staples that are often sold in organized commodity markets. Brokers receive a commission from the party they represent.
5. Export houses or trading companies may engage in both exporting and importing and perform many or all of the functions of the institutions listed above.
6. The allied company is a producing firm that agrees to market the products of another producer.

Export and/or Import Commission Houses

An export commission house places orders with home market manufacturers for the account of foreign buyers; the import commission house places orders with foreign producers for the account of home market buyers.

Export Commission Houses. The export commission house is the resident representative in the United States of foreign buyers. It receives orders or *indents*[3] from these buyers and acts as their purchasing agent in the United States. When standard goods are ordered, the commission house places the order with the designated manufacturer and attends to all details of exporting. Often, however, foreign buyers designate only the type of merchandise wanted and stipulate a price they are willing to pay. It then becomes the duty of the commission house to find the best purchase.

The export commission house was a pioneer in establishing foreign trade. It handled the bulk of United States exports during the middle of the nineteenth century. With a decline in the share of foreign trade conducted by American intermediaries, the export commission house, as such, has largely disappeared; but the function is still performed by trading companies.

Import Commission Houses. The import commission house is the resident representative in the United States for American buyers. For example, an American firm may need a particular kind of material, product, or piece of equipment abroad (Brazilian shoes, Chilean wine, or African masks), but not be knowledgeable about the markets for these goods. The American firm can make arrangements with an import commission house with offices in the United States to purchase the product required. Sometimes import commission houses receive consignments from foreign producers by whom they are paid a *selling commission*. In this case they are sales agents or brokers. Buying agents may represent several department stores, place orders abroad for the group, and receive a commission for doing so. Quite often a commission house combines exporting and importing functions.

Export and/or Import Merchants

Such merchants buy outright for their own accounts and sell, if possible, at a profit. The merchandise that is exported is usually selected by the merchant, although it may be ordered in advance by a buyer.

---

[3]Technically, *indents* are offers to purchase at prices, and under other conditions, stipulated by the prospective purchaser. In practice (trans-Pacific and African trade) indents are often synonymous with orders.

The merchant sells goods, unlike the commission house that essentially performs a buying function. Usually stocks of merchandise are maintained at home or abroad to facilitate prompt delivery; however, it has become increasingly hazardous to carry stocks of merchandise to fill anticipated demands in international commerce. Demand shifts, fashion, competition, price changes, tariff revisions, and foreign exchange and import restrictions have combined to make this practice highly speculative.

Usually merchants buy from a number of sources and have little brand loyalty unless they represent producers with strongly established franchises. They also handle competitive lines when it is profitable. Since merchants own the merchandise they usually control pricing and marketing policy in their markets. Despite these difficulties they represent a convenient means of reaching overseas markets. They usually assume the credit risks and have a strong incentive to sell merchandise they have purchased.

In the less developed countries of the world, a large portion of the export and import trade is conducted by merchants. In the developed countries merchants are not as important as exporters because the relatively standardized products originally handled by the merchants are now produced by large manufacturers who prefer to control their own distribution. Except in the case of Japan, relatively few manufactured exports are sold abroad by merchants. Imports, on the other hand, are frequently handled by merchants.[4]

Some CEMs have evolved to a merchant status and are known as Export Management Companies as discussed in Chapter 9. However, the EMC usually places orders with the manufacturer after having received an order from abroad. The EMC then pays cash, "resells" the product abroad, and invoices the customer. EMCs, compared to other merchants, have a much closer and continuous relationship with the selected group of noncompetitive manufacturers they represent. Usually the EMC controls distribution policy because of market contacts and knowledge.

Manufacturers' Export Agent

This agent represents the manufacturer in one or more markets and performs functions similar to those of a manufacturer's agent in domestic marketing. A producer may use several manufacturers' export agents, each of whom covers a separate market. The agent derives income from a commission paid on sales and usually represents more than one producer of related, but noncompetitive lines to spread marketing costs over a wider line. The agent develops a foreign market for

---

[4]Roland L. Kramer, "Export/Import Merchants," *ASIE Bulletin* (January–February, 1974).

the product, arranges for physical distribution, and may assume foreign credit risks. MEAs provide continuous coverage in the markets where they represent their clients and may be used to supplement a manufacturer's own distribution by covering specific markets. They reduce the cost of distribution to a manufacturer because the MEA's costs are borne by the entire line of products. Since payment is by commission, a manufacturer's costs are largely variable with sales volume, although some fixed costs arises from supervision and the need to provide promotional programs.

Export and Import Brokers

Brokers, by definition, bring buyers and sellers together but may act for either the buyer or seller; they are then paid a commission on the transaction. The term broker is often broadly applied, however, and so-called brokerage concerns may conduct business in several other ways. Brokers usually specialize in a selected group of staple products and may specialize in dealing with certain countries (e.g., Eastern Europe). Examples of products sold through brokers include grain, cotton, wool, sugar, and coffee. Moreover, merchandise that is consigned to a market, United States or foreign, is frequently disposed of by brokers.

The broker's primary function is to bring buyers and sellers together, but the broker's specialized knowledge is useful in providing a quick sale or in negotiating the intricacies of foreign business procedures. Some specialized brokerage firms have developed to meet specific situations such as product shortages. In 1973 barter brokers in the chemical trade facilitated the buying of products in the U.S. and the reselling of these products abroad at a high world price, but often they arranged to swap chemicals in a series of transactions to get the kinds of products their clients wanted.[5] These brokers were able to save valuable time for clients because of their worldwide connections and willingness to trade in a broader range of products than individual chemical producers. Barter brokers are also used in Eastern European trade when Western sellers agree to take Eastern goods in payment for the products they sell.

Factors and Confirming Houses

Factors, sometimes known as *del credere agents*, are intermediaries whose functions have included the financing of trade. In the United States factors are essentially financial institutions which buy accounts

---

[5]"Bartering to Beat the Chemicals Shortage," *Business Week* (October 27, 1973), p. 90.

receivable from manufacturers. Factors are active in the textile trade and have operated in the leather and lumber trade to Europe. The essential role of the factor is to carry the financing in industries where a large number of producers exist. Usually they advance funds, if needed, to manufacturers and to customers of the manufacturer. In the United States factoring also is important to the import trade. European manufacturers who do not know the American market and financing laws may turn to the factor.

The *confirming house* is primarily concerned with finance. The system orginated in the United Kingdom where approximately 20 percent of the foreign trade passes through confirming houses. When an order is placed, the house "confirms" payment to the supplier; that is, it undertakes to pay when it receives the invoices and documents of title. The confirming house arranges the terms of payment with the buyer. There is no recourse to the supplier except for the normal warranties on the product.[6]

Trading Companies

The term *trading company* is a more appropriate description of many international intermediaries than many of the separate terms previous noted (except brokers and import merchants) since many of the firms combine several functions. Trading companies buy and sell as merchants and may handle goods on consignment or act as commission houses for some buyers. Some bring together a wide variety of merchandise from many sources, others tend to specialize by commodities or regions. Financing is an important element in the service mix of the trading company. Generally they pay cash for their purchases and extend credit to their customers. In the import trade advances may be made to foreign producers of commodities. Wide lines of merchandise enable some to perform their own freight forwarding services and to avoid minimum charges for transportation by combining several smaller shipments.

Many of the well-known trading companies are European- or Japanese-headquartered and have branches wherever they do business, including the U.S. Much of their operation in the past has been with the developing countries, but some play important roles in developed countries and in importing and distributing goods in their home markets. A significant percentage of developing nations' international trade may be handled by trading firms based outside the country; thus, an estimated 40–50% of Taiwan's exports was controlled by Japanese trading companies in 1972.

One of the largest and best-known British trading companies is the United Africa Company, a Unilever subsidiary, which operates many

---

[6]Dominion of Canada, Department of Trade and Commerce, *Foreign Trade* (June 22, 1968).

wholesale and retail stores throughout West Africa. Following World War II, UAC reduced its emphasis on agricultural and local buying and began a more general trading approach which now involves such diverse products as textiles, brewery products, timber, hospital supplies, and even motor vehicle assembly.[7]

Japan is the best example of a country where trading companies dominate the country's international marketing. These Japanese trading companies are often part of a group (Zaibatsu) that maintains closely linked manufacturing, banking, and trading organizations. In 1972 the six largest trading companies had combined sales of $68 billion and accounted for 40% of Japan's exports and 50% of its imports; they also conducted 19% of the wholesale business within Japan.[8] Even large Japanese companies expect to buy through trading companies. The trading companies are important distributors of both industrial and consumer goods.

Japanese trading companies provide a variety of services for their clients. They gather market information, develop and implement marketing plans, and provide facilities for merchandise handling and wholesaling. They finance imports and exports, often making loans to or direct investment in distributors and retailers.[9] Through the extensive ties with government and other firms, the trading company organizes distribution and helps producers by storing, transporting, financing, accepting distribution risks, and marshalling wholesale and retail support for the marketing program. They are invaluable aids in penetrating the cumbersome Japanese distribution system and overcoming the many cultural and institutional differences between Japanese and Western systems.[10]

Allied Company Arrangement (Piggyback)

U.S. or foreign producers may be used as the marketing arms of U.S. companies through the allied company arrangement. Thus, Sony, the Japanese electronics firm, sells U.S. and European products in Japan. It established Sony International Housewares and distributes for Whirlpool, Schick, Regal Ware, Heath Co., and other U.S. firms. Sony provides a detailed knowledge of the Japanese market, solid promotional effort, and competent servicing for products it represents.[11]

---

[7]Robin Stoddart, "Unilever: Europe and Africa," *The International Review* (January 15, 1973), pp. 29–30.

[8]"Tackling the Traders," *Time* (February 25, 1974), p. 86.

[9]"Using Trading Companies in Exporting to Japan," Japan External Trade Organization, *JETRO Marketing Series 2*.

[10]See William D. Hartley, "Cumbersome Japanese Distribution System Stumps U.S. Concerns," *The Wall Street Journal*, March 2, 1972, p. 1.

[11]"How Sony Piggybacks Foreign Products in Japan," *Business International* (February 1, 1974), p. 38.

The Colgate-Palmolive Company is an example of an American producer selling the products of foreign firms. Colgate uses its marketing knowledge and existing distribution systems to market consumer products for a variety of U.S. and foreign firms. It buys razors and blades from Wilkinson Sword Company in Britain and distributes them in the U.S., Puerto Rico, Canada, and Scandanavia. Henkel of Germany uses Colgate to distribute Pritt Glue Stick. Alpen, a cereal widely available in U.S. supermarkets, is sold by Colgate but the manufacturer is Weetabix Company of England.[12]

The allied company arrangement is one of the simplest ways for a firm to secure foreign distribution. The above examples illustrate the essential nature of the arrangement. A producer with established foreign distribution contracts to sell the products of a second manufacturer. The distributing producer buys at agreed prices, adds the product to an existing (usually complementary) line of products, and uses a proven marketing organization to distribute the product within a trading area.

The actual manufacturer benefits from this operation by securing the marketing services of an existing system with established contacts and marketing knowledge. The arrangement provides additional revenue through exports for firms that cannot justify a continuing presence in the market because of small export potential. Piggybacking also supplements existing marketing effort by providing coverage in markets where a manufacturer is not currently represented. Piggybacking may, however, be limited to areas where distributing producers have a market for their existing line of products. The distributing manufacturer gains additional revenue from a broader line of products by effecting more complete utilization of marketing capacity.

MARKETING THROUGH AGENTS OR DISTRIBUTORS ABROAD

Many types of intermediaries discussed previously can act as agents or distributors for an exporting firm, or the firm can use wholesalers and retailers already established in the market for domestic distribution. This section describes why agents or distributors may be used, how they are selected and developed, and major provisions of a distributor contract.

Although the terms "agent" and "distributor" are often used interchangeably, there is a valid distinction between them. An *agent* is one who acts on behalf of a principal within the expressed or implied authority of the agreement. A *distributor* is an independent customer. The agent does not purchase goods, but places orders; the title to such

---

[12]"Why Colgate Sells Other People's Products," *Business Week* (April 20, 1974), pp. 108–111.

merchandise does not pass to the agent. The distributor purchases goods, acquires title, and markets the merchandise.

Why Use a Distributor?

At the time of initial entry, the market contains many unknowns for the manufacturer. Furthermore, the manufacturer is unknown to potential customers though the firm is well established at home and/or in other foreign countries. An agent or distributor can provide the initial contacts needed by the manufacturer and the final users may expect to buy from distributors or dealers from whom they currently purchase related items. The manufacturer can penetrate the market rapidly by using the distributor's marketing capability.

The services rendered by overseas agents and distributors vary greatly. Much depends upon the type of product involved, market conditions, the kind of company chosen, and the philosophy of the manufacturer. Products such as automobiles, calculators, and machine tools require distributors that can supply spare parts and provide repair services as well as well-equipped demonstration and display facilities. The distributor may carry a heavy distributive burden in large inventories, extensive credits, and local hauling and shipping. The distributor's intimate knowledge of local sources of credit information, access to sources that the manufacturer's branch or subsidiary might not be able to use, and personal knowledge of the past practices of dealers make the distributor an effective local medium for obtaining credit information.

When distributors are given exclusive rights to market the product, the manufacturer expects extra effort in promotion and service. Exclusive distributors are assured that the results of their promotional efforts will accrue to them and not be shared with others. Exporters differ in the degree to which they handle their own advertising or delegate the task to the distributor. Frequently they divide the burden under a cooperative advertising agreement.

The laws in some countries governing bidding on government contracts may make it imperative to use an agent or distributor who is a resident or a citizen of that country. Syria and Jordan, for example, prohibit representation by foreign nationals; therefore, a Mideast representative from Lebanon or Egypt could not cover these markets. Also, where trade is particularly hostile to the establishment of a U.S. branch or subsidiaries, a local agent or distributor might provide needed distribution.

Selection of Agents and Distributors

Proper selection of agents and distributors is critical since marketing depends on their effort and skill. If their efforts are ineffective, the exporter loses potential sales and may find it difficult to train distributors or costly to replace them. Moreover, the laws of some countries protect local distributor rights and make it difficult to add others once the contract is established.[13] These laws may grant agents the same rights as employees; or the laws may provide compensation for the loss of future commissions and for goodwill established by the agent during the contract.

Information regarding the capability of agents and distributors may be obtained from many sources, especially the U.S. Department of Commerce; Dun & Bradstreet, Inc.; banks; foreign trade journals; and other exporters. Before the final decision is made, however, the exporter should visit the prospective distributor to determine first-hand the facilities of the distributor and the distributor's ability to perform.

Although many firms seek distributorships for an exporter's products, some may not be very effective. Usually, since the better distributors can choose among several companies, it becomes necessary to convince them of the desirability of marketing a specific product. Exporters must convince prospective distributors of the superior value of their products, services, and marketing policies. Manufacturers can attract distributors by stressing several factors: their financial strength; the capacity to export; the marketing program; success in other markets; the basic qualities of the product; product packaging; and dealer incentives such as commissions or margins allowed, price protection, and sales quotas.

The main factors to be considered in sifting a list of potential distributors are their character, marketing capacity, financial status, reputation with the trade, the lines of product handled, sales policy, location, trade group affiliation, nationality, and political influence. All of these must be analyzed to determine both present capacity and the potential for future development.

Developing the Relationship

Selecting the distributor and signing a contract do not assure an exporter that a satisfactory marketing program will be designed and implemented. Marketing is a continuing activity in which the manufacturer and distributor must continue to cooperate and exert their best efforts if the program is to succeed. The manufacturer-distributor relationship is usually presented as a complementary one in which each cooperates to accomplish product distribution. Exporters recognize, however, that they need to continuously work with, motivate, and train distributors since the relationship also contains some elements of conflict. This is most evident when the distributor represents

---

[13]See "Central America's Distributor Laws: Companies Feel Straightjacketing Effects," *Business Latin America* (July 19, 1973), pp. 230, 231.

several manufacturers.[14] Although the mutual interest of both manufacturer and distributor is selling the product, they may differ in their choice of appropriate strategies (e.g., volume selling vs. high margins, use of advertising, amount of effort required, etc.) and in the manner in which results are divided.

The manufacturer needs to employ techniques to minimize conflict and assure continued best efforts from the intermediaries. This means the manufacturer must integrate the dealer into the channel system by contacts made by the sales force and executive visits, by effective communication, by aiding the distributor where needed, and by providing proper incentives and controls. Extensive efforts are needed to train distributors initially, to periodically update their product knowledge and marketing capacity, and to maintain enthusiastic support for the company's products. A well-planned marketing program is essential to maintain a high level of sales from distributors.

Distributor Contracts

The terms defining the manufacturer-distributor relationship usually are reduced to writing to make a permanent record of the rights, duties, and liabilities of both parties of the contract. Some manufacturers, particularly those who have long-standing arrangements, have not used a detailed written contract; instead, these manufacturers have merely confirmed terms by a letter stating a few particulars such as territory and commissions. Other problems have been decided mutually as they arose, relying on the mutual interests and goodwill of the parties. This attitude was expressed by one large manufacturer whose products are sold throughout the world: "Our agreement is quite short and rather informal. We point out to most of our people that the agreement is no better than the intent of both parties."

But it is considered better to prepare a written contract covering the important phases of the agency relationship. Sometimes a formal contract is used, but an informal presentation of terms, often on the exporter's letterhead, is more frequently found. Putting the terms of the agency into a clearly written document helps to avoid misunderstanding and later ill feelings. A written document constitutes better legal protection where large credits are extended to the agent and where the rights of third parties might be involved; it is often helpful and necessary to the agent in obtaining foreign government business or getting credit from banks.

In general the contract should stipulate items such as:

I. Manufacturer's Rights, Obligations, and Concessions
   A. Territory granted
   B. Exclusive or non-exclusive agency

---

[14]Bruce Mallen, "Conflict and Cooperation in Marketing Channels," *Progress in Marketing*, edited by L. George Smith, American Marketing Association (1964).

C. Right of manufacturer to sell certain accounts directly
D. Pricing authority
E. Procedure for handling shipments and claims
F. Terms and methods of payment
G. Legal jurisdiction and arbitration procedure
H. Assignability of contract
I. Termination procedures
J. Trademark clause

II. Distributor's Rights and Obligations
A. Best efforts clause
B. Quotas
C. Advertising responsibility
D. Inventory requirement
E. Service facilities
F. Right, if any, to handle competing lines

RETAILING AND WHOLESALING SYSTEMS ABROAD

Large manufacturers usually prefer to control their channels of distribution by contacting wholesalers and retailers overseas through their own sales force. If these multinational firms are to adapt to the existing distribution structure found in countries where their goods are distributed or if they attempt to alter the foreign structure by developing new channels, their executives must be knowledgeable regarding characteristics of the present distribution structure and reasons for its persistence. Knowledge of present channels, of the economic basis for their existence, and of cultural factors inhibiting or facilitating change is a prerequisite for the development of an effective distribution strategy. In this section two environments are discussed to show the contrasts between systems in developing and highly industrialized countries. Western Europe provides an example of the industrialized countries and further illustrates some dynamic changes that have occurred in recent years.

Marketing Channels in Developing Countries

The economies of developing countries are characterized by several factors: a large number of small producers; low per capita incomes; a large percentage of employment confined to agricultural industries; limited capital for allocation among development projects; inadequate transportation and storage facilities; and heavy reliance on imports as a supply source for equipment, industrial supplies, and durable consumer goods. As a result, a country's domestic marketing channels at this stage of economic development may be characterized by the relatively large number of intermediaries who supply many small retailers.

Wholesalers play a key role in the developing country by importing merchandise, assembling the products of the small producers, financing the marketing process, and servicing the many small retailers. Large trading companies may control most of the foreign trade in such developing situations and local manufacturers become dependent on them for exporting goods.[15] Since wholesalers have little difficulty selling their products in an economy of scarcity, they thrive by controlling imports. Because the wholesaler dominates the marketing channel, the financing of manufacturers, retailers, and other wholesalers becomes one of the major functions. This financing function provides the wholesaler with considerable control over the marketing process and its participants.

Retailing in the lesser developed economies is characterized by a large number of retailers. By modern standards these retailers typically carry very limited inventories and display merchandise poorly in the open. They stock only a few (if any) brand names, use no advertising except for a sign over the establishment, haggle over price, and depend heavily upon family labor. Often the family lives in the store building to facilitate long hours of operation. Sometimes shops handling related commodities (food) are grouped in a local area to form a concentrated market. For example, the traditional bazaar is still a significant retailing institution in parts of Asia.

As nations industrialize, the traditional marketing institutions and channels encounter continual pressure for change. As development occurs, a nation's retail institutions tend to increase in size, widen their assortments, offer less personal service, and cater to more limited specific market segments.[16] These changes radically alter the competitive structure and lead to further reforms in wholesaling, promotion, and systems for physical distribution. The parallel growth of both retailers and domestic manufacturers tends to lessen the significance of the wholesaler. Retailers form buying groups and, together with the manufacturer, circumvent the wholesaler; this compresses or shortens the marketing channel.[17] The pattern of change may, however, differ among countries. One study found little similarity in the marketing structures of countries at comparable levels of development, and found a high degree of variation among firms within a country with regard to channel relationships.[18] Thus, the international marketer should be wary of relying too heavily on generalizations when seeking or designing an effective distribution channel for a product.

---

[15]A. A. Sherbini, "Import-Oriented Marketing Mechanisms," *Business Topics* (Spring, 1968), pp. 70–73.

[16]John Fayerweather, *International Marketing* (2d ed.; Englewood Cliffs, N.J.: Prentice-Hall, Inc., 1970), pp. 61–63.

[17]For a discussion of channel changes, see George Wadinambiaratchi, "Channels of Distribution in Developing Economies," *The Business Quarterly* (Winter, 1965), pp. 77–82.

[18]Susan P. Douglas, "Patterns and Parallels of Marketing Structure in Several Countries," *Business Topics* (Spring, 1971), pp. 38–48.

Western Europe

The distribution structures of Western Europe contrast with those of developing nations. Western Europe can hardly be called a single distribution system since wide variations exist in the wholesaling and retailing structures of such nations as Germany, Spain, Sweden, Italy, and the United Kingdom. Variety exists even within the European Common Market where Italy is known for its large number of retail establishments per 1000 population while Germany and the United Kingdom have many more inhabitants per retail establishment. The advent of self-service, discounting, cooperatives, and planned shopping centers also varies among the nations. Despite such disparity, however, it is important to view the changes occurring in distribution in Western Europe, especially since the formation of the common market.

Western Europe's distribution systems more closely parallel those of the United States than those of any other group of nations. Following a long period of stagnation Europe's marketing institutions have in recent years been characterized by a high rate of change. Europe's wholesaling and retailing institutions have shown a remarkable ability to adjust to the new economic and technological environment. Large numbers of small retailers have closed down and new forms of retailing have emerged to forge a more effective distribution system for meeting the requirements of the market.

European Factors Affecting Market Structure. Several factors have had important impacts on the marketing structure. First, there was a rapid degree of economic recovery in the post-World War II period that has materially improved the standard of living for many Europeans. This, in turn, produced changes in the lifestyles of both younger and older consumers. For example, in contrast to the pre-war period a large portion of the women in Germany, France, the United Kingdom, Sweden, and Austria now work outside the home, thereby adding to family income and placing an additional premium on the use of time. Households in many sectors of Europe now have a car and, as a result, have increased mobility for shopping and leisure.

A further factor in institutional change has been the development of the European Economic Community. Lowering of tariffs has brought shifts in sources of supply so that more companies compete to provide both a broader assortment of goods and a reduction in the variation of prices among countries. Lastly, the new environment has encouraged the expansion of distributive organizations across national boundaries through mergers and through joint buying arrangements.[19]

Major European Distribution Trends. The small retailers and inefficient wholesalers in Europe have been under pressure to change or to

---

[19]National Economic Development Office, *The Distributive Trends in the Common Market* (London: Her Majesty's Stationery Office, 1973), pp. 1–2.

close their doors.[20] While large-scale retailers have been increasing
their market share, smaller retailers have sought to maintain their position by several strategies. They have joined voluntary chains and
buying groups to increase their efficiency viz-à-viz the chains or mul-
tiples. They have recognized the value of specialization and capitalized
on the boutique concept in pedestrian malls and they have participated in a unique organization called the collective department store; this
is a large selling unit owned jointly by the independent retail stores
represented. [21]

Mass retailing has become popular in Europe and takes several
forms, but most retail stores rely heavily on a price appeal and massive displays combined with self-service operations. Supermarkets are
well established in the United Kingdom and on the continent. Self-
service stores account for the bulk of food sales in Belgium, Germany,
and The Netherlands. Perhaps more significant as an indication of the
radical changes in retailing, however, is the development of the hypermarket or super store.

Canadian Consulate

---

[20]One estimate has the number of retail stores in Germany declining by 20% between 1970 and 1980, or a net closing of 90,000 stores. Francoise Civegal, "Retailing
Burst Out All Over," *Vision* (June, 1973), p. 45.
    [21]*Ibid*, p. 29.

The hypermarket is a large store covering an area of over 2500 square meters or 25,000 square feet. Both food and non-food items are sold on a self-service basis and a common checkout system is used for both food and non-food. The first hypermarket was opened in 1962 in Belgium and by 1975 the concept had spread throughout much of Europe and even to North America. By 1973 Carrefour, a French firm, operated 32 such markets in France and eight more in Belgium, Britain, Switzerland, and Spain.[22] These stores stock 20 to 50 thousand brand-name items and sell at an average markup of 11–12%.[23] The typical hypermarket offers a wide assortment of merchandise at low prices with a minimum of service.

Discounting foods in Europe has taken the form of small stores that concentrate on a limited number of the most popular items in a supermarket; the retail stores thereby concentrate on high volume items with a fast stock turnover.

The large retailers of Europe have expanded their operations by moving across national borders.[24] Retailing was once thought to be a local activity, but U.S. and European retailers have moved boldly into other countries to capitalize on the expanded market opportunities and to take advantage of knowledge gained from their national base of operations.

Many of the large retailers have penetrated the European markets through multiple strategies. Thus, department stores have developed variety store subsidiaries; mail order companies have expanded into specialty stores, department stores, and shopping centers in an attempt to gain access to different market segments.

Although slower to emerge in Europe than in the U.S., there has been considerable interest and growth in planned shopping centers designed to meet the unique needs of the various countries.[25] The potential growth of both the shopping center and hypermarket have presented a challenge to both retailers and city planners. In several countries laws are aimed at limiting the development of large-scale retail units. In Italy, for example, municipalities are required to prepare plans for the development of their areas; local retailers with a strong bias to protect the status quo have a strong influence on these plans.[26]

European distribution systems are in a dynamic state. The wholesale and retail structures serving the consumer markets are adapting to the needs of a mass consumption society. At the moment retailers

---

[22]"Carrefour: A Superdiscounter Eyes the U.S.," *Business Week* (December 15, 1973), p. 78.

[23]*Ibid*. See also, "How a Discounter Sells in France," *Business Abroad* (June 10, 1968), pp. 29–30.

[24]See Stanley C. Hollander, *Multinational Retailing*, MSU International Business and Economic Studies, East Lansing: Graduate School of Business Administration, 1970, for an account of international retailing trends and problems.

[25]"Europe's New Shopping Centers," *Business Abroad* (October, 1968), pp. 22–28.

[26]Jennifer Tanburn, *Retailing and the Competitive Challenge* (London: Lintas, Ltd., February, 1974), pp. 28–29.

and wholesalers are seeking their best strategy for growth and survival. In such a situation both domestic and foreign producers must be aware of trends and adapt their own marketing strategy to the new environment.

Retailers and service organizations from outside Europe have also responded to the changing structure. American firms such as Sears have established retail stores in Europe; others, including J.C. Penney and Jewel, have purchased interests in European companies. Still others such as the Tandy Corporation (Radio Shack), Kentucky Fried Chicken, and Holiday Inns have established franchises in Europe.[27]

Conclusion

This brief review of developments in distribution systems indicates the dynamic quality of marketing institutions in a period of rapid change. It provides only a moderate insight into the diversity of institutions that are available as possible vehicles for bringing a manufacturer's product to the market. The review warns against generalizing too much as a result of previous experience at home or in the market. Distribution systems require constant evaluation and attention from the marketing manager, especially when the manager is concerned with marketing in several countries.

QUESTIONS

1. Define each of the following intermediaries:
   a. Commission house   d. Factor
   b. Trading company   e. Agent
   c. Broker
2. An American sales manager is visiting the company's agents and distributors in the Far East. In such countries as the Philippine Republic, Indonesia, Thailand, India, and Pakistan the representatives have served the company for many years. They are European and Chinese. Nationalism is making it increasingly difficult for these firms to continue. At the same time, the sales manager realizes there is little choice of competent indigenous firms in some areas that can replace the present representatives. What can be done?
3. Under what circumstances might a broker be an efficient intermediary for a firm?
4. Why do international marketing channel decisions involve marketing within countries as well as between countries?

---

[27]For accounts of the franchising operations, see "A Radio Shack for Europe," *Business Week* (August 31, 1974), pp. 75–76; Bruce J. Walker and Michael J. Etzel, "The Internationalization of U.S. Franchise Systems: Progress and Procedures," *Journal of Marketing* (April, 1973), pp. 38–46; and Charles L. Vaughan, "International Franchising," *The Cornel H.R.A. Quarterly* (February, 1974), pp. 103–110.

5. Select a product that is produced locally and might be distributed internationally. What channel would you suggest to the local producer? What factors affected your choice?
6. What is a resident buyer?
7. How can a small manufacturer use the allied company arrangement (piggybacking) to achieve sales in foreign countries?
8. What is a trading company?
9. Some manufacturers have found it profitable to use distributors and agents as foreign representatives rather than developing their own sales force. Why? Why do other manufactuers choose not to use such foreign representatives?
10. Briefly characterize the institutional structure for distribution in developing countries.
11. What factors affected recent changes in the institutional distribution structure in Western Europe?

SUPPLEMENTARY READINGS

Cateora, Philip R., and John M. Hess. *International Marketing*, 3d. ed., Homewood, Ill.: Richard D. Irwin, Inc., 1975. Chapters 15 and 16.

Hollander, Stanley C. *Multinational Retailing*. East Lansing: Graduate School of Business Administration, Michigan State University, 1970.

Miracle, Gordon E., and Gerald S. Albaum. *International Marketing Management*. Homewood, Ill.: Richard D. Irwin, Inc., 1970. Chapters 14–17.

National Economic Development Office. *The Distribution Trades in the Common Market*. London: Her Majesty's Stationery Office, 1973.

Terpstra, Vern. *International Marketing*. New York: Holt, Rinehart and Winston, Inc., 1972. Chapters 10 and 11.

11

Physical Distribution

Having examined the nature of the international trade channels, we now turn to the related function of physical distribution. This refers to the actual movement and storage of products until they reach the final consumer. This chapter includes discussions of transportation, packing, warehousing, and the documentation needed for international movement of goods. Because of its close relationship to the physical distribution function, this chapter includes a brief description of marine insurance. Since the contents of the chapter are drawn from complex and technical subjects, our objective is to provide a sketch of the area's main concepts. Anyone inspired to conduct international commerce should at least be aware of these major considerations.

PHYSICAL DISTRIBUTION DEFINED

Often physical distribution is seen merely as transportation and the related area of storage. Actually the physical distribution function includes a broader array of activities needed to provide efficient movement of finished products and raw materials from the factory to the final user. The National Council of Physical Distribution Management, a group devoted to the advancement and study of logistics, recognized the important components when it defined physical distribution as:

> . . . the broad range of activities concerned with the efficient movement of finished products from the end of the production line to the consumer and in cases includes the movement of raw materials from the source of supply to the beginning of the production line. These activities include freight transportation, warehousing, material handling, protective packaging, inventory control, plant and warehouse site selection, order processing, market forecasting, and customer service.[1]

In this definition physical distribution is seen as an integrated system that determines what goods are needed in specific locations, performs the transportation and storage functions, processes orders, and maintains an effective information system. Bowersox offers a more

---

[1]Donald J. Bowersox, Edward Smykay, and Bernard J. LaLonde, *Physical Distribution Management* (revised ed.; New York: The Macmillan Company, 1968), p. 4.

simplified definition stressing the business activities involved to satisfy customer needs for an assortment of goods. This is the definition we use in this chapter. "Physical distribution consists of those business activities concerned with transporting finished inventory and/or raw material assortments so they arrive at the designated place, when needed, and in usable condition."[2]

TRANSPORTATION

The transportation industry is a complex of institutions that includes not only the carriers themselves (the ocean shipping companies, airlines, and truckers), but also the supporting terminal operators, stevedoring companies, freight forwarders, customs house brokers, ship brokers, financial houses, insurance firms, and engineering and manufacturing concerns. There is also an array of governmental agencies including the Federal Maritime Service, Civil Aeronautics Board, and Interstate Commerce Commission that oversee the operations of the industry and control the rates charged and services provided. Changes in any of these institutions or their foreign counterparts have ramifications on the rest of the industry and affect the service provided to the shipper of goods in international trade.

Transportation Choice Criteria

Physical distribution managers have an array of alternative methods or modes of transportation for the movement of goods across borders and within countries. Various forms of sea, air, and land transportation may be available for use singly or in combination. The manager's choice is influenced by the specific product and market characteristics. Large, bulky, low-unit-value items and basic commodities may not be capable of economically using some forms, such as air transport, except for special shipments. On the other hand, fresh flowers and perishable foods may require either fast shipment or special storage facilities. High-value items such as jewelry may be shipped by a variety of methods, but their margins permit movement by high cost rapid transportation and at less risk of theft.

Market Location. The market location affects the types of transportation that are available. Contiguous markets frequently can be efficiently serviced by truck or rail as might be the case for American manufacturers shipping to Canada or Mexico, or for most European producers selling to other Continental companies. The location and size of the market and its physical facilities may limit its access by ocean freight.

---

[2]Donald J. Bowersox, "Physical Distribution Development, Current Status and Potential," *Journal of Marketing* (January, 1969), p. 63.

Air transportation is increasingly making markets such as Iran, Japan, and Brazil quickly accessible for products that can economically employ that mode.

In order to achieve efficient movement of goods at low cost, the manager of physical distribution needs to evaluate the viable alternatives. This analysis involves investigation of not only the transportation rate structures, but also the effect of transportation on the other distribution costs: warehousing, inventory, packing, and communication. Frequently, trade-offs must be made among these various distribution functions in order to obtain the lowest *total cost* for the system as a whole. Some of the possible trade-offs within the physical distribution system itself will become apparent in subsequent sections. However, the trade-offs also involve broader marketing considerations. The performance of the distribution functions can affect a company's sales. Industrial goods buyers require assurance that supplies, component parts, and raw materials will be available to meet projected production schedules. Retailers also need assurance that products will be available in salable condition in time to conform to scheduled promotions. For both retailers and industrial buyers quick access to nearby inventories may be important in planning their own inventory levels and assortments.

Achievement of the firm's physical distribution objectives requires a knowledge of all the alternatives that are available. When selecting an appropriate mode of transportation, and the particular carrier to be used, managers evaluate the alternatives on several criteria in addition to the interaction noted above. Commonly used criteria include consideration of each method of transportation on the basis of speed, cost, dependability of performance, and services.

Speed, or rapid transportation, may be an obvious factor for perishable products, but it also is significant for other products because of its effect on inventory. Rapid transportation enables a firm to maintain a minimum inventory in float, i.e., in the movement process. Since inventory carrying charges are a significant cost factor, the reduction of float lowers the firm's investment while still providing satisfactory service. Speed also tends to lessen the losses due to spoilage and to theft. Rapid delivery shortens the period for which demand forecasts must be made. It makes possible rapid filling of customer orders, thereby lowering the inventory that a buyer must carry.

Cost. Unfortunately the use of rapid transportation modes often results in a high *transportation cost*. The higher freight rates associated with rapid transportation lead to high transportation costs per ton-mile.[3] As noted previously, however, this high transportation cost may

___
[3]The cost per ton-mile refers to the cost of moving one ton for one mile.

be partially or wholly offset by savings in packing, inventory, or other costs. Air freight, for example, does not require the packing needed to protect ocean freight and also will reduce the time in transit. The rate structure for international movement is complex and cost comparisons need to be made for specific shipments based on applicable rates for the product and shipping and receiving points.

Dependability. *Dependability* of delivery and safe carriage of goods can easily be as important as cost and speed in the transportation decision. Of prime importance to the buyer is the need to be assured that goods will be available when promised and in salable or usable condition. The buyer who can depend on delivery schedules can plan promotions and production schedules to achieve maximum sales impact and coordination of production and marketing. Dependability of transportation aids the seller in making realistic delivery promises and aids the buyer by permitting close scheduling with attendant inventory and warehouse savings.

Services. Each of the transportation modes has its unique characteristics. In addition each has developed a variety of *service* options to attract customers. Some arrange for pickup and delivery, permit diversion of freight to a second market, allow shipments to move under FAK (Freight of All Kinds) rates in which the mix of commodities is unrestricted, or provide other services to meet a customer's requirements. A firm's foreign freight forwarder can aid shippers in the selection of the most advantageous services.[4]

Modern Developments in Transportation

International marketing managers must choose from a complex, often bewildering, array of transportation methods for distributing their products between and within countries. Not only are there a large number of alternatives that may be available at a given time, but the established patterns of transportation are continually being challenged and adjusted by new technology, by changes in the infrastructure of the countries, and by changing trade patterns to which the transportation agencies adapt. Modern technology has produced the huge supertankers, lighter aboard ship (LASH) vessels, and containerships; the wide-bellied jets for air freight service; and improved trucking and piggyback facilities for land travel. In addition, governments have improved roads and port facilities as part of their economic development programs. The institutional structure of the transportation industry itself has changed to adapt to these environmental changes and the shifting economics of the industry.

---

[4]See p. 199–200.

Sea Transportation. The modern containership is a prime example of recent advances in ocean shipping. The containership is specially designed to transport shipments in relatively large boxes or containers. These containers permit the consolidation of items into standard-sized units for efficient handling and storage aboard ship. Furthermore, the containers are designed for repeated use by several modes of transportation. The container may be filled at the shipping point, carried by truck to the rail line, placed on a railcar, and transported to the dock where it is loaded aboard ship, all without intermediate loading or unloading.

The Port Authority of New York

Containerships are efficient carriers of large amounts of merchandise and have replaced smaller general cargo ships on many trade routes. They provide more efficient handling and faster turnaround times in the ports so that a smaller number of them can provide the same shipping capacity of the smaller vessels. This, in turn, has meant that many shipping firms have been forced to replace their older ships to remain competitive. Also, some ports that formerly were visited by the smaller ships are no longer able to provide the volume needed for efficient operation of the large containerships, and the routes have been adjusted so that the larger ports often serve new areas. The increasing concentration of activity in these ports has been accompanied by improved rail and road linkages between them and the interior areas previously served by other ports. The volume required to support the large vessels is indicated by the Scandinavian countries, which have found that only a few of their ports have been able to support frequent and regular containership service.[5]

Some idea of the magnitude of the effect of the containership on shipping companies is provided by changes in the North Atlantic package trade where some three dozen shipping companies with 160 to 175 ships shared the regularly scheduled trade a few years ago. By 1970 some fifty new containerships and roll on/roll off ships had been introduced and provided a capacity on these ships alone that was about one third greater than the previous total capacity.[6] The containerships, because the goods are consolidated in the large containers and not available for ready inspection of individual items, also affect the documentation and customs procedures as well as the insurance risks and rate structures of the industry. The containers, in addition, have aided the development of intermodal transport systems which integrate the use of trucks, ships, and/or planes. Thus, the new technology has influenced all segments of the industry.

Other developments in ocean freight that have provided more efficiency or better service include the gigantic supertankers, the largest of which, the ultra-large crude carriers, are 400,000 deadweight tons or larger. Following the closing of the Suez Canal the petroleum industry moved to the large tankers as a means of reducing the transportation costs. The efficiency of the newer ships led to the development of extremely large carriers that are several times the size of earlier ones. These ships require sophisticated equipment and port facilities. They also exposed the oil industry to criticism by environmentalists who feared the catastrophic effect of a gigantic oil spill in case of a wreck. The high fixed costs of operating these ships require that they be in rather continuous usage. Slowdowns in the shipment of oil in 1975 led to inactivity of these vessels at great cost to the owners.

New bulk carriers and roll on/roll off vessels are further innovations. The roll on/roll off (Ro-Ro) vessels allow the shipper to transport the entire trailer or other trucks and vehicles on their own wheels for easy loading and unloading. Roll on/roll off vessels have also been used for special transportation problems such as the carrying of helicopters from the United States to Europe[7] and the shipment of entire five-car trains for Amtrak from France to the United States. Lighter aboard ship vessels (LASH) are designed so that entire bargeloads of

---

[5]Jacob D. Merriwether and Gunnar K. Sletmo with Orville K. Goodin, "Distribution Efficiency and Worldwide Productivity," *Columbia Journal of World Business* (Winter, 1974), p. 88.

[6]S. A. Lawrence, *International Sea Transport: The Years Ahead* (Lexington, Mass.: Lexington Books, D.C. Heath and Company, 1972), pp. 175–176.

[7]"Fly-on/Fly-off Helicopters Ro-Ro the Atlantic with ACL," *Container News* (May, 1974), p. 59.

goods, along with the barge itself, are carried aboard ship. Thus, a shipper might load the barge at an up-river location and transport the load to the ocean port, ship the goods to the foreign port without unloading the barge, and at the foreign port send the barge to another river location removed from the port area — all of this without multiple handling of the merchandise. The LASH vessels further aid in loading and unloading at ports where the formation of the coast and ports requires unloading by lighter equipment rather than through direct access to the piers and wharves. Special vessels have been designed for the requirements of products such as liquid natural gas, wine, and automobiles.

Air Transportation. Although ocean freight accounts for the largest percentage of the tonnage of goods moved in international trade to and from the United States, the air carriers have long provided a viable alternative for some producers, especially those shipping products with a high value relative to their weight, that are perishable, or otherwise could profit from the great speed of the aircraft. Because of the speed factor the air carriers have been strong proponents of the total cost approach to physical distribution. Analyses of company distribution systems have sometimes shown that the higher costs of air transportation may be partially or totally offset by savings in packing, handling, inventory, documentation, delivery, and related costs. Often, however, the decision to use air transportation may reflect the service features of air carriage rather than costs. The speed of delivery may, for example, enable the customer who purchases industrial equipment to get into production at a much earlier time than when slower forms of transportation are used, thereby producing income earlier.

Recent additions of high-speed jets to the fleets of United States and foreign carriers have added to the industry's capacity. The wide-bellied jets have permitted the carriage of transatlantic loads from the United States to Europe weighing as much as 232,400 pounds (approximately 11½ forty-foot truck trailer equivalents) on a single flight and are in operation to the Far East, South America, and several other destinations.[8]

The nose-loading feature of the 747 makes possible the use of efficient loading equipment and the loading of containers and oversized cargo that could not previously be handled. The ability of the planes to carry containers may increase the ability of the air carriers to compete in the intermodal systems to further increase the value to shippers, by providing door-to-door service at lower costs and greater security to the merchandise.[9]

---

[8]"International: A Viable Alternative," *Distribution Worldwide* (October, 1974), p. 48.

[9]Warren C. Wetmore, "Seaboard Moves to Intermodal Containers," *Aviation Week & Space Technology* (November 11, 1974), pp. 32–35.

Innovations in the air cargo industry have not only included advanced airplane technology, but also improved airport facilities have been established and the carriers have introduced more efficient ground handling equipment. More flights have been added to the schedules and the carriers have sought to extend their services to a wider range of merchandise.

Land Transportation. While ocean and air transportation have provided some of the more glamorous applications of technology, land transportation has also undergone a transformation. New highways and the increased number of trucks available have improved the service of land carriers in many countries so that they now carry an increasing percentage of the inland freight volume. In Japan, for example, trucks carried almost 89 percent of the tonnage of inland traffic in 1970 compared to only 75 percent in 1960. Several reasons account for this growth in Japan: an increased demand for freight service due to the growth of the economy, the strained capacity of the Japanese railroads, emphasis on rapid and punctual delivery, improved roads, and the development of the Japanese automobile industry.[10] Some of these reasons also figure on the development of land transportation elsewhere.

In Europe, even though faced with competition from the railways and inland shipping alternatives, trucking has been significant in the fast movement of nonbulky goods. The European trucking industry has provided shippers with a flexibility that is often found when an

---

[10]Yoshimasa Yamanobe, "Surface Transport in Japan," *Distribution Worldwide* (October, 1972), pp. 70–73.

industry is characterized by a large number of small firms. In Holland, for example, 58 percent of the "for hire" firms own two or less vehicles. About 3.4 percent of the companies own 15 or more vehicles and account for 28 percent of all trucks.[11] The picture may be changing, however, as the European trucking industry is now consolidating and forming larger companies to improve efficiency.

Among the problems faced by European truckers have been the varying regulations on permitted weight and length of units among the countries, especially since it is economical to use trucks for cross-border hauling within the EEC. A related problem has been the inspections required to move goods across several country borders. A truck and its contents might be subject to several inspections and to the payment of duties or subjected to considerable paperwork. To cope with this the TIR (Transport Internationales Routiers) Convention developed a system whereby vehicles that have met certain conditions and achieved prior approval can carry merchandise across borders without examination at each. This TIR carnet procedure has greatly simplified the movement of goods by truck.[12]

Intermodal Developments. Various types of transportation have been combined to provide either low costs or improved transit time. These have sometimes resulted in a different routing for trade between widely separated points. Among these have been both sea/land combinations and air/land combinations. The so-called "landbridges" provide an interesting example of such intermodal transportation.

Container shipments from Japan to Europe may leave Japan by sea, arrive at a U.S. West-coast port, and be placed aboard a container unit train[13] which carries the goods to the East-coast port where they are again loaded aboard a ship for Europe. Similarly, Japan-bound shipments from Europe may be landed at either the East or Gulf coast for movement to Japan. Use of the landbridge may result in savings of six or seven days in travel time between Europe and Japan.[14] Some Italian companies are reported to be using the trans-Siberian rail system for connections with Japan. One Italian department store and supermarket chain reports that use of the trans-Siberian route takes only about one half the time required for sea movement.[15]

---

[11]"Europe's Highway Haulers," *Distribution Worldwide* (October, 1972), p. 74.

[12]A carnet is the customs document that allows special categories of goods to be taken across international borders at no cost. Carnets are also used for the temporary importation of samples and products for exhibition abroad under other international conventions in which the United States participates. A. G. Walker, *Export Practice and Documentation* (London: Butterworth & Company Publishers, Ltd., 1970), pp. 101–103.

[13]A unit train is one where the entire train is made up of goods shipped to a single destination.

[14]Preston Taylor, "The Mini-Landbridge," *Distribution Worldwide* (October, 1972), pp. 55–62.

[15]"Landbridge Use Increasing," *Journal of Commerce* (January 8, 1973), p. 5. See also, "World's Largest Landbridge Joins Japan with Europe," *Container News* (March, 1974), pp. 37–40.

Landbridges, or combined sea and land traffic, may involve either rail or trucks in order to speed delivery and provide improved service. Container shipments from New York to Iran can be made in 21 days using the overland service from Rotterdam provided by a Dutch trucking and forwarding firm, instead of the 35 days by sea alone. The full containers move under TIR arrangements and are sealed throughout the trip, including the 3,437 miles from Rotterdam to Iran.[16]

Shipping Companies

Shipments of general cargo move on the vessels of shipping companies. Shipments of bulk cargo, both dry and liquid, more often move on chartered ships. In the first case, a shipper usually requires the use of only a portion of the hold of a vessel, while in the second case, the shipper usually engages the entire vessel and expects to fill it with a shipment.

Shipping companies often are divided between liner companies and tramps. The main difference between the two is that the liner company advertises a scheduled service between ports. Tramp ships operate on charters wherever they can get cargo. Often the ships of the liner companies are newer and operate through an extensive network of agents. They generally serve a larger number of shippers than the tramp vessels and carry a wider range of higher valued goods.[17] Shipping companies are common carriers, while the chartered vessels used by shippers are private carriers. However, shipping companies also charter ships and operate them in common carrier service.

Shipping companies that service the United States fly the flags of all maritime nations. Some of the ships owned by United States citizens may actually be registered in other countries (e.g., Liberia). These countries provide an opportunity to register the vessel and to operate it under less restrictive conditions than under U.S. registry, thereby lowering the operating costs at times.

Shipping Conferences

Shipping companies commonly band together in the various trades in which they operate. When so banded together they are known as conferences. A primary purpose of these conferences is to establish a uniform rate structure through collective action. A *trade* is a foreign area and generally a seaboard of the United States.[18] The members of a conference may represent several nations.

---

[16]"Dutch Trucking Firm Moves the Longest Hauls of All," *Container News* (May, 1974), pp. 24–25.

[17]S. A. Lawrence, *International Sea Transport: The Years Ahead* (Lexington, Mass.: Lexington Books, D. C. Heath and Company, 1972), p. 9.

[18]Examples of trades in which conferences operate are North Atlantic United States — United Kingdom, North Atlantic United States — Continental Europe, Gulf United States — Mediterranean, and many more.

Under the Shipping Act of 1916, steamship conferences are exempt from the antitrust laws, but they are required to submit to the jurisdiction of the Federal Maritime Board. Although the conference system has been under considerable pressure in recent years from nonconference shipping, from the introduction of container services, from the rise of nationalistic feelings, and from U.S. regulations requiring that the conferences be reasonably open to qualified applicants, the conferences still control a high proportion of certain trades.

The conference sets the rates, rules, and regulations governing shipments moving in the trade in which it operates, and all members of the conference are expected to abide by these. A deposit is required from each member to assure conformance. Thus, all rates quoted by any member of the conference are set by conference agreement, and negotiations for changes in rates by shippers or receivers must be considered by the conference as a group.

The 1975 rate war among Pacific steamship companies illustrates some of the problems of maintaining the conference system. Nonconference lines, including the Far Eastern Shipping Company, operated by the USSR government, deeply undercut the established conference rate between the Far East and the United States' West coast. The result was reported rebates by members of the conference and the resignation of some companies to enable them to compete more freely. The Federal Maritime Commission even levied a $75,000 fine against one U.S. importer for accepting rebates from a shipping company.[19]

Some shipping companies refuse to join a conference, while some belong to conferences in certain trades but refuse to join conferences in others. Nonconference shipping companies sometimes, but not always, quote rates lower than the conference contract rates. A shipper or receiver therefore must decide whether or not it is desirable to sign shippers' contracts with conferences. If a contract is not signed, any shipping company desired may be used, but if a conference line is used, there will be a higher tariff rate on the shipment.

Many conferences observe two scales or rates: (1) the regular tariff rate and (2) a contract (lower) rate.

A contract rate is available to all shippers and receivers in a given trade by signing a shipper's contract. Under this contract, tendered by the conference, the shipper or receiver agrees to use conference vessels exclusively for a period of time, usually one year. The use of nonconference vessels will result in loss of status as a contract shipper, and the shipper will be required to pay the higher tariff rate and also perhaps be subject to a financial penalty.

---

[19]"The Rate War with Russia," *Business Week* (June 30, 1975), pp. 111–112. In July, 1976, it was reported by *The Wall Street Journal* (July 20, 1976, page 2) that the Soviet Union has agreed to raise its shipping rates to match those of other countries.

In a case involving the reestablishment of the contract rate system by the Japan-Atlantic and Gulf Freight Conference, the Supreme Court declared the system to be illegal. Congress later amended the Shipping Act to permit continuance of the dual rate system employed by most conferences, subject to certain restrictions. The system must not be unjustly discriminatory nor unfair among exporters, shippers, importers, or ports, or among exporters from the United States and their foreign competitors.

Freight Rate Quotations

Freight rate quotations can be obtained from a freight forwarder or from the office of a shipping company. Steamship tariffs or rate books are generally not available for public acquisition, but they are filed for public inspection with the Federal Maritime Board.

Steamship rates are commonly quoted on a weight or a measurement basis, ship's option. In other words, the merchandise is weighed and also measured. If the rate is $40 a ton and the weight ton is 2,240 pounds and the measurement ton is 40 cubic feet, a simple calculation will determine the charges. A shipment weighing 4,000 pounds and measuring 100 cubic feet would obviously yield more revenue to the carrier on the basis of measurement, since there are 2½ tons of payable freight on a measurement basis and less than 2 payable tons on a weight basis.

While 2,240 pounds is cited as the weight ton, the Far Eastern trades generally use 2,000 pounds as a weight ton. In all trades, 40 cubic feet equal one measurement ton. Some commodities (for example, iron and steel), however, are quoted on a straight weight basis. Articles of high value are sometimes quoted at a rate that is a percentage of value, such as 5 percent ad valorem.

Air freight travels under a general cargo rate or a commodity rate. When containers approved for air shipping are used, a unit load device rate is available.

Foreign Freight Forwarders

The foreign freight forwarder is in business to facilitate export and import shipments. The forwarder consolidates small shipments in larger ones and arranges for transportation from the exporter to the destination; follows the shipments to see that these move on the required routes; and arranges for switching, unloading at the port of export, repacking, and loading of the vessel or plane. The forwarder prepares the necessary government documents for shipment, including those consular invoices and other documents required by the importing country. Bills of lading and airway bills are prepared and arrangements made for marine insurance if the shipper does not have a cargo policy. The forwarder also may furnish banks, shippers, and purchasers with needed shipping notices. The forwarder's expert knowledge is available to assist the firm on general traffic management and export procedures. Both large and small firms find the forwarder useful. In practice the forwarder also may provide packing and act as a customhouse broker to facilitate the movement of goods through customs procedures.

SHIPPING DOCUMENTS

Shipping documents in international marketing include (1) commercial documents employed by shipping, forwarding, and insuring companies and (2) those required by governments.

Commercial Documents

The most important commercial document issued by shipping companies is the ocean bill of lading. (See Figure 11-1, page 201) A bill of lading is (1) a receipt for the shipments, (2) a contract for shipments, and (3) if negotiable (or "to order"), it is documentary and transferable evidence of title to the shipment. This last use is important for financing foreign shipments.[20] A clean bill of lading is usually required in all cases where financing is used. Such a bill of lading has no qualifying clauses indicating deficiency in count, description, packing, or any other factor. Since the terms of an ocean bill of lading contract relieve the shipping company of practically all liability, marine insurance companies sell this protection. Marine insurance is discussed later in the chapter.

The *air waybill* is similar in many respects to the bill of lading. It functions as a contract of carriage and is a receipt for the goods. The air waybill, however, is not negotiable.

Government Documents

On export shipments from the United States a *shipper's export declaration*, such as the one illustrated in Figure 11-2 on page 202, is required by the United States government. This declaration is a joint Bureau of Census — Bureau of East-West Trade form and is used to

---

[20]See Chapter 16.

UNITED STATES LINES CO.

(SPACES IMMEDIATELY BELOW FOR SHIPPERS MEMORANDA—NOT PART OF BILL OF LADING)

FORWARDING AGENT—REFERENCES	EXPORT DEC. No.
None	48763

DELIVERING CARRIER TO STEAMER:	CAR NUMBER — REFERENCE
Pennsylvania Railroad	PRR 78643

BILL OF LADING
(SHORT FORM)

(NOT NEGOTIABLE UNLESS CONSIGNED "TO ORDER")

SHIP American Hunter	FLAG USA	PIER 80 South	PORT OF LOADING
PORT OF DISCHARGE FROM SHIP (Where goods are to be delivered to consignee or On-carrier) If goods to be transhipped beyond Port of Discharge, show destination Here ➡ To		THROUGH BILL OF LADING	PHILADELPHIA, PA.

SHIPPER........ Cleveland Packing Company

CONSIGNED TO: ORDER OF........ Cleveland Packing Company

ADDRESS ARRIVAL NOTICE TO Emile Deschamps & Cie, 27 Rue de Napoleon, Le Havre, France

PARTICULARS FURNISHED BY SHIPPER OF GOODS

MARKS AND NUMBERS	NO. OF PKGS.	DESCRIPTION OF PACKAGES AND GOODS	MEASUREMENT	GROSS WEIGHT IN POUNDS
E D C Le Havre 1-83 Made in USA	83	Lard, in tierces Refrigerated at 35 degrees or over	--	29,880

FREIGHT PAYABLE IN   Philadelphia

$1.56 @ PER 2240 LBS.. $			
@ PER 100 · LBS.. $	466	13	
FT. @ PER 40 CU. FT. $			
FT. @ PER CU. FT... $			
TOTAL . . $	466	13	

(TERMS OF THIS BILL OF LADING CONTINUED FROM REVERSE SIDE HEREOF)
IN WITNESS WHEREOF,
THE MASTER OR AGENT OF SAID VESSEL HAS SIGNED ... 3
BILLS OF LADING, ALL OF THE SAME TENOR AND DATE, ONE OF WHICH BEING ACCOMPLISHED, THE OTHERS TO STAND VOID.

UNITED STATES LINES COMPANY

BY   (Sgd. by company)
FOR THE MASTER

B/L No.   ISSUED AT PHILADELPHIA, PA.

(Date and number perforated here)

REVISED 10-87
103933-25M PRINTED IN U.S.A.   MO.   DAY   YEAR

Figure 11-1   OCEAN BILL OF LADING

compile official U.S. export statistics and to enforce U.S. export control laws covering strategic shipments to certain countries. A violation of export license regulations could involve a charge of perjury and usually causes cancellation of license privileges.

On import shipments into the United States, the basic document is an *import entry*. Imports are subject to customs duties, but exports

U.S. DEPARTMENT OF COMMERCE – BUREAU OF THE CENSUS – BUREAU OF INTERNATIONAL COMMERCE

Form Approved O.M.B. No. 41-R0397

SHIPPER'S EXPORT DECLARATION

OF SHIPMENTS FROM THE UNITED STATES

Export Shipments Are Subject To U.S. Customs Inspection

READ CAREFULLY THE INSTRUCTIONS ON BACK TO AVOID DELAY AT SHIPPING POINT

For shipments to foreign countries, where authentication of the Shipper's Export Declaration is required, the export declaration must be presented to and authenticated by Customs and a copy so authenticated delivered to the exporting carrier prior to exportation.

Declarations Should be Typewritten or Prepared in Ink

CONFIDENTIAL – For use solely for official purposes authorized by the Secretary of Commerce. Use for unauthorized purposes is not permitted. (Title 15, Sec. 30.91(a) C.F.R.; Sec. 7(c) Export Administration Act of 1969, P.L. 91-184)

Customs Authentication (For Customs use only)

DO NOT USE THIS AREA	DISTRICT	PORT	COUNTRY (For Customs use only)
	10	01	

File No. (For Customs use only)

1. FROM (U.S. Port of Export)
New York, New York

2. METHOD OF TRANSPORTATION (Check one):
[X] VESSEL (Incl. ferry) [ ] AIR [ ] OTHER (Specify) _____

2a. EXPORTING CARRIER (If vessel, give name of ship, flag and pier number. If air, give name of airline.)
SS Mercer (American)   Pier 14

3. EXPORTER (Principal or seller – licensee)
Wilson Company

ADDRESS (Number, street, place, State)
214 Fremont Street, White Plains, New York

4. AGENT OF EXPORTER (Forwarding agent)
Miller and Sons, Inc.

ADDRESS (Number, street, place, State)
302 Lawrence Place, New York, New York

5. ULTIMATE CONSIGNEE
Gilbert Company

ADDRESS (Place, country)
11 King Street, London, England

6. INTERMEDIATE CONSIGNEE
Bryant Freight Forwarders

ADDRESS (Place, country)
650 LaSalle Place, London, England

7. FOREIGN PORT OF UNLOADING (For vessel and air shipments only)

8. PLACE AND COUNTRY OF ULTIMATE DESTINATION (Not place of transshipment)

MARKS AND NOS. (9)	NUMBERS AND KIND OF PACKAGES, DESCRIPTION OF COMMODITIES, EXPORT LICENSE NUMBER, EXPIRATION DATE (OR GENERAL LICENSE SYMBOL) (Describe commodities in sufficient detail to permit verification of the Schedule B commodity numbers assigned. Do not use general items. Insert required license information on line below description of each item.) (10)	SHIPPING (Gross) WEIGHT IN POUNDS (REQUIRED FOR VESSEL AND AIR SHIPMENTS ONLY) (11)	SPECIFY "D" OR "F" (12)	SCHEDULE B COMMODITY NO. (13)	NET QUANTITY SCHEDULE B UNITS (State unit) (14)	VALUE AT U.S. PORT OF EXPORT (Selling price or cost if not sold, including inland freight, insurance and other charges to U.S. Port of Export) (Nearest whole dollar, omit cents figures) (15)
G2W	84 Pieces: White Oak Logs (in the rough)	157590	D	242.3135	14 M.Bd.Ft.	$14,038
112-6054	15 Cartons: Woven Waterproof Nylon Raincoats, 3/4 length, Boys', New	430	D	841.1153	400 lbs.	$390
112-5254	1 Carton: Sprockets, for Mechanical Power Transmission Equipment, n.e.c.	74 lbs.	D	719.9350	---	$264
112-4842	6 Power Grader Pneumatic Tires, Rubber	984 lbs.	D	629.1050	6 each	$841

VALIDATED LICENSE NO. _____   OR GENERAL LICENSE SYMBOL _____

16. WAYBILL OR MANIFEST NO. (of Exporting Carrier)
581642105

17. DATE OF EXPORTATION (Not required for shipments by vessel)

18. THE UNDERSIGNED HEREBY AUTHORIZES Miller and Sons, Inc., 302 Lawrence Place, New York, New York
TO ACT AS FORWARDING AGENT FOR EXPORT CONTROL AND CUSTOMS PURPOSES.
(Name and address – Number, street, place, State)

EXPORTER Wilson Company   BY _____
(DULY AUTHORIZED OFFICER OR EMPLOYEE)

▶ **19. I CERTIFY THAT ALL STATEMENTS MADE AND ALL INFORMATION CONTAINED IN THIS EXPORT DECLARATION ARE TRUE AND CORRECT. I AM AWARE OF THE PENALTIES** PROVIDED FOR FALSE REPRESENTATION. (See paragraphs I (c) and (e) on reverse side.)

SIGNATURE _____
(Duly authorized officer or employee of exporter or named forwarding agent)

FOR Miller and Sons, Inc., Export Mgr.
(Name of corporation or firm, and capacity of signer; e.g., secretary, export manager, etc.)

ADDRESS 302 Lawrence Place, New York, New York

Declaration should be made by duly authorized officer or employee of exporter or of forwarding agent named by exporter.

DO NOT USE THIS AREA

*If shipping weight is not available for each Schedule B item listed in column (13) included in one or more packages, insert the approximate gross weight for each Schedule B item. The total of these estimated weights should equal the actual weight of the entire package or packages.

bDesignate foreign merchandise (reexports) with an "F" and exports of domestic merchandise produced in the United States or changed in condition in the United States with a "D." (See instructions on reverse side.)

All copies of the export declaration, bill of lading, and commercial invoice must show a destination control statement, when required. (See Department of Commerce Export Control Regulations.)

Figure 11-2   SHIPPER'S EXPORT DECLARATION

from the United States are free of duty and also free of sales taxes — national, state, and local. For example, the importers of cosmetics pay national, and often state and local, sales taxes. If exported, such taxes are not payable; if they have been paid, they are refunded upon submission of proof of export. Imports exceeding $500 in value require a *special customs invoice*. This document is prepared and signed by the foreign exporter and does not require consular certification.

Foreign governments also usually require *consular invoices* or *certificates of origin* and may also impose an import license before goods are permitted entry.

PACKING

The general considerations influencing the packing of shipments for overseas markets differ so widely from those in domestic commerce that customary domestic packing, in many instances, is not suitable. When export shipments are made by rail or motor from inland points to the seaboard, the container rules and specifications of the railroads and motor freight lines in their tariffs apply; but it is frequently essential to go beyond these requirements so as to assure safe delivery abroad and to take into account other export packing factors.

An example of the creativity needed for packing overseas shipments is provided by a shipment made to the Soviet Union. A special clause in the Russian contract stipulated that the goods must be packed to withstand one year's storage outside at temperatures ranging from 30 degrees below zero to 130 degrees above zero. If the stipulation were not met, the Russians could make sizable deductions from the payments to the manufacturer. Furthermore, the crates had to be designed to fit the smaller-sized Soviet railroad cars and to be curved on top to fit their tunnels.[21] The same export packer who handled this shipment has also been called upon to pack and ship bullet and explosion proof limousines from Cincinnati to Korea, and a 180,000 pound machine to a General Motors plant in Brazil.

Packing Objectives

The keynote of adequate packing designed to carry merchandise safely through transportation and shipping risks obviously is strength, but the required strength varies with the susceptibility of an article to damage. Locomotives may not be packed at all, and the same is true of raw materials handled in bulk. Packing also will vary with the means of transportation used. Air freight, for example, is subject neither to long exposure to salt water nor to the rolling and pitching of ocean vessels.

Whatever the product and transportation used, the packing must be suitable for the entire trip, including inland transportation at both

---

[21]"Today's Business," *The Cincinnati Post*, December 28, 1973, p. 20. Report of an interview with H. J. Hosea, Jr.

ends and the conditions to which the shipment will be exposed during the voyage. Also, the various units in a packing box must be packed so they will not damage one another.

Packing Considerations for Overseas Shipments

Among the major factors involved in designing the package are transportation and handling, climate, pilferage, freight rates, customs duties, and, most importantly, the customer's requirements.

It is well-known that the greater the number of handlings to which goods are subjected, the greater is the possibility of damage. International trade may require several such handlings. Upon arrival at the port, the shipment is either transferred to the vessel or stored until the ship arrives. If the port is not equipped to transfer the shipments directly from freight cars to vessels, additional handling may be required.

The shipment is loaded into the hold of the vessel, usually by means of the ship's own machinery, unless the weight is so great that special equipment must be employed. The shipment is then stowed as compactly as possible. Packages are placed in a position to support other packages and are necessarily subjected to a severe strain. Moreover, a certain rolling motion of the vessel enhances the package strain considerably.

Upon arrival of the vessel at the port of import, the shipment is subjected to further handling in unloading, passage through customs, and final removal to its ultimate destination. At the most important ports, unloading facilities are usually adequate for quick and safe handling of merchandise, but at smaller and less frequented ports the facilities may be less adequate.

The West coast of South America is a conspicuous example of an entire coastal stretch where, because of the formation of the coast line, the direct discharge of cargoes at piers or wharves is the exception rather than the general rule. Vessels frequently lie in the open roadstead, riding at anchor, and the loading and unloading of merchandise is hazardous. Without direct access to piers or wharves, the vessels are dependent upon lighter service for unloading. At certain seasons of the year it is extremely hazardous to attempt to discharge. Although navigation conditions on this coast are unusual, the unloading cargo with the aid of lighters, barges, junks, sampans, and other craft is common at outports of other countries.

When goods are to be delivered to some interior point, further movement and consequent handling are encountered. In some countries, for example, Colombia, the major markets are inland so that imports must be transported for some distance after arrival in the country. In other cases countries are landlocked and can be reached only through a foreign port. Bolivia and Switzerland are examples of countries of this type.

Climatic Considerations. Climate must be considered when products are readily affected by heat and moisture. It is essential that the exporter be cognizant of the climate of the country to which the shipment is destined and also the climate over the entire route which the shipment will take. Goods shipped to the southern temperate zone, for example, will cross the equator and must be protected from the heat and humidity encountered in this tropical belt. Also, the temperature changes experienced by many voyages may cause heavy sweat to form either in the ships' holds or on metal surfaces of cargoes inside their containers. Considerable damage may result if merchandise is not protected during the rainy season of tropical areas. Moisture and heat cause fungoid growths, while rust and sweating are also sources of annoyance and loss.

Climatic conditions also affect the packing problem in other ways. Sometimes a great accumulation of merchandise results from the simultaneous arrival of several vessels at a port or from even the arrival of one vessel, and all goods cannot be fully protected. The rapid growth of the Middle East markets in 1974 and 1975 strained the capacity of ports and resulted in long delays for unloading and sometimes inadequate protection.

The interior transportation of merchandise on open trucks over poor roads or by pack animals is another condition that causes goods to remain exposed to the weather. Extremes of climatic conditions may be encountered from the tropics of the lowlands to the bleak plateaus swept by wind, sleet, and snow.

Pilfering As a Packing Factor. Pilferage is an important source of loss in the shipment of products having relatively small bulk and high value. When delays are experienced in making shipping connections, when congestion holds up the passage of the merchandise through customs, or when rehandling is needed to facilitate interior transportation, the likelihood of pilferage is increased. Shipments to certain parts of the world are more likely to suffer pilferage than consignments destined to other areas. Often pilferage is high when facilities are inadequate or primitive, but it may occur anywhere along the route. The problem is continuous from the time of shipment until the safe arrival of goods at the customer's location.

The exporter can do much to prevent pilferage by concealing the identity of the contents of packages. This can be accomplished by avoiding the use of the company name or that of the merchandise on the outside of the container.

Freight Rates. The space occupied by a shipment of goods is affected by the method of packing employed. Because the railroads quote freight rates on the basis of hundredweight, the fact should not be overlooked that the classes into which shipments are placed for rating purposes are determined, among many other factors, by the space occupied by the merchandise. This space varies according to whether the goods are shipped knocked down or set up or are otherwise disassembled or reduced in volume. As noted earlier, ocean freight rates are usually quoted "weight or measurement, ship's option," and the basis that yields the larger revenue will be applied in each particular instance.

Savings in freight rates, both on land and on sea, may be made by giving careful attention to this feature of the packing problem. Bulky and irregularly shaped articles should, if possible, be reduced in bulk by disassembly. Machinery of various descriptions and automobiles are conspicuous examples of articles that have been scientifically studied to reduce great bulk. Nesting of articles of uniform shape is widely practiced in foreign and domestic trade, and the compression of merchandise to be shipped in bales is becoming more common as compression methods are improved.

In all of the efforts to reduce space it should not be forgotten that the weight of the shipment is also to be considered because rates, if based on the weight of a shipment, apply to the gross weight of both the container and its contents.

Customs Duties. When the shipment reaches the customs officials who assess the import duty, the weight of the unit is usually important.[22] The exporter has the opportunity of minimizing the charges when customs duties are levied on a basis of weight. If gross weight is applied as the basis for import duties, excessive weight becomes unnecessarily costly. When net weight is the basis, as is more often the case, heavy outside packing does not affect the import duty. This is only true, however, if the packing itself is of no commercial value.

The immediate wrapping that surrounds the merchandise (paper, boxes, bottles, cans) is included in the weight used for duty assessment in those countries which recognize legal weight. In such instances it may be more economical to ship the merchandise in bulk and make a separate shipment of the containers. Each will then be appraised separately for duty.

A further difficulty in connection with customs duties arises in packing different articles, dutiable separately, in one container. In some countries the whole shipment is assessed the duty applicable to the highest rated article in the container.

Customer's Requirements and Packing Expense. Perhaps there is no aspect of the packing problem that irritates importers more than the deliberate alteration or disregard of instructions by the exporter. When an importer transmits an order with specific instructions in

---

[22]See also Chapter 18.

regard to the routing, packing, marking, or assortment of the shipment, one should assume that it was done for a good reason. If kilo and half-kilo packages are ordered, it may be because the importer's customers are unfamiliar with pounds and half pounds; if scarlet colors are desired, then orange will not be satisfactory; if complete assortments are ordered for each case to be shipped, then breaking up these assortments to suit the packer will inconvenience the buyer.

Good salesmanship may involve the demonstration of new and better methods of packing and shipping, but once an order is received, the customer's instructions should be followed exactly. The customer often knows best the particular requirements, climatic conditions, local freight handling methods, inland transportation services, and perhaps the pilferage hazard.

The exporter should consider the cost of export packing both to the company and to the customer. Shipments should be packed to protect against normal hazards, but the safest possible packing will not always be used. Packing costs must also be considered. Many companies have been able to reduce packing and transportation costs without sacrificing reasonably safe packing.

Reconciling the Packing Factors. With such an array of problems, the export packer has no easy task. The most difficult considerations to reconcile are safety and economy. In endeavoring to guarantee safety, weights may be increased and economy sacrificed or the pursuit of economy may sacrifice safety. The task is to find a method that is both efficient and safe. Safety is the fixed factor and is of primary importance. Freight rates and customs duties should not be reduced to the detriment of security from damage or pilferage.

In studying this problem the exporter is not left entirely to individual resources. The services of expert packers and international freight forwarders may be employed, along with securing advice from several other sources. The Forest Products Laboratory at Madison, Wisconsin tests packages of various types, and studies of shipping containers are undertaken by various private testing laboratories and container manufacturers. Advice can be obtained from associations of container manufacturers, from packing engineers, and from marine insurance companies. The United States Bureau of International Commerce has published several valuable studies of export packing. Finally, the International Cargo Handling Coordination Association is active in seeking to make the packing of ship-borne cargo more efficient. It conducts symposia on various cargo-handling subjects with special emphasis on containerization.

Unitization

In order to facilitate efficient handling and to protect merchandise during shipment and storage, shippers have combined the individual cans, boxes, or units of their products into larger cartons. These cartons, in turn, have been combined into larger containers or stacked on pallets and banded together to form a single package. This unitization process permits the handling of one large package, rather than many small ones, and reduces the number of times that individual items must be handled. The larger lots — pallets or containers — can often be moved by mechanical handling equipment. Unitization strives for the reduction of handling costs as well as reduced losses from damage and pilferage.

Palletizing. Palletizing is one method of unitization that has been practiced for many years in handling freight. It is the process of stacking packages on a platform, usually of heavy lumber, elevated at the bottom to permit the use of forklift trucks. The cartons, or items to be palletized, are banded together in a manner that assures safe handling as a unit. Packages of all kinds can be palletized and stacked in the hold of a vessel, truck, or airplane.

Containerization. As evidenced in the previous discussion on transportation, containerization has become an important factor in physical distribution. While a container can be any box, bottle, bag, or similar device for holding a product, the term is used in this section in a more technical sense. By container we mean a relatively large box suitable for repeated use by several modes of transportation without intermediate loading and unloading.[23] Shipping containers usually are made of steel or aluminum, but plywood or fiberglass may also be used. The containers replace packing crates, although individual items must still be properly protected.

If the container is to achieve maximum utility, it must be designed to accommodate the requirements of intermodal transportation since most international shipments involve the use of more than one mode of transportation. Goods are often placed on rail cars or trucks at the manufacturer's plant and forwarded to the port or airport where they are put on planes or ships for movement to the foreign port. At the port they are again transferred to trucks or rail for carriage to the customer's location. If the container is to minimize the handling of individual items, it must be usable on all these modes.

In an effort to standardize the size of containers the American Standards Association and the International Association for Standards have adopted the standard sizes of 8' × 8' × 10', 20', 30', or 40'. They have also agreed on structural requirements and weight ratings. These requirements have been incorporated and extended in the American Shipping Bureau's Rules for the Certification of Cargo Containers.[24]

---

[23]See Harold K. Strom, "Containerization: A Pandora's Box in Reverse?" *Transportation Journal* (Winter, 1972), for several definitions of a container.

[24]See Albert Midboe, "Container Certification Rules Replace Earlier ABC Guides," *Container News* (September, 1974), pp. 10–12.

These standards and rules are designed to assure shippers that the containers will provide the needed protection of their merchandise and that there will be sufficient strength for handling and stacking. They also provide guidance for the development of handling equipment and vessel design. Despite the efforts at standardization, however, there are still other container sizes and designs in current use. For example, the air cargo industry has the problem of developing containers that will maximize the use of the various airplane designs and configurations. The International Air Transport Association has made its Unit Load Devices Board responsible for standardizing the airline-owned containers. The new jets have been able to utilize the twenty- and forty-foot containers commonly used in transoceanic shipments.

For the international marketer the container holds several potential advantages. The greater strength of the container reduces the possibility of damage occurring during the transportation and handling phases of distribution. Reduced pilferage results from the greater security provided by a metal container and the possibility of door-to-door service in the original container. Packaging costs are lower with containers for many items. The container revolution also promises the possibility of simplified documentation. In the case of air freight, as indicated earlier, shippers pay a standard unit load device rate for shipping in approved containers. Ocean freight, however, continues to move on commodity rates, and the use of a container may or may not result in a discount.

The use of containers has involved large investments by both shipping companies and ports. The ports have added to their handling equipment and have developed special facilities for handling the containers efficiently. Shippers and shipping companies have turned to specialized container leasing companies in many instances to overcome the high investment required in the containers themselves. It is estimated that four containers are needed at terminals for every one at sea,[25] and a single containership may have the capacity to handle 2,000 containers of the twenty-foot size. To meet the requirements of shippers and shipping companies the leasing companies have not only financed the containers, but have established a logistical system for getting containers to customers where and when they are needed. The use of leased containers aids shippers especially when they have unbalanced traffic with more going in one direction than another. CTI, one of the largest lessors, was estimated to have some 60,000 containers in 1973. They not only served U.S. companies, but also furnished containers to SovFracht, the Soviet agency responsible for chartering sea tonnage, for its North Pacific routes.[26]

---

[25]Carl E. McDowell, "Containerization: The Marine Insurer's View," *Distribution Worldwide* (March, 1974), p. 58.

[26]"The Hot Market for Leased Containers," *Business Week* (May 5, 1973), pp. 38–40.

Marketers should also be concerned with containers because of their potential for expanding the market for products and because they may provide opportunities for alternate routings. A United Kingdom manufacturer furnishes one example of containers as a tool for market penetration. The company made a cost analysis which showed a marginally higher cost for sending shipments from the United Kingdom to the Middle East using overland routes with containers rather than its previous system of ocean freight and conventional packing. However, the company reported that demand increased due to improved quality of the product. Some of the improvement was due to reduced transit times as these were more than fifty percent lower on the overland route. Furthermore, the containers with their driver-accompanied units enabled the company to maintain reliable transit schedules. Damage and pilferage were lower and the reduced transit time aided the company's cash flow.[27]

MARINE INSURANCE

Marine insurance companies and underwriting organizations are keenly interested in export packing methods and make recommendations based on their experience. One of the basic factors considered by an underwriter in quoting a marine insurance premium is the loss experience of a shipper. This is a tangible measure of the packing problems of every shipper and offers a reward to effect improvements in the loss and damage record.

Marine insurance to cover cargo risks is commonly placed on all shipments moving in international seaborne trade. The insurance may be placed for the exporter's account or for the account of the buyer, or it may be placed by the importer who has selected a particular underwriter. This is not as simple as it may sound. For example, the importer may agree to take care of the insurance. In this case, let us say that the purchase is made under a letter of credit.[28] The letter calls for furnishing an on-board bill of lading in order to collect under the credit. If a loss should occur between the time the goods leave the exporter's warehouse and before the on-board bill of lading is issued, the credit could not be used and the insurance taken out by the importer probably would not cover the loss. The exporter would be well advised, therefore, to provide protection (contingency insurance) against this kind of risk. This can be done by the issuance of an inland marine policy or by an endorsement on an open cargo policy to provide coverage for the exporter's own account until the bill of lading is issued.

There are certain advantages to the exporter who places marine-insurance. For example, when the sale is FOB vessel, Philadelphia, the

---

[27]M. Th. Slijper, "Containerization: An Appraisal," *The International Journal of Physical Distribution*, Volume 5, No. 3 (1975), pp. 165–175.

[28]Letters of credit are discussed in Chapter 17.

importer's insurance may become effective only when the goods are loaded aboard ship; hence, any loss to the shipment between the exporter's warehouse and the vessel may not be covered. To protect against such a risk the exporter would need to purchase an inland marine policy or a special endorsement for an open cargo policy. Were the exporter to sell FOB vessel, Philadelphia, with the stipulation that the marine insurance would be provided by the exporter, then the exporter would have complete protection at the importer's expense.[29]

Exporters who are not paid until delivery to destination or later are also in a more secure position with their own dollar marine insurance.

Types of Risk

Marine insurance differs from many other forms of insurance in that the insured has a choice of a vast variety of risks against which insurance can be effected. In broad categories the risks that are commonly insured against are:

1. Free of damage insurance. This is a very limited form of insurance and covers only *total* loss of the goods; partial losses are not covered.
2. Fire and sea perils. Under this coverage, FPA (Free of Particular Average) insurance, claims are paid only in case the vessel is stranded, sunk, burned, on fire, or in collision; and only if the damage is caused by fire or sea perils.
3. Fire and sea perils with average. This is the same as number 2, except that it is not necessary to show that the vessel has been stranded, sunk, burned, on fire, or in collision.
4. Named perils. This includes the fire and sea perils insurance as in number 3 and to which a number of additional perils may be added, such as fresh water damage, hook damage, fuel oil damage, theft, pilferage, nondelivery, or breakage.
5. All risk insurance. This is the most complete coverage commonly written, but it is confined to losses from physical loss or damage from any *external* cause, exclusive of war, strikes, and riots. This coverage does not include loss due to the inherent nature of goods, nor does it cover market losses due to delays in shipment, for example, missing the Christmas sales season. If insurance is desired to cover excluded perils, under certain very limited circumstances they can be included in the insurance policy by endorsement except for war risk insurance, which requires a separate policy.

All of these coverages include general average[30] and salvage charges. Marine insurance is one of the few kinds of insurance where it

---

[29]Price quotations are covered in Chapter 16.

[30]The word *average* is derived from the French word *avarie*, meaning damage; damage that is common or general to the entire venture — ship and cargo — is known as general average. *Particular average* refers to the single or individual shipment.

is permissible, in addition to insuring the value of the goods themselves, to insure profit. While the sales price of goods usually includes the exporter's profit, it does not include import duties or the importer's anticipated profit. In practice a common rule is to insure for an amount equal to all known costs plus 10 percent.

Loss Covered Under Marine Policies

Basically, there are two types of losses under marine insurance policies: (1) particular average and (2) general average.

Particular Average. Damage to the goods themselves is known as particular average and may be classified as follows:

1. Total loss. The amount stated in the insurance policy is paid.
2. Total loss of part of a shipment, for example, by theft or pilferage. The policy pays the insured value of the part lost.
3. Repairable loss. The fender of an automobile is crumpled; it is repaired in the country of importation. Loss paid is the amount of the repair bill.
4. Replaceable loss. The fender must be replaced by a new one which must be shipped by the exporter. Loss paid is the total cost of a new fender, packing, freight, etc.

In all of these situations, the limit of liability, of course, is the face amount of the insurance policy.

General Average. Loss or damage common to the entire venture is known as *general average*. If a voluntary sacrifice is made in face of impending disaster, and that sacrifice is successful in preserving at least a part of the common venture, then all who survive (ship and cargo) contribute pro rata in accordance with the value saved in order to make up the value of whatever was sacrificed.

A classic example of general average loss is by jettison, or throwing overboard certain cargo to save the ship. If 10 percent of the combined value of ship and cargo is thus sacrificed, all owners, including the owner of the jettisoned cargo, contribute 10 percent of their respective values to reimburse for the loss of the cargo that was jettisoned.

More common today is the case of water being used to extinguish a fire. The common sacrifice here is damage to cargo by water; cargo damaged by fire or smoke is not damaged as a result of a voluntary sacrifice and therefore is not subject to general average adjustment.

Insurance Policies and Certificates

There are two ways that a risk can be declared to an insurance company. The first is to send the company a copy of a certificate or a special policy, and the second is to use a short declaration insurance form.

The certificate or special policy is prepared either in the exporter's office, occasionally in the office of an insurance broker, perhaps in the office of the freight forwarder, or maybe in one of the offices of the insurance company. This certificate or special policy is necessary *only* when the exporter is required to furnish evidence of insurance to some third party, such as a bank, a customer, or a third party to whom claims, if any, are to be paid. The certificates and special policies are both negotiable instruments and hence facilitate the settlement of claims in the country of the consignee.

In this situation the exporter often takes out an open insurance policy that sets forth the risks for which there is insurance and the special policy completely reflects the open policy coverage. Every shipment that is made by the exporter under this open policy is certified to the insurance company with complete descriptions, value, and all necessary details. With this information the insurance company is in position to calculate a rate. By the use of an open policy, the exporter is protected on all shipments to the extent that the exporter advises the insurance company of every transaction.

In the second way, if there is not necessity to evidence insurance to a third party and if claims are to be paid to the exporter only, a short declaration insurance form can be used.

If terms of sale or letters of credit call for an insurance policy, a policy must be provided; a certificate, which looks very much like a policy, will not do. Provision is usually made to accept certificates.

Insurance Agents and Brokers

Marine insurance may be obtained from an insurance agent or insurance broker. The agent or broker will help select reliable marine underwriters and arrange the amount and kind of protection that is required. Brokers and agents represent the policyholder and help in the presentation of losses. They can often use their experience to make suggestions that lower a firm's losses. Since marine insurance rates are not standardized, but are determined by the risk experience and the judgment of the underwriter, the reduction in losses could help justify reduced rates.[31]

DISTRIBUTION CENTERS

The distribution center is an integral part of the international physical distribution system. The center is a warehouse that provides a merchandise assortment to meet customer requirements. Products

---

[31]*Marine Insurance: Notes and Comments on Ocean Cargo Insurance* (3d ed.; Philadelphia, Pa.: Insurance Company of North America, 1962), pp. 27, 39.

are shipped in large lots to the warehouse where they are sorted into individual customer orders. The warehouse assembles assortments, stores merchandise, and prepares and arranges delivery of customer orders. Products are stored in the distribution center to replenish customer assortments, to adjust seasonal production to demand, to prepare for erratic peak demands, and to take advantage of quantity purchases or freight rates. The emphasis, however, is on maintaining a supply to meet customer requirements rather than emphasizing long-term storage.[32]

The term "distribution center" is used in this chapter rather than warehouse because the center frequently serves as more than a storage and break-bulk point. It also serves as a control center to assure that customers' orders receive prompt attention, that adequate but not excessive inventories are available, and that necessary data are gathered to facilitate control and documentation requirements.

The multinational firm with several production points may find it advantageous to use distribution centers that are oriented toward production points as well as centers that are market positioned.

Production Oriented Centers

The production-oriented distribution center is located near the production plants or at some other point where it can act as a collection point to bring together the firm's products for consolidated shipment. Thus, the warehouse assembles customer orders involving the production of several factories. At the distribution center products are prepared for shipment; they can be containerized for protection and rapid shipment; also, the consolidated order may move at lower cost. The ready availability of the product in the warehouse also makes rapid shipment to customers possible, thus enabling them to hold less inventory.

The World Trade Distribution Center of IBM illustrates this concept.[33] Located 75 miles from New York City at East Fishkill, New York, the center controls the annual movement of more than 23 million pounds of equipment, parts, and supplies. About 70 percent of this volume moves by air, and approximately the same percentage is shipped in containers. The distribution center serves as a single control point to consolidate cost and other distribution data as well as freight. Orders sent to U.S. plants are transmitted to the center via computer-to-computer hookups. All freight to Europe is sent via the center or directly to the port from the plant, while shipments from

---

[32]This section draws heavily on material from Donald J. Bowersox, Edward W. Smykay, and Bernard J. LaLonde, *Physical Distribution Management* (Rev. ed.; New York: Macmillan Company, 1968), and Donald J. Bowersox, *Logistical Management* (New York: Macmillan Publishing Company, Inc., 1974).

[33]Based on a description of the IBM system in Janet Bosworth Dower, "How IBM Distributes — Worldwide," *Distribution Worldwide* (October, 1973), pp. 50–59.

west of the Mississippi River to Asia, Australia, or the West coast of South America are routed through San Francisco. The center also generates government and bank documents for exporting, auditing freight bills and authorizing payment, and interfacing with the U.S. Customs Service.

Market-Oriented Distribution Centers

In addition to the production-oriented distribution centers, international marketers must provide readily available assortments of their products in the countries where the products are marketed. These market-oriented centers serve primarily to replenish the inventories of the firm's distributors and retailers quickly and at low cost. The center serves largely as a break-bulk point where shipments are placed in large lots and shipped out in mixed truck or car quantities. For the multinational firm this center may provide access to major distribution points in nearby countries as well as serving the local dealers. The center may be used to consolidate assortments from a company's plants in several countries, performing services similar to those of the production-oriented distribution center.

Many American manufacturers ship directly to their distributors from their U.S. or foreign-based factories; however, when sufficient volume exists, the foreign market often can be better served with lower total transportation costs and lower basic inventories through an overseas distribution center. However, to efficiently perform the replenishment service such locations necessitate careful planning that includes the development of adequate inventory control systems. Rapid expansion of plant facilities and rapid growth of sales, especially when combined with long supply lines, have contributed to inventory losses for some American firms.[34]

The Public Warehousing Alternative

In the previous discussion there has been a tacit assumption that the owner of the merchandise operates the warehouse or distribution center. This concept is known as *private warehousing*. It is a viable approach when the demand for the firm's products is substantial and steady; however, private warehouses entail a high level of fixed expense and can be costly when demand fluctuates widely. The warehouse facility must be built, bought, or leased and personnel must be hired and trained; furthermore, the company must establish a transportation network for servicing distributors and dealers.

---

[34]See Peter Vanderwicken, "When Levi Strauss Burst Its Britches," *Fortune* (April, 1974), pp. 131–138. Inventory control systems are beyond the scope of this chapter. For more information on such systems, see Bowersox, Smykay, and LaLonde, *op. cit*.

One alternative for the firm is to use *public warehouses*. These are owned and operated by professional warehouse personnel and furnish not only space and break-bulk facilities, but also a wide variety of services related to physical distribution. The user of a public warehouse pays only for the space that is used plus the fees for services that are requested. Public warehouses will receive merchandise, store it, and assemble and deliver products as they are ordered by the customer. Public warehouses also aid the producer by issuing warehouse receipts that can be used as collateral for bank loans. Some warehouses also provide space for a firm's branch office.

Some public warehousing firms have expanded their services beyond those normally associated with physical distribution in order to provide customers with a more integrated distribution system. One Dutch firm, for example, in addition to warehousing offers customers brokerage, freight forwarding, packaging, insurance, and transportation service to all of Europe and the Middle East. In a product introduction for an American appliance manufacturer it also coordinated promotional material to assure that promotional packets and displays were available for the firm's marketing teams in the target cities.[35] In summary the public warehouse provides the shipper with the flexibility to adapt to local conditions, provide rapid service to customers, and to capitalize on local expertise regarding freight rates, tariff systems, tax and licensing laws, and business customs as well as storing merchandise.

QUESTIONS

1. Distinguish between transportation and physical distribution. What is the managerial value of making this distinction?
2. What criteria would you use in selecting a method of transportation to be used in shipping products from the U.S. to Europe? Would the application of these criteria differ when applied to grain, diamonds, or automobiles?
3. What are some of the advantages a shipper can obtain by using containerized shipments?
4. Choose one of the recent developments in ocean or air transportation and briefly indicate its implication for shippers.
5. Of what significance is a landbridge?
6. How does a shipping conference affect international marketing?
7. What is a bill of lading? Why is it an important shipping document?
8. How is a firm's packing method affected by the mode of transportation used? Climate conditions? Customer requirements?
9. What is meant by general average in the marine insurance policy?
10. How does a distribution center aid both the seller and the buyer in performing the physical distribution function?

---

[35]Tom Foster, "Warehousing Overseas," *Distribution Worldwide* (October, 1974), pp. 59–65.

11. What is a public warehouse and why should a shipper be aware of this institution?

SUPPLEMENTARY READINGS

Ballou, Ronald H. *Business Logistics Management*. Englewood Cliffs, N.J.: Prentice-Hall, Inc., 1973.

Bowersox, Donald J., Edward Smykay, and Bernard J. LaLonde. *Physical Distribution Management*, Revised ed. New York: Macmillan Publishing Company, Inc., 1968.

Bowersox, Donald J. *Logistical Management*. New York: Macmillan Publishing Company, Inc., 1974.

Container News. New York: Communication Channels, Inc., monthly.

Exporters Encyclopedia. New York: Dun and Bradstreet, Inc., annual.

Heskett, James L., Robert M. Ivie, and Nicholas A. Glaskowsky. *Business Logistics*, 2d ed. New York: The Ronald Press Company, 1973.

Magee, John F. *Physical Distribution Systems*. New York: McGraw-Hill Book Company, 1967.

12

The Product/Service Mix

Among the early and critical decisions to be made by the firm interested in international marketing is the choice of products to be offered. What products can the firm profitably market in the chosen market areas? In what market areas is the firm's existing and potential product line of value? How can the firm maximize its impact on the market by offering the most appropriate product service combination? Is the combination currently available to present customers likely to be most productive abroad or should the firm adapt its mix to the new set of market conditions? These represent but a few of the continuing questions involved in establishing and maintaining an effective product policy.

Each product to be offered must, above all, meet the needs of the potential user; therefore, each must be subjected to extreme scrutiny from the user's viewpoint before committing the company's resources to the development of products. The product decision calls for others involving the provision of production facilities and the development of effective marketing programs. The physical product itself needs review to determine its appropriateness in the overseas environment. Trademarks, patents, packaging, and promotional activities all hinge on the product decision. In addition, the decision to manufacture or sell a certain product sets the sources and types of competition that will be encountered and the investments that will be required. To cope with these complex decisions an effective marketing team must evolve that is alert to product marketing opportunities, able to screen the potential offerings, and able to design and implement an effective product introduction. It must also provide for continuous review of the product line and the elimination of products that are no longer profitable.

In this chapter we must first identify the product concept that is most useful for marketing; determine conditions that permit extension of the present product line into new markets or require adaptation; and look to the packaging, branding, labelling, and service aspects of the total product concept. In this chapter we assume that the company has already chosen the market segments it is to serve. Our concern, then, is with the development of appropriate products to meet the needs of these segments. However, in some instances a company may seek market segments with needs that can be satisfied by a product already developed for other markets. In either case the product must match the needs of the market segment to which the company will address its marketing effort.

WHAT IS A PRODUCT?

The definition of a product may be clarified with the following quotation:

> If we define a product in its simplest commercial terms it is this: A product is something people will buy — that is, in some magnitude that makes it profitable. If people don't buy it, it's not a product. . . .
>
> People spend their money not for goods and services, but to get the value satisfactions they believe are bestowed by what they are buying. They buy quarter-inch holes, not quarter-inch drills. . . .
>
> Whether the product is cold-rolled steel or hot-cross buns, whether accountancy or delicacies, competitive effectiveness increasingly demands that the successful seller offer his prospect and his customer more than the generic product itself. He must surround his generic product with a cluster of value satisfactions that differentiates his total offering from his competitors'. He must provide a total proposition, the content of which exceeds what comes out at the end of the assembly line.[1]

The concept of a product used in marketing is broader than that of an assembly of physical or chemical components in a certain size, shape, and color combination. Marketers are more inclined to view the product through the eyes of their potential customers. As the previous quotation suggests, customers are interested in the benefits they expect to receive as a result of the purchase rather than the tangible good itself. What will it do for them — provide transportation, reduce labor costs, add sex appeal? This is epitomized in the statement of Charles Revson, "In the factory we make cosmetics, in the store we sell hope." Thus, he defined the product in terms of what the customer wanted, not in terms of what the factory made.[2] This concept of defining the product in terms of demand is especially pertinent for international marketers where the temptation has often been strong to offer the same product/service mix abroad that is available at home without adequate market analysis and ignoring the possibility that the product may be viewed in an entirely different light in the overseas market. It may serve different functions or, at the very least, may be used in a very different manner.

---

[1]Theodore Levitt, *Marketing for Business Growth* (New York: McGraw-Hill Book Company, Inc., 1974), pp. 8–9.

[2]*Ibid.*, p. 66.

It is easy to slip into the view that similiar physical products perform exactly the same function for all customers, but consider the motorcycle that is a basic means of transportation in some underdeveloped countries where it is common to observe whole families riding. As many as four or five members of the family may be travelling on one cycle at a time, or the cycle may be employed as a means of hauling freight, either in its normal form or in a three-wheeled version. In contrast, in North America and Europe the cycle appears more frequently as transportation for only one person and cycling may be more of a sport than basic transportation.

The marketer's concept of the product has been variously described as an "augmented,"[3] "extended,"[4] or "total"[5] product to distinguish it from the narrower view. This total product concept is the tangible product plus the services that accompany it as expressed in Figure 12-1 (page 221). The physical product is the core value, but is extended by the addition of packaging, labelling, and branding and is accompanied by both presale and postsale services in order to provide the consumer with a maximum of satisfaction from its use. No doubt many will question the value of the extended product in the belief that the consumer receives value only from the tangible product itself. There is reason to believe, however, that these other elements do add to the benefits or utilities the consumer receives.

The brand gives the consumer assurance that a specified quality is present and can be expected every time the brand is purchased. The brand may further convey appropriate images that enhance the psychological value of the product. Labelling aids by providing information regarding the contents of the package and information as to its use and preparation; thereby providing for proper operation and efficiency in durable goods and avoiding the possibility of spoilage by improper care and preparation. The package can be a plain container that protects the product in transportation and storage, but it may also provide more convenient use through proper size and design.

Services are especially important in the sale of industrial products where suppliers may aid the buyer in determining requirements by surveying needs, providing the assistance needed to make the product effective (software for computers), or assuring that the delivery will occur at the time and place needed to main a continuous production flow. Business people may require assurance of readily available repair parts and service personnel in case there is a product failure.

For some companies there is no tangible good in the product they offer. In these firms the total product may be a service. Examples of

---

[3]*Ibid.*, p. 14.

[4]Philip Kotler, *Marketing Management*, 2d ed. (Englewood Cliffs, N.J.: Prentice-Hall, Inc., 1967), p. 424.

[5]E. Jerome McCarthy, *Basic Marketing: A Managerial Approach*, 5th ed. (Homewood, Ill.: Richard D. Irwin, Inc., 1975), p. 228.

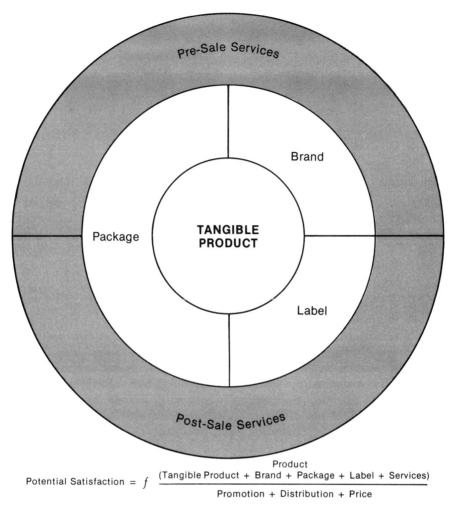

$$\text{Potential Satisfaction} = f \; \frac{\overset{\text{Product}}{(\text{Tangible Product} + \text{Brand} + \text{Package} + \text{Label} + \text{Services})}}{\text{Promotion} + \text{Distribution} + \text{Price}}$$

Figure 12-1 THE PRODUCT/SERVICE MIX

international industrial firms providing such service would include advertising agencies, marketing research agencies, management consultants, transportation companies, and insurance firms. In the consumer field many similar services exist such as automobile leasing, communication and broadcasting, travel agencies, and financial services. In these companies there is also a need to consider the total product. For example, U.S. advertising agencies operating in other countries have found that it is necessary to offer clients more than media space purchasing, art and copy ideas, and production facilities. They may differentiate themselves from local and other foreign competitors through services such as marketing research, public relations, and sales promotional aids.

When contemplating international markets a company may have a choice of selling either physical goods or services. Thus, the turnkey operations, management contracts, and licensing previously discussed as alternative strategies for entering the international markets represent methods whereby companies offer services featuring their specialties without directly selling the product. Franchising is another popular means of capitalizing on the knowledge and reputation of the firm in foreign lands without direct ownership. As discussed previously, these alternative views of the "product" often offer advantages to the international firm without substantially increasing the risks associated with inventories and/or facilities abroad. That may be the only way to enter the market.[6] For example, in 1975 Saudi Arabia imported many items directly from the U.S. and Europe but expressed a keen interest in manufacturing some of these items over the longer period, despite a present shortage of personnel for building and operating the facilities. Western firms have been able to capitalize on this latter development through management contracts and turnkey projects. The potential scope for such operations is evident in the Saudi Arabian government's plan for turning one fishing village, Al Jubayl, into an industrial complex including a three-million-ton steel mill, a half-million-barrel oil refinery, a 500,000-ton fertilizer plant, a 210,000-ton aluminum plant, a 375-million-dollar port, a desalinization plant to provide 52 million gallons of fresh water per day, and an electric plant of 1,000 megawatt generating capacity.[7] This is only one such project in the country.

PRODUCT LINE DECISIONS

Once a company has chosen the market segments to which it will cater, it is confronted with the problem of determining whether its present products are the ideal vehicles for such a move.

Should the Domestic Product Be Marketed Abroad?

The easiest decision to make is that of taking the established product abroad. By doing so the firm would capitalize on a proven product and might gain from production, R&D, and marketing efficiencies as a result of increased scale of operation. Cost savings might be obtained from longer production runs, standardized packaging, and established brand images. This easy approach is deceptive, however, for it depends on the product achieving acceptance in the overseas market before these savings can be accomplished. If the product does not satisfy the basic needs of the market, it won't sell and cost reductions are not possible.

---

[6]See Chapter 5.

[7]C. William Verity, Jr., "The Burgeoning Middle East Markets: Needs and Opportunities," Speech Before the Export Council Seminar, Miami University, Oxford, Ohio, September 10, 1975.

The logic of the dilemma, then, is to pursue a policy of product adaptation to meet the requirements of the new market segments, but such a policy also has its costs. Thus, the marketer is forced into a detailed analysis of the market to determine where and how much standardization is practical and the potential gains and trade-offs from adapting products and promotion. Often this means research on the individual products and markets to determine the specific characteristics requiring modification of the product and the associated costs. Usually some modification of the basic product, brand policy, packaging, or service is desirable to secure a better fit between the company's offering and the requirements of overseas customers, but where the firm exports only a small number of units it may not be economically feasible to achieve any substantial adaptation.

Factors Affecting Standardization of the Product Line

If market analysis is needed for information on which to base a decision regarding standardization, then what are the significant factors to be investigated? Among the factors to be considered, we can isolate several major categories: market demand, economics of operation, governmental restrictions and rules, and compatibility with company resources and policy. Each of these is discussed in turn.

Market Demand. In order to determine the suitability of a product for a given market, it is necessary first to establish the basic function of the product. What is it expected to do? Perhaps the primary function of the product is to provide transportation, shelter from the rain, warmth, cleanliness, or aid in the production of other products and services. In addition, most products incorporate qualities that are not necessary for this primary purpose. These secondary functions can play an important role in the consumer's evaluation of the product.[8] Television sets not only bring entertainment but also are status symbols in some societies. Redesigning the cabinet may have no effect on reception but can dramatically affect sales. For example, Sharp, a Japanese brand, sells in Taiwan in competition with local and other foreign brands; a recent change in the television cabinet resulted in a substantial sales increase despite a 14 percent price increase. Another example of secondary function occurred when visitors at the home of the "Muchtar," head of an Arab village in the Judean Hills, were surprised to note a shiny refrigerator which stood in the center of the spacious guest room. When asked why it was not in the kitchen, the Muchtar replied, "There, in the kitchen, the guests and neighbors

---

[8]The concept of primary and secondary functions is developed in more detail in John Fayerweather, *International Marketing*, 2d ed., *Fundamentals of Marketing Series* (Englewood Cliffs, N.J.: Prentice-Hall, Inc., 1970), pp. 48–55.

won't see it!"[9] Apparently the refrigerator served a secondary status function that is no longer present in the United States, where the refrigerator one owns carries far less ability to impress associates. In some instances the primary functions also may be different in the foreign market. Outboard motors designed for sports in the United States may be employed on fishing vessels abroad.

Even when the product serves the same functions in various countries, the conditions under which it is used may differ significantly, thus leading to product adaptation. Road conditions and traffic patterns in Japan account for some of the variation in automobile design between there and the United States. Similarly, variations in water content cause product adaptation not only between countries but sometimes within countries. More than one brand of detergent may be marketed to meet specific water conditions.

The high mobility of consumers is a factor leading some manufacturers to stress a policy of product standardization. For example, when travellers get upset stomachs in Hong Kong, they would like assurance that the Pepto Bismal purchased there is the same as at home. Likewise, people look for known quality in other products such as film because if a picture is missed through the use of poor film, the traveler may be home before it is discovered and there is no chance for a

Eastman Kodak Company

---

[9]Eliyahu Tal, "Advertising in Developing Countries," *Journal of Advertising* Vol. 3, No. 3 (Spring, 1974), p. 20.

retake. It is no happenstance that the Kodak film and package are readily recognizable in many of the world's cities. Package standardization enhances ready identification and brand similarity lends assurance of performance. Holiday Inns can also attribute some of their popularity to the similarity of service available in different countries.

The image that residents of one country have for the products of another country is an important consideration in the marketing of any specific brand. For instance, the image of Danish furniture, German beer, French wines, American cars, etc., are quite well-formed. In fact, the sales of these products likely depend heavily on their maintenance of the "foreign" quality associated with the national image. The little phrase "made in _____" can have a tremendous influence on the success of a product.[10] Manufacturers may wish to capitalize on their foreign image by exporting their product when it has a superior image.

Economics of Plant and Marketing Operations. The economics of operation usually favor standardization of the product offering. Advantages from standardizing are expected to accrue as a result of larger scale operations. If the company's plants currently are operating below their most efficient levels, the additional volume from the standardized production enables the firm to spread its costs over a larger volume of output. Standardization permits the firm to import component parts from subsidiaries and to transfer knowledge, equipment, and systems among the production points. Product development costs are minimized and some marketing efficiencies may be possible in training and advertising.

On the other hand, several factors work in the opposite direction. If there is already an established demand for a product line that has been acquired through purchase or merger, the marketing costs associated with obtaining market acceptance of the home version can be substantial. It might pay to develop the goodwill already present by maintaining the separate product in its market.

When different measurement systems are in use, it may be difficult to achieve standardization. For example, the metric system is used in all the major trading nations except the United States. Theoretically, it should be possible to merely translate American standards into the metric system but this often results in the need to buy a special part in the foreign market because the standards differ, thus increasing costs. Several American industries, including pharmaceuticals and high technology groups use the metric system, but Americans have not been especially active in establishing international standards. Although there may have been advantages in the past for insisting on American standards, the current level of international competition is rapidly changing this position.

---

[10]Ernest Dichter, "The World Customer," *Harvard Business Review* (July–August, 1962), pp. 113–122.

Governmental Effects. Governments affect the product design in numerous ways, each of which has a potential effect on decisions to make product modification. A *direct* influence is exerted through government purchases for defense, supplies and equipment, and state enterprises. The extension of governmental services in recent years has greatly increased these direct effects. Government programs for power sources, medical programs, and energy conservation represent vast markets for goods and services from private enterprise. The purchasing influence on design is exerted through specifications which must be met before a corporation can bid on government projects. The government may further restrict the entrance of firms into industries where governmental monopolies exist.

Indirect influences are exerted through laws that establish minimum standards for safety and health regulations. Government may participate in the consumer movement through information, ombudsmen, and acting as consumer advocate. Labelling laws may require specific information and sizes of containers. Building codes lay down specifications. The local content regulations that are designed to speed economic development can make modification necessary for continued production.[11] Taxes and tariffs frequently are established in a manner that gives competitive advantage to the local firms and works against foreign products, either by making them more expensive or by reducing the profit available.

Compatibility with Company Resources and Policy. Any product offered must present a reasonable compromise between the requirements of the market and the resources available to the firm. The firm seeks reasonable alignment with production and marketing capabilities as well as meeting the company's profit goals. Where production abroad is restricted by limitations on imports of raw materials and component parts, the company may find it necessary to modify the product through the use of substitutes. In some instances company policy no doubt reflects management policy to present a standard product line due to inadequate market analysis or stubborn belief that the market should want what they believe to be a superior product. However, competitive pressures from other American firms and foreign companies are likely to make this position less tenable than in the past when American products may have been the only ones available. These competitive pressures for change are likely to be strongest in the latter stages of the product's life cycle.

In Chapter 7 we discussed the self-reference criterion as a potential difficulty in developing marketing programs that are appropriate for other cultures and countries. One international company attempted to

---

[11]Local content regulations require that a specified percentage of the final product be made locally.

assure itself of deliberate and systematic examination of products by developing a checklist of major environmental factors to consider in relation to the design of its products for foreign markets. No assumptions were made about the superiority of an American-oriented product. Thirteen environmental factors considered in the analysis and their potential design implications are shown in Table 12-1.

Table 12-1   DESIGN IMPLICATIONS OF ENVIRONMENTAL FACTORS

Environmental Factors	Product Design Implications
Level of technical skills	Product simplification
Level of labor cost	Automation or manualization of the product
Level of literacy	Remarking and simplification of the product
Level of income	Quality and price change
Level of interest rates	Quality and price change (investment in quality might not be financially desirable)
Level of maintenance	Change in tolerances
Climatic differences	Product adaptation
Isolation (heavy repair difficult and expensive)	Product simplification and reliability improvement
Differences in standards	Recalibration of product and resizing
Availability of other products	Greater or lesser product integration
Availability of materials	Change in product structure and fuel
Power availability	Resizing of product
Special conditions	Product redesign or invention

Source: Richard D. Robinson, "The Challenge of the Underdeveloped National Market," *Journal of Marketing* (October, 1961), p. 22.

Many of the points in the foregoing discussion are illustrated in the recent product designs by General Motors and Ford to meet the needs of Asia and underdeveloped country markets of South America. The General Motors version, the Basic Transportation Vehicle (BTV) is a light, short-distance hauler that can be adapted as a pickup or minibus. It is being built in Malaysia, Ecuador, Portugal, and the Philippines. The car is easy to assemble with no curved body parts and the motor and drive trains are imported from England. Although the BTV is not assured of success, it does represent a major departure for the automobile firms in adapting to the less developed markets.[12] The essential features of the BTV were expressed in an advertisement appearing in the November 14, 1973 issue of *The Wall Street Journal* under the headline "How To Open Your Own BTV Assembly Plant."

> Many of the less industrialized nations of the world are in need of low-cost basic transportation. The owners of small businesses, farms, and little factories in those countries often can't afford the cost of the kinds of cars and trucks that the industrialized nations export. So we've developed a Basic Transportation Vehicle that can be made in the less industrialized countries in a plant that costs about $50,000.
>
> The assembly plants are usually owned by the people who live in those countries. We give them technical assistance at the beginning and then leave them on their own after a few weeks or months.
>
> The automobile body they make has no curved metal, so they can literally cut it out of sheet metal with a "Nipper," a kind of motorized metal shears. It's done in about the same way that a dress is cut from a pattern.
>
> We supply the difficult-to-manufacture parts (engine and drive train) from a GM plant in England, and we do it with standard parts so that there aren't any problems about the availability of replacement parts.
>
> The assembly work teaches these skills: welding, sheet-metal working, painting, work layout, quality control, scheduling and ordering, wiring, auto mechanics, carpentry, and critical path planning for production.
>
> The BTV is usually the lowest-priced 4 wheel vehicle available in the country and often the first vehicle a person can afford to buy. In some places it costs less than a good horse.
>
> Our design for the manufacture of these vehicles is labor intensive rather than capital intensive, because these countries need work for their people.
>
> All it takes to start a BTV plant is a structure about the size of a large barn, $50,000, and the national will to begin industrializing.[13]

Brand Policy

Brand policy becomes more important to the multinational firm as competition tightens in the local markets. Local producers and other foreign firms provide the impetus for sellers to seek greater control over the distribution of their product and provide a basis for an effective communication strategy. If the producer is to gain the advantage of promotional efforts, the consumer must be able to identify the product and to separate it from those of competitors. That is a function

---

[12]"GM Reaches Out for New Market with Small Multipurpose Van," *Business Latin America* (November 28, 1973), pp. 379–380.

[13]Advertisement, *The Wall Street Journal*, November 14, 1973.

performed by the brand. Part of the significance of the brand policy derives from the fact that both the seller and the buyer can benefit from branding. The essential function of the brand is that it identifies a product which stands for some quality connotation — either high or low — so the buyer has the assurance that repeat purchases will result in similar satisfactory experiences in consumption or use.

Before viewing the branding alternatives available to the producer, it is desirable to distinguish among several closely related terms used in reference to brands. The term *brand* refers to a name, term, sign, symbol, or design used to identify the goods and services of a seller and to differentiate them from those of competitors.[14] This identification may be placed directly on the product or on a label, tag, or package. Also, the brand may identify the products of a single seller (either producer or distributor) or a group of sellers. The *brand name* refers to that portion of the brand that can be spoken. Well-known examples of brand names in the world market include Ford, Norelco, Shell, and McDonald's. The *trademark* is that part or all of the brand that has been given legal protection. It is a legal term referring to the exclusive rights of the owner of the mark. The legal considerations of trademark protection will be discussed in Chapter 16 along with other features of the legal environment of world marketing.

Brand Options. The international marketer has several potential alternative brand policies from which to select. No one of these is most advantageous in all situations; therefore the producer must carefully consider the potential gains and costs of each before making a decision. This is especially pertinent in view of the heavy promotional costs that are associated with establishing the brand in a market. The various branding alternatives may be identified as:

1. A policy of selling unbranded goods, or selling goods to be resold under the brand of a distributor.
2. Establishing a single worldwide brand to identify the producer's product in all markets.
3. Establishing local brand names for the separate national markets.
4. Establishing several brands in a market to identify individual products or groups of products in the manufacturer's line. These might distinguish different types of products (e.g., food and cosmetics) or different quality or styles.

No Branding. Most marketers of manufactured products probably believe that branding is desirable, but there are a number of instances in which it is costly and difficult to establish a brand sufficiently to make

---

[14]For a more complete discussion of the terms, see Committee On Definitions of the American Marketing Association, *Marketing Definitions: A Glossary of Marketing Terms* (Chicago: American Marketing Association, 1960).

it profitable.[15] Among the conditions usually deemed necessary for effective branding, are: (1) The product must have the potential demand and margin to support the additional promotional costs and yet provide a greater profit to the brander. (2) It is imperative that the producer be able to maintain the quality connotation that has proved to be of value to the buyer. That quality may be either high or low and may be based on physical or other characteristics, but whatever the brand stands for, the customer counts on it being consistent. (3) Obviously the product also should be identifiable so the consumer can distinguish among the products in the marketplace. (4) If the producer is to gain maximum benefit from branding, the product should be consistently available to the consumer; if it is not, the promotional impact is lost and ill will may actually result when the repeat purchase is not possible.

For many of the commodities sold in international trade, the above conditions either cannot be met or would be too costly to attempt; consequently, brands are of little significance to these trades. An important segment of U.S. exports is composed of agricultural products that are produced by a large number of farmers and are sold by grade. Branding these goods would be difficult and, probably, meaningless to the prospective buyer. In the case of manufactured goods it often is possible to brand, but may still not be desirable. For instance, some products become components of a final product and are not readily identifiable to the consumer. If these items cannot be shown to provide a special advantage that is important to the final product's performance in the eyes of the consumer, or if they are not important replacement items, the manufacturer may still decline to brand them.

Private Brands. The more important case, however, is where the manufacturer fabricates items to be sold by distributors under their own brand name. This *private branding* is often resisted by manufacturers in both the international and domestic trades because the distributor, rather than the manufacturer, controls the distribution and marketing policy. To a considerable degree the manufacturer's continued sales in the foreign market are dependent not only on the marketing capacity of the distributor and market conditions, but also on maintaining a continuing relationship with the distributor. If the distributor desires to change the source of supply, the manufacturer finds that there is no contact with the market. Reliance on one or two major distributors can leave the manufacturer in a very vulnerable position.

On the other hand, private branding may provide substantial sales in the markets where the manufacturer would find penetration under its own brand difficult. The substantial sales volume and prestige of

---

[15]For a more extensive discussion of these characteristics, see E. Jerome McCarthy, *Basic Marketing*, 5th ed. (Homewood, Ill.: Richard D. Irwin, Inc., 1975), pp. 252–253.

established retailers or other distributors can be of considerable aid, especially when the foreign manufacturer is small or not well-known. Consider the case of foreign manufacturers whose products are sold in the U.S. under the brand names of Sears and Penney's. These stores display and promote electronics, appliances, and soft goods at levels that would be impossible for their suppliers to command under their own brands. Similar conditions exist abroad. The growth of large-scale retailing in Europe and Japan may add to the demand for the production of private branded goods. Private brand production may also allow the manufacturer to operate at more efficient levels of production. This efficiency can provide a base for the manufacturer to use in developing its own brands.

Worldwide or Local Brands? Options two and three deal essentially with the same issues — should the firm apply a worldwide identification to its products through the establishment of a global brand, or should it vary its brands in the local markets? The issue arises primarily because of the promotional advantages to the company if it is successful in establishing the worldwide image through the brand policy. The adoption of a policy of global brands to be applied to the company's products in all markets is most useful when the company has a reputation for quality and technical excellence that can be carried into the international markets and where brands are important to the consumer. The proponents of the global brand policy point to the ready-made base for the company's promotional effort provided by an already established brand, the preferences that exist in many countries for the foreign-made product, the desirability of better consumer recognition of the company's products, and the value of a reputation as an international firm with multinational resources and capabilities.[16] They believe the global brand leads to improved marketing communications, clearer identification of the company's products, and the possibility of better coordination of the company's worldwide advertising.

On the other hand, the proponents of a policy of varying the brand in the local markets point to the differences of both an economic and cultural nature in the various markets. Furthermore, the use of local brands helps to set the image of a local company. In some instances the company's major brand is not desirable because of its connotation in the local language. Some brand names cannot be easily translated into the local language or they may have very undesirable meanings. For example, the brand name for one American car is similar to the word for concubine in the language of an oriental country where it is sold. A brand name may already have been registered or used by another firm in the market and thus may not be available to the foreign

---

[16]These issues are discussed in "Choosing Corporate, Product, and Brand Names for Worldwide Marketing," *Business International*, Management Monograph No. 37 (1966).

producer.[17] Sometimes the company has entered the local market through the purchase of a local firm with an established product and maintains the local brand to keep the market share it has bought.

A company may seek the advantages of a worldwide image and still meet local preferences through the use of the company name or the company trademark in combination with local brands. In this manner the product is identified as coming from a company with worldwide resources and reputation; yet the policy provides the flexibility to fit the local language, traditions, and symbolic preferences.

General Foods Corporation

Multiple Brands. There are several situations in which producers are likely to establish a policy of using more than one brand in a given market. The manufacturer may produce a diverse line of products so that the quality connotation of the major brand name may have little meaning or value to other portions of the line. For example, the conglomerate may manufacture and sell industrial products and consumer goods; within the consumer line may be foods and cosmetics. It would be very difficult to convey a single quality concept for the promotion of these products; thus, several brands may be developed even though the firm maintains a family brand (one brand on related items) within each of the product groups.

Multiple brands are useful also when the manufacturer believes consumers do not have a high loyalty to any brand. In such cases competing brands may be established by the manufacturer in order to capture a larger share of the purchases of these brand switchers, or to appeal to the consumer's desire for variety within a product category. Separate brands are useful also when the manufacturer attempts to appeal to more than one market segment. Thus, the manufacturer may use an imported brand to convey the idea of high quality to appeal to

---

[17]See Chapter 17.

the higher income groups, while still producing other brands for lower income segments.

Often the producer will use an established brand in several countries on its major product while establishing diverse brands on other products. The soft drink industry is characteristic of this policy. The brand names, Coca-Cola, Pepsi Cola, and 7-Up, are widely recognized and promoted in the world markets but different brands may be employed on secondary products. Thus, Coca-Cola's orange drink and its guarana are sold in Brazil under the Fanta brand.[18]

PACKAGING AND LABELLING

The two-fold nature of the package presents the marketer with a special challenge in seeking to protect the product during its long movement from the point of production to the point of use and in seeking a package that serves as a promotional tool. Adequate performance on both of these functions is necessary if the package is to provide its maximum contribution to the firm's profit. Since the two functions do not always have the same requirements, the creative engineering talents of the packager are taxed to develop an acceptable design. Sometimes it may be possible to use the same, or similar, packages in a number of countries with only minor adjustments to take into account the local languages, traditions, and governmental requirements, thereby permitting the company to maintain a consistent image in its marketing territories and to achieve packaging efficiencies.

Four distinguishable sets of considerations that may affect the packaging requirements for the international company are:

1. Conditions of product use.
2. Cultural variations in the market.
3. Governmental influences.
4. Ecological concerns.

Conditions of Use

The packaging decision involves the choice of appropriate sizes for the convenient use of the items by ultimate buyers and for efficient handling and display by intermediate sellers. But what size is appropriate and economical? Perhaps several sizes are needed. Certainly the needs of the channel for bulk handling and display may be facilitated if the units are packed both in sizes suitable for individual purchases by consumers and are consolidated into larger units for the channel.

---

[18]"Coke Tries to Widen Brazilian Market," *Advertising Age* (August 11, 1975), p. 3. Guarana is the generic name for a sweet-tasting refreshment which holds a 29 percent share of the soft drink market in Brazil.

An English study illustrates the break-bulk problem as the product moves through the channel. Beer was distributed (1) in half-pint cans or bottles to facilitate consumer usage, (2) in six-packs to present a conveniently handled typical purchase, (3) on pallets for ease in warehousing, and (4) transported on trucks conforming to current legislation on vehicle size and load.[19]

The present discussion focuses on the issues involved in the design of packages for end use, but these must still be compatible with the total distribution system. Even within these limitations the manager of a consumer products company still has a wide range of packaging alternatives available, such as reusable packages, cook-in bags, strip packs, aerosols, tubes, gift packs, etc. A detailed consideration of the individual alternatives is beyond the scope of this chapter because of the many technical factors involved. Our attempt is to present the basic issues involved in packaging for the international, as contrasted with the domestic company. Shipping containers and protective packing for overseas shipment were discussed in Chapter 11.

Among the obvious variables affecting the packaging of individual items are the *climatic conditions* to which the product will be exposed both in the production points and markets where it will be sold and in the transportation process that may take the product through different zones. The product may be both produced and finally sold in temperate zones, but may be exposed to tropical conditions in the transportation process. The multinational firm often maintains distribution in widely diverse areas. For example, it may distribute in the Middle East with its hot and dry climate while also selling in northern Europe and in the tropics; thus, different package materials may be desirable. Both industrial and consumer goods must arrive at the customer's point of use in workable condition despite sometimes difficult transportation and improper handling. Labels must remain attached to the product for identification and information and still present an attractive appearance to the potential purchaser.

The *retailing and wholesaling systems* employed by the firm in the overseas market also affect the package design, especially when the company relies on the modern self-service segment of the system for its major distribution.[20] For example, the development of self-service operations in Europe and Japan has increased the demand for prepackaged products and placed emphasis on the promotional value of the packages. Increases in the costs of labor have added impetus to the design of packages that can be easily handled and displayed. In order

---

[19]Gordon Wills, "Packaging As a Source of Profit," *International Journal of Physical Distribution Monograph*, Vol. 5, No. 6, p. 317.

[20]In Russia the lack of prepacked items has been listed as one of the impediments to the development of self-service operations. See Thomas V. Greer, *Marketing in the Soviet Union* (New York: Frederick A. Praeger Publishers, 1973), pp. 52–54.

to accommodate this latter demand some European manufacturers have developed packaging that fits into a total system of physical handling. For example, Tetra Pak has developed a new package design for milk products that recognizes a worldwide trend toward fewer and larger retail outlets. It has developed a system for handling its specially designed milk cartons to permit the product to be displayed in the same carts used for transportation. In the store the carts function as self-service display units, eliminating the handling of individual packages by store personnel and thereby anticipating the labor-saving needs and display requirements of modern retailing.[21]

Income variations and average family size can lead to differences in the size of packages to be used abroad. By reducing the size of the package the manufacturer may be able to lower the shelf prices on products and make it possible for lower income groups to purchase them. For example, a paper products firm put seventy-five items in a package instead of the 100-200 as in the United States. With another product it put ten to a package instead of twelve or twenty-four.[22] The smaller package both lowers the shelf price for the product and meets the needs of customers with smaller families and smaller storage facilities. This is especially significant in the case of foods needing refrigeration and other products that require special storage.

Package size is also related to the company's marketing strategy. Although Royal Crown has developed a flexible approach to overseas markets to meet the competition of Coca-Cola, Pepsi Cola and other soft drink firms, its main sales appeal has been to charge a lower price than its competitors. Rather than lowering its price per bottle, Royal Crown has chosen to sell a larger bottle than its competitors for the same price they normally charge. This policy has been successful in several of the less affluent countries.[23]

The decision to use a family brand to cover several related items or to use individual brands for each product also affects package and label design. Thus, SSC International uses a family brand in the United States on a line of food products. Under the Empress label it sells sardines, asparagus, shrimp, pineapple, and mushrooms from several countries. The company's family brand actually includes over 100 items that must be coordinated on a worldwide basis. The products are packaged in containers of various shapes and sizes in many countries, but a unified identification is achieved by having the art-work for the packages designed in the United States even though the labels may be printed overseas.[24]

---

[21]*Modern Packaging* (January, 1975), p. 35.

[22]Vern Terpstra, *American Marketing in the Common Market* (New York: Frederick A. Praeger Publishers, 1967), p. 75.

[23]*Business International* (May 18, 1973), p. 157.

[24]"Showcase: New Package Ideas," *Modern Packaging* (August, 1975), p. 40.

Cultural Considerations in the Market

Even when other aspects of the package are standardized, the company frequently finds it desirable and necessary to present the information on the label in the language of the consumer. Sometimes this is required by governmental regulation but more likely it is the result of good business sense. Use of the local language facilitates the communication of essential information and represents a minimal adjustment to the needs of the customer. The label may even feature more than one language. For example, Revlon worked with the Novaya Zarya fragrance factory in Moscow to develop a product paying tribute to the Project Apollo-Soyuz (EPAS) flight. The fragrance was packaged in a distinctively designed glass bottle and called "EPAS". The embossed outer package was printed in Russian on one side and English on the other since the product was to be sold in both countries.[25] However, in some instances products such as perfumes are labelled only in the original language to accentuate the foreign atmosphere (e.g., Chanel).

The traditions, myths, and taboos that are characteristic of a people also play a role in the packaging of products for sale abroad. They are especially important in the developing nations where contacts with other cultures have been minimal. Take, for instance, the symbolism of colors. Dark red is the mourning color on the Ivory Coast rather than black; white conveys mourning to the Chinese, whereas in Ghana it expresses joy.[26] To the Chinese the symbolism of the dragon differs from that associated by the English with St. George. Use of symbols from other cultures can easily portray a completely opposite concept than that which was intended, but when carefully used they can add to the image desired.

Governmental Influences

A mandatory feature of package and label design is that they comply with the legal requirements of the countries where the product is to be sold. These regulations reflect the governmental function of protecting consumers, but some also form a basis for protecting the interests of local producers. The laws are national in character and requirements differ among the countries, thereby making difficult the standardization of packaging and labelling. Canada's Consumer Packaging and Labelling Regulations provide an example of these laws, although they are more lenient than some. The Canadian law requires bilingual and metric labelling of all except certain exempted products

---

[25]"Showcase: New Package Ideas," *Modern Packaging* (September, 1975), p. 58.

[26]Eliyahu Tal, "Advertising in Developing Countries," *Journal of Advertising*, Vol. 3, No. 2 (Spring, 1974).

such as nonfood items usually sold by count, replacement parts for vehicles, appliances, greeting cards, and games in which a knowledge of French or English is essential. In general the Canadian law requires:

1. Identity of the product by its common or generic name or its function to be shown on the principal display panel in English and French.
2. The net quantity of the product must be declared in Canadian and metric units and in the French and English languages.
3. The person by or for whom the product was manufactured must be identified sufficiently for postal purposes.
4. Special "other information" requirements are set forth for food products related to the use of artificial flavorings.[27]

Sweden provides another example of governmental influence on packaging and labelling. In Sweden the Consumer Ombudsman is concerned with complaints arising under the Marketing Practices Act which relates to "any advertising measure or any other action (undertaken in the course of marketing any goods or services) which, by conflicting with good commercial standards or otherwise, adversely affects consumers or entrepreneurs."[28] Many of the complaints to the Ombudsman concern discrepancies between the size of packages and their contents while others refer to promotional claims. This legislation provides for a reverse burden of proof in that it is the responsibility of the seller to justify marketing practice and to prove that any claims are not misleading. The Swedish government also influences labelling through grants that it provides to the Swedish Institute for Informative Labeling (VDN) whose purpose is to promote the increased use of standardized information labels by consumer goods producers and to increase awareness of such labels among consumers.[29]

Ecological Concerns

Recently ecological issues of packaging have become important in the advanced nations of the world. The "throw away" or "no return" bottles, cans, and plastics have been justified as an economic appeal to specific market segments, but environmentalists are increasingly questioning the long-run values of the practice. In many countries they are receiving support from government and influential groups. Laws have been enacted to force the use of returnables and biodegradable packaging. Recycling efforts have been advanced in both the United States and abroad, but these are dependent on procedures for collecting and

---

[27]"Laws and Rulings," *Modern Packaging* (July, 1975), p. 55.

[28]"Sweden: The Consumer Ombudsman," *EFTA Bulletin* (March, 1975), p. 17.

[29]Hans B. Thorelli, "Consumer Information Policy in Sweden — What Can Be Learned?" *Journal of Marketing* (January, 1971), p. 51.

sorting the materials. The material shortages have added to the desirability of recycling and some results have been achieved. Examples of the types of recycling abroad would include Mitsubishi Petrochemicals (Japan) which has developed a "Reverzer" to make fence posts and lumber replacements from recycled plastics, and Regal Packaging in England which forms pallets and industrial containers from wastes.[30] Packagers continue to be under pressure to have their packages conform to new environmental protection constraints, even while meeting the needs of their customers. These ecological efforts are likely to increase in the future and marketers will want to keep abreast of these developments in order to anticipate the demands of the ecological movement.

SERVICE POLICIES

The service component of the total product provides a manufacturer with an important opportunity to differentiate the product offering. Even when the physical product is similar to those of other producers, a manufacturer can gain a competitive edge by providing superior installation, repair, financing, and other services. The service element is especially important for producers of durable goods and those involving a high technology. Both industrial purchasers and final consumers are interested in what the product will do for them. This means they need the assurance that the product will continue to perform its basic functions throughout its economical life and, in turn, this implies the desirability of an adequate warranty and post-sale service by the supplier. Assurance is particularly necessary when overseas buyers are far from the factory or commercial repair centers.

The competitive edge provided by the service arrangements is difficult to evaluate. However, a recent example involving the sale of a high technology product can illustrate its significance for a specific transaction. In March, 1975, Boeing successfully concluded bargaining with the government of Iraq for the sale of six jet airliners for the Iraqi Airways. This $200-million sale was the largest commercial sale to the Middle East but before signing, the Iraqis insisted that Boeing also provide training in all phases of airline operation and management. This resulted in an additional $20-million service contract whereby Boeing will send thirteen management experts and 139 maintenance personnel to Iraq. Also, Boeing will bring almost the entire engineering staff of Iraqi Airways to Seattle for a course and 300 Iraqis to Tulsa for intensive training as aircraft mechanics.[31]

Although the size of the Boeing contract may be unusual, the basic concept behind it is not. The overseas buyer of a technical product

---

[30] Wills, *op. cit.*, pp. 331–334.
[31] "Boeing Gets Baghdad's Aircraft Business," *Business Week* (August 4, 1975), p. 35.

may need much more than the physical product if it is to be effectively employed. High technology products such as aircraft and computers are important U.S. exports. These products, however, almost by definition, are those for which the buyer needs assistance in adapting them to the production system. Neither the buyer nor the buyer's employees may be familiar with the operating characteristics of the product or the techniques required for its use or maintenance. The sale of a computer may depend on the provision of programming, installation, and maintenance services as much as the technical unit itself. Even when the product and its functions are familiar, the customer requires assurance that spare parts, together with trained service personnel, will be available to keep the product functioning properly.

To say that service is important is easy, but the provision of adequate service in overseas markets is a continuous problem for multinational marketers. Usually the firm relies on its subsidiaries and its distributors and dealers to perform the actual services. Thus, it is readily apparent that proper service facilities may be an important criterion in the selection of channel members. However, the firm itself may need to aid the distribution channel by providing training for the distributor's personnel or by supplementing the distributor's program with engineering assistance when higher technology is involved. Training of service personnel is performed either abroad at the dealer's place of business or at special training facilities. When there are relatively few key people to be trained and their training is highly technical, they may be brought to the factory; otherwise, it often is less expensive to train them at centers near their homes.

Whatever method is used, experience indicates that the manufacturer cannot rely solely on the distribution network to keep its service personnel up to date on the latest developments. Only the factory may be able to assemble the necessary information regarding its new product and service policies. Delegation of the service functions to distributors in no way relieves manufacturers of the responsibility for their performance, since the ultimate buyer is likely to assign the responsibility for product failure and ineffective service to the firm whose brand the product carries.

QUESTIONS

1. Comment on the marketing significance of Charles Revson's statement, "In the factory we make cosmetics, in the store we sell hope."
2. What is meant by the marketer's concept of total product? Of what importance is the total product concept?
3. Under what circumstances should a company sell the same product abroad that it markets in the United States?
4. What is a secondary function performed by a product? How do such functions affect the marketing effort?

5. How do governments affect product design?
6. Choose a specific product to be sold in a specified foreign country. Show how environmental factors in that country might affect product design and packaging.
7. Distinguish among the terms brand, brand name, and trademark.
8. Under what circumstances might a marketer choose not to brand a product for sale abroad?
9. What advantages do you see in the use of a worldwide brand rather than several local brands?
10. Choose a specific product and show how the conditions of use and cultural considerations would affect packaging and labelling.
11. How can an American manufacturer of transportation equipment (e.g., trucks) achieve a satisfactory level of service on products sold in foreign markets?

SUPPLEMENTARY READINGS

"Choosing Corporate, Product, and Brand Names for Worldwide Marketing," *Business International*. Management Monograph, No. 37 (1966).

d'Antin, Philippe, "The Nestle Product Manager as Demigod," *European Business* (Spring, 1971), pp. 44–49.

Fayerweather, John. *International Marketing*, 2d ed. Englewood Cliffs, N.J.: Prentice-Hall, Inc., 1970. Chapter 5.

Keegan, Warren J. "Multinational Product Planning Strategic Alternatives." *Journal of Marketing* (January, 1969), pp. 58–62.

Lightman, Joseph M. "World Patent Laws Reviewed." *Foreign Business Practices: Materials on Practical Aspects of Exporting, International Licensing and Investing*. Washington: U.S. Government Printing Office, November, 1975, pp. 31–43; *idem*, "World Trademark Laws Reviewed," *ibid*., pp. 44–45.

Terpstra, Vern. *International Marketing*. New York: Holt, Rinehart and Winston, Inc., 1972. Chapters 8 and 9.

13

Promotional Policy

The preceding chapters on international marketing management described the fundamental problems of organizing the firm for international marketing, selecting the channels of distribution, and arranging for the physical distribution of the product. The major considerations involved in product development were included in this discussion. These activities, properly performed, result in placing the appropriate product in locations for consumers to purchase when and in the quantities needed. In Chapter 13 the challenge of communicating these company and product values to the consumer is discussed.

Consumers are spatially dispersed and may not be aware of the existence of products and services that meet their needs. For this reason, the modern marketing system employs a variety of promotional methods to inform and persuade consumers of advantages derived from the use of a company's products and services.

Promotional strategy — the most effective blend of communication — lies at the very base of both domestic and foreign marketing. Advertising, sales promotion, personal selling, and publicity comprise the communication contact between the firm and its customers. As such, they are among the most visible, and probably the most controversial, of marketing efforts. Their basic nature is to inform potential customers of the value of the seller's product in order to persuade them to purchase. Consumers must perceive that the product will help them achieve a personal or social goal before they will seek out the seller's product. Promotion ensures that a company's product has a positive value to the prospective customer.[1] The promotional strategy of the firm is an integrated program to provide a unified image of the company and its products; in this way the various elements (advertising, display, personal selling, etc.) mutually reinforce each other.

This chapter is divided into three sections. The first presents elements of the promotional mix and the problems and challenges of promotion in the international context. The second section first shows the importance of advertising as measured by world expenditures, followed by a discussion of internal organization for advertising and the

---

[1] Jerome B. Kernan, William P. Dommermuth, and Montrose S. Sommers, *Promotion* (New York: McGraw-Hill Book Company, 1970), p. 8.

advertising agency alternatives. Media characteristics and the presentation of the advertising message form the last parts of this section. In the final section, personal selling and other forms of sales promotion available to the international marketer are presented.

ELEMENTS OF THE PROMOTIONAL MIX

The promotional mix is composed of four elements: advertising, sales promotion, personal selling, and publicity. (Packaging may be included in the promotional mix.[2]) The first four have been defined by the American Marketing Association:

Advertising is "any paid form of nonpersonal presentation and promotion of ideas, goods, or services by an identified sponsor."[3] Thus, advertising is paid for by a sponsor that can be identified. Frequently advertising is carried by mass media to reach wide audiences and the advertiser retains a high level of control over the message to be presented.

Personal selling is the "oral presentation in a conversation with one or more prospective purchasers for the purpose of making sales."[4] This highly flexible means of promotion can be modified to meet the specific informational requirements of the group actually present at the time of the presentation; it can be changed to meet the requirements of another group later. Personal selling is important in the promotion of highly technical products, especially where the product, financing, and other arrangements must be adapted to the individual sale.

Sales promotion relates to "marketing activities, other than personal selling, advertising, and publicity, that stimulate consumer purchasing and dealer effectiveness, such as displays, shows and exhibitions, demonstrations, and various nonrecurrent selling efforts not in the ordinary routine."[5] International trade fairs and exhibitions have proven useful in selling American industrial products abroad.

Publicity involves "non-personal stimulation of demand for a product, service or business unit by planting commercially significant news about it in a published medium or obtaining favorable presentation of it upon radio, television or stage that is not paid for by the sponsor."[6] It is the newsworthiness of the information that leads the media to discuss the product, company, or service rather than the paid sponsorship of advertising. Such publicity may be of special value because it is regarded as something other than the information provided by the firm selling the service.

---

[2]James U. McNeal, *Readings in Promotion Management* (New York: Appleton-Century-Crofts, 1966), p. 6.

[3]Committee on Definitions, American Marketing Association, *Marketing Definitions: A Glossary of Marketing Terms* (Chicago: American Marketing Association, 1960), p. 9.

[4]*Ibid.*, p. 18.

[5]*Ibid.*, p. 20.

[6]*Ibid.*, p. 19.

Packaging may be included in the promotional mix because it attracts attention through its color, lettering, and illustrations and presents a message to create interest and convince prospective consumers at the point of purchase to buy the product. The package also provides convenience of use and the possible reuse of containers. In each of these functions it serves to promote the product.[7] The promotional functions of the package are very important for many goods, especially consumer goods that are marketed through self-service stores; therefore, its value is reaffirmed here.

The promotional mix represents alternative communication channels which the international marketer can use to interpret the value of products and services to the potential foreign customer. The appropriate mix will vary with the type of product, with management's belief in the efficacy of the various elements in the specific situation, and with the alternatives that are actually available in a foreign market. Like domestic sales, the international sale of industrial goods of a high value relies heavily on personal selling, while consumer goods stress advertising supplemented by a point of sale display.

ADVERTISING EXPENDITURES AND ORGANIZATION

Advertising represents a major mode for communicating with customers throughout the world. Its impact depends in part on the environment within which it operates.

Environment of International Advertising

Every global marketer is faced with rapidly changing conditions that vitally affect the promotional strategy of the firm. Increased worldwide expenditures for advertising; the spreading consumer movement in many nations; awareness of social responsibility in matters of health, safety, advertising to children, pollution, etc.; and increased governmental regulation of promotion all combine to present the global advertiser with a need to adapt promotional strategy if the company's competitive position is to be maintained.[8] Widespread consumer dissatisfaction with business has resulted in the placement of constraints on advertising and other promotional activities in many countries. Taxes have been proposed and levied on advertising, restrictions have been established on advertising messages prohibiting comparative advertising and controlling advertising to children, "corrective" advertising has been required, and Consumer Ombudspersons

---

[7]McNeal, *op. cit.*, p. 9.
[8]See International Advertising Association, "The Global Challenge to Advertising," *Journal of Advertising* (Winter, 1974), p. 21.

and Market Courts have been established in Sweden and other Scandanavian countries.[9]

Sweden has not permitted companies to use claims ("She lost 90 kilos through the KP method") unless it can be shown that the use of the advertised product or service actually had the effect depicted. Swedish law provides for a "reverse burden of proof" in that the seller must justify marketing practices to prove that the advertising is not misleading.[10]

Products such as cigarettes and alcoholic beverages frequently are subject to special advertising restrictions, causing firms to seek other methods of promotion. In Britain television and radio advertising for cigarettes was banned in 1964. As a result some companies switched to Radio Luxembourg to beam cigarette advertising to Britain; others advertised in publications with a high readership among the young or sponsored sports events.[11] Such activities, while legal, led to increased pressure for self-regulation by the industry and for increased governmental control.

The challenges to advertising and promotion are not limited to these few examples. In the United States consumer and legal pressures mount for the control of promotional activities and in Japan, the second largest advertising nation, the Administrative Study Council has said that "advertising that exceeds the limits of necessity causes consumers to lose a sense of proportion in making reasonable product selections."[12] In a recent study European executives expressed a strong belief in the power of advertising as a tool of marketing, but expressed concern over advertising's effect on social values. The executives indicated some doubt regarding the efficiency of self-regulation, but tended to think advertising should be somehow regulated.[13] These criticisms reflect the complex environment within which promotional programs must be planned. The criticisms are most prominent in affluent countries where advertising is a popular marketing tool.

Advertising has been taxed on the basis of total advertising expenditures by a firm (India), at varying rates for the use of specific media (Austria), and upon the importation of advertising materials (Australia). Both in the United States and abroad restrictions have been placed on specific promotional techniques and messages (e.g., use of premiums and samples, and labelling requirements). Media restrictions occur in many countries. Radio is not available for advertising in Sweden, Norway, Switzerland, or Denmark and TV does not carry advertising in Sweden, India, South Africa, or Denmark.

---

[9]"Sweden: The Consumer Ombudsman," *E.F.T.A. Bulletin* (March, 1975), p. 16.

[10]*Ibid.*

[11]"Britain's No-Nonsense Attack on Cigarette Ads," *Business Week* (October 27, 1975), p. 72.

[12]International Advertising Association, "The Global Challenge to Advertising," *Journal of Advertising* (Winter, 1974), p. 23.

[13]Dick Christian, "European Views of Advertising," *Journal of Advertising* (Fall, 1974), p. 23–25.

Clearly, promotional policy is under scrutiny in many nations and the marketing manager does not have free rein in the development of his promotional program. Increasingly, the manager has to evaluate not only the constraints placed by the market, but governmental constraints and the consumer movement. It may not be desirable or possible to use copy, media, and techniques that are successful in domestic programs or that have been successful in the past. The successful promotional mix at home may need modification in overseas markets.

World Advertising Expenditures

Advertising is an important means of promotion, as demonstrated by the expenditures of advertisers around the world. The International Advertising Association and Starch INRA Hooper have provided estimates of expenditures for eighty-six countries of the free world in 1974.[14] These estimates indicate that a total of $49 billion was spent on advertising in the various media, 23% increase over 1972. Of the 1974 total expenditure, the United States alone accounted for $26.8 billion or about 55% of the total. The next largest expenditure was in Japan with $4.2 billion, followed by West Germany ($2.5 billion), the United Kingdom ($2.2 billion), France ($2 billion) and Canada ($1.7 billion). Together this group of industrial nations accounted for 80% of the 1974 total for the eighty-six countries covered by the study. Per capita expenditures in the IAA study varied from a high of $126.00 for the United States to a low of 3 cents for Ethiopia.[15]

Organization for International Advertising

The organization of international advertising is best understood as comprised of two parts: (1) the internal organization or the firm's own advertising department and (2) the external organization or the advertising agency structure.

The Internal Organization Structure. In a "built-in" export department, the domestic advertising department is responsible for international advertising as well.[16] However, when the firm establishes a separate international division, the division head or vice-president often is responsible for all foreign operations, including advertising. The international advertising manager reports to an international marketing director and is responsible for corporate advertising, product advertising, sales promotion, house publications, public relations, and

---

[14]"World Ad Total for '74 at $49 Billion," *Advertising Age* (November 29, 1976), p. 74.
[15]*ibid.*
[16]See Chapter 9.

research.[17] If a worldwide product structure is used, the corporate advertising department activities must be coordinated with the various product staffs. Often when the overseas subsidiaries are large and operate in the highly developed economies of Western Europe they have their own advertising departments and function quite autonomously within the limits of corporate policy.

The size of the advertising department is influenced by the degree to which it relies on the advertising agency for services. When the international advertising department functions through an advertising agency the department is responsible for:

1. Working with other marketing executives to establish and coordinate marketing and sales objectives, including budgets.
2. Determination of advertising strategy.
3. Evaluation of agency presentations and performance.
4. Administering departmental budgets.
5. Selling the program to company executives and related departments as well as customers.
6. Performing media functions that the agency may not be prepared to handle such as catalogs, booklets, direct mail, and displays.[18]

The international advertising department that relies heavily on agencies often is small; however, some firms prefer to rely more on a fully staffed internal organization to prepare finished or semi-finished advertisements to be placed in foreign media and used by subsidiaries. These fully staffed organizations are most likely found serving homogeneous markets through wholly-owned subsidiaries and often are found in companies with products that rely on print media for advertising.[19] As agencies throughout the world improve their production, creative, and research facilities we may expect some decline in the fully staffed department.

Control of Advertising Policy. An important policy matter to be determined is the extent to which control over advertising will be vested in representatives abroad — either distributors or subsidiaries — or centralized at headquarters. This issue is of prime importance when advertising is a significant component of the marketing plan and when companies rely on the establishment of a worldwide image for quality and service.

One policy of decentralization is followed by exporters when they give an advertising allowance to the foreign representatives in addition to any discount or margin on sales. This policy provides financial

---

[17]S. Watson Dunn, "Advertising for Multinational Markets," *Handbook of Modern Marketing*, edited by Victor P. Buell (New York: McGraw-Hill Book Company, 1970), pp. 20–52.

[18]See International Advertising Association, "Standards and Practices," *Code of Standards of Advertising Practice* (New York, 1961), pp. 20–21.

[19]Gordon E. Miracle and Gerald S. Albaum, *International Marketing Management* (Homewood, Ill.: Richard D. Irwin, Inc., 1970), pp. 502–503.

assistance to encourage local advertising. Usually representatives are expected to match the allowance with their own funds, the policy is then called cooperative advertising. The theory behind this policy is that a native representative (in Sao Paulo, for example) knows more about Brazilian advertising than an American exporter. It probably is true that the local representative is more familiar with the local scene, but the premise may be false if the local representative has little knowledge of advertising and little faith in its efficacy. In such instances the allowance becomes merely an additional discount.

The question of control over international advertising resolves itself, first, into determining the degree to which companies desire to centralize or decentralize advertising rather than assume a polar position. A second issue is the decision of which functions should be decentralized. For example, budget planning may be more centralized than the advertising agency or media selection.[20]

The proponents of strong centralization generally state that "only headquarters from its vast overall view of dealing with the history of diversified products, many countries, and markets can plan the longer term strategy and corporate advertising."[21] Although the general concept is sound, the problem really is how to centralize control to achieve corporate goals yet maintain the flexibility needed for local adaptation.

Those who favor decentralization believe that corporate headquarters can still effectively control policy while achieving substantial local adaptation. They believe that:

1. The local representative best understands the language, people, customs, and other market characteristics.
2. Today many subsidiary managers and local representatives are well qualified in advertising strategy and technique. They are quite capable of administering an advertising program within broad corporate constraints.
3. Budgets and advertising allowances can be controlled by the headquarters.
4. Cooperation has the merit of utilizing the specific knowledge of both parties; foreign advertising personnel can gain a sense of participation.
5. Media selection is not a difficult problem for local advertising, but the parent headquarters of the international firm can still retain control over regional or international advertising. Local and regional campaigns can be coordinated by means of a well-developed marketing plan. Corporate image advertising can be a part of that plan. Local and regional schedules and programs can be integrated and coordinated through headquarters in the multinational firm.

---

[20]See John K. Ryans, Jr., and Claudia Fry, "Decentralization of Promotional and Other Marketing Decision-Making — The German Experience" (Paper presented at the Academy of International Business Annual Meeting, December 28, 1974) for a comparison of U.S. and German firms.

[21]Harry E. Maynard, cited in *Export Trade* (January 30, 1961), p. 28.

In essence, the problem is one of assuring that the firms long-run advertising goals and objectives are met without stifling initiative that might generate more effective advertising programs. Harold F. Clark, Jr., of the J. Walter Thompson agency has attempted to refocus attention on the problem by stating that "we have come to a point today where most successful international marketing does not use centralization as its rationale but rather *leadership from the center*."[22] The issue is not one of imposing plans through central authority; it is instead one of the central office providing the skills and leadership that lead to cooperation from the subsidiaries using the strengths of each group.

Advertising Agencies. The advertising agency is an integral part of the structure for planning, producing, and implementing the firm's advertising program. It is considered here as an external organization, but one very closely allied to the firm. The agency is important because a significant proportion of the total amount of international advertising is developed and placed by advertising agencies. Some of these are local while others are branches of international or multinational agencies. Agencies exist in both the modern economies and in the lesser developed areas. The functions they perform, and the character of their operations, however, may differ.

Agency Functions. In the United States, Canada, and some European countries the functions performed by an advertising agency would include:

1. Close collaboration with the advertiser to study the product and its markets and distribution.
2. Conducting research involving copy testing, media, and competitive advertising in order to provide a solid foundation upon which the advertising plan can be created; and to provide a basis for evaluating the effectiveness of the plan as implemented.
3. Designing the advertising campaign, including the allocation of expenditures within the agreed appropriation; and helping to coordinate the campaign with other sales promotion and publicity activities.
4. Supervising and implementing the advertising campaign.[23]

In the United States the close relationship between agency and advertiser usually means that an agency will handle the account of only one company in an industry, thus avoiding competitive accounts and potential conflicts of interest. In Japan and some other countries, however, agencies may handle competing accounts; therefore many companies believe it is not good practice to leave the design and the

---

[22]Harold F. Clark, Jr., "Successful International Marketing Depends on Centralized Leadership," *Industrial Marketing*, (March, 1975), p. 54. [Italics added.]

[23]International Advertising Association, "Standards and Practices," *Code of Standards of Advertising Practice* (New York, 1961), p. 25.

implementation of the advertising plan in the hands of these agencies.[24] In Japan the advertiser must coordinate both in-channel (trade) and mass media promotions. Agencies in countries with limited potential may also service competing accounts. One agency in Taiwan, for example, handles appliance advertising for Sony, Sharp, General Electric, and Zenith. The agency attempts to minimize conflicts of interest by dividing its creative personnel into separate groups for each account, thereby reducing contact with competitors' campaigns.[25]

Criteria for Agency Selection. A careful evaluation of the agency is needed because both advertiser and agency hope for a long-term relationship. Furthermore, the decision to establish the advertiser-agency relationship is predicated on the ability of the agency to meet the advertiser's specific needs.

The process for choosing an agency to produce effective international advertising is similar to that of evaluating a domestic agency although some special considerations must be made.[26] The advertiser should evaluate the familiarity of the agency with the international firm's products as they are purchased and used in the country. If multinational campaigns are planned, the agency should have experience in producing and placing multilingual ads. The agency should be familiar with international publishers to supplement the occasionally meager information available on circulation of the media. It also is useful when the agency has the public relations force to coordinate the advertising and publicity. One international advertising authority has suggested additional criteria for agency selection based on:[27]

1. Quality and number of agency offices.
2. Quality of creative and media service.
3. Quality of supplementary services such as research, merchandising, etc.
4. Independence of various branches from media or suppliers.
5. Experience in the firm's product line.
6. Financial stability.
7. Ability of the agency to expand with the firm in various markets.

Donnelly and Ryans found that U.S. international advertising managers of consumer nondurable goods placed a large preponderance of their advertising through agencies. Forty-two percent of those queried said they used U.S.-based agencies with overseas branches and 38% used local agencies. The others placed ads directly with the media or used a U.S. agency without branches. Firms doing the bulk of their business in less developed countries were more likely

---

[24]*Sales Promotion in the Japanese Market* (Tokyo: Japan External Trade Organization, undated), p. 25.

[25]Personal interview with Frank Hung, Chinese advertising executive.

[26]John Moxness, "For International Ads, Pick an Experienced Agency — It's Not the Same Game As in U.S.," *Industrial Marketing* (December, 1973), pp. 68–69.

[27]Dunn, *op. cit.*, pp. 20–56.

to use U.S.-based agencies and to have major decisions for global advertising made at the home office. However, where management feels cultural and other market differences are important, companies are apt to use foreign-based agencies.[28]

Types of Agencies. The growth of multinational companies has been paralleled by growth of the international advertising function. The international marketer now has a choice among three types of agencies:

1. The international or multinational advertising agency with offices in major market areas.
2. Local agencies serving their local markets or serving international markets through advertising networks in which the agencies retain their independence but share certain international accounts.
3. House agencies.

The Multinational Agency. The multinational advertising agency has grown rapidly but American agencies such as J. Walter Thompson and McCann expanded into the European market before World War II. Following that war other agencies such as Young and Rubican and Doyle Dane Bernbach entered the European market as their American accounts expanded abroad. These agencies began also to seek local clients. A third wave of expansion occurred when American agencies purchased existing European agencies or even bought whole European networks.[29] As a result of these actions American agencies dominate several European markets holding 64% of the billings of the twenty top agencies in Germany and 72% in Britain.[30]

By 1974 American agencies had offices in fifty-seven countries and non-U.S. billings of $3.1 billion.[31] Among the motivations for this expansion were a desire to serve current clients who were moving into international markets and a desire to take advantage of a market with a large and growing potential. Initial interest by a senior executive was especially important in the overseas expansion of American agencies.[32] The desire of American agencies to expand in order to serve U.S. clients in the overseas market was most important for entry into Europe and other highly developed markets, but client service also has been a factor in the expansion of European agencies beyond their traditional national borders.[33]

---

[28]James Donnelly and John K. Ryans, Jr., "Agency Selections in International Advertising," *European Journal of Marketing* (1972), pp. 211–215.

[29]Michel Chevalier and Jean-Michel Foloit, "Which International Strategy for Advertising Agencies?" *European Business* (Summer, 1974), pp. 26–34.

[30]*Advertising Age* data reported in Chevalier and Foliot, p. 28.

[31]Arnold K. Weinstein, "The International Expansion of U.S. Multinational Advertising Agencies," *Business Topics* (Summer, 1974), p. 29.

[32]*Ibid.*, p. 31.

[33]"Europe's Admen Go Multinational," *Business Week* (May 26, 1973), p. 52.

American agencies dominate any list of the world's largest agencies in terms of billings; however, the world's largest advertising agency is Dentsu of Japan which reported $945.8 million of billings in 1975. The largest U.S. agency was J. Walter Thompson with billings of $900.1 million. The Interpublic Group of Companies, however, billed $1.1 billion in 1975.[34]

For the advertiser interested in promoting international markets through the services of an agency, the multinational agency claims several advantages over local agencies:

1. The size and resources of the multinational agency enable it to develop a full set of services including research, public relations, translation, and consulting on marketing problems in the areas served.
2. Branch offices are able to serve the local companies of multinational clients with budgets spread in numerous territories.
3. Branches often are located in the major advertising centers and cover major market areas.[35]
4. The agency has a broad base of experience and personnel available in its branches. The training of personnel and easier exchange of people among countries is a valuable asset of the multinational agency in contrast to the local agency.[36]
5. Worldwide campaigns and product introductions can be coordinated by headquarters in consultation with branches and backed by headquarters specialized services.
6. Some cost savings may be achieved by avoiding duplication of creative and production services. Also, communication may be facilitated.
7. The quality of creative and production services may exceed local alternatives in some markets.

These advantages are important but are not always present since the individual offices of the multinational agency differ markedly in creative talent, management concepts and reporting methods, and managerial capability. They sometimes lack the flexibility of the local agency in adapting to local requirements.[37] The advantages of the multinational agency have, however, been sufficient to continually add to its recent growth.

The Local Agency. The local agency has persisted and frequently prospered despite the development of the multinational agency. Not

---

[34]"Profiles of Agencies Around the World: Billings and Income," *Advertising Age* (March 29, 1976), p. 27. An annual issue of *Advertising Age* profiles the major agencies in each country providing data on total billings, income, media breakdown, and major changes.

[35]James O'Connor, "International Advertising," *Journal of Advertising* (Spring, 1974), p. 13.

[36]George Theophilopoulos, "Some Thoughts on Multinational Agencies," *Journal of Advertising* (Spring, 1974), p. 17.

[37]*Ibid.*

only does the local agency serve its local customers, but a given local agency may be the best agency within a market; the combination of creative talent and entrepreneurial incentives found in local agencies provides a powerful impetus toward superior performance. Creative personnel stifled by the managerial controls of larger international organizations may find their niche in the more free-wheeling atmosphere of the smaller organization. The less bureaucratic nature of the local agency enables it to react quickly to local competitive conditions.[38] These advantages, however, apply only to the better local agencies since some are dependent on specific media and lack familiarity with international advertising concepts. The superior local agencies pay the price for these deficiencies when they seek international clients.

To strengthen their position with international advertisers some local agencies have joined others in different national markets to form an agency network to service international clients. The network consists of independent local agencies who recognize the difficulty of serving international clients when they cannot provide multinational services. The network may be based on a cooperation agreement in which the agencies agree to share some international accounts. For example Huit, a French manufacturer, was interested in expanding into Germany. The French agency Moors et Warot selected a German, a British, and a Spanish agency to form a network to serve these markets.[39] The prime difficulty with such an alliance, however, is its temporary nature. While the network system provides advertisers with a unified group having the incentives of local management and ownership, it is essentially an unstable or temporary arrangement that has been subject to raiding by multinational agencies. A further problem lies in the difficulty of securing forceful leaders with long-run interest in the development of the network.

House Agencies. House agencies have been established by some large international firms primarily to handle their own advertising in domestic and foreign markets. These agencies provide the close coordination of a firm's promotional plan based upon intimate knowledge of the firm's products, personnel, and objectives. The large house agency can afford the hiring of capable creative production and management personnel. Potentially, at least, the house agency suffers certain disadvantages in that it can develop a protective attitude toward current advertising concepts and procedures. It may also suffer from a lack of exposure to alternative policies and procedures to which the independent agency is exposed. The house agency is not practical for many firms because of the efficiencies and creative skills offered by the multinational and local agencies.[40]

---

[38]*Ibid.*

[39]Chevalier and Foliot, *op. cit.*, p. 29.

[40]See Stuart Henderson Britt, James P. Donahoe, and Joseph E. Foley, "In-House Industrial Advertising or Outside Agency?" *Journal of Advertising* (Spring, 1972), pp. 6–8.

MEDIA SELECTION

To accomplish its persuasive purpose an advertising message must reach its intended audience. The vehicle for contacting audiences is the advertising medium. A particularly perplexing problem for the international advertiser is that of selecting the appropriate media, or more commonly, the most effective combination of media to carry out the promotional objectives. The problem is especially difficult when the company has a wide product line with unrelated product groups sold to different industrial or to consumer market segments in several countries. The problem is compounded if a lack of planning results in diffuse promotional objectives, or when specific objectives are foregone and only general goals such as "increased sales" are substituted. These are problems common to all advertisers but they may be worse for the international firms because of the knowledge they may lack regarding the market segments overseas.

In addition to these general selection problems, the international manager faces some special difficulties. The international media selection problem is magnified by these major factors:

1. A wide variety of both print and broadcast media may be available in each country. Some market segments can be reached by multinational media that have audiences in several countries. Canada has, for example, 430 radio stations, 84 television stations, 113 daily newspapers, some 200 consumer magazines, and about 500 business publications. An estimated 4.5 million copies of American publications are sold in Canada each month. In addition, almost half of the Canadian population has access to U.S. television.[41]
2. Despite the large number of alternatives, the advertiser may find that media used at home may not be available for advertising in specific markets abroad. Effective TV or radio advertising may not be possible because the government does not permit commercial use of the media. Print space and broadcast time for advertising may be limited and sales promotional techniques may be forbidden.
3. The characteristics of the media may differ from country to country in terms of their coverage, cost, quality of reproduction, political or religious alliances, etc.
4. Reliable information regarding the media may be difficult to obtain. Audited circulation data, costs, audience profiles regarding the demographics and purchasing power of readers or viewers, etc. are less available abroad than in the U.S. However, services comparable to Standard Rate and Data are available in England, France, Italy, Mexico, and West Germany.[42]

[41]"Two-Thirds of Canada is in 10 Markets," *Media Decisions* (April, 1975), pp. 128–130.

[42]James C. Baker and John K. Ryans, Jr., *Multinational Marketing: Dimensions in Strategy* (Columbus, Oh.: Grid, Inc., 1975) p. 237.

5. In some markets media rates may be negotiable so cost is difficult to predict.
6. Subjective evaluations of media are difficult. A Britisher may view TV or cinema differently than an American. The British tend to see the TV as a visual medium while the TV to an American is a visual accompaniment to words. The American views the scene but the Britisher participates in it.[43] Furthermore, advertisers need to know the image people have a specific medium and for what types of advertising it is most accepted.[44]
7. A lack of uniformity of column width and page size in the print media can increase the production expenses of an international campaign.
8. Relatively few truly multinational media exist. Most are designed for more restricted national markets or specific segments. Broadcast media such as Radio Luxembourg reach close-by markets and a few print media such as *Readers Digest, Vision, Nouveau Paris Match*, or the *International Herald-Tribune* serve multinational areas and may be important for company-wide image advertising.

Western Europe well illustrates the complexity involved in establishing an effective media program for marketers abroad. There are fourteen countries and at least ten languages. Both print and broadcast media are available but some countries do not have TV or radio; yet Belgium with no commercial TV can be reached through two Dutch, three French, three German, two English, and one Luxembourg channel.[45] In Germany, Switzerland, and France TV space is so limited the space sellers don't call on clients. Radio-France is a government broadcasting monopoly but five private stations in the Saar, Luxembourg, Monoco, and Andorra provide uneven coverage of France. The French government holds ownership shares in some of these stations.[46] Big international publications such as *Time, Readers Digest*, and *Newsweek* have substantial European circulation. In Italy TV commercials are grouped at 8:30 p.m. after the news and before the main show. Advertisers are limited in the TV time they can purchase to 100 seconds per week, and TV advertisers must agree to purchase a certain amount of magazine space.[47]

A wide variety of outdoor media are available in Europe — billboards, electric signs, bus shelters, car cards, parking lots, as well as highway signs. Cinema advertising plays a more significant role in France than in the U.S. Thirty-second to one-minute commercials are shown during intermissions to audiences, covering weekly about 7% of the total population, 17% of high executives, and 13% in the Paris area.[48]

---

[43]Stephen J. F. Unwin, "How Culture Affects Advertising Expansion and Communication Style," *Journal of Advertising* (Spring, 1974) pp. 25, 26.
[44]S. Watson Dunn, "Advertising for Multinational Markets," *op. cit.*, p. 20–59.
[45]"Media's Uncommon Common Market," *Media Decisions* (March, 1976), p. 138.
[46]"The French Connection," *Media Decisions* (March, 1976), p. 134.
[47]"How Media Is Bought in Italy," *Media Decisions* (October, 1974), p. 162.
[48]"The French Connection," *op. cit.*, p. 136.

The Coca-Cola Company

The diversity and complexity of the media choices often leads to decentralized media buying for national and local product campaigns even when headquarters retains authority to place worldwide image promotions in international media. Regardless of who purchases the media space, the buyer is interested in achieving a media schedule that provides market coverage at low cost. The media schedule itself refers both to the specific media selected and to the frequency of insertion. Again, the problem is especially difficult because of the lack of market data, media profiles, and media space or time limitations.

THE ADVERTISING MESSAGE

The effectiveness of advertising is dependent not only on the amount spent and the media chosen, but as importantly by what is said and how that message is presented. In this section we discuss two of the major issues affecting multinational advertisers.

The Research Base

Message development begins with a clear definition of the company's target markets. Each market needs analysis of the individual market segments on which the firm intends to concentrate. These segments must be identified and studied to determine usage patterns and salient attitudes toward the product, buying motives, sources from which the product is purchased, and sources the potential buyer uses to gather relevant information. Such research provides basic data for developing the theme that is to be communicated. It also clarifies any differences that may exist among the market segments or between this national market and others where the firm has experience. Differences and similarities among the markets provide a basis for determining whether a standard approach can be used or whether the advertising message must be modified for each segment. Based on knowledge of buying motives and attitudes, the advertiser can distinguish a number of possible images and messages to meet the firm's communication objectives. Various graphic and verbal symbolic alternatives can then be combined to form the final presentation.

To reach these objectives communication research should build on the economic and cultural research suggested in Chapters 6 and 7. Several specific questions may be useful to focus attention on the communication strategy.

1. What basic function or need does the product meet? This should be carefully investigated from the consumer's perspective to overcome cultural bias.
2. How is this need currently being satisfied? Consider not only directly competitive products but also alternative consumption systems. The automatic clothes washer competes with other automatic machines, wringer washers, and hand labor.
3. What are the strengths and weaknesses of the present system and how does our product or service show a relative advantage to the consumer?
4. Do different market segments have separate motivations requiring a different message (price vs. quality, status, etc.)?
5. Who influences the purchase decision? How is the decision made and what is the required information input?
6. How widely diffused is acceptance of the product? Are we dealing with a completely new product appealing to innovators and early adopters or is the product widely accepted? Are competitive models available?
7. What is the message strategy of competitors?
8. What languages must be used for effective communication? Are several dialects or languages needed for coverage of the target markets?
9. What vehicles (media) are available for presentation? Are these effective in reaching the desired segments? Can they effectively carry the graphics and verbal symbols to be used?

The reader can easily add to this list a number of questions specific to a given product or industry. The intent of the research is to ferret out the relevant communication requirements of the potential buyer to satisfy the informational input needed for the buying decision. The seller needs to know how the buyer views the product, who influences the decision, and what information is used in the decision process. For the international marketer cultural diversity creates a special hazard because each market varies from the others, yet communications may overlap.

Advertising Transferability

A major strategy question for the international advertiser is whether a given message for communication strategy can be employed in more than one market. That is, can a standardized message effectively reach multinational markets or must the message be altered for each segment? Studies of transferability are somewhat ambiguous in their results because of the variety of product and environmental conditions extant in the market.[49] The studies do, however, provide some guidance when the marketer knows the conditions faced by the company's product.

Standardized approaches have received considerable attention in recent years due to the growth of the European Economic Community and other multinational markets. This growth cultivated a view that a more homogeneous consumer might evolve. If the "European" consumer showed a willingness to accept the products of countries within the community and if that consumer was motivated similarly to those in other countries, a common promotional approach would be practical; but if national identities prevailed, separate campaigns would be more likely to succeed. Testing this approach, multinational firms have experimented with varying degrees of standardization within the E.E.C. Sometimes headquarters controlled the content of the advertisement and at other times provided prototypes which the local subsidiary adapted to its specific needs.

In a study of U.S. food, soft drink, detergent, and cosmetic companies with European connections, Wiechmann found the standardization of advertising to range from very high to very low, but three fourths of the executives felt the basic message was highly standardized.[50] From the differences among companies Wiechmann concluded that a high level of headquarter's direction and standardization of marketing programs were effective for firms whose products are culture-free; however, companies with culture-bound products needed to custom tailor their marketing program.[51] A Marketing Science Institute Study of American Marketing in the E.E.C. indicated that in 1973 sixty percent of consumer nondurables manufacturers still maintained substantial advertising adaptation to national markets, but the trend

---

[49]See S. Watson Dunn, "Effect of National Identity on Multinational Promotional Strategy in Europe," *Journal of Marketing* (October, 1976), pp. 50–57, for a review of landmark studies.

[50]Ulrich E. Wiechmann, *Marketing Management in Multinational Firms* (New York: Praeger Publishers, Inc., 1976), p. 81.

[51]*Ibid.*, p. 93.

toward standardization was more pronounced among consumer durables and industrial goods manufacturers. Increases in the degree of standardization were expected in the future for all three categories.[52]

On the other hand, Dunn found that the proportion of companies using basically the same advertisements abroad as at home was less in 1973 than in 1964.[53] He associated this trend with an increased emphasis on national identity and a search for symbols to reflect that identity.

In general it appears that successful standardization is dependent on a similarity of the motivations for purchase and a similarity of use conditions. For culture-free products such as industrial goods and some consumer durables the purchase motivations are similar enough to permit high degrees of standardization. Culture-bound products, in contrast, require adaptation. Customs, habits, and tastes vary for these products and customer reaction depends on receiving information consonant with these factors.

The increased sophistication of European advertising and variations in consumer protection regulations act as a further deterrent to standardization of advertising messages. What is legal in one country may not be in another. Language is a further barrier to transferability both because media use the local language and because of the problems of literal translation — Pepsi's "Come alive" doesn't have the same appeal when translated to "Come from the dead."

Standardization can be effective, however, when these tastes are similar across national markets as in the marketing of jeans to the teenage and young adult markets in Europe. Some degree of standardization may be possible for many products. Corporate headquarters can establish a global or regional campaign to portray a common image where services such as airlines are international. Further, advertising does not need to be identical in appearance and context in all markets but may only need a strong sense of familiarity. Similar-looking campaigns may be used in international media and a second level of attack aimed at local mass markets. The latter type of advertising looks familiar to visitors but appears local and speaks the local language. Its familiarity derives from visual elements — the Marlboro cowboy, the familiar bottle of Coke.[54] Truly international campaigns require similarity in market conditions, consumer attitudes, and product benefits but good applicable *ideas* can and do cross borders as they are adapted to local markets.[55] Care must be taken, however, to be

[52]Dagfinn Moe Hansen and J. J. Boddewyn, *American Marketing in the European Common Market, 1963–1973*, Report No. 76–107, Marketing Science Institute Working Paper (Cambridge: Marketing Science Institute, 1976), pp. 45–51.

[53]Dunn, *op. cit.*, p. 54.

[54]A. Graeme Cranch, "The Changing Faces of International Advertising," *The International Advertiser*, Vol. 13, No. 2 (1972), pp. 4–6.

[55]Rein Rykens, "International Campaigns — A Fallacy?" *The International Advertiser*, Vol. 13, No. 2 (1973), p. 9.

sure that the graphic and verbal symbols used to represent these ideas have the same meaning to all potential receivers. Concepts and illustrations that have definite meaning for an advertiser may not have the same meaning for potential buyers. A simple example may illustrate differences in communication that result when seller and buyer do not share a common frame of reference. A British-made bicycle was to be introduced in Nigeria where the seller wanted a symbol to portray the strength and endurance of the cycle. Posters were prepared showing a picture of an elephant riding the bicycle, but the campaign failed despite the "obvious" strength. Research *following* the failure produced the comment, "We have never seen an elephant riding a bicycle."[56] The advertiser did not expect that elephants would ride. The symbol simply failed to convey its intended meaning of strength. The illustration is further evidence of a need to test advertising messages for their meaning and transferability *before* launching a campaign.

SALES PROMOTION

Sales promotion, deals, and point-of-purchase displays are commonly used here and abroad to accomplish specific communication objectives. Normally, they are supplements to mass communication (advertising) and personal selling and, as such, need to be carefully integrated into the total communications program.[57] Usually sales promotion devices are viewed as short-term inducements and are designed to accomplish limited objectives such as securing display space, gaining trial of the product, introducing the product concept, or promoting immediate sale.

A wide variety of sales promotion devices are used internationally to provide immediate sales stimuli or to increase buying action by consumers. Samples, coupons, cents-off deals, point-of-purchase displays, and consumer and sales contests are illustrative. The short-term nature of sales promotion devices emphasizes the need for careful delineation of objectives before selecting an appropriate promotion. The devices may be used for the same purposes as in the U.S. and often in a similar manner, but local adaptation can increase effectiveness; in Japan the limited space leads some supermarkets to charge for displaying point-of-purchase material. The United Africa Company employed an "OMO man" to go from village to village passing out samples of Omo detergent. Each sample box top, in turn, could be used to obtain ten more samples at the local Unilever store. Thus the consumer was introduced to the product and store. Also the promotion

---

[56]A. Graeme Cranch quoted in Eliyaha Tal, "Advertising in Developing Countries," *Journal of Advertising* (Spring, 1974), p. 21.

[57]See Frederick E. Webster, Jr., *Marketing Communication* (New York: The Ronald Press Company, 1971), pp. 555–580.

was supported by radio ads suggesting the Omo man had supernatural powers to strengthen the appeal.[58] Royal Crown Cola stressed premiums to support a low advertising budget in Southeast Asia and Latin America. One approach was a bottle cap promotion where winning caps were redeemed for prizes ranging from another bottle of RC to a basketball uniform.[59] Calzados Plasticos de Mexico dropped paper parachutes weighted by three marbles in rural areas to induce purchase of its plastic shoes. The chutes contained certificates offering one free pair of shoes for every pair purchased.[60] In Eastern Europe many Western firms have organized symposia to reach potential end users who are excluded from normal contract negotiations.

The *Consorcio*, or buying club, illustrates a technique used in Brazil by the Ford Motor Company to combat the high inflation rate and the reluctance of banks to finance consumer purchases which limit the purchase of big ticket items by persons with low incomes. Members of the clubs make monthly payments pegged to the price of the car and divided by the number of members. Each member makes the full set of payments for 60 months, but a drawing is held each month for car delivery. The person whose name is drawn receives the car immediately. In this manner the consumer receives the car for current use and avoids interest payments and the company gains by having a guaranteed number of customers. In 1976 Ford expected to sell 36,000 cars by this method.[61]

Japanese producers rely on in-channel promotions to motivate wholesalers and retailers to support their consumer programs. They offer tickets to Japanese drama and trips to resorts or to foreign countries as prizes. In-store demonstrations also are popular. These devices help gain widespread distribution including small neighborhood stores.

Another important sales promotion for international marketers is the international trade fair or exposition. These organized trade fairs provide an opportunity to evaluate the market potential for a product, to line up potential distributors, to contact end users and technicians, and to promote the product. They are especially useful for the introduction of new products. Trade fairs have a long important history in Europe and represent opportunities for both selling and buying. Some fairs exhibit the products of many industries, but German trade fairs are trending toward specialized vertical fairs (toys, shoes, leather goods). Exhibitions at German fairs are even a precondition for obtaining import quota allocations for certain restricted products. The

---

[58]"Big Daddy Stays and Grows," *Time* (June 24, 1966), p. 90.

[59]"Royal Crown's Strategy Hinges on Flexibility," *Business International* (May 18, 1973), pp. 156–157.

[60]"Calzados Sells Shoes to Unshod — Via Parachute," *Advertising Age* (December 28, 1965), p. 12.

[61]This description is based on "How Brazilians Beat the Credit Squeeze," *Business Week* (November 1, 1976), p. 50.

trade fair in Canton, China (open only by invitation) is a major contact for Westerners selling to Mainland China or seeking Chinese goods.

The U.S. Department of Commerce has stimulated U.S. firms to take a more active role in these fairs since the fair is a major selling tool for the development of foreign markets at low cost. Exhibitors are provided with several incentives for participation, including reduced transportation rates, storage and display facilities, translation and stenographic services and special import procedures.[62]

The effectiveness of sales promotion devices in foreign markets is attested by their widespread use despite legal and cultural constraints. In many countries laws have been established to regulate sales promotion by limiting use of the term "free," and limiting the size and value of premiums and samples. In 1971 the Japanese Fair Trade Commission reduced the value of prizes when an apparel manufacturer offered an airplane as a quiz prize.[63] Belgium strictly regulates clearance sales and forbids premiums, but numerous exceptions are permitted such as including complementary products in a single price package or combining the principal product with accessories, samples, or even contest tickets.[64] In West Germany the Promotional Gifts Ordinance (Zugabeverordnung) prohibits give-aways except calendars and other advertising materials of minor value, marked with the company's name.[65] These and a variety of national laws make careful checking necessary before embarking on a multinational campaign.

In addition, marketers meet some resistance from wholesalers and retailers whose cooperation often is needed for the promotional device's success. Where premiums, samples, or cents-off labels are involved the traditional wholesaler or retailer may regard the promotion as a price reduction. The laws of some nations reflect this attitude as the premium constraints are part of the rules for competition or are in support of consumer protection movements.

PERSONAL SELLING

Of all the promotional methods none is more prevalent than personal selling. The ubiquitous salesperson is found at all levels of economic development performing a variety of services from peddling the products of the farm or handicraft operation to the technical sales presentations of computers and airplanes. Personal selling is conducted in streets, bazaars, wholesale and retail establishments, and offices of industrial or governmental buyers. The size of the sale varies from a few

---

[62]See Chapter 18.

[63]*Sales Promotion in Japan*, JETRO Marketing Series 7 (undated), p. 30.

[64]*Common Market Reporter* (Chicago: Commerce Clearing House, Inc., January 17, 1974), Section 21, p. 504.

[65]"Marketing in the Federal Republic of Germany and West Berlin," *Overseas Business Report*, OBR 75-52 (November, 1975), pp. 37, 38.

pennies to millions of dollars. The information and advice of the seller become important inputs in the buyer's decision-making process; yet, despite their value, salespeople often occupy a low status in society — perhaps as an extension of the bazaar-type selling, sharp practices, or a lack of appreciation regarding their function. Carson warns that, "Notwithstanding the development of more sophisticated marketing methods and techniques, personal selling remains the most important segment of marketing in all parts of the globe."[66] Self-service vending machines and catalog selling attempt to make selling less personal, but for many products personal selling is a key element in the marketing mix. Only through the face-to-face contacts of personal selling can adjustments be made to tailor products and services to the requirements of individual buyers. The effective salesperson is aware of a customer's problems and knows how to be of help.[67]

Sales Functions in International Marketing

For many exporters and subsidiary operations the primary selling function is performed by the company's independent distributors located within the foreign market. This distributor's sales force may represent the only personal contact between the company and its retailers or industrial customers. The distributor has primary responsibility for the recruitment, development, and supervision of the sales representatives. In this situation the exporter may have little control over the sales force's activities except to provide technical and sales training for distributor personnel, employ incentives for conformance to a marketing plan, or supplement the distributor's activities with a missionary sales program.

The mission of the international firm's own sales force differs among companies and industries but essentially consists of generating sales, collecting customer information, and providing customer service.[68] To perform these activities the sales representatives complement the firm's advertising and sales promotion by locating customers, making sales presentations, gathering competitive information and data on customer reaction to the product, expediting delivery, evaluating credit, and providing marketing assistance to resellers.[69]

Four types of sales missions may be distinguished in the producers' sales organization. One is *creative selling*. These sales representatives

---

[66]David Carson, *International Marketing: A Comparative Systems Approach* (New York: John Wiley & Sons, Inc., 1967), p. 398.

[67]Philip Kotler, *Marketing Management: Analysis, Planning and Control* (Englewood Cliffs, N.J.: Prentice-Hall, Inc., 1976), p. 375.

[68]Kenneth R. Davis and Frederick E. Webster, Jr., *Sales Force Management* (New York: The Ronald Press Company, 1968), p. 44.

[69]David W. Cravens, Gerald E. Hills, and Robert B. Woodruff, *Marketing Decision Making: Concepts and Strategy* (Homewood, Ill.: Richard D. Irwin, Inc., 1976), pp. 670–673.

are responsible for locating distributors to make product presentations and to secure continuing sales. They actively seek orders and sell the company's marketing program to foreign customers. They participate in the development of local advertising and sales promotion and instruct the distributors' salespeople in the merchandising of new and existing products. These representatives manage the personal selling efforts in their territory and represent a highly developed sales skill. Their task is to keep the distributive organization functioning and to improve its selling effort.

Another type of representative is the *technical expert* or sales engineer who provides back-up support for the regular sales force and the distributor. The technical expert supplements the sales activity by providing the detailed technical information needed to fit the product into a buyer's system. The expert knows the product and how it is used and, therefore, is in a position to demonstrate and install complicated equipment. These technical representatives are able to work with buyers to show how the equipment meets or can be modified to meet the buyer's needs. They may develop the supporting system for making their product effective as, for example, the software experts who can develop programs for utilizing the computer equipment (hardware).

Missionary selling is performed when a person employed by the producer assists resellers in a variety of activities. Missionary sales people help resellers set up displays, refill shelves, or accompany resellers' personnel to provide sales assistance. Any orders generated by the missionary force are routed through the reseller who receives credit for the sale. Missionary activities often supplement the distributors' sales efforts during product introductions or when promotional plans are implemented. In pharmaceuticals missionary activity is called "detailing" and involves making contact with doctors and pharmacists to acquaint them with new products. Missionary efforts are used in world markets to supplement traditional sales methods. Increased product complexity and competition plus the development of self-service stores overseas are likely to increase the need for missionary activities in foreign markets.

Some producers' sales personnel sell to *final consumers* through the firm's retail outlets or by door-to-door selling. American companies such as Avon Products, Inc., Fuller Brush, and Tupperware have used door-to-door approaches on several continents. Avon's 390,000 representatives in 16 foreign markets produced approximately $415 billion sales in 1973,[70] but selling abroad by the door-to-door method often is more expensive than in the U.S. and cultural factors force companies to vary their traditional methods. For example, foreign representatives sometimes do not like to sell to strangers so territories frequently are reduced.

---

[70]"Troubled Avon Tries a Face-lifting," *Business Week* (May 11, 1974), p. 104.

The Importance of Personal Selling in the Promotional Mix

Some product lines can best be marketed through personal selling. For example, the sale of technical products such as airplanes, computers, and machine tools requires a considerable amount of technical knowledge to explain and demonstrate their operation and advantage. The purchase of major equipment requires that many people within the buying firm be convinced of the superiority of the product. Engineers, production personnel, and technicians must be sure the product will perform properly; the financial officers need to develop a satisfactory financing plan; and major executives must be convinced of the economic desirability of the installation and must see how it conforms to future development plans for the firm. Although advertising may arouse an interest in such goods, personal contact is needed to negotiate and close the sale. Personal selling involving high-level management is essential when negotiating turnkey operations or sales to centrally planned countries.

Generally, personal selling is an important component of the promotional mix for industrial goods and for consumer goods requiring major expenditures. It also plays a significant role in those countries with a paucity of advertising media or in less developed countries where underemployment and low wages create a pool of potential sales personnel.[71] Personal selling is significant in selling to wholesalers and retailers to secure their cooperation in the implementation of the marketing plan. To reach final consumers, the exporter or manufacturer must concentrate on the improvement of selling at all levels of distribution.

QUESTIONS

1. How might the importance of each element of the marketing mix vary for the international marketer of machine tools and the marketer selling detergents? Why?
2. How has the consumer movement affected promotional programs of international markets?
3. What criteria would you use to select a multinational advertising agency? A local agency?
4. What advantages are associated with the use of a multinational advertising agency? How then does the local agency survive?
5. How does the diversity of media abroad complicate the media-buying decision of the international marketer?
6. Discuss the advantages and disadvantages of global advertising campaigns similar to Esso's "Tiger in the Tank."
7. What research information would be useful to decide whether a standardized advertising message should be used?

---

[71]Vern Terpstra, *International Marketing* (New York: Holt, Rinehart and Winston, Inc., 1972), p. 382.

8. Discuss what is meant by the statement: "Sales promotion is a supplement to advertising and personal selling and usually stresses limited promotional objectives." Cite examples.
9. What promotional objectives are met by exhibiting a product at an international trade fair?
10. How true is the statement that "personal selling remains the most important segment of marketing in all parts of the globe"? Defend your answer.

SUPPLEMENTARY READINGS

Advertising Age. Chicago: Crain Communications, Inc. (weekly)

Donnelly, James H., Jr. "Standardized Global Advertising a Call as Yet Unanswered," *Journal of Marketing*, April, 1969, pp. 57–60.

Dunn, S. Watson. "Effect of National Identity of Multinational Promotional Strategy in Europe," *Journal of Marketing*, October, 1976, pp. 50–57.

Hansen, Dagfinn Moe, and J. J. Boddewyn. *American Marketing in the European Common Market*, 1963–1973. Cambridge: Marketing Science Institute, August, 1976.

McGann, Anthony F., and Nils Eric Aaby. "The Advertising Industry in Western Europe," *Journal of Advertising* (Summer, 1973), pp. 19–24.

Media Decisions. New York: Decisions Publications, Inc. (monthly)

Terpstra, Vern. *International Marketing*. New York: Holt, Rinehart and Winston, Inc., 1972. Chapters 12, 13.

Wiechmann, Ulrich E. *Marketing Management in Multinational Firms: The Consumer Packaged Goods Industry*. New York: Praeger Publishers, Inc., 1976.

14

Pricing in the World Markets

When the marketing plan is established for the international firm, a key role is often assigned to the price policy. Although price is only one factor in the marketing mix, it may be the determining one in the firm's ability to compete. The world's major industrial markets today are highly competitive compared to the past. Even the company with a product of known technological superiority may find pricing crucial to its success. Usually competitive, though perhaps not comparable, products are available to offer the consumer a choice thereby limiting the firm's ability to command a premium price. Increased productivity has enabled firms of many nations to offer competitive prices. Furthermore, the advent of discounting and hypermarkets have forced the multinational to revise existing policy. The effect of pricing decisions is felt throughout the company, including its competitive position, production and engineering, and employment and financing. Clearly pricing is crucial to a coordinated marketing policy.

Pricing for world markets is even more difficult than for domestic strategy. In the domestic market the manager is likely to have developed an appreciation for many of the cultural and economic environmental influences on price policy. These cultural traditions are part of a manager's own heritage, but in the world market this same manager is often less sure of a decision due to unfamilarity and to the diversity of markets in which the company sells. Pricing is implemented in an environment characterized by less control and more geographical spread than at home. The importance of price in each market and its relation to promotion and distribution may be less clearly understood. Distributors and dealers need sufficient margin to spur them to the required marketing effort, yet the tasks they are asked to perform vary from market to market along with their capabilities. The customers' sensitivity and responses to pricing strategy will vary among the products in the line and among the various markets. Over time the response pattern may change as new distribution methods are used and new technology becomes available. Also, the company may be limited in its ability to control prices due to governmental restrictions on margin and prices, or because of competitive activity in the market which narrowly defines the price variation that the market will accept. Legislation may further influence the firm's attempts to control the final price of its products to consumers. For example, many countries that formerly permitted the manufacturer to establish the final price under resale price maintenance legislation have recently opened their markets to more aggressive pricing by rescinding these laws. Even the antitrust policy of the United States may deter some price activity by American companies in the overseas markets.

It can readily be seen that pricing involves the marketing manager in many difficult decisions. Pricing even in the domestic scene is far from a science, yet the international marketer often must make decisions with considerably less information that is available for the domestic decision. Despite this handicap, if the firm is to compete effectively and achieve its volume and profit goals, pricing must be adapted to the local requirements and coordinated with the other elements of the marketing mix. The various elements must work together rather than at cross purposes for maximum impact. Pricing, along with promotion, should reinforce the company's channel and the product strategies.

The international pricing manager, as with the domestic counterpart, must assess the demand for products in each of the market segments to determine how each might react to pricing strategy. In addition to the factors taken into account for domestic pricing, the international manager must consider such issues as the currency to be used for quotations, exchange rate fluctuation possibilities, governmental control over pricing, tariffs, and a host of economic and cultural environmental factors that vary from market to market.

Several aspects of pricing have already been discussed in previous chapters, especially in relation to the monetary environment (Chapter 4) and analysis of foreign markets (Chapter 6). Additional consideration will be given to the relationships between pricing and credit (Chapter 16) and the pricing effects of export cooperation and combinations (Chapter 19). In this chapter an overall view of pricing policy objectives is discussed. Then the investigation of export pricing and the adaptation of prices to the market are detailed. The intrafirm pricing problems associated with transfer pricing have become significant with the growth of joint ventures and the use of marketing subsidiaries and overseas production and marketing. The ramifications of such transfer pricing are noted and the final section of the chapter is devoted to a discussion of price quotations and their effects on both buyers and sellers.

PRICE POLICY

Many firms engaged in international trade have little control over the prices they are able to charge their customers. This condition generally occurs when the company produces or sells standardized commodities that have little or no differentiation from other products in the same class. Thus, marketers of grains, cement, and cotton may find that their prices are largely set in the world market on the basis of supply and demand as they affect prices on the organized commodity exchanges in New York, London, and elsewhere. Marketers of these products have little opportunity to use price as an active ingredient in their marketing strategy. Other marketers, however, have more discretion regarding the prices they will charge.

The Objectives of Price Policy

The firms that are able to use discretion in their pricing policy are those that have been able to differentiate their products in a manner that makes price comparisons more difficult or that establishes some special product features or service that makes their offering of special value to a class of customers. These are often manufacturers in industries with relatively few competitors so that each is conscious of the effect of its price policy on other members of the industry and on total returns to all members. Automobiles, appliances, and machine tools may be illustrative of these industries.

Even when marketers do have discretion regarding how actively they will employ price, a decision must still be made as to how the pricing strategy will be implemented. The need for coordination in the use of pricing can be illustrated by reference to the channel policy of the company. Quite different price strategies will be employed if the firm seeks distribution through mass retailers and the hypermarkets as against the traditional retail outlets.[1] Since the mass merchandiser expects to use price aggressively by seeking a low-price image, the manufacturer that wishes distribution through these outlets must also follow a price policy that enables the mass distributor to carry out a plan. Traditional retailers may be satisfied with a large margin even though it results in fewer unit sales. The concept of low-margin, high-volume retailing is emerging in many of the markets that for years relied on the small retailer's willingness to provide more service at a high margin. The rapid growth of discount selling and mail-order merchandising in many markets of Europe and elsewhere have required the reevaluation of existing price policies.

On the other hand, in many countries, and especially in the outlying markets, such merchandising methods have not been as widely accepted. Pricing in some of these situations may be controlled by custom, by government, or by trade associations. As an example, in the early 1960s McCreary noted the instance of four American businessmen in Geneva, Switzerland, who decided they would establish a dry

---

[1]The hypermarket is discussed in Chapter 11.

cleaning shop and charge $1.25–$1.50 to clean a suit in contrast to the existing prices of $4.25. They applied for a license from the city and eventually it was granted on condition that they become members of the local dry cleaning association. The one condition that the association laid down was that the new members would have to charge the going price in the market.[2] Obviously the entire basis for the operation was demolished.

The significance of price in the international marketing strategy is clear from the results of a recent survey of 511 large U.S. multinational firms. When asked to rank six elements of marketing strategy (advertising, product policy, channel, credit, packaging, and price) in terms of their importance in nondomestic markets, the executives ranked price second, but immediately below product policy. Pricing was considered most important by 45 percent of the respondents.[3] No indication was provided in the study to indicate whether this percentage was concentrated in particular industry groups. This same study indicated that product managers or middle management personnel make the international pricing decision in 56 percent of the responding companies. Twenty-one companies reported that the pricing decision was made in the overseas operations, while twenty said the decision was centralized in the U.S. home office. The authors conclude that pricing is a key marketing tool overseas.[4]

Price Strategies

The term *price strategy* is used in this text to refer to the firm's general price policies rather than to the tactics used in a specific time and place. Price strategy refers to the basic policy established in the marketing plan. Thus, the strategy may be to establish low margins to secure volume, to meet competitors' prices, or to use a skimming policy to recover expenses early. Tactics refer to the means of implementing the policy; price is $100, FOB New York.

As an element in the basic marketing strategy of the firm, pricing policy should reflect the firm's goals and objectives. If the company is seeking maximum market penetration, then the pricing policy should support this effort. Likewise, the pricing strategy probably should differ when a company seeks other goals such as target rate of return, stability of market share, or maximum profit.

As one might expect, the international firm can strive for the same goals in the world market that it seeks at home. There is no need, however, for the firm's objectives to be the same in all the markets it

---

[2]Edward A. McCreary, *The Americanization of Europe* (Garden City, N.J.: Doubleday and Company, Inc., 1964), p. 32.
[3]James G. Baker and John K. Ryans, Jr., "Some Aspects of International Pricing: A Neglected Area of Management Policy," *Management Decisions* (August, 1973).
[4]*Ibid.*

serves. In some markets the company may be introducing its product line for the first time, while in others it may be well established. Seeking market penetration initially may well call for quite different pricing strategies than seeking further penetration in a market that already approaches saturation. Furthermore, in the overseas markets the company may be aiming at different market segments. Products that may be widely accepted for mass distribution in the advanced countries may have only limited elite markets in some developing nations. A common illustration of such a product would be the automobile. Often such a product is available to only a small portion of the population with high incomes or to people holding important government positions in the developing countries, as in Asia and Africa.

The use of pricing as an active element in the marketing strategy requires that marketers be aware of the limits to their ability to control the final prices charged to consumers, and sometimes to industrial buyers. Indeed, some marketers focus their price policies on the prices to be charged to their distributors on the assumption that the distributor will follow appropriate policies. Especially when the firm is new to exporting is it likely to rely heavily on its distributors in the local markets. Similarly, reliance on distributors is high when the market potential in the area is limited. Even among the more experienced exporters, though, the use of independent middlemen may lead to a lack of market knowledge as a result of little contact between the firm and its final customers. Even the establishment of discount structures for distributors and dealers provides little assurance that the underlying price policies are being effectuated in the market. Dealers may shade margins or charge higher prices when they see this is an appropriate strategy for themselves, even though such a policy may not be in the best long-run interest of the exporting firm. Somewhat more control may be exercised when the firm is producing and marketing overseas through the use of its own production plants and sales force.

Some marketers seek to establish themselves in the market by following a *penetration pricing* policy. Firms using this strategy set prices low in order to quickly achieve a large market share. The intent of this policy is to establish a market position rapidly that will make competition difficult. Especially when the overseas market is seen as having a limited market potential, the low profit margin per unit combined with a small market potential in the remainder of the market may deter competitors. The penetration policy is attractive when the market is responsive to a low price appeal and when production or other cost savings are substantial as a result of volume.

Alternatively, a firm might follow a *skimming* policy by entering the overseas market with a high price to reach only a limited market segment that is not particularly price sensitive. Then when the product is established, a lower price might be introduced to attract a wider market segment that is responsive to price. The skimming policy may be employed when the product is new to the foreign market but has easily sensed values for the purchaser. Initial buyers may represent a market segment that has a very inelastic demand, for example, a small pocket or layer of very affluent among the nation's elite. After the product is accepted by the elite, the demonstration effect may lead others to desire the product. They may, however, not be able to enter the market until there are price reductions.[5]

The appropriate pricing strategy for a firm's products may also vary over the product's life cycle. In Chapter 2 we pointed out the existence of an international product cycle.[6] According to this concept a product might be in a growth or maturity stage in the country where it was originated, while still in the introduction or early growth phases in other nations. The life cycle theory, thus, would indicate the possibility of varying the price policy among nations at a single point in time. Such differential pricing would imply that the company was able to keep the two markets separated for marketing purposes and that the price elasticities differed in the two markets. This product life cycle concept coincides in many respects with Joel Dean's concept of a deterioration in a product's distinctiveness over time due to competitive inroads.[7] Thus, there is a need to continually adjust prices as changes occur in the market. A recent example of this process is the electronic calculator. Initially it provided clearly superior advantages over its mechanical counterpart in performance and size. Yet the rapid changes that resulted from research and development, plus the widespread competition from many producers of components and final instruments, quickly brought about a series of reduced prices as the calculator became a standard item. Four function calculators that were the equivalent of those selling for $100 in 1972 sold for less than $10 in 1976.

Price strategy varies not only over time but also in the individual geographic markets. *Business International* reported the results of a study of the European Economic Community involving 35 branded consumer goods such as foods, radios, tape recorders, and electric appliances. The researchers found that there was a wide disparity in the prices of these goods within the Community. On nine prepared foods, costs were least in The Netherlands and greatest in Italy. Germany had the lowest prices for radio and television sets. These differences were ascribed to differences in the wholesale and retail distribution structures of the individual countries as well as market size and saturation.[8] Italy, for example, has 1 food shop for every 100 people, while West Germany has 1 for every 350 people. Although further integration

---

[5]Penetration and skimming policies for products with perishable distinctiveness are discussed in more detail in a classic treatment by Joel Dean in his *Managerial Economics* (Englewood Cliffs, N.J.: Prentice-Hall, Inc., 1951), pp. 410–424.

[6]Chapter 2, p. 24.

[7]Dean, *op. cit.*, pp. 410–427.

[8]"Why Common Market Does Not Mean Common Prices," *Business International* (February 2, 1973), p. 47.

and development of cross-border distribution systems may have narrowed the range, some variations probably continue to exist. Even more disparity would be expected among nations where no integration has occurred.

International retailing furnishes further examples of the need to coordinate price policies with the market segments to be served. In comparison with indigenous retailers, the international retail firms selling luxury items are usually found in the higher prevailing price ranges.[9] But even such merchandisers as supermarkets in developing countries do not try to compete with the local marketplace. Instead they cater to the upper income groups and provide different assortments and service than are available in the local market. Mass merchandisers such as Sears, Woolworth's, Migros, and Jewel's Super Bazaar tend to emphasize value rather than price. Some international retailers do see themselves as price leaders, but Hollander notes that international merchants can suffer when their prices are too low. He states that:

> Entirely aside from the problem of competitive or political reprisals, consumers' suspicions and doubts about the quality of the merchandise in foreign-seeming or innovative stores can easily be identified if the prices seem unbelievably or unreasonably cheap. Moreover, foreign markets will often reject "low end," i.e., low-priced, low-quality products. Some highly publicized ventures organized around price appeals, such as GEM (American discount stores in England) and INNO-France (Belgium department stores in France), have been marked failures.[10]

ESTABLISHING THE EXPORT PRICE

Two approaches to pricing can be identified. One starts with the costs of a product and desired profit margins to determine the price, while the other starts with prices in the market to determine whether, at those prices, the firm can earn a profit. These two approaches must be reconciled if a proper decision is to be made since the price must be one at which the market will buy, yet it must be high enough to cover costs at the projected volume. Considering market factors alone might lead to prices that do not cover basic costs, but cost consideration in isolation can lead to a price that is not acceptable to the consumer.

When costs cannot be covered by a price the market is willing to pay, the company needs to reexamine its offering to see if changes in

---

[9]This section on international retail price policies draws heavily from the excellent study of Stanley C. Hollander, *Multinational Retailing*, Division of Research, Graduate School of Business Administration, Michigan State University, 1970. See especially pages 162–172.

[10]*Ibid*, p. 169.

product, production, marketing, or channels of distribution might make the price fall within an acceptable range.

Price in Relation to the Domestic Price

Export prices are generally based upon some domestic price that has produced a satisfactory profit. While there is no reason to quote a higher or lower price to a prospective customer simply because the customer is foreign, there is good reason to question the appropriateness of the domestic price if it is used without adjustment. The use of the domestic price as an export base price would be tantamount to establishing a worldwide base price. Even though management may perceive this price as a price which recovers all costs, such a system has been questioned on several bases. The worldwide system of pricing ignores the following: (1) certain of the costs in the domestic system which are not properly assignable to the export market (examples include the domestic sales and promotional costs as well as certain administrative expenses); (2) differences that may exist in the costs of researching the various markets; (3) the competitive position of the firm differs in the individual markets; and (4) exporting may require additional expenses in packaging, documentation, etc.[11] Furthermore, the use of the domestic price may result in a price that is too high for the overseas market.

In a relatively few instances the export base price may be set at a higher level than the domestic price. Such a policy might occur when the export market is seen as a special opportunity or when the market is risky. This is a somewhat opportunistic price policy whereby the overseas customer pays more as a privilege of buying the imported product. A special example occurs in times of shortage and of war when export prices may be much higher than domestic prices to reflect both the limited supply and the added risk.

Alternatively, the export base price may be set lower than the domestic for several good reasons. For example, the overseas market may be one in which purchasing power is low; as a result sales may be possible only at a reduced price. Or competition may be such that prices may be reduced in order to compete. Also, the exporting firm may have calculated that the cost of producing exported products is lower than for domestic products on the theory that overhead costs have already been absorbed in domestic prices, and the export market is an added or extra market that does not have the domestic overhead to bear. On this last basis the export market is seen as a marginal market. If there are unused facilities, such a marginal pricing concept

---

[11]For a discussion of the worldwide base price in more detail, see Richard D. Robinson, *International Business Management* (New York: Holt, Rinehart and Winston, Inc., 1973), p. 73.

may be appropriate, but if the overseas market requires additional investment, a full costing approach may be more correct.

Quoting export prices at levels lower than domestic prices is technically known as *dumping*, which is against the law in a number of industrial countries. Antidumping laws in these nations have been enacted to prevent foreign manufacturers from selling their products at prices that are detrimental to the interests of local manufacturers. Antidumping laws generally require that products be offered for sale at prices that are no lower than those in the country of manufacture. The United States and Canada are among the nations having such legislation.[12] When a company has been found to be dumping, the penalty is usually increased duties or fines that result in higher prices to the importers.[13]

Demand-Based Prices

It may be argued that the proper starting point for developing export prices is the price that consumers or industrial buyers are willing to pay rather than the relationship between export and domestic prices or the relation of export prices to cost. This approach argues that a price acceptable to the final buyer is of crucial importance to the export marketing program.[14] When prices are set by demand, it is the task of market research to supply the data needed to evaluate the market demand. Once the firm has determined the range of prices that will be acceptable to the buyers, it works backward to find the net price to the firm. This is accomplished by subtracting from the final price that buyers will pay, the margins that must be paid to channel members, taxes and duties, transportation charges, insurance costs associated with exporting, export handling costs, and other export related costs. The result is the export base price.

Assuming that the resulting export price provides an acceptable return, the firm is in a position to export. If, however, the resulting price is not satisfactory, the firm can see if modifications in the product, production, or marketing plan can be made to result in a more satisfactory price. The firm also can reevaluate its pricing requirements and settle for the lower price and return, or the firm can decide not to export.

---

[12]See Chapter 17 Import Management, for a discussion of American antidumping legislation and its effects on American importers.

[13]In the inflationary period of the early seventies the U.S. laws came under some criticism on the grounds that protection of the domestic producers should not be permitted to thwart inflation fighting — that is, antidumping duties should not cut imports when U.S. producers cannot meet domestic demand. See Boyd France, "A New Look at the Antidumping Rules," *Business Week* (May 18, 1974), p. 25.

[14]Franklin R. Root, *Strategic Planning for Export Marketing* (Scranton, Pa.: International Textbook Company, 1964), p. 56.

A critical factor in the development of demand-based pricing is the demand estimate at the various price levels. When the firm is new in the international market, or in a particular market, the required facts may not be known. In such a case the firm must undertake a research effort to produce the needed information. Such a study may involve contacting final users or intermediate buyers to determine the prevailing market prices and the levels of consumer satisfaction. Some information regarding the market may be obtained from the United States Department of Commerce and its contacts with U.S. embassies abroad, from the embassy of the foreign country in Washington, from the Chambers of Commerce here and abroad, from banks, and from other commercial sources. A particularly important source may be the firm's distributors and dealers.

LEASING

Recent years have seen the expansion of equipment leasing as a factor in international marketing. Although common in the United States for many years and recently popular in Europe and Japan, leasing lately has been expanded to cope with the unique problems of Asia and Africa. Leasing is an alternative to owning the product. As such, leasing represents payment for controlling the use of the product — in effect, leasing is a payment for the services rendered by the product rather than payment for the product itself. For many users ownership is of little importance. What does count is that they can employ the equipment either for personal use or to foster the production of goods and services. Why own machinery or equipment if it is cheaper to lease, capital requirements are lower, and the risk of obsolescence is minimized?

There are a number of reasons for the increased popularity of leasing in both the industrial and developing nations in recent years. One major reason has been the difficulty that firms in many countries have had in obtaining financing for purchasing the product. The tight money market in these countries has prohibited firms from budgeting the full amount needed for outright purchase of necessary equipment. Leasing permits the lessee to make smaller annual payments than are necessary when purchasing the equipment. It also eliminates the need for budgeting large amounts of capital for investment. Additionally, the lessee's risk associated with rapid obsolescence in such products as computers is minimized. The lessee knows that after an initial period a shift to newer models or continued use of the present equipment at minimal cost can be accomplished. Leasing is also an advantage in products, such as shipping containers, where the leasing company may be able to better utilize the containers through its worldwide logistic system than could an individual firm.

From the standpoint of the producer, leasing also has advantages. It may permit entrance to markets that would otherwise be closed due to the shortage of capital. Once the product is introduced into the market through leasing, other potential customers may become familiar with its advantages over current products. Leasing provides the producer with some control over the conditions of use of the product. When satisfactory performance is dependent on proper maintenance and service, the lessor is able to provide the quality of maintenance that is needed. Where preventive maintenance is not an accepted policy, as is true in many sections of the world, this maintenance contract can have an important influence on the product's performance.

Leasing does, however, also have disadvantages for both the lessee and lessor. For the lessee the total payments over the lease may be greater than the cost of purchase and maintenance. This is to be expected both because the lessor retains title and bears ownership risks, and because the lessor normally provides more services under the lease than when an outright purchase is made. Lessors obviously have more capital invested in a leasing program and accept more risks than under purchase plans. Furthermore, there is considerable difficulty in establishing a proper price for the lease or rental value. The lease must produce over its life a return for the product, for the additional services, and for the additional risks. Even under stable price levels it is difficult to set such a price, but in conditions of inflation it is even more of a problem. Unless the inflation rate is taken into account the lessor may find that the lessee is being subsidized in the latter portion of the lease period. Pricing must consider also the duration of the lease and forecasted economic conditions over the entire period.

There is always the possibility that the lessee may not follow through on the contract and the producer or leasing firm may be stuck with equipment that was designed for a special purpose. An example is that of TAW International Leasing, Inc., one of the pioneers in leasing to African countries with about $40 million worth of equipment on lease in Africa. In 1973 when Rhodesia closed its borders to Zambian trade, TAW worked out a contract to lease 330 tractors and 400 trailers to the Zambian government to be delivered in September. When heavy U.S. demand for trucks and a shortage of components delayed production, TAW diverted some equipment from West Africa, but later the Zambian government cancelled its deal to lease the tractors and trailers. Suddenly TAW found itself with 330 unwanted trucks and 400 trailers that had been specially built for heavy duty on inferior roads.[15]

In some instances companies have sought to combine the advantages of both leasing and outright purchase through the use of contracts that permit the lease payments to be applied against purchase if

---

[15]"Zambia: The TAW Truck Deal Runs Out of Gas," *Business Week* (April 27, 1974), p. 56.

the lessee so desires. This allows the lessee to use the product on a rental basis, and if the equipment and finances later permit, the lessee can purchase by paying the balance due.

Leasing in the international market has been of particular significance for products such as computers, transportation equipment, containers, and some industrial machinery. The French government, for example, proposed leasing plans for the Concorde supersonic jet liner and other French-produced aircraft to facilitate marketing. The plan was to get Concorde into use so the plane would be established by the time the lease expired, at which time airlines might either purchase or renew their leases.[16]

Often the producing firm does not directly participate in the lease, but rather, as in the TAW illustration, an independent leasing company performs the leasing and servicing functions.

TRANSFER PRICING

Up to this point we have been primarily concerned with the problems of pricing goods for sale to unrelated firms and customers. However, the expansion of multinational firms through the establishment of owned production facilities abroad, the use of separate marketing subsidiaries for international sales, and joint ventures have pushed another important problem into the foreground. What prices should be charged for transferring goods from one of these associated units to another? This is the issue of transfer pricing. *Transfer prices* refer to the prices assessed on transactions involving goods, services, loans, and property between such related units.[17] The problem would be significant if only because it deals with a very large volume of trade. We have seen that for many American firms their foreign subsidiaries represent a substantial export market. The problem is significant, however, for other reasons.

Transfer pricing vitally affects the information system on which management relies to make decisions regarding the effectiveness and efficiency of its operations.[18] Through its effect on the information system, transfer pricing influences the appraisal of executives in both the producing and marketing divisions as well as those in charge of overseas subsidiaries. While transfer pricing can be used to enlarge the

---

[16]"Concorde Leasing Plan to Facilitate Marketing Is Approved by France," *The Wall Street Journal*, August 17, 1973, p. 18.

[17]Warren J. Keegan, "Multinational Pricing: How Far Is Arm's Length?" *Columbia Journal of World Business* (May–June, 1969), p. 57.

[18]Excellent appraisals of transfer pricing and systems appear in *Business International*, "Solving International Pricing Problems" (1965), *Business International*, "Setting Intercorporate Pricing Policies" (1973), and Jeffrey S. Arpan, "International Intracorporate Pricing: Non-American Systems and Views," *Journal of International Business Studies*, (Spring, 1973), pp. 1–18.

profit of the company as a whole, it is likely that such systems often produce opposite results. High or low transfer prices may so distort the profit of a subsidiary that it acts in a manner not in the best interests of the entire corporation. Thus, a high transfer price might cause a subsidiary to seek other sourcing for its needs even though total profit for the firm might be maximized by sourcing through the parent or another subsidiary. Executives of overseas operations can become dissatisfied when the pricing system limits their ability to show a profit or provides other units with unwarranted gains since their pay and evaluation for promotion may be vitally affected.

Transfer pricing systems sometimes lie at the root of the problems between the international firm and the host governments in countries where it operates. While all the ramifications of transfer pricing are not immediately observable, there are some obvious points at which the firm and the various governments might find themselves at odds. These include issues regarding income taxes, customs duties, antitrust laws, antidumping statutes, technology transfers, exchange controls, and profit repatriation. Potentially, at least, the transfer price system can affect taxes by shifting recorded profits from high to low tax countries when high transfer charges are made on products sent to subsidiaries in the high tax nation or low transfer prices are set on goods exported from these subsidiaries. Customs duties are often based on value, and therefore the transfer price directly affects the amount of duty owed. Transfer prices also interact with antidumping laws and price controls. If the country has a price control law that is based on the imported value, then the final price is determined by the transfer price. When host countries place restrictions on profit repatriation by not making exchange available, the firm may be able to repatriate some of its profits through the transfer mechanism.

Claims regarding the extent to which transfer pricing has been used to accomplish these and other objectives inimical to the host countries have proliferated in recent years. One issue of *The Wall Street Journal* provides the following instances of governmental action against multinational companies:[19]

1. West Germany's Cartel Office is investigating paper and drug prices that multinationals charge their subsidiaries in Germany.
2. In Britian the government issued a new set of tax regulations to tighten rules under which companies can determine transfer prices for their oil.
3. In the U.S. the Federal Energy Administration alleged that Gulf Oil had overcharged itself for oil purchased from subsidiaries in Nigeria and Cabinda. (Gulf denied the charge.)
4. International Business Machines Corp's practices have been questioned in a number of nations.

---

[19]William M. Carleym, "Investigations Beset Multinational Firms with Stress on Pricing," *The Wall Street Journal* (December 19, 1974), p. 1.

5. Roche, the Swiss drug maker, has had prices for its tranquilizers Librium and Valium scrutinized in Britain, West Germany, Australia, and the Common Market Commission.

Regardless of the validity or invalidity of the above claims, it is obvious that the international firm must be prepared to defend its transfer prices. This will require systems that provide for fair evaluation of a subsidiary's operations, fair allocation of the profits, systems that do not destroy the incentive of employees, and systems that meet the varying requirements of the United States and the host governments. This is indeed a Herculean task and, even if it could be accomplished, it would only mitigate but not remove the controversies within the organization and between the company and host governments. Some of the arguments surrounding the transfer prices reflect differences of opinion regarding underlying policy rather than difficulties with the pricing system per se. For example, no transfer pricing system can overcome the belief that a firm should no longer charge for a technology transfer once it has recovered its costs as has been claimed by nationalists in some lesser developed countries.

PRICE QUOTATIONS

Export price quotations may be made in terms of the currency of the exporting country, that of the importing country, or that of a third country.

Foreign Currency Quotations

Price quotations in terms of a native currency are advantageous to the exporter because they reduce foreign exchange risks, facilitate the prompt determination of profits, and, if the exporter's own currency is stable, reduce the necessity of frequent price changes. The exchange risks, when quoting in foreign currency, may in many instances be minimized by hedging in the foreign exchange market or by taking the other precautions discussed in Chapter 4. Hedging may be impossible, however, because of the expense or the absence of an open exchange market, and other precautions may be unreliable or difficult to execute.

The importer may favor price quotations in the currency of the exporting country if an additional speculative profit is foreseen due to an expected exchange fluctuation before settlement, or because the importer believes that the assumption of exchange risks will affect the price quotation favorably. The importer frequently prefers purchasing at prices quoted in the importer's national currency, however, and in order to promote sales, the exporter may grant the request. Quotations in the currency of the importing country shift the risk of exchange fluctuations to the exporter. They enable the importer to compute profits, to announce resale prices promptly, and also more readily to compare price quotations received from the competitive exporters of different foreign countries. Custom, moreover, may largely determine the prevailing practice in particular trades, and the danger of non-payment of bills due to unfortunate exchange speculation by importers may cause the exporter to favor foreign currency price quotations.

The practice of quoting prices in the currency of a third country is at times dictated by custom, but when the currencies of both the exporting and the importing country are unstable, or when the banking facilities of a third country are depended upon for financial settlement, it may be rational to quote prices in the currency of a third country. Pounds sterling, for example, were widely used by all countries prior to World War I, and United States dollars immediately following World War II.

Price Quotation Elements

Price quotations are the basis not only for determining the amount to be paid, but also to reflect the ways in which the responsibilities and costs for the shipment will be split between buyers and sellers along with the duties and liabilities that each assumes. Thus, the quotation should be carefully read for its total impact. International price quotations and terms define for the buyer and seller the following:

1. The basic price.
2. The place of delivery.
3. The transportation and related charges and cost items included in the price.
4. The respective duties of the seller and buyer.
5. Buyer and seller liability in case of loss or damage.

Quotations can be varied to cover costs at any stage of distribution. These are defined and illustrated in the appendix at the end of the chapter. The appendix provides verbal descriptions to distinguish among the terms on the basis of the previous five elements. It should be noted that no single quotation is best for all situations and that the marketers can utilize a wide variety of terms to meet their specific needs. Furthermore, the buyer and the seller may have quite different preferences for the manner in which the duties and responsibilities are to be split. For example, buyers may well prefer to have the seller accept all responsibility for the shipment until it arrives at the buyer's place of business, while sellers might prefer FOB plant terms. To some extent these differences will be factors involved in the negotiation process, but sometimes either the buyer or the seller has particular advantages that enable performance of the duties more efficiently. In any case, few exporters can insist upon a particular quotation if another is requested by customers.

International Price Quotations and Terms

Many of the technical terms used for quoting prices in international marketing are different from those used in domestic trade. Frequently the international terms are more complex to reflect the greater distances and costs that may be involved. Not surprisingly, a lack of uniformity regarding the terms still prevails throughout the world despite the efforts of several international agencies to standardize and clarify them, but two sets of definitions are important for American marketers. In 1941 a joint committee of the Chamber of Commerce of the United States, the National Council of American Importers, and the National Foreign Trade Council adopted the *Revised American Foreign Trade Definitions — 1941*.[20] Although these definitions have no legal status unless there is specific legislation providing for them or unless they are confirmed by court decisions, the joint committee recommended that sellers and buyers agree to their acceptance as part of the contract of sale. These definitions would then become legally binding upon the parties. These definitions are similar to those published by the International Chamber of Commerce but differ somewhat.[21]

Even with the wide acceptance of the definitions mentioned above, price quotations may still be interpreted differently by American buyers and sellers. Further confusion results from interpretations placed upon American importers and exporters by foreign marketers. Some requests for quotation by foreign traders may ask for the use of abbreviated terminology that is not common in the United States. In the case of importers the problem is potentially great because the prices are quoted by overseas manufacturers and exporters. Because of these issues exporters and importers are well advised to be sure that there is agreement on the meaning of the terms that are employed in order to minimize the chance for misunderstanding and the consequent loss of future business or an involvement in arbitration or litigation.

Other Quotation Components

The international price quotation should specify the quantity of items being quoted. This may be based either on a specific unit or on the shipment as a whole. Unit prices are prevalent, but it is important

---

[20]*Revised American Foreign Trade Definitions — 1941*. This source has been used throughout this chapter unless otherwise indicated.

[21]International Chamber of Commerce, *Trade Terms (1929); International Rules for the Interpretation of Trade Terms (1936)*.

that the unit of quantity be definite. When the price is per automobile, lathe, tractor, or appliance, the product itself constitutes a definite unit, but when prices are quoted in terms of weight or volume there may be ambiguity. One portion of the ambiguity lies in the definition of the unit itself. For example, does the term, ton, refer to a short ton (2,000 lbs.), a long ton (2,240 lbs.) or a metric ton (2,204.6 lbs.)? Similarly, does a gallon refer to the American gallon (4 quarts) or the imperial gallon (5 quarts)? Also, weight quotations require the specification of whether the stipulated weight is gross weight of the commodity and container or net weight.

Quality of the product should also be a part of the quotation. The price quotation may definitely indicate particular grades, standards, percentage of mineral content, or other quality standards. It may also indicate quality by specifying the brand and model of the product. In some instances specifications may need to be developed.

Credit terms are an important part of the quotation. These are discussed in Chapter 16.

Definite or fixed prices are the most prevalent in international marketing. The sales contract may, however, provide that the settlement shall be the price that is current at the time of delivery. Periods of inflation lead buyers to desire fixed prices, but sellers, especially when the product must be manufactured to order or involves a long-term contract, desire some protection against cost increases. In such cases they may seek to tie the price of the item to some established index.

GOVERNMENTAL INFLUENCE OVER PRICE

Except for transfer pricing, much of the preceding discussion implicitly assumed that the individual firm is free to set any price that will enable it to reach the company's objectives subject only to market acceptance. In many situations, however, the company finds that its ability to freely establish prices is circumscribed by both law and governmental policy. Governments intervene in the pricing process as part of their overall programs to contain inflation, to improve their balance of payments, to support local producers of agricultural and manufactured goods, and to directly affect profits and income distribution. They operate in a variety of ways in order to accomplish these goals. Some influence on prices is exerted through antitrust policy, through direct controls on specific products, through the output and pricing of government-owned enterprises, through manipulation of strategic stockpiles of critical materials, and through various subsidy and price-support programs.

Direct price controls have been instituted by many nations, including the United States, as parts of programs designed to cope with problems of continuing inflation, shortages, or balance-of-payment problems. In the United States price controls have been established in war periods and most recently, in 1971, to cope with balance-of-payment problems. Controls over energy-related products have continued as the nation sought to lessen the impact of rapid price increases in imported supply. The United States has also been active in supporting its agriculture through price-support programs that set an artificial level of domestic prices above the level of international prices on the world market. The government has also participated in a number of international commodity programs to help control the export prices of coffee, sugar, nitrates, and rubber.

Many governments abroad exercise similar types of controls and often see price controls as a more continuing influence on the national economy. Thus, for example, Brazil is a country that has had a continuing inflation problem. In 1973 the government announced a goal of holding the cost of living increases to 12 percent. Part of the program for containing the inflation required firms seeking price increases to make application through the Interministerial Price Commission (CIP). The commission had been established in 1969 and charged with the responsibility of holding down prices. Companies negotiating with CIP for price increases were subjected to an analysis of their profit margins and costs. Some companies felt they were caught in a price-cost squeeze when prices were not permitted to rise as rapidly as costs, thus the companies were under pressure to cut costs by improving efficiency or by the use of substitute materials.[22]

Mexico furnishes a further example. For many products the prices in Mexico had theoretically been frozen for years; yet in 1974 the government imposed new controls on products such as foods and industrial goods. Prices on 29 of these food and related items could not be increased for an indefinite period and the Ministry of Industry and Commerce was permitted to order retail price cuts on these items. The new measure provided heavy fines for companies that did not comply and was prompted by the high inflation rate in Mexico.[23]

In the European Economic Community the agricultural program has been at the heart of many difficult negotiations between the members, and between the EEC and other countries. The variable import duty that is levied by the commission has the effect of supporting the Community's agricultural producers and making outsiders residual suppliers to the Community. The high consumer prices that result from the EEC policy have been an issue in the British referendum in 1975 regarding their continued membership. For many Britains, EEC membership and the support program are seen as primary influences

[22]"Firms Operating in Brazil Appear Caught in Cost-Price Bind," *Business Latin America* (December 19, 1973), pp. 407–408.
[23]"Mexico Curbs Price of Various Products Due to Inflation Rate," *The Wall Street Journal* (October 4, 1974), p. 2.

on the high cost of living in their country in contrast to their previous purchases from Commonwealth suppliers.

Essential products such as foods and drugs are particularly susceptible to price controls as these products are politically sensitive in almost every country. The prices on imported drugs in some European countries may be controlled to permit only a very small markup — one that is not sufficient for a company to carry out the kind of promotional campaign that it might deem necessary. Drug prices can also be influenced by the policies of the national health plans in some countries where the government is a major purchaser and supplier of drugs for large portions of the population. Countries that have experienced hyperinflation in the past are likely to be especially cognizant of the need to control prices on basic commodities.

QUESTIONS

1. How does an international price strategy differ from a pricing tactic? Illustrate.
2. Distinguish between skimming and penetration pricing. Under what circumstances would you employ each policy?
3. Why might a single worldwide base price not be the most desirable price?
5. Why should an exporter be aware of antidumping laws? Why do industrial countries establish such legislation?
5. What is demand-based pricing?
6. Why has leasing become an important pricing tool in overseas markets?
7. If the transfer price is the price at which products or components are transferred between units of the same company, the company is free to choose any transfer price it desires. True or false? Why?
8. Define the meaning of the price quotation symbols FOB, FAS, and CIF.
9. Under an export quotation "CIF Rio de Janeiro" on a shipment through the port of New Orleans, Louisiana, where does the exporter's responsibility end?
10. What advantages do you see in the quotation of prices in the currency of the buyer's country?
11. Why would an exporter hesitate or refuse to quote prices in a foreign currency?

SUPPLEMENTARY READINGS

Arpan, Jeffrey S., "International Intracorporate Pricing: Non-American Systems and Views," *Journal of International Business Studies.* (Spring, 1972).
Business International. "Solving International Pricing Problems." 1965.
Business International. "Setting Intercorporate Pricing Policies." 1973
Carson, David. *International Marketing: A Comparative Systems Approach.* New York: John Wiley & Sons, Inc., 1967. Chapter 14.
Cateora, Philip R., and John M. Hess. *International Marketing.* Homewood, Ill.: Richard D. Irwin, Inc., 1975. Chapter 14.

Exporters' Encyclopedia. New York: Dun & Bradstreet, Inc. Annual.

Hollander, Stanley C. *Multinational Retailing*. East Lansing: Graduate School of Business, Michigan State University, 1970.

Miracle, Gordon, and Gerald Albaum. *International Marketing Management*. Homewood, Ill.: Richard D. Irwin, Inc., 1970. Chapter 22

Root, Franklin R. *Strategic Planning for Export Marketing*. Scranton, Pa.: International Textbook Company, 1966. Chapter 4.

Terpstra, Vern. *International Marketing*. New York: Holt, Rinehart and Winston, Inc., 1972. Chapter 14.

Terpstra, Vern. *American Marketing in the Common Market*. New York: Frederick A. Praeger, Publishers, 1967. Chapter 6.

APPENDIX

This appendix contains examples of common price quotations used in international trade. All quotes are based on the *Revised American Foreign Trade Definitions — 1941*. An example of each abbreviated quotation is given with a description to clarify and explain the term. All prices are quoted in U.S. dollars.

The assumed costs are held common in each example. These are as follows:

Value of shipment, including export packing, FOB factory, St. Louis, Missouri	$1,000.00
Rail freight to Philadelphia	150.00
Ocean freight charges	235.50
Marine insurance	2.50
Freight forwarder fees	12.00
Import duties in The Netherlands	200.00

Note: If credit is granted on the transaction, interest costs would be added. If war risk insurance is desired, the cost of such insurance would be added.

(1) Ex (Point of Origin) Price. The price quotation under which the exporter's liability for loss or damage, the exporter's duties, and the costs included in the export price are at a minimum is the ex (point-of-origin) price.

Example: Price quoted is $1,000, ex factory, St. Louis, Missouri.

The seller's responsibility and costs end at the factory. Although the buyer literally is called upon to pick up the shipment, the seller does render assistance at the buyer's request. This assistance comprises the shipment of the merchandise from St. Louis and obtaining a clean bill of lading covering the same. The route to the seaboard is to be selected by the buyer who, again, may seek the seller's assistance.

(2) FOB (Free on Board) Prices. In international marketing several FOB prices are quoted. Some require loading of the product on cars, lighters, or other conveyances at the seaboard, while some require delivery on board other carriers.

(a) FOB (Named inland carrier at a named inland point of departure).

Example: Price quoted is $1,000, FOB cars, St. Louis, Missouri.

Here, the seller is *responsible* for placing the merchandise on the kind of carrier named and for providing a clean bill of lading. There may be a hauling charge or a heavy lift charge or a delay that might entail penalties (demurrage) before the merchandise is placed in the custody of the carrier; therefore, this quotation would include more costs than in the base of the ex warehouse quotation, and the price would be increased to include such costs. Thus, the use of the FOB price quotation does impose more responsibility on the seller than the ex (point of origin) price.

(b) FOB (Named inland carrier at named inland point of departure, freight prepaid or allowed).

Example: Price quoted is $1,150, FOB cars St. Louis, Missouri, freight prepaid (or allowed) to Philadelphia, Pennsylvania.

The quotation is basically the same as the simple FOB cars St. Louis, Missouri, quotation. The seller, however, prepays or allows for the freight to Philadelphia. No responsibility for the shipment from St. Louis to Philadelphia is assumed by the seller, only the cost of shipping. This is a noteworthy distinction. Losses may occur en route, and even if they are fully compensated by the carrier, certain procedures and waiting are required in order to present a claim.

Under the "freight prepaid" version of this quotation, the railroad freight charges are included in the price, as witnessed by a prepaid clean bill of lading. In the case of the "freight allowed" version, the freight charges are also included in the price but they are paid by the buyer, who then deducts these charges when paying the invoice. Therefore, under freight prepaid, the buyer's *net* price is $1,150; while under freight allowed, it is $1,000 ($1,150 less allowance of $150).

(c) FOB (Named inland carrier at named point of exportation).

Example: Price quoted is $1,150, FOB cars Philadelphia, for export.

In this quotation the seller not only includes the transportation costs from St. Louis to Philadelphia, but also assumes the responsibility for this movement. Billing the shipment "for export" assures two things: (1) that the shipment will be delivered at the pier or railroad lighterage point at no extra expense (although there could be), and (2) that the export freight rate will apply on the rail haul. This rate may be lower than the corresponding domestic rail rate.

(d) FOB Vessel (Named port of shipment). The previously named FOB quotation, (c), should not be confused with the FOB vessel (named port of shipment) quotation.

Example: Price quoted is $1,150, FOB vessel Philadelphia.

Here the seller pays the costs and assumes the responsibility for the shipment from the factory in St. Louis to a place on board a vessel in Philadelphia. The actual price quoted is the same as quoted for the FOB cars Philadelphia, for export price quotation. This is on the basis of no extra costs from the cars to the place on board the vessel. There could be a difference in cost, however, if special loading (grain) or any heavy lift were required and charged for. There may also be a long and expensive interval between the arrival of freight cars at the port of Philadelphia for export and the loading on a vessel in Philadelphia. For example, a sudden waterfront strike could delay loading. The exporter (seller) is responsible for placing the merchandise on the vessel, regardless of delays at the port. Moreover, the $12 forwarder fee is added to the charges (or absorbed) but does not appear in the price quotation.

In bulk trades, such as grain and coal, the buyer generally furnishes the vessel. In ordinary business the seller may ship on any common carrier. If the seller is a contractor with a shipping conference operating in the trade in question, then goods must be shipped on one of the vessels of the member lines.

(3) FAS (Free Alongside) Price.

Example: Price quoted is $1,150 FAS vessel Philadelphia.

This quotation differs from the FOB vessel quotation since the time and cost of loading, if any, are not included in the FAS price quotation. In ordinary trade, FAS is equivalent to FOB where costs are concerned, but there may be great differences otherwise. If the merchandise is on a pier waiting for a vessel on which to load it, this waiting may be expensive. Under FOB price quotations, the seller pays for the waiting time; under FAS terms, the buyer pays for it.

In bulk trades where a buyer charters and furnishes the vessel, the differences can be very great. Vessel demurrage charges are expensive and idle time not chargeable to the vessel is paid by either the buyer or the seller, depending upon the quotation.

(4) CIF (Cost, Insurance, and Freight) Price. In contrast with the above price quotations, there are several which carry delivery and costs beyond the port of exportation. The most commonly quoted of these is the CIF (named point of destination) quotation.

Example: Price quoted is $1,400, CIF Rotterdam.

This quotation includes the costs from St. Louis, Missouri, via Philadelphia, Pennsylvania, to Rotterdam, The Netherlands. The responsibility of the seller, however, ends at Philadelphia, either on board the vessel or alongside the vessel, depending on whether an on-board bill of lading or a received-for-shipment bill of lading is called for.

The costs included in the quotation are the FAS or FOB vessel Philadelphia costs, plus ocean freight and marine insurance to Rotterdam. While the buyer is responsible for war risk insurance and fees for foreign government documents, these are commonly paid (advanced) by the seller and added into the calculation of the CIF price.

If a vessel should sink with CIF cargo on board, the buyer (not the seller) would be obliged to present claims. Sellers, however, may prefer to handle these claims if, according to the method of payment, title has been retained in the name of the seller or the seller's bank.

(5) Miscellaneous Price Quotations. The revised American rules contain definitions of two additional price quotations. Both carry the transaction beyond the points referred to in the previously mentioned quotations.

(a) Ex Dock (Named Port of Importation).

Example: Price quoted in $1,600, ex dock Rotterdam.

This quotation adds to the cost included in the CIF quotation, the war risk insurance, foreign government documentary fees, import duties in The Netherlands, and unloading costs, if any, in The Netherlands. It also adds to the responsibility of the seller who is now responsible until the expiration of free time on the dock in Rotterdam. In this particular example, war risk insurance was not requested and there are no government documentary fees.

(b) FOB (Named Inland Point in Country of Importation). Another price quotation is the FOB (named inland point in country of importation) quotation that includes all transportation costs to the inland point abroad at which delivery is to be made. It also includes all the other costs included in the ex dock quotation. The seller's liability for loss and damage continues "until arrival of goods on conveyance at the named inland point in the country of importation." The buyer is required to take delivery promptly from the freight car or other conveyance at the inland destination, to bear any costs that may arise after arrival there, and to be responsible for loss and damage occurring after arrival.

15

Financing World Marketing

Finance and marketing are inseparable in the conduct of international business. The relationship between the two functions permeates the entire marketing plan, reaching into almost every marketing activity. Pricing, for example, must consider the financial aspects of the transaction if the sale is to be profitable. The credit terms may be even more important than the price in a given transaction. Promotional expenditures and themes must be coordinated with financial practicality. The establishment of overseas branches, subsidiaries, and marketing channels requires both long-term expenditures and working capital.

The large size of many international transactions, the great distances involved, the many sovereign nations, and the limited knowledge about customers all combine to require close coordination between the financial and marketing departments. Furthermore, marketers need more than a casual knowledge of the financial considerations in each of the transactions they propose. This is especially true in international marketing since the sources and instruments used there are different from those used in domestic trade.

This chapter describes some of the major sources of funds for international marketing and the principal instruments that are used. The final section of the chapter deals with credit policy and the various means available for reducing the risk to the international seller.

SOURCES OF FUNDS FOR INTERNATIONAL MARKETING

As might be surmised from earlier discussions of the different marketing strategies that can be employed by the multinational firm, there is likewise, a variety of capital requirements that must be satisfied to support these approaches. Funds are needed by firms with foreign subsidiaries for physical facilities and for working capital to supply inventories, credit, and operating expenses. Even when the company limits its international activity to exporting, it needs funds for inventory, credit, and the promotional activities. These many needs are met from a variety of sources, some within the corporate structure and some external to the firm.

Internal Sources of Funds

The multinational firm with subsidiary, joint venture, or other affiliate operations abroad may be able to raise a portion of the required funds internally. Some of these funds may be obtained from the parent company's operations and investments, while others might be generated by the affiliate itself or other subsidiary operations within the corporate structure. The parent organization is an important financial source as it provides equity for the subsidiary or loans funds directly to the local unit. In some cases these loans may take the form of credit extended for inventory or equipment. The parent organization also has the opportunity to aid its subsidiaries by guaranteeing any loans that the affiliate negotiates with local financial sources.

External Sources of Funds

Usually the financing of international marketing requires funds in excess of those that can be allocated from the parent company. Thus, the firm turns to outside sources of both a private and governmental nature to meet these needs. Over the long course of international trading history a variety of financial institutions has evolved to aid the firm in supporting its marketing activities. Some of these are private sources, but others have been developed by the United States government and multinational sources.

Commercial Banks. Banking is one of the most important facilities for the conduct of international as well as domestic marketing. Until World War I, banks of the United States were engaged primarily in the development of the agricultural and industrial resources of the country. The United States was a borrowing nation and depended largely upon the banking facilities of other countries for support of its international marketing. Overseas business was transacted largely in sterling; the dollar was little known abroad. The reliance on European banks for transacting international business continued up to World War II despite the development of a few foreign branches of U.S. banks. The war, however, along with the extended worldwide depression between the two world wars, greatly affected the international banking structure. In the postwar period America emerged as a powerful economic factor in the world market. Many firms developed into multinational corporations and American banks developed worldwide operations to better serve these customers who had moved abroad. Some of the major banks not only evolved an extensive system of branch banks in foreign countries, but they also began to expand the number and types of services they offered to meet the needs of the emerging multinational firms.

The international firm can choose from a number of banking sources for its foreign operations. American banks have developed different types of facilities to extend credit and otherwise support the overseas operations of their customers. When the international firm makes its choice of banks, there are several possibilities that are open: (1) The American firm may choose to do its banking through the international department of a United States bank. This bank may carry out its functions through correspondent banks abroad or it may have its own subsidiaries or branches abroad. (2) Alternatively, the firm may choose to route certain transactions, perhaps at the request of its customers, through the local banks in the foreign markets. (3) One additional possibility that has emerged in recent years is to work with one of the consortia formed by banks of several nations. Each of these has special advantages for certain situations and companies.

The International Department of a Commercial Bank. The growth of international business has led many American banks to form international banking departments to service their customers' overseas operations and as a service to attract new accounts. These departments frequently are found in regional banks as well as the major commercial banks of New York and San Francisco.

The international departments perform all the necessary functions to finance imports and exports. They make payments as requested by correspondents or branches and cash drafts drawn against them; handle inquiries received from correspondents or branches; provide foreign credit and business information; issue commercial letters of credit for imports into the United States and all other countries; handle export credits opened by foreign purchasers for shipment of commodities from the United States; handle export drafts for collection or discount; purchase and sell drafts and cable transfers; make contracts for the purchase and sale of foreign exchange; make loans on commodities stored in the United States for ultimate shipment abroad; accept drafts for customers' accounts; accept drafts for foreign branches or correspondents to create dollar exchange; handle the purchases and sales of acceptances drawn on banks and institutions payable in the United States; dispose of refused merchandise shipped under financial arrangements negotiated by branches, correspondents, or themselves; and generally seek to promote international marketing by undertaking market surveys and preparing trade reports and lists of prospective foreign distributors. They also advise Americans contemplating business overseas and foreign business people coming to the U.S.

In addition to the export-import related services indicated above, the commercial bank is an important source of short- and medium-term financing. In their overseas operations U.S. banks often combine the functions of investment banking and commercial banking in order to underwrite security offerings or make long-term loans.

International banking facilities are available in a large number of locations throughout the United States. Many regional banks offer a wide range of international services, sometimes comprising all those listed above. This is important to many industrial and commercial firms because they have already developed contacts with these institutions to meet their domestic needs and find them to be effective in servicing international requirements as well. Regional banks have sought the international business in their territories and have developed knowledgeable personnel in their departments. In the last decade cities such as Chicago, Houston, Miami, Los Angeles, and San Francisco have developed their international banking facilities and are able to provide an extensive array of international services.

Overseas Arrangements of American Banks. A number of arrangements are used by American banks to provide worldwide services to their clients. Among the more significant are the development of correspondent relationships with banks in New York, San Francisco, London, Paris, and other financial centers; the establishment of overseas branches; and the formation of Edge Act corporations.

Correspondent Banks. When banks establish correspondent relations with other banks they enter into agreements for the reciprocal exchange of business. This is important to the international marketer because it means that a local bank has connections which enable it to do business on a worldwide basis. The correspondent bank may be one of the large multinational American institutions such as Citibank, Bank of America, or Chase Manhattan; or it may be a foreign bank.

Foreign correspondents usually are very familiar with the local business customs and laws of their territory. They have already established themselves in their communities and have contacts with local firms. Furthermore, they may not be subject to certain restrictions imposed on banks from abroad. They have the facilities for conducting the financing of business within their area without requiring the additional investment that would be needed if an American bank were to set up its own branch. A major advantage of the foreign correspondent for the marketer is the familiarity with local conditions.

But working through correspondents also has its hazards. A foreign bank may, for example, be quite lenient in handling documents by permitting inspection of merchandise prior to acceptance or payment of a draft or by holding a draft until arrival of the merchandise, regardless of instructions to the contrary. A foreign bank may not be impressed with the necessity of gathering complete information in connection with a refusal of acceptance or payment. In still other respects, such as the issuance of credit reports, the correspondent may have different concepts of banking service from those practiced in the United States. It is important to note that an American bank is not considered to be responsible for the acts of its correspondents.[1]

Citibank, N.A.

Foreign Branches and Subsidiaries of U.S. Banks. The growth of U.S. multinational firms has been accompanied by the development of foreign branches of U.S. multinational banks. These branches are located in the major financial centers of the world. The branch system differs from the correspondent system in that the branch is a part of the parent organization. Thus, the home office completely backs the branch and cannot disclaim responsibility for acts of the branch. The bank functions as a unit and a higher degree of coordination is possible for lending, handling deposits, and gathering information than

---

[1]Article 12 of Uniform Customs and Practice for Documentary Credits (1962) states:

Banks utilizing the services of another bank for the purpose of giving effect to the instructions of the applicant for the credit do so for the account and at the risk of the latter.

They assume no liability or responsibility should the instructions they transmit not be carried out, even if they have themselves taken the initiative in the choice of such other bank.

The applicant for the credit shall be bound by and liable to indemnify the banks against all obligations and responsibilities imposed by foreign laws and usages.

when correspondents are used. The unity of interest between the branch and its parent is advantageous to the international marketer in that the branch gathers a wide array of information that is transmitted to the home office and becomes available for improving the research base of the parent. The data are available to the marketer as a client of the worldwide organization. Also, within the local regulations, banking practices are likely to be more uniform and the range of services more consistent with American practice than when correspondents are used.

When American banks establish branches abroad, they become subject to the laws of the foreign countries. Many nations place few restrictions on the establishment of branches, but in others the branch may be subject to restrictions on its functions, capital requirements, investment of funds and surplus, or other matters. Sometimes strong nationalistic feelings may make it difficult, or impossible, for American banks to establish branches. In such instances, correspondent banks must be relied upon for service.

Edge Act Banks. The Edge Act, which was enacted in 1919 as section 25A of the Federal Reserve Act, provides for the federal incorporation of concerns to engage solely in international or foreign banking or in other types of foreign financial operations. Originally the Act provided for two types of banks: commercial banks, performing functions relating to the exportation and importation of merchandise such as issuance of drafts and letters of credit and dealing in foreign exchange; and investment banking houses, buying and selling foreign securities and issuing their own debentures secured by bonds, stocks, etc., of foreign corporations or governments. Now, however, Edge Law banks can combine the commercial banking and investment business in one enterprise. Thus, the Edge Act subsidiaries of American banks can make long-term loans and also purchase equities of foreign firms. These banks provide capital for the financing of business outside the continental limits of the United States. They participate in financing operations alone and with other banks and industrial concerns. By this means, medium- and long-term financing is provided. Such longer term development projects usually are initiated by local businesses and referred to the Edge Corporation by the parent.[2] The Edge Act permits a U.S. bank to establish international subsidiaries outside the bank's home state. In 1965 there were only 37 Edge Act operations, but these had expanded to 116 by 1975.[3]

United States Government Financial Agencies. The United States, along with most of the industrial nations, has established a number of

---

[2]David K. Eiteman and Arthur I. Stonehill, *Multinational Business Finance* (Reading, Pa.: Addison-Wesley Publishing Company, Inc., 1973), p. 89.
[3]"The Edge Is Off the Edge Act Banks," *Business Week* (April 7, 1975), p. 42.

financial agencies to support its export expansion programs. In many instances international marketers may not feel concerned with these agencies because the agencies deal directly with the foreign buyers. The U.S. firm may sell its product, draw drafts, and collect its funds without even being aware that the purchase was financed by a loan from the United States government. However, the alert marketer should be knowledgeable regarding these financing sources as a means of promoting the sale. The marketer can sometimes improve the chances of getting the order from the prospective buyer by helping make the necessary contacts.

Export-Import Bank of the United States (Eximbank). Since its establishment, the Eximbank has filled an expanding role in international finance. The bank's predecessor, the Export-Import Bank of Washington, was founded in 1934 to expand trade with the Soviet Union. At that time the country was also embarking on a Reciprocal Trade Agreements Program and, finally, the expansion of exports was seen as a means of relieving some of the impact of the depression.[4] The aim of the Export-Import Bank has always been to promote the exportation of United States products. During World War II the bank financed a number of activities for allies. Following the war the bank extended loans to Europe for purchase of U.S. equipment for reconstruction and also financed projects in developing countries. At the present time it is active in export financing to make credit available so U.S. exporters can compete effectively with those of other nations.

The Export-Import Bank now functions in three different financing fields: (1) Direct loans — these are loans made by the bank directly to buyers outside the United States for purchases of U.S.-made goods and services. The loans are used to pay U.S. suppliers and must be repaid in dollars by the borrowers. The direct lending program of the bank aims to supplement private sources of funding when the private sources cannot or are unwilling to assume the commercial and political risks involved, to extend longer terms of credit, and to provide terms that will enable U.S. suppliers to be competitive with suppliers of other nations who may be supported by similar programs.[5] In some instances the bank participates with private sources in making the loans. In general these loans must be for economically and technically sound projects, must have a reasonable assurance of repayment, and must not adversely affect the economies of the U.S. or the country in which the project is located.

(2) Guarantees and insurance — under its guarantee program the Eximbank assures repayment of credits extended by private lenders to

---

[4]See "Eximbank Programs, Volume 1," *Export-Import Bank of the United States* (April, 1973), for a more complete discussion of the history and programs of the bank.
[5]*Ibid.*, p. 30.

purchasers of U.S. goods and services who are outside the U.S. This guarantee is available to both U.S. and non-U.S. financial institutions. The commercial bank makes the loan to the exporter and is protected by Exim's guarantee against political and commercial loss. When the shipment is made, the commercial bank advises the Eximbank that it has purchased the buyer's promissory note without recourse to the exporter and Eximbank issues its guarantee. Thus, the exporter is relieved of the risk of loss and receives the funds. The commercial bank is also protected.

The Foreign Credit Insurance Association, a group of private casualty and property insurers, has offered credit insurance to U.S. exporters in cooperation with Eximbank since 1962.[6]

(3) Discount loans — the bank offers both a medium- and short-term discount program to commercial banks. Under these programs the Eximbank does not purchase the export obligations (e.g., promissory notes). Instead, it lends funds to the commercial banks to assist the banks in financing current exports.

Agency for International Development (AID). Another U.S. governmental agency involved in financing international trade is the Agency for International Development. AID was established as an agency in the Department of State under the Foreign Assistance Act of 1961. AID's assistance programs are designed to help less-developed countries develop their human and economic resources, increase productive capacities, and improve the quality of human life. The programs of the agency include: (1) promoting economic development through loans to less-developed friendly countries; (2) assisting in the development of human resources through programs of technical cooperation; (3) issuing guarantees to eligible U.S. investors assuring against loss of loan investments in self-liquidating housing projects; (4) furnishing both loan and grant assistance to promote the economic development of countries and areas in Latin America (Alliance for Progress); and (5) in cooperation with the Department of Agriculture, participating in the sale of agricultural commodities on concessional terms under Public Law 480.[7] Imports financed by AID loans must come from the United States, but exceptions can be made if the products are not available from here. The sale of agricultural commodities results in holdings of local currency that may be loaned to U.S. firms or their affiliates. These so-called Cooley loans, however, cannot be made for the manufacture of goods to be exported to the United States to compete with U.S.-produced goods.

---

[6]The FCIA insurance will be discussed later in this chapter in more detail.

[7]*United States Government Manual 1973/74* Office of the Federal Register, National Archives and Records Service (Washington: General Services Administration), pp. 343–344.

Multinational Agencies. Among the most significant sources of financing through multinational agencies are those of the World Bank group and the various regional development banks.

The World Bank Group. This group of three financial institutions is especially important for the financing of projects in developing countries that are related to infrastructure.

The International Bank for Reconstruction and Development. The World Bank is the central institution of the group. Founded in 1946 it has since made loans in excess of $20 billion. The bank's functions as set forth in its articles are:

1. To assist in the reconstruction and development of its member countries by facilitating the investment of capital for productive purposes, and thereby promote the long-range growth of international trade and the improvement of standards of living.
2. To make loans for productive purposes out of its own funds when private capital is not available on reasonable terms.
3. To promote private foreign investment by guarantees of, and participation in, loans and investments made by private investors.

The bank makes loans on conventional terms for basic development projects chiefly to governmental bodies in the borrowing countries or for government guaranteed loans to private interests. Approximately one third of these loans has been for electric power; another third for transport improvement; and the other one third for agriculture (particularly irrigation), for industry (especially steel products), and for general development purposes. In recent periods lending has been significant to Africa, Latin America, Asia, and the Middle East. American marketers benefit from the bank's activities through their participation in the development projects themselves and through increased market potential from the developing nations.

The International Finance Corporation (IFC). This organization was formed in 1956 to assist in the economic development of its member countries by promoting the growth of the private sector of their economies. The corporation is to supplement and assist the investment of private capital and not to compete with it. It is a development agency that is to finance only enterprises which are productive in the sense of contributing to the development of the economies of the member countries in which they operate.[8] The IFC has participated in loans involving pulp and paper products, construction materials, textiles, steel, motor vehicles, fertilizers, food, mining, and tourism, among others.

---

[8] IBRD, "Articles of Agreement of the International Finance Corporation and Explanatory Memorandum," (April 11, 1955), pp. 31–32.

The International Development Association (IDA). The third member of the world bank group, IDA, has the primary objective of creating a supplementary source of development capital for countries whose balance-of-payments prospects would not justify their incurring external debt on conventional terms. IDA credits are repayable in foreign exchange, but on very lenient terms. A government entity is usually the borrower. Credits may be repayable over a period of 50 years, including a grace period of 10 years. Compared with conventional loans, these terms substantially alleviate the repayment problems of the borrowing countries and bear less heavily on balances of payments.[9]

Regional Development Banks. Various regional development banks have been established to promote the development of underdeveloped areas through the provision of intermediate and long-term loans. Of the numerous banks so established only the Interamerican Development Bank and the European Investment Bank are discussed as examples.

The Interamerican Development Bank (IDB). This bank came into being in 1959 to promote the economic development and regional integration of the Latin American republics. The bank is a result of pressure exerted by the Latin American countries to provide a financing facility that would be less strict than the Export-Import Bank. IDB carries out three types of loan activities: (1) Loans repayable in the currency loaned are made available for 10- to 20-year maturities to private and governmental entities of member countries. (2) Soft loans at low interest rates and long maturities are made for both economic and social projects. These rates are adapted to the specific requirements of specific countries. (3) IDB administers special funds established by member and nonmember countries, including the United States, Canada, Sweden, United Kingdom, and West Germany. Funds received under the first two programs may be used for purchases anywhere in the free world, but funds from the Special Progress Trust Fund (3 above) are to be spent in the donor nations.[10]

The European Investment Bank. This bank was designed to facilitate the economic integration of the Common Market. It assists in the financing of projects that involve two or more national governments, aids in the adjustments required by integration policy, and aids the underdeveloped regions of the Common Market. The bank seeks to cooperate with the financial institutions in the various countries, thereby pooling the financial resources of the several nations.

---

[9]IDA, *Annual Report 1961–62* (Washington: U.S. Government Printing Office, 1962).
[10]J. Fred Weston and Bart W. Sorge, *International Managerial Finance* (Homewood, Ill.: Richard D. Irwin, Inc., 1972), pp. 165–166.

Other development banks have been established including regional banks such as the Asian Development Bank, the African Development Bank, and national development banks such as the Nacional Financier South Americano of Mexico.

INTERNATIONAL COMMERCIAL PAYMENTS

International commercial payments may be broadly grouped into the following categories: (1) cash, (2) open accounts, (3) bills of exchange, and (4) letters of credit.

Cash

Cash is both a method of payment and a term of payment, but as a method of payment it is rarely used in international marketing. As a method of payment, the international marketing firm may use checks as in domestic trade. If accounts are maintained in banks in various countries, checks may be drawn and paid in a variety of currencies. Or cash may be remitted by means of an international money order for small amounts.

Banks in the United States have deposit accounts abroad, and foreign banks have deposit accounts in United States banks. Funds may be paid from any of these accounts for purposes of financing trade, yet an exporter in the United States receives dollars for the merchandise that is sold, regardless of whether the price was stated in United States dollars or in some other currency. If, for example, the price were stated in Italian lira, then the American bank's lira account in Italy is increased and the Italian bank's dollar account in the United States bank is reduced. The conversion of the lira into United States dollars is a foreign exchange transaction taken care of by banks. Of course, Americans can accept foreign currencies in payment, but they usually do not care to do so.

Cash also is a term of payment. Cash may be called for with the order, or against certificates of manufacture as work on a complicated piece of equipment progresses. One exporter declared in 1958 the discovery of the perfect terms of payment. "We have the best inducement in the world. Since we deal with a high value item, we require a deposit with the order. If full payment is not received when shipment is ready, the deposit is forfeited. Our terms are strictly cash upon delivery." This position may have reflected America's position in 1958, but today credit is increasingly demanded.

Cash payment is not attractive to buyers since they bear the entire burden of financing the shipment. The buyer loses the use of funds for a considerable time before the goods are received, incurring a loss in the use of working capital as well as loss of interest. There may also be resentment of the view that the buyer is unworthy of credit.

Furthermore, the buyer is dependent upon the honesty, solvency, and promptness of the exporter in the business deal. Today cash payment will probably be used when the importer is of doubtful credit standing, when the exporter is financially weak, on orders requiring special construction, or when the exporter is not cognizant of the competitive situation faced by manufacturers of other countries.

Open Account

The open account method of payment for export shipments is the opposite of the cash method. Under the open account, goods are shipped without documents calling for payment — the commercial invoice of the exporter indicating the liability. Since no documentary evidence of ownership or obligation exists, the open account presents difficulties because of differences in the laws and customs of countries which make it difficult to safeguard the interests of the exporter. In the open account method the burden of financing rests upon the exporter. This requires a greater amount of working capital than other forms of payment and the exchange risks are assumed by the exporter. Despite the disadvantages of the open account, competitive pressures have forced many American producers to use this method after years of selling on more secure terms. The United States government has recognized the competitive advantage of this form of credit in the system of credit guarantees it has established to aid American producers in competing with their European counterparts.

Bills of Exchange

One of the common methods of payment in international trade involves the use of bills of exchange. Bills of exchange, also known as drafts, provide documentary evidence of obligation, and the financial risk of the transaction is more widely spread.

Bills of exchange are drawn by sellers of products, calling upon buyers either to pay or to accept for payment a designated sum of money at a determinable future time. Acceptance consists of an acknowledgement to this effect written across the face of the bill and signed by the drawee (buyer), obligating the drawee to provide payment of the amount stated within the period of time designated. When accepted, a draft becomes a trade acceptance. This method of payment provides the documentary evidence of obligation that is readily transferable.

A draft drawn without collateral documents attached is known as a clean draft, while one with certain stipulated documents of shipment, insurance, etc., is known as a documentary draft. In international marketing it is the documentary draft that is employed most commonly.

There are three parties to the draft as shown in Figure 15-1.

1. *The drawer* — the person who executes the draft (exporter, Malcolm Ewo).
2. *The drawee* — the person on whom the draft is drawn and who is required to meet the terms of the document (importer, Grant Simpson).
3. *The payee* — the party to receive payment (exporter or exporter's bank, The Philadelphia National Bank).

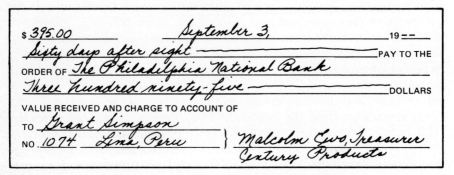

Figure 15-1 DRAFT (BILL OF EXCHANGE)

The drawer is the person to whom payment is due and is therefore the seller or exporter. The drawee is the person who owes the payment — the buyer or importer. In international payments the payee is usually the exporter (also the drawer), but it may be a bank that is named as payee on behalf of the exporter.

The time at which payment of a draft is to be made is known as a tenor or issuance. A *sight draft* calls upon the drawee to accept and pay the draft upon sight or presentation. This may mean that the draft is payable before the goods arrive because the draft is sent through the mails while the goods move by freight. The marketer should be aware, however, that in some countries it is an accepted custom for a bank to hold a draft until the arrival of the goods before presenting it to the drawee. An *arrival draft* calls for payment upon the arrival of the merchandise. The *date draft* calls for payment on a specified date, or at so many days after date.

In addition to the time designation in a quotation involving the use of drafts, there is also a declaration of the mode of transfer of documents covering shipments. The fundamental commercial documents required in international marketing are:

1. *Bills of lading.* The bill of lading serves three purposes. It is a receipt for a product, a contract with the carrier, and evidence of title. If it is a negotiable bill of lading, the holder is the lawful owner of the shipment.

2. The *marine insurance certificate*, or policy, protects the owners against marine and other insurable perils.
3. The *commercial invoice* indicates the types of goods, quantities, prices, terms, and other matters which relate to the shipment.

Other documents that may be required are packing lists, inspection certificates, consular invoices, and certificates of origin. Since the possession of essential documents is so important, their transfer is an integral part of financing.

When trade bills or drafts are drawn in international trade, the exporter may dispose of them by discounting, by borrowing, or by placing them for collection. The accepted draft can be discounted or sold to a bank or an advance or loan may be obtained from a bank, using the accepted draft and collateral documents as security. If the exporter is not seeking to discount or to borrow on a draft, the draft and all documents attached are sent to the bank with instructions to send them abroad for collection.

The draft method of payment, as has been pointed out, places the final responsibility upon the exporter, as the exporter is subject to recourse until the drawee has paid. Therefore, the necessity for securing adequate credit data on the drawee is apparent. In addition, the exporter runs the risk that the importer may reject the merchandise. In this case the importer will not accept the draft and the exporter is faced with the problem of disposing of the merchandise by forced sale abroad, storage, shipment to another country, or bringing the merchandise back to the home country.

Appendix A at the end of this chapter provides a detailed illustration of the process by which bills of exchange are used in international marketing.

Letters of Credit

The letter of credit is a means of payment that provides the exporter with more security than open accounts or bills of exchange. A *commercial letter of credit* is issued by a bank at the request of a buyer of merchandise whereby the bank itself undertakes to honor drafts drawn upon it by the seller of the merchandise concerned. Thus, the letter of credit substitutes the bank's promise to pay for that of the importer. Before the seller can receive payment, however, all the requirements specified in the letter of credit must be met, including the furnishing of documents, delivery dates, product specification, etc. Figures 15-2 (page 304) and 15-3 (page 305) illustrate features of letters of credit.

There are three essential parties to a commercial letter of credit:

1. The *opener or importer* — the buyer who opens the credit.
2. The *issuer* — the bank that issues the letter of credit.
3. The *beneficiary* — the seller in whose favor the credit is opened.

WINTERS NATIONAL BANK & TRUST CO.
INTERNATIONAL BANKING DEPARTMENT
40 NORTH MAIN STREET, DAYTON, OHIO 45401

CABLE ADDRESS:
" WINBANK"

PHONE: AREA 513
449-8657

IRREVOCABLE CREDIT NO. 69801-C

TWX: 810-459-1604

DATE: 5 March 19*

ANSWERBACK: WINTERS DTN

Southern Tool Co. Inc.
9654 Southern Blvd.
Dayton, Ohio 45440

Dear Sirs:

We are instructed to advise you of the establishment by Bank of the
United Arab Emirates of their irrevocable credit No. 18436 in your
favor, for the account of Arjan I Brahim Esmat for U.S. $3,000.00
(Three Thousand U.S. Dollars) available upon presentation to us of
your drafts at sight on us, accompanied by:

—Commercial invoice in triplicate, covering one pressing machine as
per purchase order 1274 dated 7 March 19*
—Consular invoice in triplicate, all signed and stamped by the Consul
of the United Arab Emirates
—Negotiable insurance policy and/or underwriter's certificate, endorsed
in blank, covering marine and war risks
—Full set of straight ocean Bills of Lading showing consignment to the
Bank of the United Arab Emirates stamped by United Arab Emirates Consul
and marked "freight prepaid" evidencing shipment from United States Port
to Kalba, Sharjah

Except as otherwise expressly stated herein, this credit is subject to
the Uniform Customs and Practice for Documentary Credits (1974 Revision)
International Chamber of Commerce, Brochure No. 290.

The above bank engages with you that all drafts drawn under and in
compliance with the terms of this advice will be duly honored if
presented to us on or before March 31, 19* on which date this credit
expires.

We confirm the foregoing and undertake that all drafts drawn and
presented in accordance with its terms will be duly honored.

VERY TRULY YOURS,

FOR WINTERS NATIONAL BANK & TRUST CO.
INTERNATIONAL BANKING DEPARTMENT

73-044. 5/72

Figure 15-2 IRREVOCABLE LETTER OF CREDIT

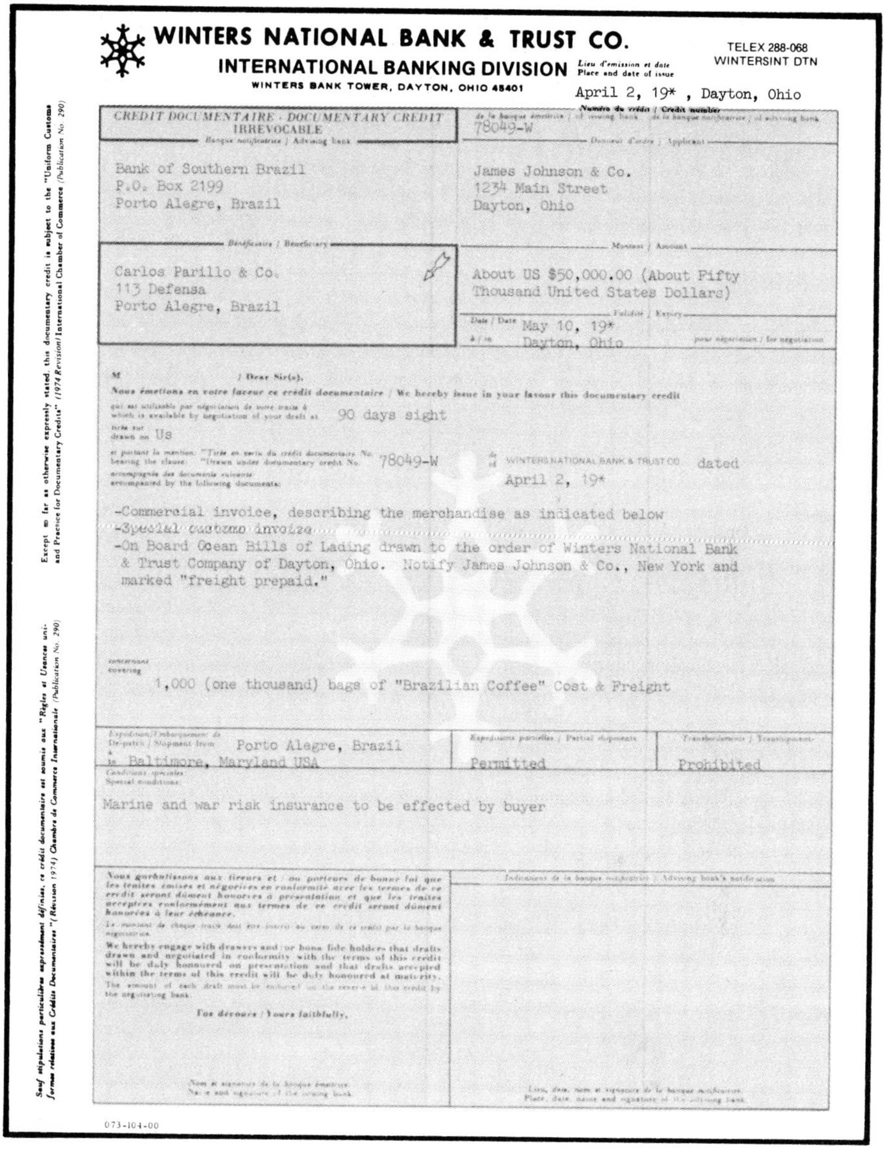

Figure 15-3 IRREVOCABLE LETTER OF CREDIT

In practice, however, there may be additional parties introduced in order to perform certain necessary functions. The *confirming bank* is a bank in the beneficiary's country, which at the request of the beneficiary guarantees the payment and/or acceptance of the seller's draft. The *advising bank*, located in the beneficiary's country, notifies the seller of the opening of the credit. The advising and confirming banks may be the same. The *paying or accepting bank* is the one on which the drafts are to be drawn.

Types of Letters of Credit. Letters of credit are of various types to fit differing conditions. Therefore, the exporter should carefully scrutinize them to determine the responsibilities of the parties.

Letters of credit may be either *revocable* or *irrevocable*. The privilege of revocability refers to the right of the issuing bank to revoke its promise to honor drafts drawn upon it. When the letter is revocable the issuer can cancel or change an obligation at any time prior to payment. Revocable credits are not legally binding undertakings between banks and beneficiaries.[11] When the letter is irrevocable the issuer agrees not to cancel or modify the credit without the permission of the beneficiary.

In addition, the letter of credit may be either *confirmed* or *unconfirmed*. If the letter of credit is confirmed, the irrevocable obligation of the issuer is guaranteed by a confirming bank in the beneficiary's country. Thus, in a confirmed letter of credit payment is guaranteed by both the issuing and the confirming bank. An exporter may seek confirmation because of dissatisfaction with the security offered by the issuing foreign bank.

It is perhaps obvious that letters of credit might take various combinations of the above. Thus, they might be revocable and unconfirmed, irrevocable and unconfirmed, or irrevocable and confirmed. While an irrevocable and confirmed letter of credit is a virtual guarantee of payment from the standpoint of the responsible banks, it is no guarantee that the conditions of the credit will or can be met. For example, accidents, strikes, or government allocations of material may delay the production of the order so that the expiration date of the credit cannot be met.

When payment authorized by a letter of credit is designated in funds of the country of the beneficiary, the credit is said to be in *local currency*. The converse of this is *foreign currency*. Although usually made for a fixed sum of money, a letter of credit may be renewable, and it is then known as a *revolving letter of credit*. Finally, in authorizing the type of draft to be drawn under a letter of credit, the letter may be either for cash payment or for payment at a definite future date.

---

[11]International Chamber of Commerce, *Uniform Customs and Practices for Commercial Documentary Credits*, Article 2 (1962).

Under conditions of shortage of exchange, the letter of credit may be used to assure the availability of dollars or other currency.

Checking Export Letters of Credit and Documents. Exporters are encouraged to check letters of credit carefully to be sure there is no later misunderstanding. The beneficiary should check for the following:[12]

1. Has the correct title been used in addressing you as beneficiary?
2. Has the correct title of the buyer been used?
3. Is the amount sufficient? Take into consideration the terms of the sale and possible addition of any charges.
4. Is the tenor of the drafts the same as your quotation to the buyer?
5. Is the credit available at the banking institution or in the locality requested by you?
6. Are the documents required in the credit in accordance with your arrangements with the buyer and can such documents be furnished?
7. Is the description of the merchandise correct? (Check unit price, trade definition, point of shipment, and destination.)
8. Do you agree with any special instructions which may appear in the credit?
9. Is the expiration date and place of expiration satisfactory?
10. Is the credit confirmed by a domestic bank, or is an unconfirmed credit satisfactory?

Since the terms of a commercial letter of credit are so exacting and the payment under the credit depends upon meeting all of the letter's requirements, the beneficiary cannot be too careful in checking every step of the transaction.

Advantages of Letters of Credit to Buyers. Although the burden of financing is placed upon the buyer under a letter of credit transaction, this method of payment also provides certain advantages:

1. Perhaps the greatest practical benefit derived by the buyer is the protection of setting a definite date by which the seller is required to ship the order. The buyer, accordingly, may figure on prompt delivery, as the credit will expire on the date set unless an extension is granted.
2. The buyer can receive low prices when a letter of credit is submitted, since contingencies are so fully guarded against that an exporter finds it unnecessary to cover them in the price.
3. Advance orders, or orders running throughout a period of time, are also well protected by reason of the expiration date of the letter of credit as well as by the limitation of the sum of money for which it is drawn.
4. Finally, an attractive cash discount may be offered to importers for providing letter-of-credit payment.

---

[12]George W. Tomlinson, *Pointers on Export Letters of Credit* (Philadelphia, Pa.: The First Pennsylvania Banking and Trust Company, 1953), p. 11.

In order to facilitate an understanding of the process by which the letter of credit operates, an illustration is provided in Appendix B at the end of the chapter.

CREDIT EXTENSION

One of the ever-present problems in international marketing is the extension of credit. Whenever international marketing groups assemble and the subject turns to marketing conditions in particular countries, the question inevitably raised is: "What terms do you grant?" The differences in the terms are often due to the products for which the terms are cited. There are also differences in the way marketers appraise a particular market. Therefore, it would appear that the appraisal of the credit situation of a buyer in a particular market is determined by a number of factors. Before looking at these factors, however, it would be well to examine closely the meaning of credit.

The Meaning of Credit

Credit usually refers to the procedure of surrendering title to merchandise without immediate payment. In other words, credit means trusting the buyer to pay for goods after title to them has been obtained by the buyer. Under the various credit and payment terms described earlier, a buyer would receive credit under open account and under all draft transactions. Under a letter of credit, the exporter (beneficiary) is assured of payment; therefore there is no credit risk.

There is another aspect of credit, however, that should also be considered. This is the credit — or better, the financial — needs of the firm that is engaged in exporting merchandise. It refers to the fact that under the terms of sale, there is usually a period of time elapsing between the shipment of the order and the time that payment is received. A payee of a draft may discount or borrow against the draft before its maturity but in so doing, interest for the period of time that the funds are advanced must be paid. Moreover, there is no assurance that the draft will be eventually paid by the drawee.

The inference may easily be drawn that under all credit and payment terms except open account, a payee (exporter) has valuable documents that can be used to obtain immediate finances, if such finances are required. Such is not the case because banks will not discount or loan against accepted drafts beyond a certain point, and this point is the line of credit that the bank has set up for each individual customer. The line of credit establishes a maximum amount that will be loaned to a customer. A limit may be placed on the dollar value of discounting or borrowing that an exporter will be permitted to receive.

Evolution of Export Credit by United States Firms

A common criticism of American exporters is that they are unwilling to grant the liberal credits that are offered by some European competitors. If it is true that legitimate credit extension is predicated upon adequate information, then the general absence before World War I of foreign credit data in the United States may be cited as one reason for the failure of American exporters to extend liberal credit at that time.

European countries, particularly Great Britain, with an early start in overseas business, promptly developed the means of extending foreign credit. This was accomplished not only through sources of information but also by the creation of a banking system that would advance funds on trade documents. Until 1913, when the Federal Reserve Act was passed, this facility was not generally available to American exporters. At that time the United States was very active in developing domestic resources and business. Export trade was actively solicited only by exceptional concerns that saw a limit to their domestic market. Export commission houses and merchants handled most of the business; and these, together with the manufacturers that were engaged directly in international marketing, granted credit in many instances. The manufacturers who took business as it came, without solicitation, rarely granted credit as they were not forced to do so.

With the development of interest in international marketing and the growth of sources of information and changes in banking methods, American exporters are more free to extend foreign credit. Perhaps it is true that Americans do not grant as liberal terms as do European competitors. In the past they did not find it necessary to grant long-term credit. However, recent competition in the world markets has changed this. Now credit is an important competitive tool. American producers who formerly sold only on irrevocable confirmed letters of credit are finding it necessary to extend credit.

Conditions Influencing Foreign Credit Extension

There are several conditions peculiar to international marketing that require an exporting firm to view foreign credit differently from domestic credit. These conditions are:

1. Supply of banking capital.
2. Interest rates.
3. Diversification of production.
4. Time in transit and business turnover.
5. Exchange rate fluctuations.
6. Competition.
7. Customs.

At the outset it is well to emphasize that the influence of these conditions varies from country to country. While in Canada credit conditions are practically identical with those in the United States, except for foreign exchange rates and tariffs, the conditions influencing credit extension are different in Mexico. The supply of capital varies greatly among countries and is highly dependent on the nation's natural resources and past production.

Importers located in underdeveloped areas have depended upon foreign sellers to finance their purchases of consumer goods, transportation, automobiles, or infrastructure improvements because local bankers were unable to provide the financing. The supply of capital is quite meager in these countries.

Interest rates in nonindustrial areas usually are substantially higher than in industrial countries. In such circumstances the wisdom of an importer borrowing abroad at relatively low interest rates and lending the funds at home, where interest may be from 10 to 30 percent, becomes apparent.

The lack of developed business systems is another factor entering into the foreign credit situation. In underdeveloped or developing areas of the world, intensive specialization in commodity or functional lines may not be warranted, and the business person may frequently combine several types of business ventures in order to earn an adequate income. This imposes a heavy financial responsibility. A further factor accentuating this condition is the lack of diversified production. Many countries have only certain primary products for export such as sugar, rubber, coffee, etc. It is quite conceivable that a crop failure or a low price could cause an economic collapse. If this occurs, not only the grower, but also business people, bankers, and others may be placed in precarious positions.

Because of the length of time elapsing between the date of shipment by the exporter and the time goods are received by the importer, there may be a considerable period during which, in the case of cash payment, the importer is without both funds and goods. If credit of sufficient duration is granted to enable the importer to obtain the goods before making payment, the exporter bears the financial burden of the import transaction, but the sluggishness of turnover may leave the goods in the hands of the buyer for a considerable additional period of time, during which the buyer's funds would also be tied up. This condition is of little significance in domestic trade where shipments may be made quickly, but in international marketing it presents an important problem. It may be weeks or months before the importer located at an inland destination receives the merchandise. Moreover, customs duties and transportation charges may be paid before delivery. In addition, distance and time compel importers to place orders for substantial quantities goods long before the selling season opens.

Still another condition influencing credit extension in international marketing is the fluctuation in foreign exchange rates. Whenever a buyer receives quotations and accepts prices in a currency other than the native currency, the buyer assumes a speculative risk against which protection may or may not be obtained.[13] If the buyer has agreed to pay for the purchases by sight draft, the latest that payment can be postponed and possession of the goods received is upon their arrival. An exchange loss sufficiently great to eliminate the anticipated trade profit may be incurred.

Credit may also be extended for competitive reasons. As a means of promoting sales, liberal credit terms may be offered. Moreover, it may be difficult for an exporter to refuse credit terms at least as liberal as those customarily granted by rival suppliers.

Finally, credit extension is influenced by the credit customs of the foreign market. Certain terms are often established in each market along commodity lines, and they are to be recognized by exporters selling in those markets.

Foreign Credit Policy and Management

Whether or not credit will be extended on export sales is a matter that will be decided more by the policy of the firm than by the foreign market, the foreign importing firm, or even product conditions.

If domestic credit terms are 2 percent cash discount in 10 days, 30 days net, a firm may be reluctant to consider any export credit terms that would prevent returns from reaching them for a period longer than 30 days. In international marketing, however, such a period may constitute no credit at all for buyers because of the longer delivery time.

Any large exporter finds that continuous supervision of credit through foreign credit departments is essential. Such a department is charged with the following functions:

1. Investigating and authorizing credit. It must assemble credit data and decide the terms, amounts, and methods of credit extension.
2. Making collections, maintaining customer respect and goodwill.
3. Recommending credit policies dealing with exchange restrictions, exchange rate fluctuations, export credit insurance, trade disputes, and the refusal of shipments.
4. Cooperating with other departments. For example, in the appointment of agents abroad, the credit department may aid the sales department by collecting data on prospective representatives.

Sources of Foreign Credit Information

The foreign credit manager uses several sources of credit information. References received from foreign customers are contacted and

---

[13]See Chapter 4 for further discussion of foreign exchange rates and the risks involved in international buying and selling.

salespeople are asked to forward whatever credit information they have. If the firm maintains branch offices or subsidiaries, the credit manager may receive valuable credit information from them. Indeed, a considerable degree of credit control may be transferred to the foreign branches because of their knowledge of local conditions. When an exporter sells through foreign agents or representatives, these become a source of credit information. The firm's own credit files are an important source of information on the firm's regular customers.

Mercantile Credit Agencies. The export credit manager may obtain credit reports from *mercantile credit agencies* whose primary activities consist of gathering and disseminating credit information. For example, Dun & Bradstreet, Inc., has offices abroad in most communities of commercial importance. It depends primarily upon its foreign reporters, whose reports are supported by investigations of American sources such as banks, manufacturers, and others having foreign connections and outlets. In the gathering of data the reporters are somewhat handicapped, as are all others seeking foreign credit information, by the unwillingness of many foreign business people to provide the necessary information. The reports are as factual as possible, but they also contain opinions obtained from the local trading community. Dun & Bradstreet also publishes *International Market Guide* — *Latin America* with a listing for 220,000 Latin American companies, and *International Market Guide* — *Continental Europe* with marketing profiles of over 372,000 companies. Figure 15-4 (page 313) is an example of a typical Dun & Bradstreet international report.

Banks. Many American banks gather foreign credit information for the use of their clients. Their reports are prepared mainly on the basis of information received from foreign correspondent banks, from branch banks, and from information incident to the bank's foreign transactions. Therefore, the banks' data are less dependent upon trade opinion or commercial investigation.

Interchange of Ledger Experience. Export credit information sources quite different from those referred to previously are organizations that depend primarily or wholly upon an *interchange of ledger experience* among the exporters themselves. An informal exchange of ledger experience occurs when an exporter consults with other credit managers, while a more organized, but still informal, method of interchange occurs at the periodic meetings of various local world trade or credit clubs.

A more formal interchange of credit information and experience has, however, been organized. The Foreign Credit Interchange Bureau of the National Association of Credit Management is a nonprofit

INTERNATIONAL REPORTS CONTAIN THE FOLLOWING POINTS OF INFORMATION

1. SUMMARY — Condenses the information needed for a sales or credit decision. Highlights significant facts. Credit data, on the right, shows year business started, trend of payments, annual sales, net worth, number of employees. RATING, upper right, indicates estimated financial strength and composite credit appraisal.

2. HISTORY — Identifies owners and their commercial experience, describes the background of the business. Enhances understanding and makes it easier to establish confident business relations.

3. FINANCES — The financial condition, how a firm is progressing, capital in use and borrowing record. Analysis covers ability of the concern to meet its obligations.

4. OPERATION — What the concern does, lines of merchandise and class of trade sold, facilities and equipment. Is it a profitable outlet for your goods and services? Can they supply your needs?

5. TRADE — How they pay their bills, the answer to one of your most important questions. A concise record of trade payments, high credits received, amounts owing and, if any, past due, terms, and pertinent comments from suppliers.

Source: *Dun & Bradstreet International* brochure "Guides to World-Wide Markets," undated.

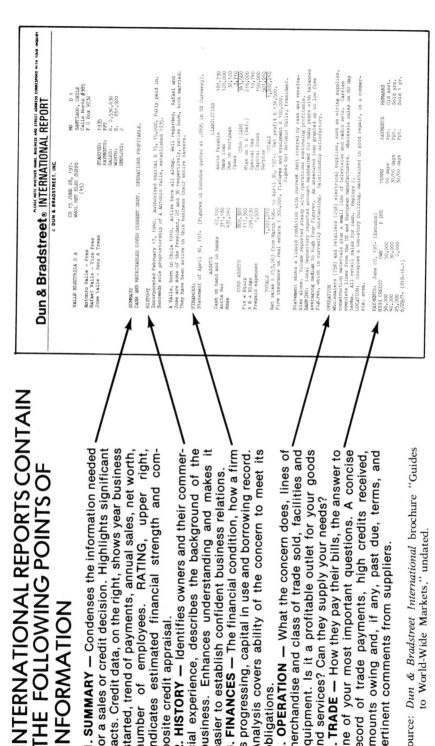

Figure 15-4 INTERNATIONAL REPORT

cooperative bureau whose members agree to furnish to the bureau information regarding its experience with foreign customers. Based upon the experience of approximately 36,000 members, the bureau is in a position to provide its members with valuable individual credit reports such as that shown in Figure 15-5.

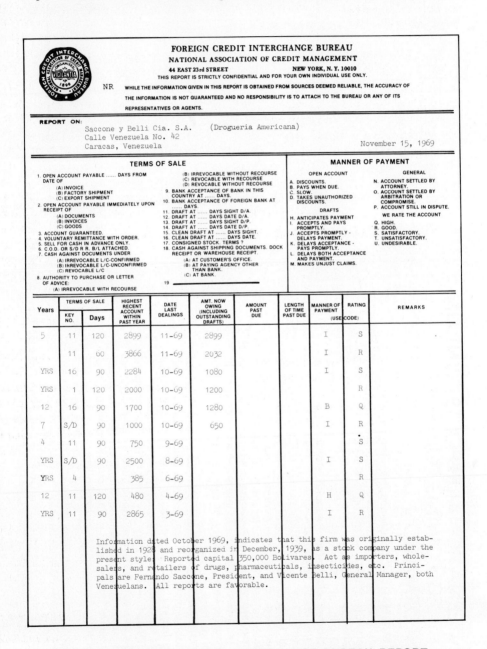

Figure 15-5 FOREIGN CREDIT INTERCHANGE BUREAU REPORT

In addition to issuing foreign credit interchange reports, the FCIB also conducts monthly round-table conferences covering current foreign credit, collection, and exchange problems; it operates a world-wide collection service to aid in collecting deliquent accounts; it issues a *Weekly Bulletin* which reports current changes affecting foreign credit, collection, and exchange conditions; and it offers a consultation service for the benefit of members.

U.S. Government. By including the United States government as a source of foreign credit information, it is not to be inferred that the government is in the credit reporting business. However, among its activities relating to the promotion of international marketing and coming within the scope of what is known as *commercial intelligence* is the provision of certain data for the benefit of American exporters. This information is obtained by Foreign Service representatives and is found in the World Trader Data Reports prepared by the Bureau of International Commerce. These reports are described more fully in Chapter 18. Some credit data are also available from the Export-Import Bank.

Foreign Collections

It is one thing to decide upon a policy for granting credit but quite another to determine what to do when a customer fails to pay.

If payment is not made when due, prompt steps are to be taken, but the marketer should remember that failure to pay may be due to several reasons. It is essential to know the reason that applies to a particular case before adopting a definite plan of action.

The buyer may, for example, have fair or unfair claims against the exporter and thus not pay. In such cases, if a reasonable adjustment is made, the payment may be made. Still, a thorough investigation is advisable to determine, if possible, the legitimacy of a claim and where to place the responsibility. If the buyer is merely seeking to evade payment, or is taking advantage of some technicality, the exporter may try to obtain protection. Legitimate claims are, however, the general rule and if the claims are not resolved, some form of conciliation or arbitration is highly advisable for making settlement.

A shortage of liquid capital is a reason for failure to make payment, and here the collection policy, at least at the beginning, can be sympathetic. Trying to rush such a case may lead to total loss, whereas cooperation may result in payment and, if not, will retain a customer. Extended financial embarrassment may finally result in insolvency. If this happens, the fortunate creditor is the one who insisted on and received payment. Impending insolvency, however, can usually be discerned from up-to-date credit reports and, in such cases, the collection policy will try to obtain funds before the crash. When insolvency occurs, it is highly desirable to place the case in the hands of a capable lawyer, or to instruct the bank to take the necessary steps, or seek legal recourse in other ways. Laws relating to bankruptcy vary widely and the greatest care is essential.

Sometimes nonpayment is caused by exchange restrictions over which the buyer has no control. Then the exporting firm will have to determine its policy with respect to outstanding accounts and the methods to be pursued in connection with future sales to customers in that country.

Assistance in Making Collections. Several kinds of organizations can aid the firm in making foreign collections. Assistance can be obtained from organizations such as the National Association of Credit Management. Foreign collections may be undertaken by American or foreign collection agencies, and banks may press claims for payment. The foreign branches of American banks are especially valuable in this connection.

In draft transactions the bank located abroad will, if so instructed, enter official protest in case of nonpayment of a draft. This step is often necessary to support subsequent court action.

Foreign Service Officers of the Department of State, while unable to assist directly in the collection of debts because of Foreign Service regulations, can use their good offices to aid in the adjustment of trade disputes. For example, a delinquent debtor abroad may be approached informally to determine whether a misunderstanding exists. By such information methods, delinquency problems are frequently solved.

Litigation. Legal action may provide the necessary collection power, but it should be employed only as a last resort. As a widely accepted policy, it is advisable to avoid litigation in foreign courts unless the amount involved is large enough to warrant this procedure. There are many objections to lawsuits in international trade, among the most significant being the delay and expense incurred, loopholes in foreign laws favorable to the delinquent, reaction against the exporter because of nationalistic feelings, and possible political immunity of the defaulter. At a minimum legal actions are long and costly.

Credit Guarantees and Insurance

Certainty of payment may at times be obtained by means of guarantees. There are several sources of credit guarantees.

Credit Guarantees by Banks. The oldest and most widely known method of shifting the credit burden by means of a guarantee is known as *del credere* — a term really synonymous with guarantee. *Del credere* transactions, in one sense, consist of discounting drafts drawn with the words "without recourse" placed under the signature of the drawer. The party (bank) that buys the paper thus becomes responsible under the bill and the drawer is entirely relieved. For this service a commission is charged which measures roughly the risk that is incurred in the guarantee.

The payment of credits in international trade may also be assured by means of the irrevocable and confirmed letter of credit, under which the issuing and confirming banks are both responsible to the drawer of the drafts. Letters of credit, however, are not obtainable everywhere and at all times.

Credit Guarantees by Factors. Another financing facility that provides guarantee of payment under credit extension is the *factor*. Factors relieve manufacturers and merchants of the time and expense involved in administering their receivables. In a given transaction the factor will handle all of the customer's credit checking, accounts receivable, bookkeeping, and collections; assume all credit and political risks; and, when required, provide necessary financing. For a fee the factor takes over the credit operation for a seller of merchandise. Financing for the seller is provided by buying receivables on a nonrecourse basis; that is, if the factor can't collect, there is no recourse on the seller.

Credit Guarantees by Sales Agents. In another type of *del credere* arrangement, sales agents assume the risk. An exporter may employ the services of a commission sales agent abroad, and the agent may assume the entire responsibility, including credit risks, to customers. In such an arrangement, the exporter generally extends credit to the customers but looks to the agent for a part or all of the funds due under credit extensions in case the customer fails to make payment. For this service the agent receives a *del credere* commission in addition to the usual salary and/or commission.

Credit Guarantees by Individuals. Credit may also be guaranteed by individuals, but this practice has developed to a marked degree only in certain countries where the prevailing banking and commercial structures have failed to provide adequate protection of the rights of sellers. With the development of banking facilities this system is declining, but until satisfactory means of obtaining adequate credit data on national merchants are available and until security of the rights of sellers is provided, some such form of personal credit guarantee may remain of importance.

Self-Insurance of Export Credits. Self-insurance takes the form of a reserve set aside for bad debts — a practice followed in domestic as well as in international trade. The reserve is computed on the basis of past credit experience and is set at an amount sufficient to offset prospective losses on accounts receivable, the assumption being that future losses will average the same as in the past. However, the failure of this statistical expectation to work out uniformly has wrecked many self-insurance plans.

Export Credit Insurance. Export credit insurance today involves two concepts: (1) insurance against commercial credits and (2) insurance against "political" risks. These political risks are exchange transfer (inconvertibility) hazards that rarely can be anticipated by exporters. In recent years the United States government has helped by protecting against these political risks; exporters, however, generally have preferred to take care of the commercial credit risks themselves through private credit facilities if such protection becomes necessary.

The subject of credit insurance is important because many overseas customers are attracted by the liberal credit terms offered by exporters of competing countries. A brief review of export credit insurance practices in the United States and in other countries is helpful in appraising this situation.

Export Credit Insurance in the United States.

In the fall of 1954, the Export-Import Bank of the United States began an expanded program of exporter credits by financing without recourse. This program was slow in getting started and by the end of the fiscal year 1956, only $8.1 million in 65 exporter credit lines had been made, plus $3.9 million in 11 new exporter credit lines. But exporters began to show greater interest in this means of financing capital exports, and the net amount of exporter credits as of December 31, 1957, was $180 million.

In early 1962 the Foreign Credit Insurance Association (FCIA) was established in collaboration with the Export-Import Bank. This association is a voluntary group of private insurance companies interested in the insuring of foreign credits. With the aid of the Foreign Credit Insurance Association, medium-term credit was offered by U.S. commercial banks.

The Export-Import Bank assumes responsibility for political risks and, together with FCIA's member companies, shares the policy obligations with respect to commercial credit risks. *Political risks* are defined as inconvertibility of foreign currency to United States dollars, expropriation, confiscation, war, civil commotion or like disturbances, and cancellation or restriction of export or import licenses. *Commercial credit risks* are defined as insolvency of a buyer and the buyer's protracted default.

The FCIA offers several types of policies, and even these can be varied to meet the needs of exporters.

Master Policy. A master policy provides coverage for both political and commercial risks. It is written to cover all, or a reasonable spread, of an exporter's eligible shipments during a one-year period. It covers both short- and medium-term credits up to five years. Usually FCIA insures 90 percent of the gross invoice value of the shipments, while the exporter retains the other 10 percent. There is also a deductible provision on the commercial risk, but this does not apply to the political risk coverage. A special master policy can be obtained at a reduced premium to cover political risk only.[14]

Short-Term Policy. A short-term policy also requires the exporter to insure a reasonable spread of the eligible short-term export credits. It covers commercial risks and political risks on terms up to 180 days.

Medium-Term Policy. A medium-term policy covers capital and quasi-capital goods that are made in the U.S. and sold on terms from 181 days to five years. In contrast to the other policies, this one is written on a case-by-case basis. Under this policy the buyer must make a minimum cash payment on or before delivery of at least 10 percent and the remaining portion is covered by a promissory note that provides for equal installment payments. Payment is to be made in dollars at a U.S. bank. Normally the policy covers 90 percent of both commercial and political risks.

Combination Policy. The combination policy combines coverage of short- and medium-term risks and is designed especially to meet the needs of transactions with overseas dealers and distributors. It provides protection in three areas: (1) parts and accessories on terms up to 180 days, (2) inventory financing where the exporter ships under a floor plan, and (3) receivables financing with terms up to three years.

Recent Changes. Since foreign credit insurance is relatively new in the United States, many changes are being made to increase its effectiveness. For example, the FCIA now covers risks on the sale of technical services abroad by U.S. firms, such as architectural services, design, engineering studies, and economic surveys.

The need for credit information led to the development of a Management Information Systems Department to provide a data base for the evaluation of overseas customers by FCIA underwriters. In 1974 this Buyer Data Base became operational. It contains data on about 88,000 foreign buyers and is updated every 24 hours. An underwriter may request information by individual buyer, country, or market levels according to a particular need.[15] This should aid marketers by cutting the time needed to process credit data and by helping FCIA tailor its policies to specific requirements.

---

[14]These descriptions are based on FCIA, "Export Credit Insurance: The Competitive Edge" (undated brochure).

[15]*FCIA News*, Issue No. 85 (April, 1975), p. 1.

Additional benefits of Foreign Credit Insurance have been pointed out by the FCIA: "On the security of this insurance, the exporter may be much more active in competing with his foreign competitors on credit terms, when in his good judgment it is necessary and desirable for him to do so. This security also makes it much easier for him to obtain bank credit on the basis of the assignment of the proceeds of the policy. Further, this insurance will undoubtedly make it possible for exporters to expand their sales and it should also attract new firms into the export business, which is an objective very much desired by our government in order to promote our general economy and to help correct our balance of payments problem."[16]

QUESTIONS

1. What services are offered by the international division of a commercial bank? Which of these are peculiar to international marketing with no counterpart in domestic trade?
2. How can a bank in Kansas City, Missouri, offer international services to its clients?
3. What is an Edge Act Bank? Define its functions.
4. Of what interest to international marketers is the activity of the United States government in financing?
5. Describe the financing operations of the Export-Import Bank of the United States.
6. Why was the International Bank for Reconstruction and Development (World Bank) established? Why should marketers be interested in its activities?
7. Distinguish between the activities of the IFC and the IDA.
8. Why are the loans from the IFC and IDA generally for long periods of time and at low interest rates?
9. Why is the matter of the currency which is to be borrowed and the currency in which repayment is to be made of such importance?
10. Define a bill of exchange.
11. Explain the purposes of the essential documents used in a documentary draft transaction.
12. What choice does the exporter have in disposing of the documentary drafts drawn to cover international transactions?
13. In what way does a commercial letter of credit provide a means of substituting bank credit for mercantile credit?
14. What advantages does the exporter gain in obtaining a confirmation of an irrevocable letter of credit?
15. How important is the checking of the terms of a letter of credit and the documents when the time comes to receive payment under the credit?
16. Why were U.S. exporters slow in developing export credit?

---

[16]Foreign Credit Insurance Association, *Introducing Exporters, Bankers, and Industry to Foreign Credit and Political Risk Insurance Through FCIA* (undated pamphlet).

17. What major sources of credit information are available to the international marketer?
18. Define political risk.
19. Of what value is credit insurance to the American exporter?

SUPPLEMENTARY READINGS

Dowd, Laurence P. *Principles of World Business*. Boston: Allyn & Bacon, Inc., 1965. Chapters 21, 22, and 23.

Eiteman, David K., and Arthur I. Stonehill. *Multinational Business Finance*. Reading, Pa.: Addison-Wesley Publishing Co., 1973. Chapters 5, 6.

Ewing, John S., and Frank Meissner. *International Business Management — Readings and Cases*. Belmont, Calif.: Wadsworth Publishing Co., 1964. Chapter 20.

Exporters Encyclopedia. New York: Dun & Bradstreet, Inc., annual.

Goldner, Jack. *Foreign Trade Accounting and Management Handbook*. Chicago: Commerce Clearing House, Inc., 1967. Chapters 1, 3, and 10.

Morgan Guaranty Trust Company of New York. *Export and Import Procedures*. New York: Morgan Guaranty Trust Company of New York, 1968.

Vernon, Raymond. *Manager in the International Economy*. Englewood Cliffs, N.J.: Prentice-Hall, Inc., 1968.

Wasserman, Max J., Charles W. Hultman, and Laszlo Zsoldos. *International Finance*. New York: Simmons-Boardman Publishing Corp., 1963. Chapters 8, 9, 10, and 11.

Weston, J. Fred and Bart W. Sorge. *International Managerial Finance*. Homewood, Ill.: Richard D. Irwin, Inc., 1973. Chapters 8 and 9.

Appendix A
BILLS OF EXCHANGE

In order to gain a better understanding of the process by which the bill of exchange operates, Figure 15-6 (page 322) traces a transaction using a 60-day sight draft.

1. The American exporter makes shipment to a British importer with the billing made out to the name of the exporter.
2. The exporter delivers the draft and shipping documents to the American bank which sends the draft and shipping documents to the British bank.
3. The British bank notifies the importer that the documents have arrived and presents the draft to the importer for acceptance, payment in 60 days.
4. Upon accepting the bill of exchange, the shipping documents are surrendered to the importer and the shipment can now be claimed.
5. The accepted bill of exchange is returned to the American bank by the British bank.
6. The exporter discounts the draft and receives advance payment.

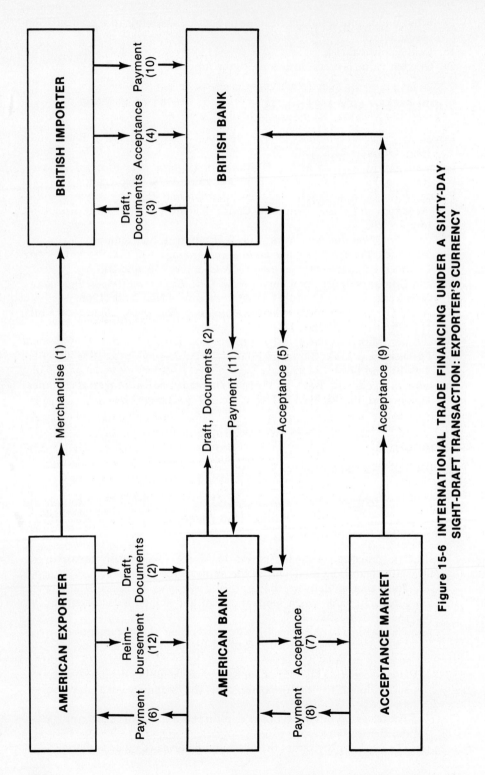

Figure 15-6 INTERNATIONAL TRADE FINANCING UNDER A SIXTY-DAY SIGHT-DRAFT TRANSACTION: EXPORTER'S CURRENCY

7. The American bank, in turn, disposes of the bill of exchange in the acceptance market.
8. Upon receiving such funds, the American bank is now in a liquid position again.
9. When the 60-day maturity approaches, the bill of exchange is sent to the British bank by some financial institution that had purchased it from the American bank.
10. The British bank receives payment from the British importer in pounds sterling and the conversion of sterling to dollars is made by the British bank.
11. The funds are transmitted to the present holder of the trade acceptance.
12. The American exporter settles with the American bank to complete the transaction.

Appendix B

OPERATION OF A LETTER OF CREDIT TRANSACTION

Figure 15-7 (page 324) may clarify the previous discussion and show several additional features of the operation of a letter of credit transaction, an illustration of international trade financing under an irrevocable, confirmed letter of credit, and a 60-day sight draft drawn in the exporter's currency. It should be observed that the burden of arranging the letter of credit falls upon the importer.

(1) A commercial letter of credit (60 days, irrevocable, confirmed) is mutually decided upon as the method of payment for goods ordered by a Brazilian importer; the price is quoted in American dollars.

(2) The importer (opener) arranges the credit with a bank in Brazil and fills out a formal application. (This application may be forwarded by the bank to a correspondent in case the former has no foreign connection.)

(3) If the application is accepted, the letter of credit is signed and the Brazilian bank becomes the issuer. This contract protects the bank by guaranteeing payment of all sums expended by the bank under the credit. Security is required by the bank in accordance with the standing of the importer.

(4) The preliminary steps now having been completed, the credit is made available by preparing the (import) letter of credit in favor of the exporter (beneficiary). Because it is irrevocable, it cannot be rescinded by the issuer without the consent of the beneficiary. The document is sent to the advising bank.

(5) The advising bank informs the beneficiary by means of an *advice of letter of credit* (export credit). As the credit is to be confirmed, the adviser is instructed by the issuer to add its name to the obligation,

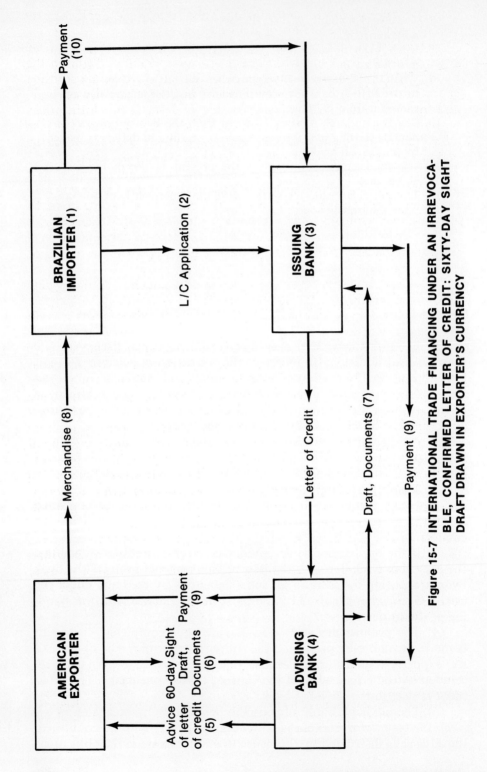

Figure 15-7 INTERNATIONAL TRADE FINANCING UNDER AN IRREVOCABLE, CONFIRMED LETTER OF CREDIT: SIXTY-DAY SIGHT DRAFT DRAWN IN EXPORTER'S CURRENCY

guaranteeing the latter's undertaking. There is now available an irrevocable and confirmed letter of credit.

(6) When the shipment is ready, within the time limit fixed by the letter of credit, the beneficiary draws a draft at 60 days' sight on the issuing bank and presents it with documents attached to the advising and confirming bank. The letter of credit may be "specially advised" and thus indicate the bank or banks that will honor the draft; otherwise the exporter is obliged to locate a bank that will discount it. The advising and confirming bank is required to check carefully all of the documents presented and to determine the authenticity of the credit.[1] As the draft is drawn upon the issuing bank, the negotiator must look to it for reimbursement, and any discrepancies in the documents may be grounds for refusal of payment on the part of the issuing bank. (If the letter of credit is opened in a currency foreign to the beneficiary, it is often customary to draw the draft on the foreign correspondent of the issuing bank and the correspondent is then known as the paying or accepting bank.)

(7) The draft is now sent, with documents attached, to the issuing bank for payment or acceptance, depending on whether the letter of credit is for cash or acceptance. The case under consideration is an acceptance credit.

(8) The merchandise is shipped to the importer in Brazil, but with the documents made to the order of the beneficiary, who endorses them either in blank, or to the confirming bank that, in turn, will endorse them to the issuing bank. The issuing bank accepts the draft and releases the merchandise to the importer, upon the signing of a *trust receipt*. This document, widely used in the United States and in Great Britain, is an acknowledgment by the importer that the ownership of the goods remains with the bank, possession only being transferred; and guarantees disposal of the merchandise solely as specified in the trust receipt. In most foreign countries a document known as a *warrant* is employed in lieu of a trust receipt. This is in the nature of a duplicate warehouse receipt (not indicated in Figure 15-7).

(9) At the expiration of the 60-day period following acceptance of the draft by the issuing bank, payment is reimbursed by the Brazilian importer and by the issuing bank. Should the importer fail to meet this obligation, there would be no recourse upon the exporter as long as either the issuing or the confirming bank honors the draft. In this respect the credit is a virtual guarantee of payment.

---

[1]Regarding the responsibility of a bank seeking to determine the authority of a credit, Article 9 of *Uniform Customs and Practice for Commercial Documentary Credit* states that there is no liability or responsibility "for the form, sufficiency, accuracy, genuineness, falsification, or legal effect of any documents, or for the general and/or particular conditions stipulated in the documents or superimposed thereon; nor do they assume any liability or responsibility for the description, quantity, weight, quality, condition, packing, delivery, value, or existence of goods represented thereby. . . ."

Since the transaction was a 60-day acceptance, the draft is probably returned to the advising bank as soon as it is accepted by the issuing bank. This would be done if the advising bank desired to rediscount the draft and place itself in a fully liquid position. In any event the draft or bill of exchange will make a round trip from the advising bank to the issuing bank and, finally, back to the advising bank with the payment.

16

Legal Aspects of International Marketing

The problem of adjusting private trade disputes, although not peculiar to the international field, is especially significant to international marketing. Commercial disputes are more difficult to avoid because foreign as well as American commercial customs and laws are involved. There is a greater likelihood of damage in transportation and there is more dependence upon samples, grades, or descriptions as the basis for sales. When commercial disputes occur in international trade, adjustment is complicated by the distance between buyer and seller, as well as differing trade customs and laws.

The number of trade disputes tend to be reduced by several factors: growing experience on the part of international marketing enterprises; more careful selection of foreign agents and distributors; more precise and carefully drawn contracts; and the establishment of foreign branches. However, the very nature of marketing transactions inevitably cause some misunderstandings. Many, of course, are adjusted directly between the buyer and seller; others require arbitration or litigation.

When international marketers transact business abroad, they are subject to the laws of the countries in which they operate. Foreign law is in many respects different from the law with which the domestic marketer is already familiar. It is the purpose of this chapter to indicate some of the more substantial differences which may become problematic for international marketers. Identification of the differences will not, however, eliminate international trade disputes. Consequently, the latter portion of this chapter is devoted to the methods by which trade disputes may be settled. The material in this chapter hardly eliminates the need for legal council. Its purpose is to provide enough information about the significant legal concepts in order to avoid many of the legal pitfalls associated with international trade. This chapter deals with five elements: which law governs, common and code laws, industrial property rights, commercial law, and settlement of disputes.

JURISDICTION AND COMMERCIAL USAGE

Perhaps the most basic question is: Which law governs in a particular transaction between the foreign and domestic marketer, such as, an American and an Argentine? In case of dispute, two different jurisdictions are involved. One way to determine which law governs is to agree beforehand, in the sales contract or in the agency or distributor agreement, which law is to apply. For example, an American exporter might stipulate that all conditions will be interpreted according to the law of some designated state of the United States. The *jurisdictional clause* shows the intent of the parties to the contract and this is likely to be honored by the court.

If no jurisdictional clause exists, the question of jurisdiction will be decided by the courts where the case is tried. Each court follows its own procedure to determine which law is to apply. Rules have been adopted to determine where and when foreign law will be applicable. Some courts apply the law of the place at which the contract was *entered into*; thus, if an American contracts in Argentina to purchase Argentine linseed oil, the Argentine law governs the transaction. On the other hand, some courts hold that the law of the place of contract *performance* is to govern. This is often a different country from that in which the contract was entered into. Thus, an American salesperson might visit an Argentine importer of machinery and receive an order which the exporter delivers in New York. Contract *performance* would then take place in New York; the place of contract would be in Argentina. Since there is no uniformity in private international law, either principle might be involved in a particular case. Thus, if the parties can agree beforehand, there is merit in inserting a jurisdictional clause to convey their intent.

Another problem facing the courts is the interpretation of specific contract terms. Some of these terms may be based on customary trade practice. Courts of law recognize established principles of trade (commercial usage) and accept them as binding upon merchants. When the intent of the parties is determined, the courts logically assume that business people know the customs in their trade that are applicable to particular products and specific countries. Thus, a quality designation of "fair average quality of the season" is interpretable not by law, but by usage. Other examples of commercial usage include the right to inspect merchandise before accepting a draft or the definition of a ton (2000, 2200, or 2240 pounds) of cargo. The international trader is expected to know the customary usage of trade terms.

COMMON LAW AND CODE LAW

The countries of the Free World may be grouped into common law and code law countries on the basis of their legal systems. The distinctions between the two have important implications for marketers. For example, trademark protection depends on registration in code law countries, while a company may have to show it was the first user in common law countries. Or code law countries define such contract terms as "Acts of God" differently than common law. A strike may be an "Act of God" in code countries but not in common law nations.

Common or *community law* developed in England following the Norman Conquest of 1066. The common law is a body of unwritten principles, based on customs and usages of the community, that is recognized and enforced by the courts. Common law applies in the United States, United Kingdom, and other countries that now or formerly have been associated with British legal thought. A fundamental basis of commercial law in these countries is found in the precedence of court decisions.

On the other hand, the remaining countries of the world generally adopt the principles of code law. *Code law*, as distinguished from common law, consists of compiled laws, assembled into groups of identical or similar subject matter, thus constituting a code.

Some codification of commercial law occurs even in common law countries to establish uniform rules of conduct. In the United States an important example of such a code is the Uniform Commercial Code covering sales, commercial paper, bank collections process, letters of credit, warehouse receipts, bills of lading, documents of title, and investment securities. The code is the law of all the states except Louisiana.[1]

Trademark Law[2]

In common law countries, ownership of a trademark is predicated upon use; while in code law countries, ownership is acquired by *registration*. In code law countries, the first person to register the mark owns it. There are registration laws in common law countries, but registration is recognized only as *prima facie* evidence of ownership that was already acquired by use. Thus, in case of a conflict over trademark rights, the burden of proof falls on the party who had not registered the mark. From the standpoint of international marketing, however, there is additional value in trademark registration in a common law country since some foreign countries will not register a mark for a citizen of the United States unless it is registered in the United States.

Trademark registration in a code law country is a comparatively simple matter and is the means of acquiring title. Prompt registration

---

[1]Harold J. Grilliot, *Introduction to Law and the Legal System* (Boston: Houghton Mifflin Company, 1975), p. 305.

[2]Parts of this discussion rely heavily on Joseph M. Lightman, "World Trademark Laws Reviewed" in the U.S. Department of Commerce publication *Foreign Business Practices* (Washington, D.C.: U.S. Government Printing Office, November, 1975), pp. 44–55.

is advantageous for exporters in all countries where they intend to do business to lessen the possibility of infringement. *Infringement* is the appropriation of a trademark owned by another or adopting a mark so similar in appearance, phonetic qualities, or meaning as to constitute effective infringement. For example, an American manufacturer of hosiery was informed that an authorized person in Peru had adopted a label almost identical in design to that used by the American marketer for a number of years. Many customers purchased the inferior product, believing it to be the genuine American article.

An automobile manufacturer failed to register a trademark in a foreign country, perhaps because the market did not seem to warrant the expenditure of approximately $100. Later, a market developed through the efforts of the manufacturer's agent in the country. However, the trade name of this automobile had been registered in the agent's name. Problems did not arise until the American manufacturer decided to select a new agent and discovered that it would be necessary to market the automobile under a new name, or otherwise pay several thousand dollars to the previous agent for the transfer of a registration that could have been obtained for $100.

The J.C. Penney Company has been involved in a dispute with Penney's Ltd. over use of the Penney name in England. A Canadian investor had purchased a Dublin company and renamed it Penney's, Ltd. In 1973 Penney's Ltd. expanded into England where J. C. Penney had been selling goods under its own name since 1962. An appellate court sustained an injunction that prevented the Irish firm from putting the Penney name on its merchandise. This case illustrates the problem of adequately protecting a trademark in foreign jurisdictions since the dispute has occurred in several markets where courts have ruled both for and against the U.S. firm. The U.S. company won in Hong Kong, lost a preliminary hearing in Ireland, and had action pending in a Scottish court in 1976.[3]

Protection from Trademark Piracy

In common law countries where registration is regarded as *prima facie* evidence of ownership, an application to register a trademark may be defeated by proving that the trademark was used previously by another. In code law countries, however, the problem is far more serious since registration provides the sole basis of ownership.

Trademark and patent attorneys retained by American companies watch for applications to register trademarks in certain foreign countries. However, unless the American trademark is registered in the United States Patent Office, there may be no basis for opposing someone else's application for registration in many code law countries.

---

[3]*Business Week* (February 2, 1976), p. 27.

After a trademark is registered in a code law country, there is usually no way to defeat the registration unless fraud can be proved.[4]

International Conventions Relating to Industrial Property

International conventions have been formed to reconcile the differences that exist among the users of trademarks, designs, and commercial names.The United States is a party to some of these. The international marketer is protected by such conventions.

The International Union for the Protection of Industrial Property was drafted in Paris in 1883 and now embraces about eighty of the commercially and industrially important countries of the world. The headquarters of the Convention is located in Berne, Switzerland. Under this Convention the signatory countries agree to:

1. Register and protect the trademarks of the citizens of other signatory states to the extent that national trademarks are protected.
2. Register trademarks of citizens of other signatory states in the form in which they are registered in the country of origin.
3. Acknowledge the property rights residing in trade names without the formality of registration.
4. Grant a priority period of six months from the date of application for registration in the country of origin for making application for registration in any signatory state. Thus by filing first in the U.S. and within six months in another member country the second filing is given the same status as if the application had been filed on the same date as the first.

The *General Inter-American Convention for Trademark and Commercial Name Protection* of Washington affords similar protection for the signatory republics of the Western Hemisphere. It grants the right of a trademark owner "to apply for and obtain the cancellation or annulment of the interfering mark upon proving. . . (1) that he enjoyed legal protection for his mark in another of the Contracting States prior to the date of the application for registration or deposit which he seeks to cancel," and either (2) that the present holder "had knowledge of the use, employment, registration or deposit in any of the Contracting States," or (3) that the rightful owner has used the mark in the country where registration has been made by an unauthorized party, prior to filing application for such registration or prior to adoption and use.

The *Madrid Agreement Concerning the International Registration of Trademarks* provides centralized protection in about 23 countries by means of an "international" registration. The trademark owner registers the trademark in the country where the owner is domiciled. The

---

[4]The Bureau of International Commerce publishes up-to-date information on the protection of industrial property rights in most foreign countries.

international registration is issued by the International Bureau of the World Intellectual Property Organization (WIPO) in Geneva, Switzerland. This registration is filed in the trademark offices of the member countries which examine the application in accordance with their own laws. Although the U.S. is not a party of the agreement, U.S. firms can take advantage of it when they have bona fide industrial or commercial establishments in a member country. A branch office or an American subsidiary could get an international registration. A single fee of 400 Swiss francs is assessed for the registration and the period of protection is 20 years. Registration may be renewed for additional 20-year periods.[5]

Patents

Patent laws of the various countries differ more widely than do those relating to other industrial property. Edward J. Brenner, U.S. Commissioner of Patents, characterized the present system as one of "current chaos in obtaining effective patent protection in international markets."[6]

The International or Paris Union referred to above includes all the industrialized and many developing countries. Also, there is the Inter-American Convention for the Protection of Inventions, Patents, Designs and Industrial Models to which the United States and 12 other countries adhere. "United States businessmen are entitled also to certain other advantages in the member countries, such as protection against arbitrary forfeiture of their patents for nonworking, and preservation of filing rights on an invention for one year after first filing a patent application thereon in the United States. Thus, they can file corresponding applications in other member countries and receive on the latter the benefit of the first United States application's filing date (right of priority)."[7]

Some countries require prior registration of the patent in the home country and a few countries provide no patent protection. To improve the situation, a draft patent treaty was announced in 1968. This was prepared by BIRPI (United Bureaux for the Protection of Intellectual Property) which is the intergovernmental agency serving as Secretariat of the Paris Union. This treaty is a procedural rather than a legal effort. "It is intended to be an aid, not a substitute, for national laws, by simplifying international filing for applicants and by providing participating governments with search and examination assistance."[8] The

[5]Vincent Travaglini, "Protection of Industrial Property Rights Abroad," in *Foreign Business Practices* (Washington, D.C.: U.S. Government Printing Office, November, 1975) pp. 25–30.

[6]*International Commerce* (August 5, 1968).

[7]*International Commerce* (June 3, 1968).

[8]*Ibid.*

system outlined below is not exclusive. An applicant may choose to file patent applications on a country-by-country basis. Use of the treaty, however, would provide an alternative international patent filing procedure consisting of four basic features:

1. A single filing of an international application prepared according to a uniform format to replace the many separate and diverse national filing procedures now required.
2. An international search report made available promptly to the applicant to improve the assessment of the applications position which is sent to designated countries to assist and expedite national examination.
3. Deferral, without loss of rights, of the most substantial expenses of foreign filing (for example, translations, national fees) giving businesses more time to assess and evaluate patentability and commerical desirability of foreign patent programs.
4. An international preliminary examination report, optional for applicants and adhering countries, which will provide an additional deferral of time and further assistance in evaluating patentability for the applicant and receiving patent offices.[9]

COMMERCIAL AND CORPORATION LAW

The body of commercial law applies to a special social group known as traders. A *trader* is usually defined as one who is habitually engaged in commerce as a profession; all other persons are *nontraders*. Essentially, the commercial code has been instituted to establish relations between these two groups as well as among traders.

Commercial Register

One of the primary obligations imposed upon traders in code law countries is to enroll in the commercial register of the city or locality in which their business is transacted. These registers are usually maintained by the commercial courts or chambers of commerce. The information to be entered in the commercial register usually includes:

1. The firm or individual name.
2. A statement concerning the nature of the business.
3. The address or place of business.
4. The name of the manager or employee in charge of the business.
5. At times, the amount of capital subscribed in the business together with the amount contributed by each member.

---

[9]*International Commerce* (August 5, 1968). For a concise review of patent laws in various countries, see Joseph M. Lightman, "World Patent Laws Reviewed" in *Foreign Business Practices, op. cit.*, pp. 31–43.

Other information may be required such as powers of attorney granted to other persons; declarations of bankruptcy or suspension of payments; and even documents relating to marital status and attendant property settlements of a firm's members. Deeds and titles to real and industrial property may be recorded in the commercial register.

Failure to register incurs penalties such as a fine or, more often, certain legal disabilities. In the event of litigation involving an unregistered firm, it might then be necessary to prove legal existence which theretofore had not been established. Indeed, recourse to law courts may be refused an unregistered foreign company; petitions of bankruptcy may be held up or refused; books of account may not be accepted as legal evidence; and other serious impediments might be incurred as a result of failure to register.

Business Organizations

There are several types of business organizations that are recognized under foreign law. In many ways they are counterparts of business organizations found in the United States but in some respects they are entirely unlike those found in the United States.

General Partnerships. Most business organizations in foreign countries are smaller than in the United States. For this reason partnerships occupy a more important position. *General partnerships* are authorized by the laws of all countries in the Free World and the liability of members is the same as under English common law. The partners have joint and several liability for the debts of the association. The contract of partnership may be entered into privately or, as generally is the case under Spanish and Latin American law, it is formally drawn up, notarized, duly recorded in the commercial register, and published in the daily press of the locality.

Limited Partnership. The unlimited liability feature of a general partnership has greatly restricted its use thus giving rise to the *limited partnership*. The limited partnership (society en commandite — French; *S. en C. — sociadad en comandita* — Spanish; *Kommanditgesellschaft* — German) combines two types of partners: (1) those who possess the same joint and several responsibility as those of the general partnership; and (2) those who have restricted their liability to a definite amount of capital, as witnessed in the articles of agreement. The "sleeping" partners of the second class possess only a financial interest in the enterprise; they do not exercise the administrative function and their names may not appear in the firm name.

Limited Liability Companies. A further departure from the general partnership organization occurs in *limited liability companies*. These are essentially partnerships but resemble a corporation. An extensive development of this type of concern is found in the German *G.m.b.H. (Gesellschaft mit beschraenkter Haftung)*. The limited liability company and the corporation are contrasted later in this section.

Corporations. The business corporation, as known in the United States, is found in all countries of the world. It is known in Britain as a limited (liability) company (Ltd.), in France as *societé anonyme* (S.A.), in Spain as *sociadad anonima* (S.A.), and in Germany as *aktiengesellschaft* (A.G.). General corporation laws have been enacted in practically all countries.

The corporation, contrasted with the types of organization previously discussed, is an association of capital and not of persons. It possesses an independent identity and exists for a definite or indefinite period of time regardless of the life of the organizers and members. A corporation may often be formed in foreign countries by agreement of a minimum number of persons. The text of the articles of incorporation, the bylaws, and any other documents are notarized and registered in the commerical register. The key documents are then published in the official gazette. Usually, the general features of corporation law in foreign countries are similar to those of American corporation law.

The corporation, as it is organized in code law countries, is particularly well adapted to the demands of large business involving considerable amounts of capital, but it often is too unwieldy and rigid for a modest-sized concern. Business abroad is frequently more personal than it is in the United States, and units are smaller. The limited liability company can be formed by fewer organizers, each of whom may participate actively in the affairs of the company. Formal requirements for organization are simple and greater flexibility is afforded with regard to organization and operation.

A limited company, compared to a corporation, is a private concern. In fact, it may be a "one-person corporation." Shares are generally held privately without the widespread distribution typical of a public corporation.

Power of Attorney

The *power of attorney* confers authority to perform specific acts in behalf of the grantor. Abroad, it is necessary to establish the precise authority granted to salespeople, agents, and attorneys to transact business for a foreign concern. Meticulous care is required in the preparation of powers of attorney for use in code law countries; the law is often strict with respect to form and authentication. Particularly complicated requirements may arise in connection with powers of attorney carried by representatives of corporations. In such instances it may be necessary to establish not only the right of representative to act but also the power of the corporation to confer such a right.

The precise authority to be conferred should be clearly stated in the power of attorney. General powers of attorney are acceptable in some countries, but in others nothing is recognized unless it is specifically set forth. Although a power of attorney may be acceptable if written in English, it rarely is admitted as legally binding unless translated into the language of the foreign country. Two or three witnesses may be required to guarantee the authenticity of a power of attorney.

Bankruptcy

The laws of the different countries as they relate to this important subject vary considerably. In some countries the primary object of the bankruptcy law is to punish the debtor. In other countries efforts are made to assist an unfortunate debtor to make a settlement of obligations and to start anew in business. Moreover, "many legal systems afford inadequate protection to creditors, and the available security devices are either antiquated, cumbersome or illusory. A marketer should determine whether the law provides for either real or chattel mortgages and, if so, whether a foreign corporation may hold or enforce rights thereunder."[10]

Due to the registration system abroad and the juridical position occupied by traders as a class, it is necessary for a bankrupt to be rehabilitated as well as discharged. *Rehabilitation* refers to the bankrupt's reestablishment to the status of merchant with the capacity to carry on business again; the term *discharge*, as generally employed, refers merely to the settlement arranged with creditors.

The bankruptcy laws of many countries are more stringent than those in the United States, particularly regarding the discharge of bankrupts. Full payment of debts or composition with creditors may be required to obtain discharge and, in case creditors fail to agree upon a composition, the debtor is still liable for payment of all obligations. If bankruptcy has been tinged with fraudulent conduct of any description, a debtor is not rehabilitated in many countries until a period of years has passed. This does not refer to discharge from bankruptcy which may be accomplished by financial settlement of one's debts.

Taxation

In general, a foreign concern whose business is handled by a local dealer in the dealer's name is not considered "doing business" in that

---

[10]*Foreign Commerce Weekly* (June 11, 1962), p. 1038. One of a series entitled "A Management Checklist for Overseas Business."

country and, therefore, is not taxable. However, taxes may be levied when branches are operated, when an agent works in the name of the company represented, or when local business firms are purchased.

The tax problem may be especially serious where it is claimed that an exporting firm in the United States is "doing business" in a certain foreign country and accordingly is subject to taxation on its *whole* worldwide business. Foreign branches of American firms may consist of separate corporations, partly because of the likelihood of such taxation. Another problem is that of international double taxation which is the concurrent taxation by two or more countries on the same income, whether derived from business or from investment. This latter often is part of the bilateral negotiations between countries in their Treaties of Friendship, Commerce, and Navigation. Businesses should be aware of differences in the tax structure of the countries in which they operate and in the reciprocity arrangements among the countries.

Generally speaking, taxes are imposed irrespective of nationality but a law may impose a greater burden upon foreign than upon domestic concerns. Often when this has occurred, the effect has been to force foreigners to organize companies abroad. The alternative may be withdrawal from the market.

SETTLEMENT OF COMMERCIAL DISPUTES

When a commercial dispute arises, there are several ways by which it may be resolved. These arrangements include conciliation, mediation, and arbitration as "peaceful" methods of settling disputes, and litigation as a "belligerent" method of settlement.

Conciliation and Mediation

When the parties to a transaction are unable or unwilling to adjust a trade dispute by dealing directly with each other, an effort is frequently made to conciliate or mediate. This may be merely an attempt to bring the disputants together; or it may mean that a trade association executive, an individual business person, a business firm, or an agency acting on the request of one of the parties or upon the mediator's own initiative will attempt to adjust the dispute. Foreign Service Officers of the United States government sometimes act in this capacity without, however, having any power to compel an adjustment. Some organizations such as the International Chamber of Commerce provide facilities and rules governing commercial arbitration and encourage conciliation or mediation.

Trade disputes are sometimes adjusted directly between the parties concerned or through the medium of third parties, even after they have been submitted for arbitration or after they have been taken to court. If the disputing parties agree upon a settlement during the course of an arbitration proceeding, they frequently request that the arbitrators give their mutual agreement the status of an award. This binds the agreement in case either party later becomes dissatisfied. Often arbitrators accede to such requests. Courts of law often suggest the direct settlement of a trade dispute that has become the basis of litigation.

Commercial Arbitration

When disputing parties fail to resolve their problem directly or through a conciliator or mediator, the alternative is either litigation in the courts or arbitration.

Advantages of Arbitration. Commercial arbitration is usually voluntary. It is dependent upon the inclusion of an arbitration clause in contracts or, in the absence of such a clause, upon the voluntary submission of the dispute after it occurs. Arbitration is becoming more popular because of the disadvantages of litigation in matters involving trade. Litigation is costly, subject to long delays during which business capital is tied up and trade is at a standstill, and disruptive of business relationships. Juries, moreover, may be inclined to compromise disputes. Both juries and judges may lack appropriate knowledge when a fair adjustment depends on complete understanding of a complicated business transactions.

Many trade disputes are not matters of law but of fact. In many instances the questions of law that arise are of secondary importance. Commercial arbitration often uses unbiased expert arbitrators or business people who are familiar with the practices that arise in the course of a trade dispute. Compared to court litigation, commercial arbitration claims the advantage of lower cost, speedier decisions, fewer instances of permanent loss of customers, and more intelligent understanding of the nonlegal points at issue in trade disputes.

More extensive use of commercial arbitration is also the result of improved arbitration statutes and the efforts of commercial organizations. These organizations conduct campaigns to educate traders in the value of arbitration, publish carefully devised arbitration rules, set up permanent arbitration machinery, and place their facilities at the disposal of international businesses.

Types of Commercial Arbitration Tribunals. Commercial arbitration tribunals for the adjustment of private trade disputes may be classified as temporary or permanent.

Establishing a temporary tribunal to arbitrate a specific dispute is a long-established practice, but one that has given way to the utilization of permanent machinery created in advance. When a contract does not contain an arbitration clause, or when the arbitration clause

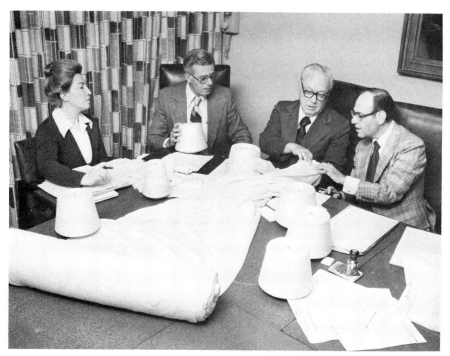

American Arbitration Association

does not specify a tribunal already in existence, the parties concerned may agree to create a temporary tribunal. They may agree upon a single "umpire" or upon all of the members of a larger tribunal.

Commercial arbitration in international marketing increasingly uses the facilities of permanent arbitration tribunals. Organizations such as the International Chamber of Commerce, the London Court of Arbitration, the Chamber of Commerce of the United States, and the American Arbitration Association are typical organizations that have adopted arbitration rules and that maintain committees or tribunals to facilitate the arbitration of trade disputes.

Many organizations with specialized interests also provide for commercial arbitration in their particular fields. Grain, cotton, coffee, sugar, rubber, jute, and other organized commodity exchanges commonly provide for the arbitration of trade disputes resulting from exchange transactions. A large number of trade associations also maintain facilities for the arbitration of disputes in their respective trades or industries. Various British trade associations are active in the commercial arbitration movement and their services are at times utilized by American traders.

Permanent organizations assist the disputing parties in the selection of arbitrators or undertake the actual appointment of arbitrators. They maintain staffs to accomplish this purpose and, in some instances, to supervise the arbitration proceedings.

Selection of Arbitrators. The number of arbitrators that may comprise an arbitration tribunal is not uniform. There is, moreover, no uniform standard regarding qualifications of arbitrators. Often each party will appoint an arbitrator to act as an advocate and they agree to a mutually satisfactory third arbitrator to decide the issue. However, arbitrators in the United States tend to be disinterested and unbaised. The more recently enacted arbitration statutes, in which the parties are interested if they wish to be assured of the legal enforcement of the award, discourage the appointment of biased arbitrators.

If the trade dispute of an American business is to be arbitrated abroad, the selection of arbitrators may be governed by the laws of a foreign country. These laws may contain provisions regarding the selection of the arbitrators if the awards are to be enforceable in courts of law. Sometimes trade agreements recommend arbitration procedures. For example, the Bureau of East-West Trade noted that:

> The trade agreement entered into between the United States and the Soviet Union in October 1972 recommends that the parties to international commercial transactions provide in their contracts for arbitration of any disputes which may arise. Arbitration was also recommended in an exchange of letters between the United States and Poland in November 1972.
>
> The U.S. — U.S.S.R. agreement recommends that parties provide for arbitration under the Arbitration Rules of the Economic Commission for Europe; that they designate an Appointing Authority in a country other than the United States or the Soviet Union to name the arbitrator, or arbitrators, if the parties cannot agree on the designation; and that they specify a neutral country in which the arbitration is to take place. In addition, the agreement contemplates that parties, rather than using the ECE Rules, "may decide upon any other form of arbitration which they mutually prefer and agree best suits their particular needs." The exchange of letters between the United States and Poland contains similar recommendations and also includes as a further alternative the possibility of using the Rules of the International Chamber of Commerce.[11]

Commercial Arbitration Clauses. Definite clauses providing for the arbitration of trade disputes are, to an increasing extent, being inserted into sales and agency contracts. Experience has shown that better results can be obtained if arbitration is agreed upon before a dispute arises. The number of countries in which such clauses are legally valid and irrevocable is growing.

The general arbitration clause of the American Arbitration Association is an example of the type of clause that might be included in a

---

[11]U.S. Department of Commerce, Bureau of East-West Trade, *Information and Assistance Available Through the American Arbitration Association to U.S. Corporations Engaged in East-West Trade* (Washington: U.S. Government Printing Office, April, 1973), pp. 1–2.

contract. It states that "Any controversy or claim arising out of or relating to this contract or the breach thereof, shall be settled by arbitration, . . . in accordance with the Rules of the American Arbitration Association, and judgment upon the award rendered by the Arbitrator(s) may be entered in any court having jurisdiction thereof."

Legal Aspects of Commercial Arbitration. Commercial arbitration has been practiced for many years, both in domestic commerce and in international marketing. However, the progress that has been made recently is due, in part, to the enactment of statutes that (1) establish a legal basis for the validity of contract clauses providing for arbitration of a future dispute, as well as of agreements to arbitrate an existing dispute; (2) stay action in courts of law during the life of the arbitration clause or agreement; and (3) provide a means for the enforcement of awards in courts of law.

Under common law in the United States and Great Britain, an arbitration award in an existing dispute can, as a rule, be enforced in a court of law; but an arbitration clause in a contract providing for the arbitration of a trade dispute that may arise in the future is not legally binding, and agreements to arbitrate existing disputes are revocable. Either party may refuse to appoint arbitrators, may revoke the authority of arbitrators who have been appointed, and may resort to court litigation. Arbitration under common law rule, therefore, depends upon the integrity of the parties concerned.

The handicap described in the preceding paragraph has been largely removed in the United States and in Great Britain through the enactment of arbitration statutes. In the United States prior to 1920, many states had enacted laws that facilitated the enforcement of awards but which did not materially change the common law rule regarding revocability. The New York State Arbitration Act of 1920[12] was the first definitely to remove the handicap. It provides that "A provision in a written contract to settle by arbitration a controversy thereafter arising between the parties to the contract, or a submission hereafter entered into of an existing controversy to arbitration . . . shall be *valid, enforceable, and irrevocable*, save upon such grounds as exist at law or in equity for the revocation of any contract."

The Act further provides legal machinery to enforce the specific performance of arbitration clauses and agreements; makes provision for the appointment of arbitrators by the Supreme Court or a judge thereof, upon request of either party to an arbitration agreement in case the other party fails to name them; directs the court to stay court proceedings brought in violation of an arbitration agreement or submission; and authorizes either party to apply to the court for an order

---

[12]*Laws of 1920*, Chapter 275; *Laws of 1923*, Chapter 341; *New York Civil Practice Act*, Article 84.

confirming the award and to obtain judgment for enforcement. Similar state arbitration statutes have since been enacted in other states.

The United States Arbitration Act of 1925 is "an act to make valid and enforceable written provisions or agreements for arbitration of disputes arising out of contracts, maritime transactions, or commerce among the states or territories or with foreign nations."

The legal status of commercial arbitration agreements and contract clauses, their validity and irrevocability, and the enforcement of awards is, of course, complicated in international marketing because disputes involve citizens and laws of different countries. Many of the countries of continental Europe have fortunately enacted arbitration laws providing for the enforcement of arbitration awards rendered within those countries. Some of these European countries enforce awards as court judgments and others as contracts. The legal enforcement abroad of arbitration awards rendered in the United States depends upon the laws of particular foreign countries.

Avoidance of Litigation

Should litigation in code law countries become necessary, extreme care must be taken. Indeed, the decision to carry a matter into the courts is itself a weighty one. The admonition now generally accepted regarding the wisdom of avoiding litigation, if possible, applies emphatically when foreign code law country litigation is considered.

One experienced attorney expresses it this way: "I have had the experience abroad of watching lawsuits firsthand and, although several of them ended in nominal victory, the cost, frustrating delays and extended aggravation which these cases involved were certainly more oppressive, by far, than any matters of comparable size I have watched in the United States."[13]

QUESTIONS

1. In case of dispute between an American citizen and the citizen of another country, how is the governing law determined?
2. Define: (a) common law and (b) code law.
3. Cite the law concerning trademarks to illustrate the basic difference between common law and code law.
4. How can United States international traders best protect their property rights in trademarks and labels for use in other countries?
5. What is the meaning of the letters "S.A." following many Spanish and Latin American business names?

---

[13]Andrew W. Brainerd in *Export Trade* (June 13, 1961), p. 32.

6. What is the meaning of the suffix "Ltd." in British business names? What is the meaning of "A.G." in German business names?
7. Contrast the business corporation of the United States and the limited liability companies commonly operating in foreign countries.
8. In the event of an international marketing dispute, how could settlement be reached by means of mediation or conciliation?
9. Why is arbitration frequently more effective than litigation in settling commercial disputes?
10. The Esterbrook Pen Company of Camden, New Jersey, found that Japanese-made pens sold in the Philippines carried such trade names as "Easterbrook," "Easterlook," "Easterbook," etc. These pens sold at a lower price than the legitimate Esterbrook Pen. The Esterbrook Pen Company has its trade name registered in the United States Patent Office and also in the Philippines. It also knows that a treaty exists between Japan and the United States which guarantees the reciprocal respect of each other's property rights.

    This has become a serious matter; what do you advise the company to do?
11. You have been waiting for a remittance of $5,000 from a customer in another country. The merchandise has been delivered, but payment has not been made on the assertion that the merchandise shipped was not the same as that described in your firm's catalog. You have since learned that this customer has overbought and is therefore in financial difficulty. The customer offers to submit the dispute to arbitration. Will you accept this offer? If so, why? If no, why not?

SUPPLEMENTARY READINGS

The Arbitration Journal. New York: American Arbitration Association, quarterly.

Domke, Martin (ed.). *International Trade Arbitration — A Road to Worldwide Cooperation*. New York: American Arbitration Association, 1958.

Dowd, Laurence P. *Principles of World Business*. Boston, MA.: Allyn & Bacon, Inc., 1965. Chapter 9 and 10.

Exporters' Encyclopaedia. New York: Dun & Bradstreet, Inc., annual.

Foreign Business Practices. Washington, D.C.: U.S. Government Printing Office, November, 1975.

U.S. Department of Commerce, Bureau of East-West Trade. *Information and Assistance Available Through the American Arbitration Association to U.S. Corporations Engaged in East-West Trade*. Washington, D.C.: Government Printing Office.

CHAPTER 17

Import Management

Importing refers to the purchase of foreign products for use or sale in the home market. It involves searching foreign markets for acceptable products and sources of supply, providing for transfer of the product to the home market, arranging financing, negotiating the import documentation and customs procedure, and developing plans for use or for resale of the item or service. Thus, successful importing depends on more than good buying; it requires planning for acceptance of the product and delivery of the promised benefits. The importing firm has the responsibility to determine whether the foreign product or service will meet the needs of the home market.

THE IMPORT PROCESS

Importing has been considered in several places in this text. The present chapter serves: (1) to organize the various aspects of importing by presentation of the import process, (2) to describe major importing institutions, (3) to portray the minor problems confronting U.S. importers, (4) to elucidate major facets of the customs law and procedure, and (5) because of its close relationship to customs arrangements, to present the concepts and utility of foreign-trade zones. The discussion should aid the reader in conceptualizing the import process and should provide a somewhat different perspective on U.S. commercial policy.

Earlier sections of the text presented many of the tariff, quota, exchange, and administrative barriers to exporting. The usual interpretation of Americans is that such obstacles are placed by foreigners against U.S. exports. Now we need to take a closer look at some barriers that foreigners meet in exporting to the U.S., or otherwise stated, what are the problems found by foreigners or U.S. nationals in importing into the U.S. market? Chapter 18 will indicate many of the activities of the federal government in promoting trade; this chapter presents many of the obstacles. Such inconsistencies in foreign commercial policies are common. It is appropriate to analyze the import system and to inquire into the ramifications of the federal systems with which importers must deal.

Essentially the import process comprises the following five stages:

1. Determining market demand and purchase motivation.
2. Locating and negotiating with sources of supply.
3. Securing physical distribution.
4. Preparing documentation and customs processing to facilitate movement among countries and organizations.
5. Developing a plan for resale or use.

Determining Market Demand and Purchase Motivation

Importers can have a distinct advantage over foreigners in the home market, because often they know or can more easily learn the requirements and nuances of the market. They are closer to the market, may live there, and may be native to the market. They are familiar with information sources and institutions. This knowledge can, however, be a disadvantage when familiarity leads to carelessness and individuals assume a level of knowledge that does not really exist. Enthusiastic exclamations of family and friends over souvenirs from abroad are no substitute for careful market analysis. Studies similar to those proposed in Chapter 6 or described elsewhere in standard marketing research texts are needed also by the local importer to achieve realistic estimates of market potential and as a basis for development of the promotional plan.

Raw materials and component parts are imported for use by home country manufacturers in fabricating their own final products. The potential for such materials and parts is determined by the expected sales of the manufacturers who use them. A careful analysis of trade reports and business conditions will aid importers in determining the market potential for both final products and components. Manufacturers may not only buy crude materials from abroad but may operate mines and processing plants abroad from which they import to meet their requirements.

Foods are imported in great volume to meet the tastes and needs of the public. These may be staples or foods that add variety to the meal. Manufacturers, packers, and numerous marketing agencies participate in this business where potential is determined by population and standard of living as well as taste.

Affluence and the lifestyles of the population affect the level and types of manufactured products imported by merchants for resale. Some equipment and supplies are imported to facilitate and make more efficient our manufacturing, commercial, educational, and governmental processes.

Locating and Negotiating with Sources of Supply

Importers must develop dependable supply sources in order to assure customers and themselves of their ability to deliver promised goods at the negotiated time and place and in the correct quantity and quality. Various types of sourcing strategies are available ranging from a constant scouring of the foreign market by the importer, the resident buyer, or middlemen to the ownership and control of supplying firms. The choice among the various options is dependent on supply market characteristics, the product involved, and the importer's ability to finance and manage the operation. Department stores and importers of fashion and novelty items must constantly cover the market to anticipate their requirements. Sometimes they establish foreign buying offices. Manufacturers may buy from a variety of sources, but often they can make long-term contracts with suppliers and may even import from subsidiaries.

The importer and the importer's customers are interested in supply sources that are capable of producing the quantities and quality levels needed as well as having financial stability and dependability. Where possible, sources should be operating in an environment that is conducive to satisfactory future performance if the relationship is expected to continue.

Product quality is partly a technical matter of specifications or conformance to samples or description. It also has another dimension. Foreign products may be perceived differently than local ones. Some foreign products from some countries may be seen by Americans as being of higher quality than local products, (e.g., Rolls Royce automobiles) while other foreign products find it difficult to overcome an image of poor quality. The quality perception can change over time, but importers should, at least, be aware of the potential differences perceived by their customers.

Price, financial arrangements, terms of trade, and promotional aids are among other factors for negotiation. Even among parent companies and their subsidiaries negotiation may be needed to establish policy on transfer pricing, priorities, product line, and deliveries.

Physical Distribution

The logistics of supply including delivery dates, transportation modes, inventory policy, and claims servicing are the responsibility of either the buyer or seller or both — and may be subject to negotiation. These considerations affect the ability of the importer to deliver goods to customers or the assembly line on time and they affect the landed cost. Risk management policies will vary with the negotiated results.

Documentation

Documentation is important in international trade. The distances between trading partners and the sovereign rights of nations require more elaborate systems than those in domestic trade. Each business-person desires to protect a personal interest and each nation wishes to be certain its laws are upheld, its revenues protected, and its sovereignty maintained. Previous chapters have indicated some of the documents needed to support these systems. The individual importer has little choice but to conform — at least in the short-run. Failure to carry out documentation procedures exactly can be costly and result in non-delivery. Exporters who require irrevocable confirmed letters of credit will not ship merchandise on revocable unconfirmed letters. Customs procedures are especially relevant and will be discussed in a later section of this chapter.

Developing a Plan for Resale or Use

Goods well bought are not yet sold, nor do they necessarily fit the production and use systems of a specific business firm or institution. It behooves the importer to have a plan for convincing others of the merits of a product or service. The distribution channels, promotional activities, pricing, and financing should be organized for orderly and effective marketing because selling in the home market may be even more competitive and difficult than in foreign markets. There is no reason to expect that the majority of foreign products will sell themselves anymore than it would be true for domestic goods. Competitive products and sources make a marketing plan necessary for successful selling if resale is contemplated. Witness the automobile industry and the penetration of foreign-made cars; also, the competition among these importers for significant market segments. The inroads on the American market by successful foreign automobile producers were facilitated by carefully planned strategy.

TYPE OF IMPORTERS

Four basic types of importing institutions are found in most countries: private traders, end users, government agencies, and facilitating agencies. These are augmented by many agents of foreign suppliers.

Private Traders

Private traders represent wholesalers and retailers who buy and sell for their own account. Unless the country is centrally controlled, there usually are numerous private traders, some large and many very small. In Western countries these traders may carry on a significant portion of the import business while in the less developed countries the activities of traders may be hampered by governmental attempts to achieve economic development goals. Restrictions such as the following are not unusual:

> Private traders are precluded from importing any items on the controlled list, and they are often unable to get government approval to import on deferred payment terms. Except for industrial raw materials, traders must pay by letter of credit (L/C), payable within 14 days after the import license is granted.[1]

American retailers find it desirable to import many goods to supply variety to the U.S. market and to appeal to Americans' desire for fashion goods. Many durable items made abroad have appeal because of their special features (sports cars), luxury image, workmanship (handicrafts, limited production items), or price. Much of the actual buying in merchandise lines is conducted through overseas channels, including resident buying houses, or by buyers from the home country who have extensive knowledge of their product lines and who are also responsible for selling the merchandise.

End Users

End users are manufacturers, public utilities, hospitals, schools, etc., who buy for their own use. They purchase raw materials, supplies, machinery, and equipment to facilitate their own operations and gear the level of their importing to their expected level of operations. Imports of this group often constitute the major source of imports for a country.

Traditionally U.S. industrial buyers purchased from abroad only when the domestic suppliers could not service their requirements. Recently, however, the growth of multinational companies, improved transportation and communication, supply shortages, and increased exposure to foreign firms have led to increased use of foreign sources.[2]

Some of the chief reasons for foreign sourcing in recent years are:

1. To secure lower prices.
2. To ensure supplies of materials during long strikes, i.e., steel and copper.
3. To benefit from advanced technology.
4. To ease foreign exchange problems when a U.S. company exports its products.

---

[1]U.S. Department of Commerce, *Taiwan: A Market for U.S. Products* (Washington: U.S. Government Printing Office, 1967), p. 10.

[2]Wilbur B. England, *Modern Procurement Management: Principles and Cases* (5th ed.; Homewood: Richard D. Irwin, Inc., 1970), p. 464.

5. To help the plant of a foreign subsidiary develop economic production volume.
6. To reduce lead times on materials in short supply.[3]

Governmental Agencies

Governmental agencies constitute a separate class of importers because of their operating characteristics, usually being subject to an extensive budgeting process, detailed procedures for bidding and ordering, and attempted close coordination with governmental development and social plans. The exact role of governmental agencies varies among countries.

The U.S.S.R. Ministry of Foreign Trade controls the activity of all Soviet organizations that are authorized to operate in the foreign market. The chief Soviet agencies directly concerned with foreign commercial activity are specialized foreign-trade associations which represent all branches of Soviet industry. They are the major contact for those wishing to bring goods into the U.S.S.R. since the All-Union associations are authorized to conclude import transactions through direct contact with foreign organizations.[4] These associations are organized on a commodity sectorial basis and some deal only with relationships between the U.S.S.R. and selected countries, for example, Mongolian People's Republic, Afghanistan, etc. Many of the agencies handle exporting as well as importing as indicated in the description of responsibilities for V/O "Aviaexport."

> Exports & Imports: aircraft, helicopters, aircraft engines, aircraft units, aircraft instruments, aircraft electrical equipment, radio navigational aids, control and testing apparatus and aircraft spare parts; ground equipment for the maintenance and servicing of airplanes and helicopters.[5]

In some countries purchases by government agencies and government-owned corporations account for a large percentage of all imports. This is true in LDCs where the emphasis is on developmental plans and conservation of foreign exchange. For example, in the middle 1960s purchases by government agencies and corporations in Taiwan accounted for approximately 23 percent of all imports financed with government foreign exchange. These were channelled through only two government trading agencies.[6]

Purchasing by U.S. governmental agencies is more decentralized. A wide range of goods is purchased ranging from major equipment and

---

[3]*Ibid.*, p. 76.
[4]Nikolai Patolichev, *Foreign Trade* (Moscow: Novosti Press Agency Publishing House), pp. 10–14. See also Chapter 20 of this text.
[5]*Sovetskie Vneshnetorgovye Organizatsii* (Moscow: Vneshtoryizdat), pp. 23–24.
[6]U.S. Dept. of Commerce, *loc. cit.*

construction to office supplies. These are purchased at all levels of government and by various units at each level. Utilities may do their own purchasing of equipment, including foreign-made. Often these governmental agencies are required to give preference to local or nationally produced goods as exemplified by the "Buy American" provisions requiring the purchase of nationally produced goods unless the foreign advantage exceeds 6 percent. While the degree of preference varies from time to time, the idea clearly is to give domestic bidders on federal contracts an advantage over foreign bidders.[7]

Facilitating Agencies

The various types of import facilitating agencies were described in Chapter 11 and 12 under distribution systems and logistics. Two additional agencies are of special interest to U.S. importers — bonded warehouses and customshouse brokers.

Customshouse Brokers. For the routine associated with clearing merchandise through customs as well as in resolving controversies that may ensue, an importer may engage the services of a customshouse broker. These middlemen are registered by the Treasury Department and are experts in the complicated paperwork connected with customs procedures. They often combine functions and serve also as freight forwarders.

Customs Bonded Warehouses. Importers may not always want to take immediate possession of imported merchandise. They can postpone the payment of duty by storing dutiable imports in customs bonded warehouses where they may clean, sort, repack, and make certain changes in the condition of merchandise.

Customs bonded warehouses are in the charge of a customs officer who, jointly with the proprietor, has custody of all stored merchandise subject to detailed customs regulations. Imported merchandise may be withdrawn from the warehouse (1) for consumption (upon payment of import duties and accrued charges); (2) for transportation and exportation; or (3) for transportation and warehousing at another port.

THE UNITED STATES CUSTOMS SERVICE

The customs service of a country administers regulations governing the movement of persons, ships, vehicles, and merchandise across

---

[7]John Fayerweather, *Facts and Fallacies of International Business* (New York: Holt, Rinehart & Winston, 1962), p. 33.

national boundaries. In line with this general statement the primary activities of the U.S. Bureau of Customs include:

> The assessment and collection of all duties, taxes, and fees on imported merchandise, the enforcement of customs and related laws, and the administration of certain navigation laws and treaties. As an enforcement organization, it engages in combating smuggling and frauds on the revenue and enforces the regulations of numerous other Federal Agencies.[8]

The Bureau of Customs is part of the U.S. Treasury Department. The Bureau is headed by the Commissioner of Customs and is organized into regions, districts, and port levels. These offices include the fifty states, Puerto Rico, and the Virgin Islands.[9] District offices are scattered throughout the states but tend to be more common where foreign trade is significant. Ports of entry are found in all border states and in many interior states to facilitate the movement of passengers and freight. A detailed consideration of the Bureau's structure and operation is beyond this text. Here we concentrate on several major facets of the customs procedure that affect importers: entry of goods, valuation and appraisement, controversies, and the Bureau's responsibility relative to special laws affecting importers.

Entry of Goods

Careful adherence to customs procedure is necessary if foreign goods are to be brought into the United States. Among the first requirements is one that states the goods must be formally "entered" by the consignee. An entry is filed with the district or port director of customs by submitting (1) a special customs, commercial, or pro forma invoice, (2) a bill of lading, and (3) a declaration that prices and other data in the invoice are correct.

In the entry the consignee declares the value of the merchandise, indicates the rate of duty (if any) and tariff classification of the merchandise, and designates how the goods will be disposed. If the goods are to be released from customs custody immediately, a *consumption entry* is filed. In this situation a deposit is made with customs equal to the estimated duty, and when the duties are finally determined, a refund or an additional payment is made. A *warehouse entry* permits merchandise to be placed in a customs bonded warehouse. This postpones the release of dutiable goods and postpones payment of duty.[10]

---

[8]U.S. Dept. of the Treasury, *Exporting to the United States* (Washington: U.S. Government Printing Office, 1971), p. 2. This section on the Customs Service borrows heavily from this source.

[9]*Ibid.*, pp. 2–6.

[10]See Bonded Warehouses, p. 350.

Dutiable Status

All goods imported into the United States are subject to duty unless they are specifically exempted. In the U.S. duties may be assessed on an ad valorem, specific, or compound basis according to classifications and rates in the Tariff Schedules of the United States. If information on the classification and rate for goods is desired, the importer may obtain it from the customs service by furnishing the necessary information. The decision of the Bureau of Customs may be relied upon as a basis for placing orders for goods to be imported. There is no provision under U.S. law for prepayment of duty or taxes prior to the importation of goods as liability for the payment of duty is fixed at the time goods are entered.[11]

Appraisal of Merchandise

When a shipment is classified as dutiable it must be appraised by customs officials to determine the value for duty purposes. The importer is responsible for ensuring that all the statements and information in the documents filed with customs officials are correct to the best of the importer's knowledge. If a package contains several articles subject to different rates of duty, the assessment may be at the rate applicable to the highest dutiable product in the package, but this assessment usually is avoided by separating the different articles. This is another indication of how seemingly minor variations can affect the final cost of imported goods.

Customs Values

Another factor affecting cost is the value placed on merchandise by customs. In the United States imported merchandise may be appraised on several bases. These various bases are significant to the importer because along with classification and rates, they determine the amount of duty that will be paid and have ramifications on the importer's price and competitive position. The bases used are:

1. Export value.
2. U.S. value if export value cannot be determined.
3. Constructed value if neither 1 nor 2 can be determined.
4. American selling price (only for certain merchandise — this is not an alternative method of valuation).

Export value is the market price at which the imported goods are freely sold, i.e., offered for sale for exportation to the United States *in*

---

[11]U.S. Department of the Treasury, *op. cit.*, p. 9.

the principal markets of the country of exportation in the usual whole-sale quantities and in the ordinary course of trade. *U.S. value* is the price at which such or similar merchandise is freely sold or offered for sale in the United States in usual wholesale quantities less allowances for specified expenses such as customs duty, excise taxes, transportation and insurance costs, commissions, and profits and expenses usually made. *Constructed value* is the cost of producing the merchandise packed ready for shipment to the United States.

The American selling price is the U.S. selling price of the article produced in the United States when sold for domestic consumption. This base usually results in higher duties and is applied to a limited group of products including coal-tar products, canned clams, and low-priced knit gloves and mittens. This basis for valuation has been important in negotiations for removal of trade restrictions. Europeans have asked that it be abolished in return for specific changes in tax laws affecting American products.

Controversies Over Valuation

Controversies over valuation, classification, and other customs matters are common; therefore a procedure for resolution has been established. An importer may protest a decision within 90 days of liquidation[12] and get an administrative review within customs. If the protest is denied, the importer can appeal to the U.S. Customs Court where a final decision is made.

SPECIAL LAWS AFFECTING U.S. IMPORTERS

The importation of many goods is either restricted or prohibited by the federal government. Such laws and regulations are administered by one or more governmental agencies and are enforced by the U.S. customs service. Importers must be aware of these laws since shipment of restricted items can result in seizure or forfeiture of the goods. The restrictions pertain to a wide range of goods including obscene, immoral, and seditious matter; drugs; alcholic beverages; arms; counterfeit coins and currency; food items; fabrics; and wild game.

Imported autos must meet safety and emission standards and television receivers are subject to the Radiation Control for Health and Safety Act. The Consumer Product Safety Act aims at reducing or eliminating product hazards. Under this Act importers will not be permitted to enter a foreign product into the U.S. even under customs bond while the product is undergoing safety tests.[13]

---

[12]Liquidation is the final ascertainment of the rate and amount of duty due.
[13]*Journal of Commerce* (January 24, 1973), p. 1.

These are merely examples of the range of laws and products that may be subject to restriction. Protectionist measures such as the proposed Burke-Hartke bill would penalize importers by curbing or rolling back the level of imports into the United States. Such bills have considerable support from some sectors because of trade deficits and claims of preserving American jobs.

Import Quotas

U.S. import quotas are of two types: tariff-rate and absolute. Tariff-rate quotas permit the importation of a specified quantity of the product at a reduced rate of duty. After this volume of imports is reached, additional imports during a designated period of time are assessed higher rates of duty. As of January, 1971, the United States had tariff rate quotas on certain cattle, whole milk, fish, potatoes, and brooms. Because it is difficult to determine when the level of imports is nearing the quota level, importers are not sure what rate of duty will be assessed on specific goods and customs may require deposits based on the higher rate of duty.

Absolute quotas place a strict quantity limit on the amount of an item that may be imported during an annual period. No importation is allowed beyond that quantity at any rate of duty. Cotton, peanuts, wheat, condensed milk, animal feeds, and ice cream are among the products subject to absolute quotas. Imports in excess of the quotas may be exported or detained for entry in a subsequent period. Often the quota status of a commodity cannot be established in advance of entry since many of these quotas are filled shortly after the opening of the quota period. Some are filled on the same day.

Antidumping Act

Under the Antidumping Act the Secretary of the Treasury investigates to determine whether foreign merchandise is being sold to purchasers in the United States at less than fair value. If it is found that this is the case, the U.S. Tariff Commission (now the International Trade Commission) is advised. The Commission, in turn, determines whether such importation injures, or is likely to injure an industry in the United States. If the Commission finds injury, imports of that class of merchandise become subject to special antidumping duties. For the purposes of this Act fair value is based on a comparison of FOB factory prices to U.S. importers and to buyers in the home market.

U.S. importers recently were affected by this law when the Electionic Industries Association filed suit to convince the Trade Commission that undervalued Japanese color TV picture tubes had forced American manufacturers to reduce prices and suffer a profit loss. The Treasury Department found that dumping existed and importers of these products were required to post a 12 percent dumping duty bond in addition to a regular 15 percent duty. The Trade Commission reversed the Treasury and ruled that dumped tubes had not damaged domestic industry, thus permitting return of the dumping bond to importers. The commission noted that Japanese imports accounted for less than 2 percent of the U.S. color-tube market and that only a small percentage of these were imported at unfairly low prices.[14] During the period of the 12 percent dumping duty, American importers not only had their capital tied up but also were unsure of the final cost to be considered when setting price and predicting margins.

FOREIGN-TRADE ZONES

The United States has 18 foreign-trade zones as shown in Figure 17-1 on page 356. Some 600 companies used these zones in 1974. The value of merchandise moved to and from the zones exceeded $400 million during that year. [15]

To the general public the zone appears merely as another warehouse in Brooklyn or a wharf terminal in Toledo, Ohio, but to the international marketer it has special significance. Geographically and legally the zones are within the United States, but for customs purposes they are outside. The zones are operated as public utilities established under grants of authority from the Foreign-Trade Zones Board. They operate under the supervision of the United States Customs Service.

Foreign-trade zones facilitate import and the reexport trade.[16] They permit foreign goods to be held in the zone without being subject to customs entry, payment of duty or tax, or bond. Merchandise may be stored, sold, exhibited, repacked, assembled, sorted, cleaned, mixed with other foreign and domestic merchandise, or manufactured in the zone. Later the goods may either be exported or transferred into customs territory. If the merchandise is entered for consumption, duties and taxes are assessed.

A foreign-trade zone has no resident population but is furnished with facilities for loading and unloading; for storing goods, both foreign and domestic; for processing operations; and for reshipping goods. If reshipped to foreign ports, imported merchandise leaves the zone without payment of duty.

U.S. Importers who use foreign trade zones gain a number of advantages.[17]

---

[14]*Merchandising Week* (January 8, 1973), p. 43.

[15]U.S. Department of Commerce, *A Basic Guide to Exporting* (Washington: U.S. Government Printing Office), pp. 50–51.

[16]Reexport refers to imported merchandise that is subsequently exported.

[17]See "Lawyer Lists Advantages of Foreign Trade Zones," *Cincinnati Enquirer*, January 4, 1976, p. B-1. "How U.S. Free Trade Zones Help Cut Costs," *Business International* (January 4, 1974), p. 5.

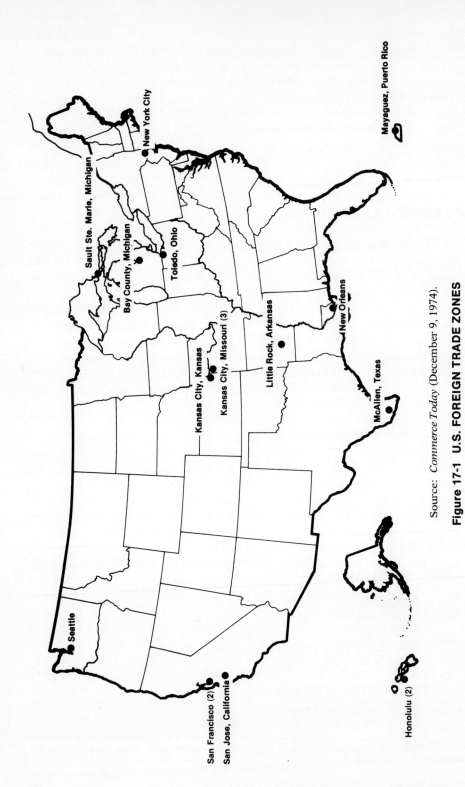

Source: *Commerce Today* (December 9, 1974).

Figure 17-1 U.S. FOREIGN TRADE ZONES

1. U.S. quotas, duties, and bonds are not applicable within the zone; therefore, goods can be landed quickly without full customs formalities.
2. Merchandise may be displayed in the zone's showroom so prospective buyers can examine it.
3. Duty is not paid until goods leave the zone, nor are internal revenue or state taxes applicable on goods held for export.
4. Merchandise can be repaired, altered, relabeled, or remarked to meet federal or local requirements. It can be processed to qualify for lower duty or freight charges.
5. Merchandise subject to import quotas may be held within the zone until the next quota period. Storage also allows marketers to hold goods until market conditions improve within the U.S., or to ship the goods abroad if U.S. buyers are not found.
6. Components may be imported from several countries and assembled within the zone. Duty will be paid only on the assembled products that enter the U.S., but not on those that are shipped to other countries.[18]

QUESTIONS

1. What activities are involved in importing goods into the U.S.?
2. What advantage, if any, does the importer have over foreign exporters in determining market potential for a product?
3. Distinguish among the four types of importing institutions.
4. Why have some U.S. manufacturers turned to imports as a source of raw materials, supplies, or equipment?
5. What is a customshouse broker?
6. Why might an importer place goods in a customs bonded warehouse?
7. How is the value of imported merchandise determined for customs purposes?
8. How does an import quota differ from a tariff?
9. Why does the United States have an antidumping act?
10. How can importers gain from the use of foreign-trade zones?

SUPPLEMENTARY READINGS

Custom House Guide. New York: Budd Publications, Inc., annual.

Export and Import Procedures. New York: Morgan Guaranty Trust Company, 1968.

" 'In' But 'Out' Foreign-Trade Zones Merit Community Attention Today," reprinted from *Commerce Today*, (December 9, 1974), pp. 12–14.

Goldner, Jack. *Foreign Trade Accounting and Management Handbook*. Chicago: Commerce Clearing House, Inc., 1967.

---

[18]Foreign Trade Zones are also found in many other countries. For a list of countries and the functions of their foreign trade zones, see "How Free Trade Zones Facilitate Global Marketing," *Business International* (October 26, 1973), pp. 339–351.

Keegan, Warren J. *Multinational Marketing Management*. Englewood Cliffs, N.J.: Prentice-Hall, Inc., 1974.

U.S. Department of Commerce, *A Basic Guide To Exporting*. Washington: U.S. Government Printing Office, June, 1975.

U.S. Department of the Treasury, Bureau of Customs. *Exporting to the United States* Washington: U.S. Government Printing Office, 1971.

Part 4 Special Issues

4

18

Trade Promotion

The international marketing environment is strongly influenced by governmental policy and trade promotion. Marketers must be aware of such activity both because it affects the competitive conditions under which trade occurs and because trade promotion by government can provide substantial aid to the marketer who participates in the world market.

National, state, and local governments strive to expand exports to improve their balance of payments, to develop their industrial capacity, and to provide additional employment for their citizens. They furnish information, help new exporters, organize overseas trade exhibitions, and facilitate financing of exports. Governmental efforts also affect investment opportunity and the choice of marketing strategy. A national government also may view trade as an extension of the country's foreign policy.

International business is not new to Americans. It is part of their business heritage. International trade between the Colonies, Great Britain, and other nations existed even prior to the American Revolution. Among the governmental agencies, the U.S. Department of State has played the primary role in conducting foreign relations, including those of a commercial nature. As the United States has been drawn, increasingly, into world affairs, additional agencies of the federal government, such as the Departments of Commerce, Agriculture, Treasury, and Interior, and various specialized commissions, have sought to promote international marketing. Some of the individual states have actively aided their producers by promoting and facilitating trade missions to foreign countries. The trade missions are used to determine marketing opportunities and to establish contacts with foreign manufacturers and distributors. A few states have even established "mini-embassies" or trade offices abroad. The state of Ohio, for example, has offices in Dusseldorf and Brussels. These offices continuously represent Ohio's interests both in promoting Ohio international trade and investment. They promote exports, help find distributors for Ohio products, and seek investment from European firms by promoting Ohio as a factory or headquarters location. They also serve to make the state's trade missions more effective.

Foreign governments also energetically support their traders' efforts to expand trade. Such international institutions as the United Nations, Regional Economic Groups (e.g., EEC), and the Organization of American States also seek to develop the trading positions of their members. Many foreign governments promote trade through their embassies and by establishing trade promotion offices in major markets.

Trade promotion is also a function of various private associations such as the International Chamber of Commerce, the Chamber of Commerce of the United States, local World Trade Clubs, trade centers, banks, and international transportation companies.

The combined impact of these groups can alter the international environment, thereby making international marketing easier by promoting exports, educating businesses regarding export opportunities, aiding in establishing overseas contacts, and aiding in the settlement of commercial disputes. This chapter outlines briefly some of the more significant services of these agencies as they affect international marketing — concentrating on those of most interest to American firms whether exporters or overseas producers.

PROMOTION BY THE UNITED STATES GOVERNMENT

The Departments of State and Commerce are among the U.S. agencies most actively involved in trade promotion and are described here in some detail.

Department of State

The principal responsibility for the execution of the policy of the U.S. government in relation to international problems revolves around the Department of State. Some of the more vital decisions on questions of foreign affairs are made by the President, but the day-to-day negotiations with foreign countries, the specific measures for the protection of American interests, the promotion of friendly relations between the United States and other countries, and the conduct of the voluminous correspondence with the diplomatic and consular representatives of the United States, as well as with representatives of foreign powers accredited to the United States, are delegated to the Department of State.[1]

Striking changes have taken place in the international position of the U.S. during the present century, and the sharp increase in global responsibilities is reflected in the organization and work of the Department of State. Figure 18-1 depicts the complex structure to support

---

[1] "The Department of State of the United States — Functions, Organization, and Recruitment of Personnel" (Undated mimeographed brochure of the Department of State).

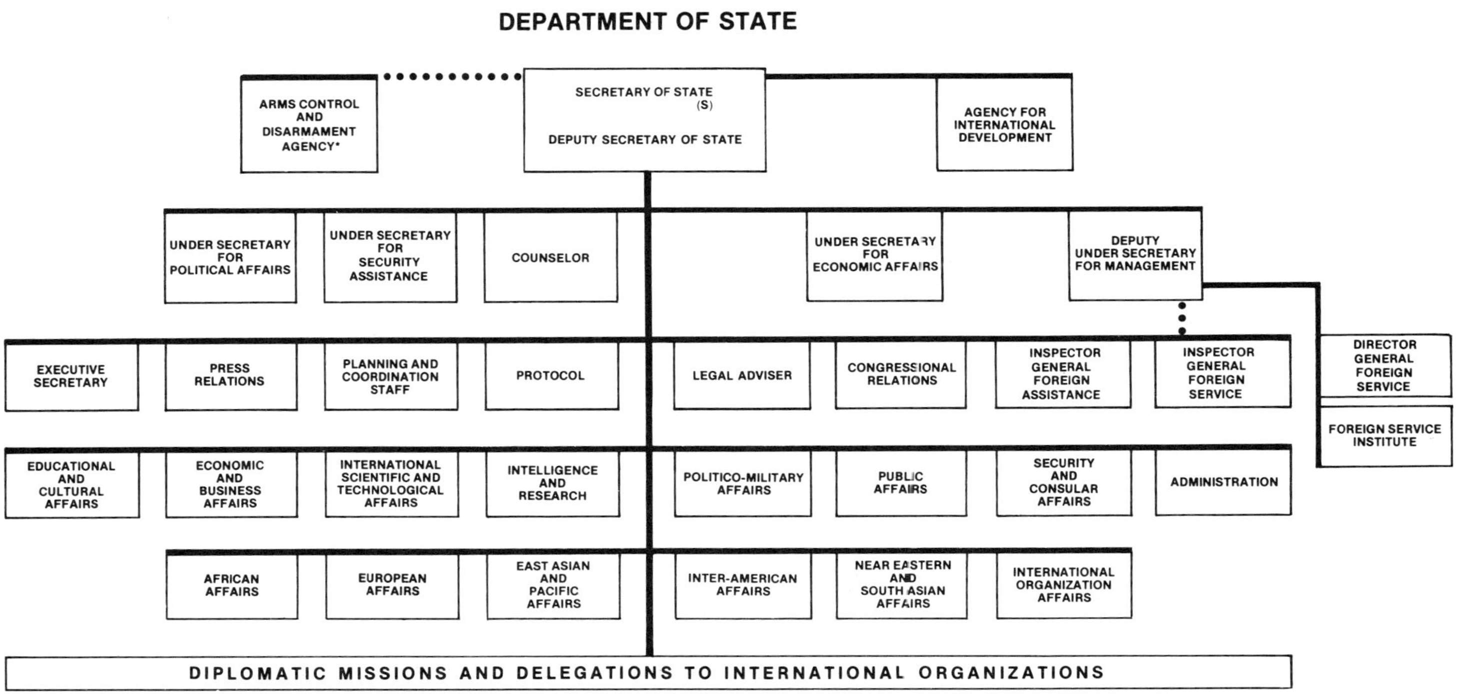

DEPARTMENT OF STATE

DIPLOMATIC MISSIONS AND DELEGATIONS TO INTERNATIONAL ORGANIZATIONS

*A separate agency with the director reporting directly to the Secretary and serving as principal advisor to the Secretary and the President on Arms Control and Disarmament.

Source: *United States Government Manual*, 1973/74, p. 334.

Figure 18-1 ORGANIZATIONAL STRUCTURE OF DEPARTMENT OF STATE

our representatives at 127 embassies, 9 missions, 69 consulates general, 45 consulates, 3 special offices, and 12 consular agencies throughout the world.[2] Of special importance to marketers is the fact that these worldwide operations provide a base for gathering significant information regarding foreign marketing opportunities. Foreign Service personnel, especially the attaches (commercial, agricultural, etc.) at the embassies are responsible for promoting American business, facilitating business contacts, and protecting American interests. Even ambassadors are active in the development of trade in addition to their political functions.[3]

Economic Activities of the Department. The economic activities of the State Department that affect marketers extend over the following important fields:

Economic Assistance Policy. Economic assistance policy involves the use of foreign aid to stimulate production abroad and to improve economic conditions in underdeveloped areas so as to strengthen the ability of free nations to resist aggression from without and subversion from within. Economic aid to Europe, Asia, and Africa has expanded marketing opportunities for U.S. businesses.

International Trade Policies. International trade policies include the promotion of prosperity through commercial interchange; the furthering of the international exchange of technology and related data; the application of export controls and other security measures; and the conduct of activities with reference to specific commodities, including not only strategic commodities traded on world markets but also those commodities of which the United States is, or may be, a competing exporter and which bulk large in the total trade of friendly foreign countries. The Bureau of International Scientific and Technological Affairs formulates and implements policies for U.S. international science and technology programs. The Agency for International Development promotes economic development through loans and technical cooperations grants, and cooperates with the Department of Agriculture in the sale of agricultural commodities under Public Law 480.

Financial and Development Policy. Financial and development policy relates to the protection and encouragement of United States investment abroad and the investment and development programs and policies of foreign governments; foreign loans and grants, and

---

[2]*U.S. Government Manual* (1973–1974), p. 339.
[3]For an example see "World Trade: A U.S. Ambassador's New Business Role," *Business Week* (December 16, 1973), p. 38.

other international financial matters, including the convertibility of sterling and other currencies, the balance of payments, the relaxation of exchange restrictions, and exchange rate adjustments.[4]

Trade Promotion Functions. The Foreign Service is engaged in the promotion and the protection of the foreign trade of the United States. It performs these trade promotion functions by:

1. Keeping alert for concrete trade opportunities for American importers and exporters.
2. Reporting on the potentialities of overseas areas as a market for American products, as a competitor of American products in other countries, and as a source of supply to the American economy.
3. Endeavoring to create a demand for American products within their districts.
4. Reporting on factors affecting the production and exportation to the United States of local products that might be desirable for import.
5. Investigating for World Traders Data Reports on the capacity of foreign firms within their districts. World Traders Data Reports provide data to American business persons on firms and individuals engaged in business — selling or buying.[5]
6. Preparing trade lists of commercial firms within their districts.
7. Maintaining commercial reading rooms for the use of local business people.
8. Supplying information to American citizens traveling abroad on business and to sales people, buyers, and other representatives of American manufacturers and exporters and importers abroad.
9. Answering trade inquiries received from firms and individuals.

Trade Protection Functions. The functions of trade protection that are performed by the Foreign Service are to:

1. Protect the national commercial reputation of the United States.
2. Observe and attempt to remove discriminations against American interests in other countries.
3. Guard against the infringement of rights of American citizens.
4. Furnish information regarding national and local laws, administrative regulations, and governmental and private monopolies operating in restraint of trade.
5. Report on restrictions upon commercial travelers.
6. Endeavor to adjust and obtain settlement of trade complaints filed against American exporters.
7. Aid in the arbitration of trade disputes by submitting names of individuals considered competent to act as arbitrators (but may not themselves act as such arbitrators).

---

[4]"The Department of State of the United States — Functions, Organization, and Recruitment of Personnel" (Undated mimeographed brochure of the Department of State).
[5]See page 368.

Department of Commerce

The Department of Commerce functions to foster, serve, and promote the economic development and technological advancement of the nation. Its services to industry have earned it the title of "the business person's department." It has long functioned to serve not only private industry, but also states, regions, and local communities. Figure 18-2 shows the organizational structure of the department.[6] Although all organizational units support the activities of the department, our immediate interest settles on the Domestic and International Business Administration — its bureaus and field operations. These deal directly with the international marketer and help in the day-to-day conduct of international business affairs.

Domestic and International Business Administration.[7] The Domestic and International Business Administration was formed in 1972. Among its functions are promoting the growth of U.S. industry and commerce and stimulating the expansion of U.S. exports. It brings together the formerly separate domestic and international trade activities of the department, thereby acknowledging the close relationship between domestic and foreign operations in the modern corporation. Units of the department cooperate to assist U.S. firms with a broad range of information services to facilitate international operations. They also aid in promotion of business through trade missions and trade fairs. Activities of the DIBA are carried out through four bureaus and extensive field operations.

The Bureau of International Commerce has the major responsibility for the department's export expansion program. Three major fronts characterize the Bureau's many services.[8] First, it helps to keep American products competitive by assisting in the negotiations for reduction of trade and investment barriers and by developing export financing policies. Secondly, export awareness activities are aimed at the 92 percent of U.S. firms that do no exporting to inform them of the foreign potential.[9] Thirdly, it offers export assistance through Trade Centers and trade fairs, trade missions, and conferences. Market information gathering and dissemination are important facets of this last thrust.

The Bureau of East-West Trade helps business establish trade with Socialist countries by conducting market analyses, publicizing business opportunities, giving contract advice, and establishing contacts

---

[6]*U.S. Government Manual*, 1973–1974, p. 126.

[7]Tilton H. Dobbin, "DIBA: New Organization for Exports," *New York Times*, September 30, 1973, Section 12, p. 4.

[8]Marinus van Gessel, "Exporting Help Is Available," *New York Times*, Advertising Supplement, September 30, 1973, Section 12, p. 7.

[9]*Ibid.*

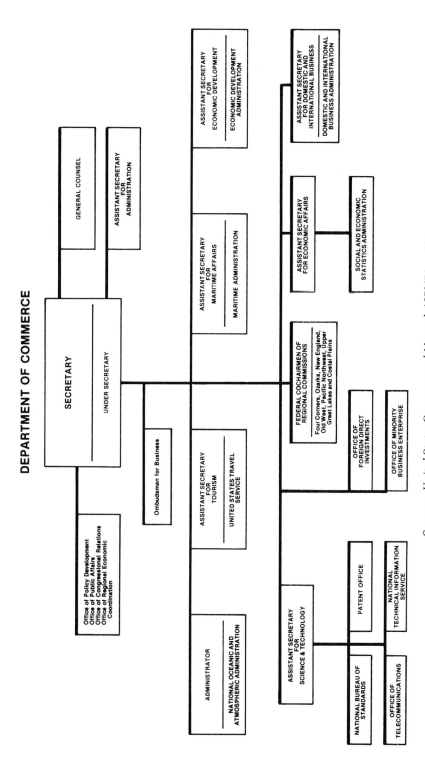

DEPARTMENT OF COMMERCE

Source: *United States Governmental Manual, 1973/74*, p. 126.

Figure 18-2 ORGANIZATIONAL STRUCTURE OF DEPARTMENT OF COMMERCE

with the proper authorities in the Foreign Trade Organizations which conduct the Socialists' trade with foreign countries. The Bureau also can assist U.S. business people with the clearance procedures of the U.S. government.[10]

A Bureau of Resources and Trade Assistance administers the trade adjustment assistance for firms adversely affected by imports resulting from trade concessions made by the U.S. It also analyzes the effect of imports on American markets and handles special import problems dealing with specific categories of products.

The Bureau of Competitive Assessment and Business Policy collects and analyzes data on U.S. industries to assess their competitiveness in international markets.

The Office of Field Operations provides major contact between the Department and the business community through its forty-three District offices throughout the country. These offices are located in the major industrial and commercial cities. They implement the Department's plans within the U.S. and make available a ready source of information and counselling on international marketing.

Major Trade Information and Promotion Services. The Foreign Traders Index maintains information on more than 130,000 foreign importing organizations in 112 countries. The data are assembled by the U.S. Foreign Service of the State Department. The Index makes it possible for the Department to offer Export Mailing Lists classified by products/industry groups and by country. A Data Tape Service is available for firms wishing to retrieve the data through their own data processing systems.[11]

The Trade Opportunities Program (TOP) is computerized to furnish sales leads and information on possible foreign sales representation. The American business specifies the products and markets where leads are desired. These specifications are matched against the information from the Foreign Service and the American marketer receives a report similar to Figure 18-3.[12]

The Agent-Distributor Service helps identify potential agents or distributors for a specific product. Commercial Officers overseas will identify up to three foreign firms that are interested in the specific proposal.[13]

World Traders Data Reports (formerly known as World Trade Directory Reports) provide a profile of commercial and financial information on specific foreign firms. Data include year of establishment,

---

[10]See Chapter 20 for a more extended discussion of East-West trade.

[11]"The Export Mailing List and FTI Data Tape Services" (Pamphlet of the U.S. Department of Commerce, May, 1973).

[12]"Announcing TOP Trade Opportunities Program" (Undated brochure of the U.S. Department of Commerce).

[13]"Agent-Distributor Service Now Going Worldwide," *Commerce Today* (March 5, 1973), pp. 12–13.

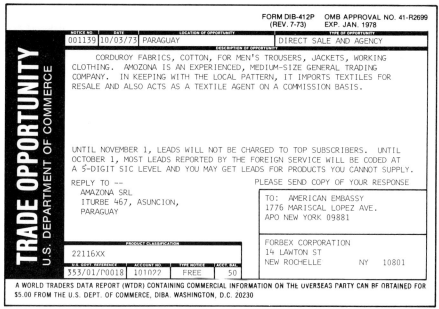

Source: Department of Commerce bulletin "Announcing TOP (Trade Opportunities Program)," undated.

Figure 18-3 TRADE OPPORTUNITY REPORT

size, method of operation (e.g., importer), product lines handled, and credit sources. Figure 18-4 is a sample of such information.

The publications of the Department of Commerce provide a means of researching individual markets before making a major investment in a marketing program. The "Checklist of International Business Publications," available from the District offices, indexes the main publications. Of special note are the monthly foreign trade statistics produced by the Bureau of Census in its "FT" series. These data show exports and imports by commodity and country to aid prospective marketers in determining trade patterns and opportunities. "Country Market Digests" is a series of reports on individual countries thought to have favorable conditions for marketing U.S. products. "Overseas Business Reports" contain country information showing basic economic data, market factors and specific information on climate, customs, transportation, commercial practices, and economic structure. These reports may be purchased or examined in the District offices. The Department's magazine, *Commerce America*, formerly *Commerce Today*, discusses current commodities, policy, and trade.

The monthly *Survey of Current Business* contains a wealth of statistical data and analyses, including trade and balance of payments data. The annual *Statistical Abstract of the United States* is a mine of statistical and historical data gathered from hundreds of governmental and private sources.

DEPARTMENT OF COMMERCE · UNITED STATES OF AMERICA

World Traders Data Report

This report, submitted by the U.S. Foreign Service, under the direction of the Secretary of State, is transmitted in confidence. No responsibility can be assumed by the Government or its officers for any transactions had with any persons or firms herein mentioned. The report is not for publication. All correspondence relating to information in this report should be addressed to the Export Information Division, Bureau of International Commerce, U.S. Department of Commerce, Washington, D.C. 20230. SECONDARY DISTRIBUTION PROHIBITED.

R 221345Z JAN 73
FM AMEMBASSY LONDON
TO USDOC, WASHINGTON
UNCLASS LONDON 1454

REF WASH USDOC 113

SUBJECT: WTDR - MAGRUDER AND SONS TRADING COMPANY

1. ADDRESS: P.O. BOX 322, 226 BARTON STREET, LONDON E.C. 2. CABLE: MAGTRCO, LONDON. TELEX: 664321, PHONE: 844-3472, OFFICER: G.M. MAGRUDER, PRESIDENT.

2. MEDIUM SIZED FIRM ESTABLISHED IN 1922, EMPLOYS 220, OF WHICH 30 ARE IN SALES. ACTS AS IMPORTER, AGENT AND DISTRIBUTOR OF CONSTRUCTION, MINING AND MATERIALS HANDLING EQUIPMENT, DIESEL ENGINES, CONCRETE PRODUCTS MACHINERY AND EQUIPMENT, PUMPS, AIR-CONDITIONERS, AND WOODWORKING MACHINERY. PROVIDES SALES AND SERVICE IN ENGLAND, SCOTLAND AND IRELAND.

3. FINANCIAL REFERENCES: BARCLAYS BANK, STRAND SQUARE, LONDON, E.C. 2, AND BANK OF AMERICA (LONDON BRANCH), GROSEVER SQUARE, LONDON, E.C. 2. TRADE REFERENCES: GENERAL MOTORS CORPORATION, 220 WEST 42ND STREET, NEW YORK; FEDDERS WORLD TRADE CORPORATION, P.O. BOX 2204, WOODBRIDGE, NEW JERSEY: BRITISH REFRIGERATED WAREHOUSES LIMITED, 1422 WEST CHAPEL LANE, LONDON, E.C. 4., AND ANGLO AMERICAN CONTRACTORS, WESTGATE PARK, DUBLIN, IRELAND.

4. MAJOR FOREIGN FIRMS REPRESENTED: FEDDERS WORLD TRADE CORPORATION, P.O. BOX 2204, WOODBRIDGE, NEW JERSEY, ROOM AIR CONDITIONERS, AGENCY ACQUIRED IN 1950; GENERAL MORORS CORPORATION, 220 WEST 42ND STREET, NEW YORK, NEW YORK, DIESEL ENGINES, AGENCY ACQUIRED IN 1954; REX CHAIN BELT COMPANY, 4300 MADISON STREET, MILWAUKEE, WISCONSIN, CONSTRUCTION, MINING, CONCRETE PRODUCTS MACHINERY AND EQUIPMENT, AGENCY ACQUIRED IN 1960; MANNESSMAN AG., 211 FELDSTRASSE, FRANKFURT AM MAIN, GERMANY, PUMPS AND WOODWORKING MACHINERY, AGENCY ACQUIRED IN 1960; HENKEL MACHINERY GMBH., 43 DUISBURG STRASSE, 7110 STUTTGART, GERMANY, MATERIAL HANDLING EQUIPMENT, AGENCY ACQUIRED IN 1954.

5. THIS FIRM IS ONE OF THE LEADING TRADING FIRMS IN ENGLAND FOR THE PRODUCTS LISTED IN THIS REPORT. THE FIRM MAINTAINS ITS HEAD OFFICES IN LONDON WITH BRANCH SALES AND SERVICE OFFICES IN DUBLIN AND GLASGOW. THE OWNERS HAVE HAD CONSIDERABLE TECHNICAL AND ADMINISTRATIVE EXPERIENCE IN THEIR LINE OF BUSINESS AND ARE WELL RESPECTED IN THE LOCAL BUSINESS COMMUNITY. THE FIRM ACTS AS AGENTS AND DISTRIBUTORS OF THE PRODUCTS IT IMPORTS. THE COMPANY REPRESENTS A NUMBER OF LEADING U.S. AND FOREIGN MANUFACTURERS AND ITS SALES ABILITY IS CONSIDERED GOOD THROUGHOUT ENGLAND, SCOTLAND AND IRELAND. BANKING AND TRADE SOURCES REPORT THAT THE FIRM HAS GOOD FINANCIAL REPUTATION AND THEIR OBLIGATIONS ARE MET PROMPTLY. IT IS HIGHLY RECOMMENDED AS A TRADE CONTACT FOR INTERESTED U.S. FIRMS.

6. DATE OF INFO: 01/73

Figure 18-4 SAMPLE OF WORLD TRADERS REPORT INFORMATION

The United States maintains permanent Trade Centers in major cities of Europe, Asia, Australia, and Latin America for the display and promotion of American products. These Centers provide an excellent and inexpensive means for entering a new market. Major exhibitions are built around a product theme that has been identified through market research. Prior to the exhibitions the Center staff conducts a promotional campaign to identify prospective customers and agents in the market area and makes direct mailings and individual sales calls on the most promosing prospects to invite them to the show. About six to nine major product exhibitions are held at each center annually. The Department claims that the immediate sales of an exhibitor can range as high as $1 million and that later sales from these contacts may substantially boost the total. The cost to the American exhibitor involves shipment of the product, provision of a representative to staff the booth, and a participation contribution.[14] Table 18-1, derived from

Table 18-1 RESPONSIBILITIES OF THE DEPARTMENT AND THE COMPANY

The Company Must:	The Department of Commerce Will:
1. Provide products for display	1. Identify by name and promote the attendance of qualified buyers and agents
2. Supply handout technical and promotional literature	2. Provide exhibit space and utilities
3. Ship the product	3. Design and construct the exhibit
4. Assign a representative qualified to man the booth and transact business	4. Advise on shipment of products to site
5. Make the specified contribution	5. Unpack and position display
	6. Provide necessary show hospitality
	7. Provide meeting rooms for exhibitor-customer conferences
	8. Pay the cost of returning exhibit items to the United States if not sold at the show

Source: U.S. Department of Commerce, *U.S. Trade Promotion Facilities Abroad* (August, 1973), p. 11.

---

[14]For further information on the Trade Centers and effective methods for using them, see "U.S. Trade Promotion Facilities Abroad," "How to Get the Most from Overseas Exhibitions," "Overseas Trade Centers and Fairs" (Undated brochure of the U.S. Department of Commerce).

Commerce sources, summarizes the responsibilities assumed by the exhibitor and those of the Department. The exhibits present a unique opportunity to meet with a concentration of potential buyers and representatives at a modest cost. Representatives should know the product, its applications, and the terms under which it will be sold.

The Centers are available between the major shows to trade associations and individual companies for conferences, product promotion, and seminars. The Department of Commerce also sponsors U.S. exhibitions at well-known international trade fairs such as the Paris Air Show. They also sponsor their own trade fairs. In 1974 the Department operated major trade centers in Beirut, Buenos Aires, Frankfort, Mexico City, Milan, Paris, Singapore, Sydney, Stockholm, Teheran, Tokyo, Vienna, Warsaw, Taipei, and Seoul.

General Motors Corporation

The Major Projects Program concentrates on contracts with an export value in excess of $4 million. Specialists around the world notify American companies of impending projects for which they may be qualified. Assistance is provided to enable the company to make a successful bid. Many of these projects involve major infra-structure (schools, transportation, power) investments.

The Department's District offices are manned by knowledgeable people in foreign trade. International trade specialists are available for consultation on issues ranging from "How do I get into international marketing?" to technical questions on licenses and trade regulations.

Other Federal Government Agencies

Numerous other federal departments and agencies facilitate international marketing. Many of these are discussed in the context of their major function in other parts of this text. Several, however, warrant mention here because of their special significance.

The Department of Agriculture develops foreign markets for the products of our farms. This includes continued appraisal of marketing opportunities abroad and of competition and trade barriers. It also includes efforts to improve trade conditions for U.S. agricultural products. The Agriculture Department is a source of current information on world agricultural commodity and trade policy gathered by agricultural officers stationed in all principal countries, in addition to special studies sponsored by the Department. In one study of pet foods in Germany, the agricultural attache proved to be the person with the necessary information rather than the commercial attache.

The Treasury Department, through the Customs Service, administers all customs regulations, imposes import duties, provides import/export statistics published by the Department of Commerce, and assures compliance with export license regulations. The Office of International Affairs advises on international financial, economic, and monetary policies; monitors developments in gold and foreign exchange operations; and coordinates policies of bilateral and multilateral development lending programs.

The International Trade Commission is charged with the administration of the flexible provisions whereby tariff rates may be changed. It advises the President as to the probable economic effect of a reduction in the import duty or other restrictions. It investigates charges of unfair competition in the import trade and hears appeals from allegedly injured producers claiming excessive imports under reduced tariffs.

The Export-Import bank promotes U.S. exports through direct loans to buyers abroad, including U.S. enterprises, for financing the export of capital goods. It further assumes 100 percent responsibility for political risks and shares the commercial risks under the U.S. export credit insurance program.[15]

PROMOTION BY STATE AND LOCAL UNITS

The trade promotions sponsored by the Federal government functions nation-wide. Individual states, however, are interested in

---

[15]See Chapter 15 for details of the credit program and operations of the Export-Import Bank.

promoting the welfare of the citizens of those states. Responding to significant export opportunities, the states have developed a variety of promotional efforts on their own and in concert with federal and foreign programs. State Development Agencies have been charged with the responsibility of fostering economic growth. Other state groups and port authorities promote tourism, analyze and influence legislation affecting the states' trade, and help develop a supporting infrastructure.

One study classified the activities of states that affect the buying, selling, and transportation functions as: informational, enabling, supportive, constructive, protective, and negotiational.[16] Informational functions include the promotion of tourism, state products and facilities by the provision of data, advertising, and personal contract. Enabling activities involve the passage of legislation conducive to trade. Supporting may require financial aid or gaining access to federal funds to support projects. Constructive activities include the development of such infrastructure as roads, airports, and port facilities; while negotiation may involve state intervention in transportation rates, commercial laws, and tariff changes. This range of functions involves numerous state departments and agencies. One problem of state commercial policy is the effective integration of these efforts.

One means of integration is to concentrate the major thrust of state governmental efforts in the State Development Agency. The International Trade Division of the Ohio Department of Economic and Community Development, for example, provides a comprehensive program to business. The major objectives of the program are:[17]

1. To increase the overall international sales/profit base of Ohio companies, be they manufacturing, agriculture, or service.
2. To create employment opportunities through increased international trade expansion.
3. To attract new investment to Ohio both internationally and domestically.

In order to accomplish these goals the department's program provides sales leads and business opportunities for specific products, international market research reports, international trade consultants, a library on foreign trade, state sponsored trade missions and trade fairs, and representation overseas through local offices and travelling personnel.

Several states and port authorities have established offices outside the United States in order to generate sales leads, promote trade, and

---

[16]John L. Hazard, "Michigan's Commerce and Commercial Policy Study," *Michigan State University International Business Studies*, Division of Research Graduate School of Business Administration, Michigan State University, East Lansing, 1965, p. 151–153.

[17]This section is based on printed material from the Ohio Department of Economic and Community Development and discussion with Merrill Katz from the Office of International Trade.

increase the use of harbors.[18] These "mini-embassies" promote trade through personal selling, advertising, trade fairs, and speeches to various industry groups. While early efforts were aimed primarily at export expansion, dollar devaluation in the early seventies provided an increased opportunity to attract foreign capital to the state — the so-called reverse investment function — and state agencies and overseas offices actively sought such funds.[19]

PROMOTION BY PRIVATE AGENCIES

In addition to the governmental trade promotion activities, international marketers are aided by scores of private organizations which function independently or through government channels. Some of them are interested in government policy related to international trade while others perform services for the exclusive benefit of members or subscribers. In this section we have selected several major institutions to reflect the range of activities.

National Foreign Trade Council, Inc.

This council may be regarded as the business person's representative for American foreign trade. It provides "coordination of industrial, commercial, transportation, and financial interest of the United States for the purpose of developing American foreign trade and investment policies on a sound basis."[20] Committees represent various technical trade fields. They study and recommend action on a range of legal, financial, governmental, and economic factors affecting trade. The Council staff also makes investigations and provides trade information to members. Current international marketing problems are discussed at an annual convention.

American Importers Association, Inc.

This council represents the import trade areas as a whole and strives to bring about equitable adjustment of the laws and regulations governing the entry of imported merchandise. It supplies members with accurate information on matters affecting imports, including tariff and customs questions, transportation and insurance problems, etc.

---

[18]See James D. Goodnow, "American Overseas Business Promotion Offices," *Michigan Business Review* (January, 1970, for a survey of the functions of these offices.)

[19]See Gerald Albaum, *State Government Promotion of International Business*, University of Arizona, 1968, for a study of state programs. See also *The Journal of Commerce*(January 15, 1973) for a series of articles describing state programs to attract foreign investment.

[20]*Exporters Encyclopedia* (1966), p. 1546.

Chambers of Commerce

The Chamber of Commerce of the United States represents small and large businesses on a variety of fronts. The International Department carries out the international trade promotion activities of the Chamber. It studies legislation and governmental administrative procedures in world trade. Many of the local chapters maintain World Trade Clubs and other facilities to enhance trade.

The International Chamber of Commerce brings together thousands of businesses and associations in many countries. The United States Council is the American affiliate. The ICC is a spokesman for business where they can pool their experience and form a common policy. The ICC, in turn, brings this policy to bear on individual governments, the United Nations, and world public opinion.

American Chambers of Commerce abroad seek to protect American interests by opposing discriminatory legislation; arbitrating trade disputes; publicizing American ideals, institutions, and policies; and promoting U.S. trade.[21] The membership of these organizations is composed primarily of Americans living and operating in other countries.

PROMOTION BY SUPRANATIONAL ORGANIZATIONS

In addition to the activities of private and governmental agencies, world trade is promoted through the activities of the United Nations, the Organization of American States, and various other supranational organizations.

The United Nations

While individual countries promote their own trade and investments, the United Nations is interested in the development of trade of all countries.[22] A primary instrument for UN programs is the Economic and Social Council. The Council has observed that long-term development of trade, particularly for the less developed countries, depends on their ability to export and upon policies of the industrial nations — including trade in addition to basic commodities such as manufactured goods.

The Commission on International Commodity Trade is concerned with the stability of trade in primary products. UNCTAD, or the United Nations Conference on Trade and Development, deals largely with the problems of lesser developed countries. The UN International

---

[21]Edward F. Feely, "How The American Chamber of Commerce Abroad Helps the American Foreign Trade," *American Chambers of Commerce Abroad* (Washington: Chamber of Commerce of the United States.)

[22]*United Nations Yearbook* (various editions).

Trade Center helps these lesser developed countries find markets for their exports by providing information on export markets and marketing development and by export promotion services and the training of personnel.

The UN publishes a wealth of information for world markets such as the *United Nations Yearbook*, the *UN Statistical Yearbook*, the *Direction of International Trade*, and a host of special studies from its specialized agencies on production, agriculture, and health and technical assistance.

Other Supranational Agencies

Numerous regional organizations exist to promote and facilitate the trade of their members. Some of them carry out extensive publication programs that can provide data and insight regarding marketing conditions and methods within the member's territories. The Organization for Economic Corporation and Development (OECD) is made up of over 20 European countries, plus the United States, Canada, and Japan. It conducts research related to the economic problems of its members. An extensive publications program provides valuable marketing data and insights. The organization maintains a U.S. office.[23]

Western hemisphere information is available from the Organization of American States through its Secretariat, the Pan American Union.

EVALUATION OF TRADE PROMOTION BY GOVERNMENT

Before leaving the topic of trade promotion, it is well to make several salient points regarding its effectiveness and its limitations. The preceding material has shown that extensive efforts are involved in these activities. Many functions and institutions have been shown to provide potential aid, but some people question the effectiveness of the activities, especially as they relate to export expansion.[24]

(1) Trade promotion by governmental agencies is extensive and pervades the international scene. Numerous promotional events and contacts occur. These are effective in producing sales for the private sector when marketers are knowledgeable about the available services and use them. Trade promotion by government is an effective supplement to private marketing efforts.

(2) Export expansion and direct investments can be facilitated by trade promotion only when basic economic conditions are conducive

---

[23]Organization for Economic Cooperation and Development, 1700 Pennsylvania Ave., N.W., Washington, D.C., 20006.

[24]See William A. Dymsza, "Export Expansion — American Style," *Michigan Business Review* (May, 1971), pp. 16–22.

to international business. However, the competitive position of American exports is also dependent on American productivity; management, marketing and production skills; and comparative advantages. Trade promotion by government cannot overcome any deficiency in these resources. Recent years have seen the loss of some markets for standardized goods to Western European, Japanese, and other Asian countries. Our comparative advantage now lies in high technology items such as computers and aircraft, miniaturization, and in agricultural products that capitalize on our available land and technology. Governmental agencies have supported exports in these fields to the advantage of the private sector.

(3) Governmental trade promotion is designed to supplement, not replace, private initiative in seeking out new markets and adapting product and services to those potentials. The private sector still bears the primary responsibility for developing international business in the American society.

(4) Trade promotion activities by government often are impeded by other governmental policies. Trade may be subordinated to political and social issues. This is not to say it should be otherwise, but at least recognition should be given to the potential conflicts, even when foreign policy may favor expanded trade.

(5) Finally, no amount of governmental promotion can succeed unless the basic commercial functions of the firm satisfy its customers better than the products and services available from domestic and foreign competitors.

QUESTIONS

1. Define the functions of the United States Department of State in trade promotion.
2. Why do commercial nations try to promote their export trade?
3. What are the major trade promotion functions of the United States Department of Commerce?
4. Select a specific product and show how the U.S. Department of Commerce could assist in marketing that product abroad.
5. How can a marketer benefit from World Traders Data Reports?
6. How can an American firm utilize the U.S. Trade Centers in Europe or Asia?
7. How do the various state agencies promote the products of their state in overseas markets?
8. How can an American firm use the United Nations to aid its marketing abroad?

SUPPLEMENTARY READINGS

Exporters' Encyclopedia. New York: Dun & Bradstreet, Inc., annual.
Small Business Administration. *Export Marketing for Smaller Firms*, 3d ed. Washington: U.S. Government Printing Office, August, 1971.

Stuart, Robert Douglass. *Penetrating the International Market*. New York: American Management Association, 1965.

United Nations Yearbook. New York: United Nations, annual.

United States Department of Commerce. *A Basic Guide to Exporting*. Washington: U.S. Government Printing Office, June, 1975.

United States General Services Administration, National Archives and Records Service, Office of the Federal Register. *United States Government Manual*. Washington: U.S. Government Printing Office, annual.

CHAPTER 19

Export Cooperation in The United States and Combinations Abroad

As discussed in this chapter, cooperation in exporting from the United States means the voluntary combination of *independent* and *competitive* business concerns, each of which retains its identity, for purposes of mutual development of foreign markets. Such combinations are illegal under the federal antitrust laws for domestic American enterprises and import trade; however, the Webb-Pomerene, or Export Trade Act in 1918 removed this illegality for export trade.

Cooperation among competitive independent economic enterprises has been more common in foreign countries than in the United States. Antitrust policy in some countries has been much more lenient than in the United States. Wars and depressed business conditions cause great strain upon international combines which represent producers of several nations. When nationalism becomes dominant, international understandings are avoided. Nevertheless, the desirability of stabilization in production, exports, and price leads to national and international combinations when legislation tolerates or encourages such action.

Germany and Japan have favored combinations in industry and trade. World War II was expected to bring an end to these practices but the tendency to combine as a means of controlling competition is again evident.

EXPORT COOPERATION AMONG AMERICAN EXPORTERS

The specific reasons for removal of the antitrust ban on American export trade were revealed in a survey conducted by the Federal Trade Commission at the time the Export Trade Act was considered. The Commission declared that: "In seeking business abroad American manufacturers and producers must meet aggressive competition from powerful foreign combinations, often international in character."[1] Continuing, the Commission held that: "If Americans were to enter the world markets on more nearly equal terms with their organized competitors and customers . . . they [have] to be free to unite their efforts."[2] In conclusion the Commission found:

1. That other nations had marked advantages in foreign trade from superior facilities and more effective organizations.
2. That doubt and fear as to legal restrictions prevented Americans from developing equally effective organizations for overseas business and that the foreign trade of American manufacturers and producers, particularly the smaller American concerns, suffered in consequence.[3]

On the basis of this report of the Federal Trade Commission, the Webb-Pomerene Act was enacted by Congress.

Provisions and Interpretation of the Webb-Pomerene Act

Export trade is defined in the Act as "solely trade or commerce in goods, wares, or merchandise exported, or in the course of being exported from the United States or any Territory thereof to any foreign nation." By its very nature, production is excluded but the question as to what constitutes "in the course of being exported" depends upon the interpretation adopted by the Federal Trade Commission which administers the Act. In 1924 this phrase was defined by the Commission which administers the Act in answer to questions submitted for interpretation by the silver producers of the United States. In accordance with this opinion, it is considered legal for export associations to allot export orders among their members or to fix the prices at which their individual members shall sell in export trade.

The Commission further ruled that "there is nothing in the Act which prevents an association formed under it from entering into any cooperative relationship with a foreign corporation, for the sole purpose of operation in a foreign market." This view opened the door to international cooperation between American associations and foreign concerns.

In 1955, however, the Federal Trade Commission warned against the practice of price-fixing arrangements between Webb-Pomerene associations and foreign competitors, declaring that such practice is not necessarily exempt from the antitrust acts. In other words, this specific practice is not to be interpreted as coming within the meaning of

---

[1] Federal Trade Commission, *Report on Cooperation in American Export Trade*, Part I (1916), p. 4.
[2] *Ibid.*, p. 8.
[3] *Ibid.*, p. 3.

the phrase "in the course of export trade." Sales made to export houses located in the United States are authorized if the product sold is intended for, is actually marked for, and enters into export trade.

Geographical Area

The Act permits cooperation in exporting from the United States or any U.S. Territory to any foreign nation. The associations may, therefore, be organized in territories of the United States and may ship to foreign countries, but not to the United States or to other American possessions or territories. Moreover, associations formed in the United States may not ship to any American possession or territory. Thus, even if individual companies serve Puerto Rico through their international division, a Webb-Pomerene association cannot legally do so.

Provisions of the Export Trade Act

When considering the provisions of the Act, it is well to remember that the general intent is to retain the long-established antitrust policy at home and to alter it only for purposes of export trade.

The Sherman Antitrust Act does not apply to export associations formed under the Export Trade Act provided their activities cause (1) no restraint of trade within the United States, (2) no restraint of the export trade of any domestic competitor, (3) no effect on prices within the United States of the commodities exported by the association, or (4) no substantial lessening of competition or restraint of trade within the United States.

Section 4 provides that the Federal Trade Commission Act shall extend to unfair methods of competition against competitors engaged in export trade even though such acts take place outside the territorial jurisdiction of the United States.

This section obviously aims to enforce the same standard of commercial morality on American enterprises engaged in trade at home or abroad. As interpreted by the Federal Trade Commission, unfair methods include the use of misleading labels, misrepresentation, full-line forcing, and unfair discounts. The Commission has stopped the practice of misleading labels on condensed milk exported to Mexico. It also has considered complaints filed by the foreign buyers of American products.

This feature of the Act is evidence of the intent of Congress to place American exporting combinations on a legal parity with foreigners, but not to lower the standards of American business practice. This position tended to allay the suspicions in some countries that discrimination against foreigners was authorized by permitting business practices abroad which the law prohibits at home.

Failure to comply with any request of the Commission for information contemplated in the law removes from an association the benefits of the provisions and makes the association liable for a daily fine. The enforcement of the Webb-Pomerene Act is provided for in this simple manner.

The Commission has made several cooperative associations change their methods of operation. In a number of cases, associations were required to cease agreeing upon export sales prices and terms with American nonmembers. In one case, the association was charged with agreeing on export market quotas with nonmembers. One association was advised not to hold stock in any companies in foreign countries engaged in the manufacture of the product in which the association dealt, and not to sell any products of non-American origin. In still another case, the association was accused of seeking to keep nonmember competitors from entering export markets.

One case heard by the Supreme Court involved charges of efforts to eliminate competing imports by foreign members of the association; restrictions or elimination of exports by domestic producers from the United States to many world markets; prevention of independent domestic producers from competing in export; restriction of United States production; and price fixing in the United States.[4]

Activities of the Webb-Pomerene Associations

An association includes "any corporation or combination, by contract or otherwise, of two or more persons, partnerships, or corporations." Thus, a wide range of organizational forms are possible.

A study of the number of associations formed under the Act indicates there was an initial interest, followed by a slump, and then a steady and declining level. The number of active associations has never been large; in the period 1959–1965 the number was consistently below thirty. Most of the associations have been short-lived. The typical association deals in producer goods and standard products.

Associations provide a number of services for their members. In one study of twenty-three active associations, three acted as export merchants by buying the product and performing the entire merchandising function. Five others acted as agents for the products and eleven were involved in price setting and/or market allocation. Four provided marketing information, aided in financing sales, or developed a uniform sales contract.[5] Table 19-1 provides more detailed information regarding the activities of associations in 1962.

---

[4] *United States Alkali Export Association v. United States*, 325 U.S. 196 (1945).
[5] Federal Trade Commission Survey, *Export Trade Associations*, 1963.

Table 19-1 ACTIVITIES OF WEBB ASSOCIATIONS IN 1962

Function	Number of Associations Performing Function*
Price setting and market allocation	19
Foreign sales offices and/or agents	13
Market research and information	9
Selling agent	8
Sales to United States government	9
Freight and insurance	8
Negotiating with foreign governments and international agencies	7
Promotional activities	6
Publications	6
Representing member firms before United States government agencies	5
Statistical services	4
Engineering and related services	4
Distributing and licensing activities	4
Market development	3
Foreign storage facilities	2
Financing exports	2
Credit information	1
Uniform sales contract	1

Source: Federal Trade Commission Survey, *Export Trade Associations*, 1963.
*Data based on 23 active associations in 1962. Each of these associations performed two or more of the functions listed.

Price Administration. Export Trade Associations generally establish minimum export prices, while their foreign agents set actual prices as affected by conditions. Since associations that operate a central selling agency generally export larger quantities of merchandise than any single member, it is often possible for the export association to fix export prices that will hold longer than when each member individually ships smaller orders. Some associations leave export price control to the individual members, but at least one association establishes prices abroad and supervises agents by means of a traveling official of the association. Another plan is to place control over prices and terms of sale under jurisdiction of the export association's price committee.

Allocation of Orders. The allocation of orders among the members of Export Trade Associations often is determined by a quota. Some of these export quotas are predicated on capacity or production but they also may be determined by the quantity of merchandise that members report will be available for export. When several different products are handled, quotas may be assigned for each type.

Finally, there is the very difficult question of how to handle shipments above or below the quota assigned. In some agreements each member must supply the market as orders arise; failure to do so results in the loss of a turn.

Advantages of Webb-Pomerene Associations. Several advantages have accrued to associations operating under the Act. These include:

1. Stabilization of export prices.
2. Reduction of selling costs so that small companies which cannot individually penetrate foreign markets can pay their share of expense.
3. Standardization of grades, contract terms, and sales conditions. (The Walnut Export Sales Company, for example, established a uniform brand "WESCO" and maintains quality by careful inspection.)
4. Prompt and efficient filling of orders.
5. Elimination of harmful practices.
6. Combating combinations of buyers that might play one exporter against another.
7. Storage of seasonal products, thus averting oversupply and consequent low prices.
8. Consolidation of cargoes for better service and lower transportation costs.
9. Joint advertising.
10. Adjustment of claims.
11. Bidding on and securing large orders.
12. Filling orders for a variety of products by allocating orders among the members.
13. Division of territory.
14. Use of direct exporting channels.

Problems. The Webb-Pomerene Act has been particularly suited to the needs of exporters of raw and bulky products, while the manufacturers of finished products are less attracted. In the case of raw and bulky products individual attention to particular brands or qualities is not required since raw materials may be mixed without affecting their marketability. When goods are sold by brand or trademark, however, cooperative export marketing is much more difficult.

An inherent problem for some associations is the fundamental inability of the members to cooperate. Dissension in the domestic market cannot always be overcome in the interest of cooperation for export. Sometimes exports prove to be a heavy burden. Often it is difficult for the association to represent a whole industry. Some associations have suffered from poor management and have been discontinued. Some began with a great deal of enthusiasm and optimism but failed to attract a sufficient number of members and were dissolved. Still others encountered such keen competition abroad that, in spite of their combined front, they could not compete effectively. Finally, many manufacturers of branded products found the difficulties of adequately representing individual interests insurmountable. Nevertheless, associations have represented some differentiated products as in the machine tool and TV film industries.[6]

Shortcomings of the Act

Certain shortcomings of the Act are apparent. It is generally felt that the elimination of all of our territorial possessions is an unfortunate limitation. Some possessions of the United States, in practice, are distinctly foreign markets. Undoubtedly, the greatest deficiency of the law, however, is the restriction of its provisions to the export trade. At first, the Federal Trade Commission's interpretation of export trade was narrow. The later expansion of this interpretation under the Silver letter of 1924 enabled cooperative associations to engage in important activities formerly believed to be forbidden, but the exclusion of the import trade from the application of the law remains. Furthermore, the position of architectural, engineering, financing, and management project firms is still not clear.[7]

The FTC viewed fifty years of experience under the Act as follows:

> "A half century of experience with the Webb-Pomerene Act reveals that associations have not proved to be effective instruments either for the expansion of overall United States exports or for the expansion of exports by small firms. As a whole, the business sector of the economy appears to be disinterested in organizing cooperative associations to promote exports."[8]

Some students of the law, including the Justice Department and the Federal Trade Commission, have advocated repeal of the Act or amendments that would restrict the current approach to easy formation of Webb-Pomerene associations. These students are suggesting that the statute has not been effective in attracting smaller firms into export trade. A "need" test has been proposed for granting permission to form an association.[9] This latter derives partly from the heavy participation of large American firms in association activity. Further, the large size of many of these American corporations relative to their

---

[6]"Defanging Antitrust for Foreign Trade," *Business Week* (April 21, 1973), pp. 26–27.
[7]*Ibid.*
[8]Federal Trade Commission Economic Report, *Webb-Pomerene Associations: A 50-Year Review* (Washington: U.S. Government Printing Office, June, 1967), p. 61.
[9]Thomas J. Leary, "Acquisition Activity of Webb-Pomerene Member Firms, 1951–1958: A Policy Suggestion," *The American Journal of Economics and Sociology* (July, 1972), pp. 259–269.

foreign competitors indicates a quite different environment than that existing in 1918 when the Export Trade Act was passed.

MARKETING COMBINATIONS ABROAD

The attitude of many countries toward combinations of industrial and commercial firms differs radically from that of the United States. Despite the Webb-Pomerene exemption for export trade, the U.S. has pursued a basic policy of promoting competition. Some other governments, in contrast, have either permitted or fostered the elimination of competition to develop their industrial base.

The domestic antitrust operations of the U.S. Department of Justice and the Federal Trade Commission are well-known, but less well-known is the application of U.S. antitrust law to American firms operating abroad. Several times U.S. law has been extended beyond the national boundaries by legal authorities in breaking up American companies' participation with foreign business interests.

Continental European governments frequently have permitted combinations of firms that enable them to achieve market control. Historically, Germany has been a leader in concentration movements by encouraging and occasionally participating officially in restrictive agreements; however, the Treaty of Rome and the antitrust rules of the Common Market have changed this situation materially.

Antitrust Policy of the EEC

The European Economic Community appears to be moving toward a more vigorous antitrust policy than that pursued by some of the individual members. The basis for this antitrust philosophy of the EEC is laid down in Articles 85 and 86 of the Treaty of Rome.

The treaty prohibits certain practices that may affect both contracts with European agents, licensees, and distributors as well as American companies operating in the Common Market. Specifically, Article 85, paragraph 1 prohibits such practices as:

1. The direct or indirect fixing of purchase or selling prices or of any other trading conditions.
2. The limitation or control of production, markets, technical development, or investment.
3. Market-sharing or the sharing of sources of supply.
4. The application of unequal conditions to parties undertaking equivalent engagements in commercial transactions, thereby placing them at a commercial disadvantage.
5. Making the conclusion of a contract subject to the acceptance of additional goods or services which by their nature or in commercial usage have no relation to the subject of such contract.

However, Article 85, paragraph 3 appears to take much of the sting out of the prohibitions of paragraph 1. Paragraph 3 declares that such practices outlawed in paragraph 1 will not be invalid if they contribute to the improvement of the production or distribution of goods or to the promotion of technical or economic progress, while reserving to users an equitable share in the profit resulting therefrom, and which do not:

1. Subject the concerns in question to any restrictions not indispensable to the achievement of the above objectives.
2. Enable such concerns to eliminate competition in respect of a substantial proportion of the goods concerned.

Thus, the practices in paragraph 1 are not to be considered illegal per se. Rather the treaty seems to suggest that they should be judged by their effect. If beneficial by contributing to technical or economic progress, they may be permitted; yet the precise interpretation of the nature of these provisions is not certain and will require numerous administrative decisions by the Common Market Commission's Antitrust Division as they implement the treaty.

Article 86 refers specifically to monopolies or quasi-monopolies already in existence. These are declared to be incompatible with the Common Market if, by reason of their dominant position, they improperly exploit their position. Practices such as the following are specifically outlawed:

1. The imposition, direct or indirect, of any unfair purchase or selling prices or of any other unfair trading conditions.
2. The limitation of production, markets, or technical development to the prejudice of consumers.
3. The application of unequal conditions to parties undertaking equivalent engagements in commercial transactions, thereby placing them at a commercial disadvantage.

The Common Market Commission is issuing regulations pertaining to these and other conditions of the Rome Treaty. Some of these have been tested in the courts. One of the most significant of such cases testing Article 86 was that of the Continental Can Company, a U.S. company with subsidiaries in Europe.[10] As a result of its holdings of Schmalbach-Lubeca-Werke, AG and Thomassen and Drijver, the Commission found that Continental had a dominant position in cans for meat, fish, and seafood and in caps for glass bottles that led to the practical elimination of competition. Continental appealed to the European Court of Justice. The court agreed with Continental that its subsidiaries did not dominate the market, but the court also appeared

---

[10]Peter Vanderwicken, "Continental Can's Intercontinental Tribulations," *Fortune* (August, 1973), pp. 74–79.

to give the Commission power to prohibit mergers, joint ventures, or acquisitions that would increase a company's dominant share.

Types of Combinations Abroad

Unhampered by legal obstruction in some countries, international marketing combinations have taken various forms. First to be considered is the *cartel*. A cartel aims to control the market; it tends to create a monopoly although it rarely succeeds in doing so. Cartels were especially active in the period between World War I and II.

Cartels. A cartel may be defined as a combination in restraint of competition in industry and trade that is implemented through agreements among enterprises maintaining separate identities and separate ownership, stock controls, and management.[11] United States industries have participated at one time or another in cartels. These include producers of aluminum, alkalies, electrical equipment and appliances, fertilizer (phosphates and potash), petroleum products, steel products, and sulphur.

From the threat of overproduction in basic mass-production industries, the cartel form of organization has expanded into other fields of activity, so that a classification of cartels includes not only (1) those organized to limit output, but also (2) those established to maintain prices, (3) to agree upon sales territories, foreign as well as national, (4) to agree upon uniform documents, credits, and other collateral phases of merchandising, or (5) to undertake centralized selling.

National Combines. In the United Kingdom combinations have been formed in certain lines in spite of traditional individualism. Some of these result in mergers as in the United States while many others are distinct cartel agreements. In Japan traditional combinations such as the undertakings of a firm like Mitsui or Mitsubishi, for example, often cover production, financing, and trading units. Cartels have been formed by Japanese firms in response to the government's desire to nationalize industry and to strengthen Japanese firms during periods of recession.

Despite the breakup of the large Japanese industrial combines at the close of World War II, some have since been reorganized and again represent vast commercial power.

International Combines. In the international sphere, combinations have been the outgrowth of national combines. Indeed, the establishment of international control over production or distribution is chiefly

---

[11]United States Federal Trade Commission, *Annual Report, 1946*, p. 13.

predicated upon extensive national control; therefore, a favorable legal attitude on the part of the governments involved is most important for the development of international combinations. Cheapness and ease of transportation and communication over great distances have been cited as conditions favorable to international agreement.[12] Other factors are the existence of standard articles of mass production; large supplies of materials or labor, or patents; or large minimum and optimum size of plant.[13]

Characteristics of International Combinations

With few exceptions international combines have been concerned chiefly with raw materials and basic manufactured products or articles supplied in bulk or in a few recognized grades.[14] One list of international cartels and other industrial understandings included eight classifications: mining industries, metal industries, chemical industries, ceramic industries, metal industries, chemical industries, ceramic industries, electrical industries, textile industries, miscellaneous industries, and insurance and traffic.[15]

Insofar as details permit analysis, these combines attempted one or more of the following activities: allotment of sales territories; allotment of sales quotas; establishment of common sales agencies and common purchase agencies; price fixing; regulation of terms of sale; regulation of production; pooling of profits; and patent pooling and cross-licensing.

Of increasing importance in world trade are international marketing agreements relating to raw materials. This new emphasis derives from the needs of the raw-material-producing countries. Many of these are in the less developed category and the country's internal economic conditions are directly related to the volume and price of raw material exports. These exports are generally shipped to the developed countries which are the markets for raw materials and foods. Fluctuations in the volume and prices of these products have adversely affected the economic stability of the exporting countries. Concern for the welfare of the less-developed countries has led to marketing agreements to stabilize prices of their exports. Some of these nations also have formed organizations to improve their marketing positions. The oil-producing countries represent a current illustration of governmental cartel action by producing nations.

---

[12]Alfred Plummer, *International Combines in Modern Industry* (2d ed.; London: Sir I. Pitman and Sons, Ltd., 1938), p. 64.

[13]Theodore J. Kreps, *Hearings of Temporary National Economic Committee* (Sir I. Pitman and Sons, Ltd., 1938), p. 64.

[14]Plummer, *op. cit.*, p. 64.

[15]Dr. Heinrich Friedlaender, quoted by Theodore J. Kreps, *op. cit.*, pp. 13,368–13,369.

Examples of Cartel Action — International Commodity Agreements

The following examples of present and past cartels illustrate the forms and operations of commodity cartels.

Organization of Petroleum Exporting Countries (OPEC). The oil embargo of 1973–74 and consequent success in raising oil prices brought attention to OPEC. It was formed in 1960 to exert more control over the international oil companies operating in the producing countries.[16] At that time Venezuela and Iran joined the Arab producers to form a group which also is open for membership to other producing nations. By 1975 twelve such nations belonged to OPEC[17] which has the twin objectives of (1) raising the taxes and royalties earned by member countries from oil production and (2) gaining more control over production and exploration.[18]

The nations of OPEC produce about 85 percent of the world trade in oil and, thus, are in a position to control supply and prices in the short run, especially in view of the high oil demand in the industrialized consumer nations. However, the embargo and subsequent activity have fostered energy conservation programs, development of substitute fuels (coal), and increased oil development in the consuming countries as they attempt to reduce their vulnerability to future production or marketing restrictions by OPEC nations.

Despite the divergent interests of its member nations OPEC had been successful in maintaining a unified position from its formation to the post-embargo period. However, the pressure for a split in policy was evident in early 1975.[19] Some of the OPEC nations, such as Iran and Algeria, needed maximum immediate revenues to implement their development plans while others, such as Kuwait and Saudi Arabia, were interested in the long-run prospects since current revenues exceed immediate investment requirements.[20]

The success of OPEC naturally has stimulated the interests of other basic raw material producers in cartel formation, and associations have been proposed or formed in several products, but these had not yet achieved the success of OPEC by early 1977. The iron ore, bauxite, and copper industries are examples of potential cartels. However, the

---

[16]"The Birth of OPEC, and How It Grew," *Business Week* (January 13, 1975), pp. 78–79.

[17]Mexico apparently has decided to stay out of the cartel but to maintain the prices set by OPEC. "Oil Gives Mexicans a Boost, But They Plan to Stay Out of OPEC," *The Wall Streert Journal*, February 11, 1975, p. 1.

[18]"OPEC: The Economics of the Oil Cartel," *Business Week* (January 13, 1975), p. 77.

[19]"OPEC Heads of State to Meet Tomorrow to Set Stand for Talks with Oil Buyers," *The Wall Street Journal*, March 3, 1975, p. 7. Also, "Signs of Strain in Oil Cartel," *U.S. News & World Report* (March 10, 1975), p. 32.

[20]"OPEC: The Economics of the Oil Cartel," *op. cit.*, p. 80.

Association of Iron Ore Exporting Countries suffers from the lack of support from several major exporters and the International Bauxite Association had not yet acted as a unit by late 1974.[21] The copper-producing countries formed the Conseil Intergouveremental des Pays Exportateurs de Cuivre (CIPEC) in 1967 and were reported to be attempting to control production and establish a price system.[22] These organizations suffer basic problems in forming cartels sometimes because they do not include some major producers. In some there are many small producers making cooperative effort difficult. For some products substitutes are plentiful or the product demand is unstable over the course of the business cycle.

Diamonds. Doubtlessly the most closely monopolized trade in the world is the diamond trade. De Beers Consolidated Mines, Ltd., exercises control through a group of companies affiliated with it. Probably 95 percent of the gem and industrial diamonds produced in the West are in the hands of this combine. It not only participates in production but it also purchases the output of companies that are not members of the combine. London is the wholesale market where two companies — Diamond Trading Company and Industrial Distributors, Ltd. — market both gem and industrial diamonds. The de Beers diamond combine made news in 1960 when it succeeded in negotiating a contract with the Soviet Union to purchase and market the diamonds produced in the Soviet Union that were to be exported.

Coffee. International Commodity Agreements of the post-World War II period have often differed from the preceding examples because they included consuming nations as well as producers. The United States government refrained from joining other international agreements designed to stabilize world trade in raw materials; however, in 1963 the Senate approved the United States entry into the International Coffee Agreement. The coffee agreement had been initiated in 1959 and included the major producing countries in Latin America and in Africa, but it originally excluded important producers in Asia and Africa that were later admitted in 1968. The agreement attempts to stabilize trade by establishing export quotas, but this method generally has not been successful and prices of coffee have not been stabilized. In 1967, however, the U.S. signed the International Coffee Agreement in response to pressure from the Third World.[23]

Sugar. While the United States controls the quantity of sugar to be allotted to domestic producers and foreign suppliers, it has not

---

[21]"Cartels for Basic Raw Materials?" *Business in Brief* (October, 1974).

[22]"Is the OPEC Epidemic Spreading?" *Business International* (November 22, 1974), pp. 369–370.

[23]*The Wall Street Journal*, April 21, 1976, p. 1.

become a member of the International Sugar Council. The Council includes both producing and consuming nations; yet the absence of the United States, as the biggest consumer, has hindered the effectiveness of the agreement. The sugar agreement operates on a basis of export quotas supplemented by voluntary production restrictions; however, these production restrictions have not been effective and the international price of sugar has not been stabilized. The elimination of Cuba as a supplier of the United States market caused wide disturbances in the world sugar trade because Cuba was forced to sell its surplus to Communist countries which, in turn, dumped some of their purchases on the world market at low prices. In 1974, by contrast, sugar prices rose rapidly.

Tin. An International Tin Council embracing seven producing countries has been operating since 1956 but has not always been able to control prices. Inherent in this scheme is the establishment of a central buffer stock with funds provided by the individual member nations. When a surplus of tin developed in 1958, the buffer stock method failed because the members did not have the funds to pay for the metal that would go into the buffer. Export quotas were then decreed, but world prices of tin continued to fall. With production curbs in effect, the supply was decreased and when demand increased in 1961, producers were unable to increase output rapidly. As a consequence, the price of tin rose to a high level. In 1974 the International Tin Agreement's price policy was not operating because of tight supply.[24]

Benefits of Cartels

The benefits claimed for cartel agreements may be set forth in outline as follows:[25]

Lower Costs of Production.
1. Methods of production are standardized by means of mutual agreement.
2. Rate of production is kept at a more uniform level.
3. Competitive overexpansion is reduced.
4. Risk premium is less. Less stock is necessary to meet unexpected demands.
5. Cartel research institutes are established, patents and processes pooled.
6. Problems of management are solved in mutual conference.

Lower Marketing Costs.
1. Advertising is done by cartel rather than by individual enterprise.
2. Terms of trade are uniform, preventing unfair competition.

---

[24]"Cartels for Basic Raw Materials?" *loc. cit.*
[25]Kreps, *op. cit.*, pp. 13,081–13,082.

3. Transportation expenses to uneconomical markets are eliminated through allocation of markets.

Smoothing Cyclical Variations.
1. Greater equilibrium between productive capacity, production, and consumption is obtained.
2. Rate of employment is less subject to severe fluctuations.
3. Prices are kept at a more stable level.

Obstacles to Success of Cartels

As the foregoing examples illustrate, the cartel is subject to serious limitations as a means of restraining competition. Not the least of these is the independence of members which gives rise to difference of opinions on policy. As a result some national combines are riddled with internal dissensions and constantly threatened with disintegration. This condition is accentuated when the concept is extended to the international field, such as when the International Steel Cartel had to contend with overproduction by German manufacturers. Another problem arises when quotas are established since it may be more profitable for a member to produce in excess of quota because the fines incurred are less than the losses incurred by curtailing production.

Another obstacle to the success of a cartel is the incentive of each member to produce in excess of allotments during one period in order to support a contention for a larger quota during a subsequent period. This difficulty is especially present in pooling arrangements. Unless effective disciplinary measures can be imposed, a member may at any time violate an agreement and precipitate open competition. An historical example of cartel instability is provided by the International Zinc Cartel which was forced to disband late in 1929 because of "overproduction by the new plants in Norway, France, and Silesia and the announced intention of one of the American producers to change Mexican shipments to Europe from 70,000 tons of concentrate to 30,000 tons of refined metal annually. . . ."[26] Reconstructed in 1931, the cartel was again dissolved in 1935 due to rising nationalism and monetary difficulties. Constantly changing economic and political world conditions make it difficult to stabilize industry positions for extended periods of time.

Difficulties of international agreements are further intensified by differences in the conditions prevailing in each of the constituent countries. Such differences make it difficult to negotiate an agreement and leads to continuous dissension which often results in dissolution of the agreement.

Government policies sometimes present disturbing problems for the members of a cartel. Such policies may relate to protective tariffs

---

[26]*Commerce Reports* (March 3, 1930), p. 556.

or to efforts encouraging the establishment of national industries free of foreign affiliation or control. For example, (1) British interests in several international cartels and agreements have been hindered when the British government refused to give its sanction, and (2) the absence of American producers from direct participation in some cartels is partially traceable to uncertainty caused by the antitrust laws in the United States.

The difficulties inherent in loose forms of agreement have led firms to seek more effective forms of combination. The highest degree of such combination is the merger, a phenomenon that is especially characteristic of the United States and has been increasingly important in Great Britain and other industrial countries. The merger is not necessarily a monopoly, but it is a combination in which the merged companies lose their independent identity. Many multinational firms are the result of such mergers by American and other firms.

This chapter has attempted to present the chief characteristics of trading combinations with which American firms must either compete or collaborate. In the case of industrial raw materials, the United States and other industrial nations are the buyers of these products and are thus directly affected by any agreements to stabilize trade or prices.

The strength of any national industry in world competition is dependent upon its strength within its own national sphere. The strength of American firms, faced with national and international combines of the scope described, derives partly from the powerful organizations that have developed in this country within the framework of antitrust legislation and from the facilities provided by the Webb-Pomerene Act. The success of these multinational organizations is recognized throughout the world, but, increasingly, they are being subjected to competitive pressures and to governmental restrictions.

QUESTIONS

1. Why did Congress pass the Webb-Pomerene Act and give American exporters privileges they do not have in domestic trade?
2. What gains would American firms expect from participation in a Webb-Pomerene association? What limitations on their marketing policy might result from this participation?
3. Why have Webb-Pomerene associations not become more numerous?
4. What changes appear to be occuring in European antitrust policy that might affect U.S. multinational firms?
5. What is a cartel?
6. How does OPEC affect the marketing of oil?
7. Why might the U.S. as a major consuming nation enter into international commodity agreements with producing nations?
8. What kinds of internal pressures sometimes cause cartels to be less effective than their proponents desire?

9. Why have most international combines been concerned with raw materials and basic manufactured products rather than innovative high technology products?
10. What is the current status of the agreements on oil, coffee, tin, and sugar? Does the U.S. participate in any of these agreements?

SUPPLEMENTARY READINGS

"The Birth of OPEC and How It Grew." *Business Week* (January 13, 1975).

Leary, Thomas J. "Acquisition Activity of Webb-Pomerene Firms, 1951–1958: A Policy Suggestion." *The American Journal of Economics and Sociology* (July, 1972).

Martin, Everett G. "Protecting Prices: Tin Pact May Emerge as a Model for Future Raw Materials Groups." *The Wall Street Journal*, April 21, 1976.

U.S. Federal Trade Commission. *Annual Report*.

U.S. Federal Trade Commission. *Webb-Pomerene Associations: a 50 Year Review*. Washington: U.S. Government Printing Office, June, 1967.

U.S. Federal Trade Commission. *Export Trade Associations, 1963* Washington: U.S. Government Printing Office.

20

Marketing to Centrally Planned Economies

U.S. trade with Eastern Europe and Socialist Asia represented only 2.3% of U.S. exports in 1974 and 1% of its imports. These trade statistics, however, understate the interest of American entrepreneurs. Trade with the Socialist nations has grown with the thaw in the Cold War, albeit in an irregular fashion. Detente brought hopes for increased trade built upon expectations resulting from the immense population of these countries, spurred by a desire for economic development, and aided by the wealth of natural resources within these countries and their emerging purchasing power. Recently, conditions have modified some of the American optimism following detente.

This chapter provides a brief history of East-West trade and a discussion of its present potential and obstacles. The structure for foreign trade organization in Russia and the People's Republic of China is presented to show strategy alternatives and the methods of demand creation. Marketing to these countries is emphasized since the internal marketing structure and policy is largely outside the influence of foreign entrepreneurs.[1]

A separate chapter was devoted to the Socialist countries because of their unique character resulting from government ownership or control of resources and the emphasis placed on central planning. In this discussion the Eastern countries include Bulgaria, Czechoslovakia, German Democratic Republic, Hungary, Poland, Romania, the USSR, People's Republic of China, Mongolia, North Korea, and Vietnam. Although the countries differ in the structure of their economic relations with the West, it is convenient to discuss them as major markets: the USSR, China, and Eastern Europe (excluding the USSR).

---

[1]For a discussion of marketing *within* the Eastern European and Soviet countries see Thomas V. Greer, *Marketing in the Soviet Union* (New York: Praeger Publishers, 1973) or Charles S. Mayer, "Marketing in Eastern European Socialist Countries," *University of Michigan Business Review* (January, 1976), pp. 16–21.

EAST-WEST TRADE IN PERSPECTIVE

The United States had maintained trading relationships with the Eastern countries, both before and after their emergence as centrally planned socialist economies. Commerical exchange with China began as early as 1784 when the *Empress of China* unloaded a cargo of ginseng at Canton.[2] Similarly the U.S. had traded with Czarist Russia before the Bolshevik Revolution. The U.S. also traded with these nations in the early periods of their present governments. In 1950 the U.S. share of China's total trade was 22.5 percent and two-way trade totaled $191 million. In 1931 the USSR absorbed over 60 percent of U.S. machine tool exports and three fourths of our tractor and forging equipment exports.[3] In fact, the U.S. Export-Import Bank was formed in 1934 to expedite trade with the USSR. World War II disrupted normal trading relations with the Soviets and Eastern Europe and trade was further stymied by the Korean War and the Cold War tensions of the 1950s.

The U.S. began a program to control exports of U.S. goods and technology to the East as part of an economic containment policy. This was formalized in the Export Control Act of 1949 and reinforced by the formation of COCOM (a coordinating committee made up of NATO allies, excluding Iceland and including Japan) which established a standard list of items that were not to be exported to Communist countries. In 1950 a total embargo was placed on exports to the People's Republic of China and the most-favored-nation status for Communist countries was revoked by the Trade Agreements Extension Act of 1951.

During the late fifties and sixties U.S. trade with the East fell behind that carried on by Western Europe, which had expanded its trade with Eastern Europe by purchasing oil and raw materials while exporting capital goods. In the 1960s Canada, Japan, and Western Europe extended most-favored-nation treatment, provided credits for the Russians and Eastern Europe, and began lowering import restrictions. In contrast, in 1964 the U.S. cut off government credits for agricultural exports to communist countries and in 1968 prohibited export credits for the duration of the Vietnam War.

A change of American policy began to emerge in 1969 when the Export Administration Act was passed, endorsing trade in peaceful goods with any nation with which the U.S. had commercial relations.

---

[2]William Clarke and Martha Avery, "The Sino-American Commercial Relationship," *China: A Reassessment of the Economy*. A compendium of papers submitted to the Joint Economic Committee Congress of the United States (Washington, D.C.: U.S. Government Printing Office, July 10, 1975), pp. 502–509.

[3]Rogers Morton, *The United States Role in East-West Trade: Problems and Prospects* (Washington, D.C.: U.S. Government Printing Office, August, 1975), Appendix A.

As amended in 1972, the act exempted wide categories of exported goods from the validated licensing requirements.[4]

In early 1972 the Shanghai Communique was signed during a presidential visit to China as the U.S. and the PRC moved to facilitate bilateral trade. The communique stated that "Both sides view bilateral trade as another area from which mutual benefits can be derived, and agree that economic relations based on equality and mutual benefit are in the interest of the peoples of the two countries. They agree to facilitate the progressive development of trade between their two countries."[5] Following this communique Americans were invited to the Chinese Export Commodities Fair at Canton, and by June 1973 both the U.S. Liaison Office in Peking and the PRC Liaison Office in Washington had opened to assist business and promote trade.

A U.S.-USSR Trade Agreement in 1972 provided that (1) the Soviets would place large orders in this country, (2) government commercial offices would be opened in Moscow and Washington, (3) office facilities for private firms and government trading would be established, (4) both governments would cooperate to avoid disruption of their domestic markets through exports from the other country, and, most important, (5) each country would treat exports from the other country in a non-discriminating fashion (most-favored-nation status).[6] Another agreement was signed whereby the USSR would be treated equally with other countries by the Export-Import Bank. As a result of these agreements, and Russian grain and technology requirements, U.S. exports to Russia climbed sharply from $161 million in 1971 to $1,188 million in 1973. Later the Jackson-Vanik Amendment to the trade act denied MFN status and Export-Import Bank loans to countries denying their citizens the right to emigrate or imposing more than a nominal tax on emigration. Furthermore, Congress limited extension of Export-Import Bank credits to the USSR to $300 million over a four-year period. In January 1975 these Congressional actions led the Soviets to reject the 1972 U.S.-USSR Trade Agreements.

U.S. trade restrictions have had little effect on the volume of total East-West trade, but there is some evidence that Western Europe and Japan have gained relative to the U.S., since Russians and East Europeans bought where they were able to obtain export credits from local governments. Sometimes they purchased from the subsidiaries or licensees of U.S. multinationals in Europe and Japan.[7] In other

---

[4]"Trading with the U.S.S.R.," *Overseas Business Report, OBR 74-01* (Washington, D.C.: U.S. Government Printing Office, January, 1974), p. 9. A validated license authorizes exportation of specific goods to certain countries. It is used to control shipment of strategic goods and is issued only upon formal application.

[5]Clarke and Avery, *op. cit.*, p. 534.

[6]Morton, *op. cit.*, pp. A9–A10.

[7]"The U.S. Trade Lag with Eastern Europe," *Business Week* (February 23, 1976), pp. 44–51.

instances American traders have had to arrange for private short-term credit with U.S. banks or by discounting Russian Foreign Trade Bank notes.[8]

Trade with centrally managed socialist nations has always been strongly affected by political as well as economic needs; recent trade is no exception. Yet trade is important to both the East and West. Concerning the USSR it has been said that:

"The potential for substantial trade between the U.S. and the U.S.S.R. is no longer just a theoretical possibility. It may be an ordeal for both parties, but the market and the mutual needs are there. A few years ago, when U.S. economic power was at its peak and American products and dollars were valued throughout the world, we did not need the Russians. But faster than almost anyone could have predicted, the international economic climate has changed and now in many respects the U.S. needs Soviet business almost as much as the U.S.S.R. needs American grain and technology."[9]

Soviet Party General Secretary Leonid Brezhnev in a speech to the 25th Party Congress in 1976 clearly explained the interrelationship between trade and politics when he said, "In foreign economic relations politics and economics, diplomacy and commerce, industrial production and trade are woven together. Consequently, the approach to them and management of them must be integrated, tying into one knot the efforts of all departments, and our political and economic interests."[10]

MARKET POTENTIAL

Researching the potential market in centrally planned economies is difficult. Theoretically, the country plans should provide information for foreign markets, but changing technology and market conditions can make a five-year plan obsolete before its completion. With regards to the Chinese, the plans are considered State secrets. Consequently international marketers observe progress reports on plan fulfillment, monitor trade statistics showing exports from other nations, and check themes and products offered at trade fairs to determine future trends in purchases and assess market potential.

---

[8]"Soviet Union: A Cash Pinch Slows Trade with the U.S.," *Business Week* (December 1, 1975), p. 33.

[9]Marshall Goldman, *Detente and Dollars* (New York: Basic Books, Inc., Publishers, 1975), p. 267.

[10]Quoted in Jack Brougher, "U.S.S.R. Foreign Trade: A Greater Role for Trade with the West," in the Joint Economic Committee Report, *Soviet Economy in a New Perspective* (Washington, D.C.: U.S. Government Printing Office, October 14, 1976), p. 686.

Exports and Imports: 1968–1975

Table 20-1 (page 402) presents export and import data from 1968 to March 1975 showing U.S. trade with individual Socialist countries. The data indicate a rapid increase in U.S. exports to these countries, rising tenfold during the period 1968–1974. During the same period imports from these countries increased fivefold. Thus, the U.S. increased its favorable balance of trade with the East. The increase in both total exports and imports is steady, but there is variation in the individual country totals.

Growth of U.S. exports is attributable to a number of factors. Some of the structural and political factors were discussed in the previous section. In addition, the dollar devaluations in 1971 and 1973 made U.S. goods less expensive. A large demand for technology to modernize the Eastern economies has been a major factor in the growth of U.S. exports. Export gains in agricultural products to meet crop shortages have been substantial as illustrated by the USSR grain purchase in 1972.

In 1974 Eastern Europe accounted for slightly over one third of U.S. exports to Socialist countries. Romania and Poland, the only two Socialist countries having most-favored-nation status with the U.S., represented 80 percent of this market. They are eligible for Export-Import Bank credits.

Data for the People's Republic of China show the non-existence of trade before 1972, but a very rapid growth until 1974 when exports to the PRC almost equalled those to Eastern Europe and, in that year, exceeded exports to Russia.

Trading Relations of the Centrally Planned Economies

Figure 20-1 (page 403) illustrates the trading relations of the USSR and Eastern Europe in 1973. The largest volume of trade occurred between the USSR and Eastern Europe but significant trade took place between the Industrial West and both Russia and Eastern Europe. Much of the Russian and Eastern European trade is conducted under bilateral trading agreements and is influenced by country commitments as members of the Council for Mutual Economic Assistance (CMEA), a group of European Socialist countries designed to promote and integrate trade among themselves. Under these agreements the USSR supplies Eastern European countries with fuel and raw materials and in return imports machinery and manufactured goods from them. These long-term bilateral agreements specify the products to be exchanged. Figure 20-1 illustrates that in 1973 the U.S. had a very small share of the trade; only $2.3 billion of the total trade of the USSR and Eastern Europe involved the U.S.

Table 20-1   U.S. EXPORTS TO AND IMPORTS FROM SOCIALIST COUNTRIES: 1968–1974, AND JANUARY–MARCH 1975 [Thousands of Dollars]

Country	1968	1969	1970	1971	1972	1973	1974	Jan.–Mar. 1975
Exports, including reexports[1]								
Total	215,024	249,288	353,645	384,242	882,690	2,490,711	2,239,070	618,082
U.S.S.R.	57,728	105,547	118,712	162,013	542,214	1,194,651	609,248	276,323
East Europe	157,296	143,739	234,932	222,212	276,909	606,416	822,388	271,522
Albania	8	18	4	16	217	221	485	554
Bulgaria	4,036	4,645	15,294	4,353	3,543	6,474	22,260	11,469
Czechoslovakia	13,956	14,363	22,512	38,726	49,993	72,087	48,860	12,294
Ger. Dem. Rep.	29,047	32,373	32,545	25,441	17,473	28,025	20,913	2,146
Hungary	11,194	7,252	28,263	27,873	22,613	32,956	56,446	30,167
Poland	82,375	52,694	69,915	73,271	113,642	350,039	395,642	140,941
Romania	16,680	32,394	66,399	52,532	69,428	116,614	277,782	73,951
PRC	—	—	—	—	[2]63,537	689,596	807,425	70,236
Mongolia	—	2	1	2	19	31	9	1
North Korea	—	—	—	—	—	—	—	—
North Vietnam	—	—	—	[3]15	[3]11	[3]17	—	—
General Imports								
Total	200,755	197,819	226,514	228,522	353,957	592,940	1,006,856	242,147
U.S.S.R.	58,453	51,504	72,312	57,225	95,536	220,072	350,223	78,994
East Europe	139,976	143,953	153,463	165,792	225,034	306,152	540,428	124,930
Albania	283	396	151	279	470	488	484	1,477
Bulgaria	3,731	1,598	2,431	2,614	2,872	4,458	8,399	9,377
Czechoslovakia	23,756	24,063	23,892	23,597	27,972	35,162	45,562	10,980
Ger. Dem. Rep.	5,934	8,018	9,394	10,136	10,336	10,516	14,129	2,905
Hungary	3,848	4,077	6,224	7,751	12,725	16,736	75,407	13,261
Poland	96,871	97,835	97,946	107,641	139,172	182,856	265,931	68,918
Romania	5,553	7,966	13,425	13,774	31,487	55,936	130,516	18,012
PRC	[4]	24	1	[5]4,922	32,422	64,874	114,680	38,072
Mongolia	2,326	2,338	738	583	965	1,842	1,525	151
North Korea	—	—	—	—	—	—	—	—
North Vietnam	—	—	—	—	—	—	—	—

Source: *East-West Foreign Trade Board Report* (Washington: GPO, First Quarter, 1975).

[1]In this table, the term "reexport" refers to an export from the U.S. of foreign origin goods. Elsewhere in this report "reexport" refers to the shipment of U.S. origin goods from one foreign country to another.

[2]This figure does not include shipments of about $550,000 from Guam, which are not considered to be U.S. exports in Bureau of Census statistics.

[3]Data are for surgical supplies shipped under validated license.

[4]Less than $500.

[5]No imports were received directly; all came by way of third countries.

Note. — Exports are shown by area of destination. Imports are credited to the area in which the merchandise was originally produced, not necessarily the area from which purchases and shipments were made. General imports represent merchandise entered immediately upon arrival into merchandising of consumption channels plus commodities entered into bonded customs warehouses for storage.

U.S. exports to North Korea were embargoed in July 1950, and those to People's Republic of China, Manchuria, and Outer Mongolia were embargoed the following December. On July 26, 1954, exports to North Vietnam were embargoed. In February 1972, a list of commodities eligible for export to the People's Republic of China under general license, parallel to the general license list for Eastern European countries, was published and other commodities were made eligible for consideration for validated licenses.

Imports from North Korea and the People's Republic of China were placed under license control on December 17, 1950 through the Foreign Assets Control Regulations of the Treasury Department. On May 5, 1964, license control of imports from North Vietnam was added to these regulations. In June 1971, a general license was established authorizing importation without restriction of goods from the People's Republic of China. Under the regulations in effect prior to June 10, 1971, the importation of goods from the People's Republic of China was prohibited without license by the Treasury Department and it was generally contrary to the policy of that agency to license such imports, except goods for noncommercial purposes which, effective December 22, 1969, were permitted by general license. Some items of People's Republic of China origin, however, continued to appear in the statistical records of U.S. imports. In U.S. import statistics, goods originating in the People's Republic of China are credited to that country regardless of the last country from which they were shipped.

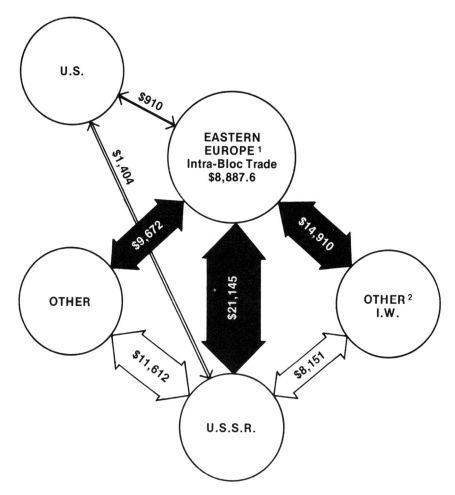

1. **Bulgaria, GDR, Czechoslovakia, Poland, Hungary, Romania.**
2. **Canada, W. Germany, France, United Kingdom, Belgium-Luxemburg, Sweden, Norway, Switzerland, Italy, Denmark, Austria, Netherlands, Japan.**

Source: Morton, *The United States Role in East-West Trade: Problems and Prospects* (Washington, D.C.: U.S. Government Printing Office, August, 1975), Appendix A.

Figure 20-1 MAJOR EASTERN EUROPEAN TRADING RELATIONS — 1973

Figure 20-2 (page 404) illustrates similar trade relations for the PRC in 1973. Again the U.S. share is small, although a larger share is held by other Western nations. The small share between the PRC and the USSR reflects the adverse political relations between these two countries. In the 1950s about one half of China's trade was with the USSR, but this share declined sharply following the split between the two countries. China's dependence on the USSR during the 1950s is explained by its political sympathy for the USSR, the advantage of conducting trade between planned economies, the availability of the Soviet market and Soviet credit, and to some degree the existence of trade controls by the Western nations.[11] Most of these advantages did not exist in 1973.

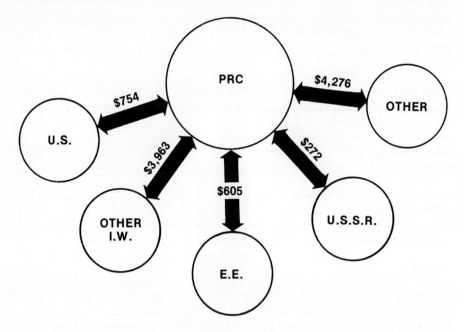

Source: Morton, *The United States Role in East-West Trade: Problems and Prospects* (Washington, D.C.: U.S. Government Printing Office, August, 1975), Appendix A.

Figure 20-2 MAJOR PRC TRADING RELATIONS — 1973 (Millions of Dollars)

U.S. Department of Commerce Estimate of Trade Potential

The Department of Commerce has estimated potential trade between the U.S. and the socialist countries for 1980. The estimate assumes normalized trading conditions among the countries, aggressive effort by U.S. business to foster trade, and continued efforts by the socialist countries to modernize their industry by importing technology. Table 20-2 illustrates the department's estimates.

In 1980 it is estimated that the U.S. will export $7.2 billion to socialist countries while importing $3.9 billion. Thus, a favorable trade balance of $3.3 billion is expected. Manufactured goods should account for 62.5% of U.S. exports and represent 67.7% of exports to the USSR. Total trade with Eastern Europe ($4.2 billion) is assumed to approximately equal that with the USSR ($4.4 billion), but imports

---

[11]Feng-hwa Mah, *The Foreign Trade of Mainland China* (Chicago: Aldine Atherton, Inc., 1971), pp. 19–21.

from Eastern Europe are expected to be greater ($1.8 billion vs. $1.2 billion) while exports to the USSR should exceed those to Eastern Europe. The department estimates total trade with China to be about $1.7 billion or 2.7 times its level in 1974. Exports to the PRC are expected to be twice the level of imports and it is anticipated that manufactured exports will be almost double the exports of agricultural products.

Table 20-2 POTENTIAL LEVELS OF U.S.-SOCIALIST COUNTRY TRADE IN 1980, ASSUMING NORMALIZED TRADING CONDITIONS (Billions of Dollars)

U.S. exports to:	Eastern Europe	USSR	PRC	Total
Total	2.4	3.1	1.7	7.2
Manufactured goods	1.3	2.1	1.1	4.5
Agricultural goods	1.1	1.0	.6	2.7
U.S. imports from:	1.8	1.3	.8	3.9
U.S. trade balance	.6	1.8	.9	3.3

Source: Morton, *The United States Role in East-West Trade: Problems and Prospects* (Washington, D.C.: U.S. Government Printing Office, August, 1975), Appendix A, p. C-3.

Barriers to Trade

Before accepting the above estimates, however, U.S. marketers should recognize several barriers:

1. Trade between the East and West always has been and continues to be strongly affected by the political as well as the economic considerations.
2. The estimates assume "normalized" conditions, however, in 1976 only Poland and Romania were accorded most-favored-nation status. Both U.S. and Eastern country tariffs currently limit trade.
3. Financial handicaps to trade exist since the U.S. does not provide credit to support export sales to the degree that government credit is available to English, French, and Japanese companies. Furthermore, the Johnson Debt Default Act limits Eastern countries' ability to raise funds in the U.S.
4. The data indicate a continued dominance of U.S. exports over imports from these countries, thereby reducing the supply of hard currency in the Eastern nations.
5. The physical location of the U.S. relative to the socialist countries is a deterrent to trade relative to nearby countries.

6. The organization for trade and business practices within the socialist countries is not as well-known to American marketers as the structure and practices in Western markets. This last barrier is being overcome, albeit slowly.

TRADING ORGANIZATIONS

State trading organizations differ from the arrangements found in the free market. The State has a monopoly on foreign trade and controls the trade to conform to its overall plans. In this section the USSR and PRC organizations are described as examples of State trading.

Soviet Foreign Trade Organizations

Foreign trade in the USSR is a state monopoly administered by the Ministry of Foreign Trade. Figure 20-3 indicates the major Soviet organizations involved in foreign trade. An overview of the primary functions of these organizations is useful for understanding the marketing situation and procedures.

The USSR is a centrally planned economy. A major responsibility of the State Planning Committee (Gosplan) is the development of long-range, five-year, and annual plans for the economy, including foreign trade. The five-year plan sets targets for production, investment, and output mix for the economy. The annual plan is more specific and details production quotas and resource allocations for industries and regions. These plans are established using estimates of production and input requirements of the enterprises which are, in turn, coordinated by the planning agencies and formulated into preliminary plans. Final plans are approved by the Council of Ministers and have the force of law.[12]

There are three major foreign trade plans: (1) the plan for exports and imports; (2) the plan for delivery of equipment and materials for projects outside the Soviet Union; and (3) a balance of payments plan.[13] These plans are important in coordinating foreign trade with the other economic plans, although exports and imports do not always conform to these plans and some plans are adjusted to meet changing foreign market conditions or revised national plans. Thus, a marketing opportunity may arise although a firm's products were not involved in the original plan.

---

[12]"Basic Data on the Economy of the Union of Soviet Socialist Republics," *Overseas Business Report*, OBR 74-25, pp. 4–6.

[13]Lawrence J. Brainard, "Soviet Foreign Trade Planning," in Joint Economic Comittee Report, *Soviet Economy in a New Perspective* (Washington, D.C.: U.S. Government Printing Office, October 14, 1976, p. 699.

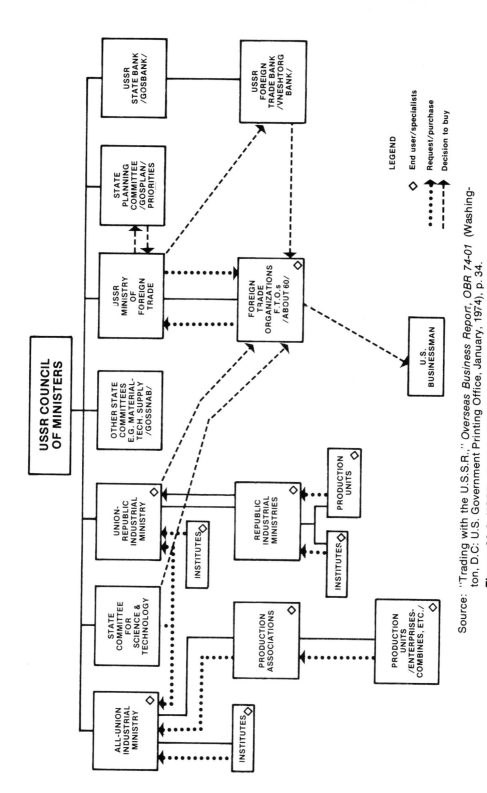

Source: "Trading with the U.S.S.R.," *Overseas Business Report, OBR 74-01* (Washington, D.C: U.S. Government Printing Office, January, 1974), p. 34.

Figure 20-3 USSR ORGANIZATIONS IN FOREIGN TRADE

The State Committee for Science and Technology is responsible for supervising all scientific and industrial research in the USSR. It is influential in selecting foreign suppliers of technology and equipment for high priority projects.

The Ministry of Foreign Trade has primary responsibility for planning and administering all foreign trade. It establishes commercial relations with foreign countries and carries on such activities as directing the work of Soviet trade representatives abroad and regulating trade payments and customs policy. For the foreign trader, a most important group of agencies is the Ministry's All-Union Foreign Trade Organizations (FTOs). The FTOs specialize in the export and/or import of specific commodities and act as intermediaries between the foreign seller and the Soviet end-user. They are responsible for negotiating contracts with foreign companies and, in general, operate under normal commercial principles. Westerners must approach the appropriate FTO and carry out negotiations with it. The FTO acts as an independent organization conducting business in its own name for end-users. Soviet end-users provide the FTO with an import requisition and the FTO contacts foreign firms to select a supplier. Although the FTOs negotiate contracts with foreign firms, actual buying decisions are made by end-users.

Vneshtorgbank is in charge of all payments related to foreign trade. The Soviet Foreign Trade Bank issues credit to the FTOs, provides advice on financial terms in contract negotiations, and guarantees commercial paper issued by the FTO. The bank has correspondent relations with banks in more than one hundred countries.

The USSR Chamber of Commerce and Industry is composed of more than 1500 members including FTOs and industrial enterprises. It promotes Soviet foreign trade by organizing trade fairs abroad and in Russia, helps foreign marketers contact the appropriate FTO, handles patents and trademarks, and aids in adjusting commercial disputes by means of its Foreign Trade Arbitration Commission.

Contacting the Soviet Market

The United States marketer can make direct contact with Soviet Foreign Trading Organizations in Moscow or may contact one of the Soviet representatives in the U.S. Contact may be made through Amtorg, a Russian-owned firm based in New York. This company represents the FTOs and knows their needs. It seeks buyers for Soviet products and contacts American manufacturers to supply merchandise needed by the FTOs. Approaching the Soviet market by means of Amtorg is less time-consuming and less expensive than direct contact in Moscow; however, it is not always useful to companies seeking licensing or turnkey operations. [14] The Kama Purchasing Commission, also

---

[14]Robert E. Weigand, "Selling Soviet Buyers," *Business Topics* (Spring, 1976), p. 17.

located in New York, functions as a channel for FTOs involved in automotive procurement projects.

Two other approaches may be used to contact the Soviet market. (1) For smaller firms consultants and sales agents from the U.S. and Western Europe can be used. These agents obviate the need for the substantial investments required for direct contact. Although the USSR often prefers direct contact, these agencies may be familiar with Soviet bureaucracy and thus facilitate sales. (2) The Soviet market also may be approached through European subsidiaries of American firms when the subsidiary's country has an established trading relationship with the USSR.

The People's Republic of China

Trade between the U.S. and PRC was effectively shut off from 1950–1971. Since the Shanghai Communique it has grown rapidly.

Recent Trade Trends. Traditionally the Chinese have viewed exports as a means of payment for necessary imports and the PRC has striven for a balance between exports and imports. However, during the early 1950s the PRC developed an unfavorable balance of trade as it exported minerals, agricultural products, and consumer goods for Russian raw materials and machinery including complete factories. Later trade surpluses were used to repay the Soviet debts and import industrial equipment. Since 1972 the PRC has turned to heavy purchases of complete factories and equipment in order to develop its technology bases.[15] Imports from the U.S. have included eight large ammonia plants, ten Boeing 707 jets and accessories, as well as automotive gear-cutting equipment, satellite earth stations, petroleum explorations, and off-highway trucks. The major portion of U.S. exports to the PRC, however, have been agricultural products. In 1974 the seven leading U.S. imports from China were cotton fiber, tin, rosin, artworks and antiques, fish, and clothing. These represented about sixty percent of U.S. imports from the PRC.

PRC Trade Organization.[16] Foreign trade is a state monopoly in the Peoples' Republic of China and is controlled through the Ministry of Foreign Trade (see Figure 20-4). Foreign Trade Corporations of the Ministry act as agents for end-users and conclude all contracts with foreign firms. The national economic plans are the ultimate authority

---

[15]Clarke and Avery, *op. cit.*, p. 515.

[16]See Eugene E. Theroux, "Legal and Practical Problems in the China Trade," *Joint Economic Committee Report* (Washington, D.C.: U.S. Government Printing Office, July 10, 1975), pp. 535–549; Central Intelligence Agency, *People's Republic of China: International Trade Handbook* (Washington, D.C.: U.S. Government Printing Office, Sept., 1974); U.S. Department of Commerce, "Trading with the People's Republic of China," *Overseas Business Report 73-16* (Washington, D.C.: U.S. Government Printing Office, May, 1973).

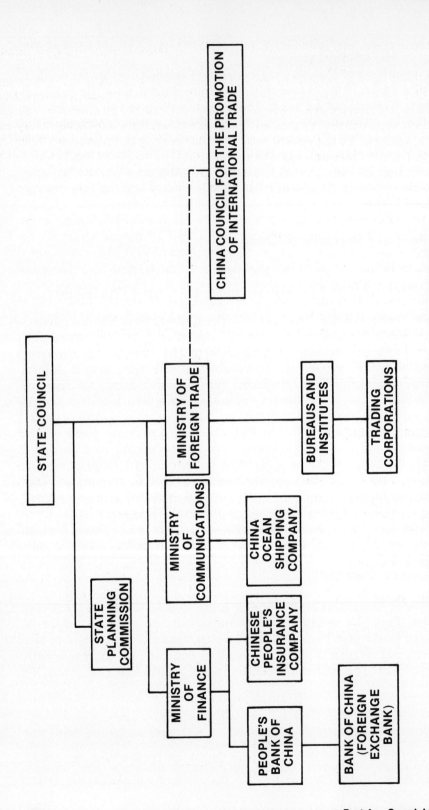

Figure 20-4 FOREIGN TRADE ORGANIZATION OF THE PEOPLE'S REPUBLIC OF CHINA

Part 4   Special Issues

for these contracts. (The fifth Five-Year Plan began in 1976.) Details of these plans are State secrets and are never released; thus they provide no guidance for the foreign marketer who desires to export to the PRC.

The China Council for the Promotion of International Trade (CCPIT) has a Legal Affairs Department to advise the CCPIT's Foreign Trade Arbitration Commission, Maritime Arbitration Commission, and other agencies of any trade-related legal developments abroad. The council assists foreign companies and countries in setting up exhibitions and symposia in the PRC and is responsible for China's trade exhibitions abroad. It also publishes periodicals on China's foreign trade.[17]

The appropriate FTC in Peking is the main contact for the foreign marketer in negotiating with the PRC. This FTC can be contacted directly or through agents of the FTC in Hong Kong. The U.S. Liaison Office in Peking can aid marketers with advice on contacting FTCs and appraising commercial opportunities in China.[18] Any proposal submitted to the FTC should include (1) information on the firm's background, including corporate structure and product lines; (2) a concise, but comprehensive proposal to allow technical evaluation and stressing benefits to PRC; (3) technical information, and (4) expression of a desire for invitation to the Chinese Export Commodities Fair or a desire to invite a PRC delegation to the U.S. or an offer to take a delegation there.

TRADE PROMOTION

Developing the market for Western products in the centrally planned economies presents special problems. The planning process itself, the relative inaccessibility of end-users and government influentials, a dearth of market information, and differences in promotional facilities and techniques all require special attention from Western marketers. Various forms of trade promotion are used to overcome these obstacles.

Trade Fairs

Trade fairs play an important promotional role in the Soviet Union, Eastern Europe, and the PRC. Many Western companies consider the trade fair one of the most effective ways to present their products to a large number of end-users and government personnel. The fair facilitates face-to-face contact between the firm's representatives and members of the FTOs' relevant industrial ministries and

---

[17]Theroux, *op. cit.*, pp. 539, 540.
[18]U.S. Department of Commerce, *Trading with the People's Republic of China, op. cit.*, p. 5.

planning authorities, as well as technical experts. The fair also provides information on competitive products that are exhibited.

At the large international trade fairs in Leipzig, Poznan, Brno, and Budapest both domestic and foreign participation are permitted. In Eastern Europe specialized international exhibitions built around a theme or industry are of interest to Western marketers because they may indicate which industries are to be given priority in the current plan.[19] These specialized fairs attract technicians interested in learning the latest available technology of their industry. So-called national exhibitions are organized around the products of a single foreign country. These may carry a variety of consumer and industrial goods or be limited to the products of an industry.

The importance of the trade fair is nowhere more evident than in the PRC.[20] The Chinese Export Commodities Fair (also known as the Canton Fair) is held bi-annually and combines trade negotiations with exhibits. Attendance is by invitation only and is limited to business representatives in market economies. The largest representations have been from Hong Kong and Japan, but some 220 American firms attended the Spring 1975 Fair. As a measure of its importance, the Fair has accounted for 35–40 percent of annual Chinese exports; however this percentage may decrease since the Chinese planned 10–12 "minor" fairs in 1976 in several cities and representing specific industries.[21]

Company Seminars and Exhibits

Lectures and seminars at fairs and exhibits and company organized symposia have been effective promotional tools in Eastern Europe to present technical data on a company's products. Attendance may be restricted to potential purchasing influentials, and presentations do not include competitive products. The seminars require detailed planning to assure attendance; the very success of this tool has prompted widespread use and fair attendees have only a limited time for participating. Poor attendance has led a number of companies to develop mobile displays that visit end-users at factory or office sites to deliver a company message designed to meet specific needs of the end-user.[22]

Advertising

Advertising was long opposed by traditional Marxists who considered Western advertising to be a means of solving a problem of

[19]Business International, *Doing Business with the USSR* (Geneva: Business International S.A., 1971), p. 69.

[20]Theroux, *op. cit.*, pp. 543–555.

[21]"China Augments Its Big Kwang Chow Fair with Shows in Other Cities in Push to Put '76 Trade Balance in Black," *Marketing News* (November 5, 1976), p. 3.

[22]Business International, *Eastern Europe Report* (May 28, 1976), pp. 163, 164.

underconsumption. These traditionalists thought planning could be used instead to coordinate production and consumption. Indeed, little advertising was needed for consumer goods that were in short supply prior to recent years. However, beginning in the 1950s Soviet Bloc advertising became more receptive to Western advertising techniques when a conference of the Bloc declared advertising benefits to be "molding taste, developing demand, forming new tastes, broadening the knowledge of consumers, speeding the turnover of goods and services."[23] Recently advertising has been used to adjust consumption to output and, in some instances, has even been used to reduce demand for specific items.

Despite some recent growth the advertising effort in the European Socialist countries still is weak by Western standards. Its role is considered educational and informative but must not create competition among brands;[24] yet some forms of "competitive" advertising are appearing in the Soviet Union. *Business Week* reported one instance of a TV advertisement in *Commercial Bulletin*, a Soviet magazine for the marketing trade: a front cover illustration of a TV was labelled "The Novelty of the Year — Horizon 107" and copy for another model claimed it was "the only first-class TV set in the country."[25] Such developments and past increases in advertising expenditures, portend a greater role for advertising in the socialist marketing systems.

Advertising agencies exist in Eastern Europe. These, too, are government monopolies and all advertising by foreign exporters must be channelled through the agency. The agency generally restricts its services to advertising functions such as media selection, copy and art work, public relations, organization of symposia, and direct mail.[26] It seldom conducts market studies or consumer surveys often associated with the American or European agency. Hungary and Czechoslovakia each have two agencies with equal access to media. The Soviet advertising agency, Vneshtorgreklama, was established in 1964 both to publicize Soviet products in foreign markets and to publicize foreign goods in the USSR.

A wide range of advertising media is available in Eastern Europe. Costs for advertising in these media tend to be low according to Western standards as the media do not rely on advertising for revenue. Print media include mass circulation newspapers, specialized periodicals aimed at trade officials, and technical and industrial journals. Television, radio, newspapers, cinema, and outdoor advertising can be

---

[23]D. Levy, "Advertising Comes to the Soviet Union," *Canadian Business* (December, 1962), pp. 60–67. Quoted in Leslie Szyslaki, "Advertising in the Soviet Bloc," *Journal of Advertising Research* (June, 1974), p. 14.

[24]Charles S. Mayer, *op. cit.*, p. 20.

[25]Russia Discovers Madison Avenue," *Business Week* (September 8, 1975), p. 41.

[26]International Trade Center UNCTAD/GATT, *Exporting to the Socialist Countries of Eastern Europe: a Guide to Marketing Techniques*, (Geneva: International Trade Centre, 1971), p. 213.

used to reach consumers. For industrial goods the technical and industrial journals, company catalogs, and direct mail are useful. In Russia the State Committee for Science and Technology maintains a State Scientific Library network (SSTL) that distributes industrial catalogs received from private companies to approximately 10,000 information bureaus throughout the Soviet Union; these catalogs inform end-users of technical developments. Similarly the Committee reviews, translates into Russian, categorizes by end-user industries, and publishes in the *New Industrial Catalog* much advertising that appears in foreign publications.[27]

Personal Contact and Negotiation

Advertising in Soviet and Eastern European publications, direct mail, and industrial catalogs are important informational media sometimes serving as supplements to exhibitions in trade fairs, but they are not sufficient substitutes for personal contact with agencies and users. Negotiating sessions inevitably involve personal contact. Negotiations over major contracts require Western export representatives capable of answering technical questions and having the authority to negotiate.

Both the Chinese and Russians have reputations as hard bargainers. They usually possess a thorough knowledge of the background and product line of the foreign firm and pay vigorous attention to contract details. The specific language of the contract must be analyzed in detail since both Russians and Chinese adhere strictly to the written contract terms and expect sellers to do likewise. Provisions such as "force majeur," guarantees, arbitrations, etc., need to be explicit since interpretations differ widely as do patent and trademark rights.

Negotiators for Western firms often are high company executives but continuity of representation also is important in developing business relationships with the bureaucracy. Negotiations over licensing and turnkey contracts can take several years. To maintain relations some firms expecting large sales to Russia may even request permission to establish a Moscow office. However, such offices are expensive, sometimes costing $250,000 to several million dollars per year to staff and support them.[28]

PROSPECTS FOR EAST-WEST MARKETING

The opening of trade with the People's Republic of China, detente with the Russians, and recent technology sales caught the imagination

---

[27]Weigand, *op. cit.*, p. 19.

[28]"Soviet Trade: The Disappointments Continue," *Business Week* (December 6, 1976), p. 100.

of American marketers. Many saw a large, relatively untapped market for American goods. Recent events have somewhat discouraged such speculation. Although some companies have achieved commercial success, many American firms are re-evaluating their commitments to the Eastern markets.

Major obstacles to increased Chinese trade involve consideration of the status of Taiwan, the settlement of American claims for assets that were nationalized and blocked Chinese assets held under Foreign Asset Control regulations, most-favored-nation status for the PRC, as well as a lack of information regarding Chinese plans. Individual marketers have problems in assessing Chinese demand and market conditions and conforming to trade regulations. Nevertheless, it seems apparent that mutual benefits can be gained if marketers heed the following advice:

> "Americans should be quick to realize that China is not a market for 50 million automobiles or refrigerators, but a highly selective one dependent on the dictates of Peking's planning. To the extent the PRC chooses to emphasize rapid, national economic growth in the years ahead, the market for some American products, particularly those of a more advanced nature appears good. To be successful, and there are successful American businessmen in the China trade, one requires large amounts of patience and a fine appreciation of Chinese decision making and commercial practice."[29]

Similarly, trade with the USSR and Eastern Europe indicates considerable long-run potential but is subject to political influences, including the emigration issue and American refusal to establish most-favored-nation status to most of these countries. A major limitation to trade growth has been the restriction on governmental trade credits available to the USSR and the rapid growth of indebtedness of some Eastern European countries.

During 1971–1975 Soviet world trade doubled, but trade with the developed Western countries tripled. Soviet leaders now appear to believe that trade can facilitate both Soviet economic development and Soviet participation in world affairs.[30] They have initiated new forms of industrial cooperation and proposals have been made to improve foreign trade planning and to relate Soviet domestic production costs to world prices. In addition the Soviets attempted to diversify by exporting more manufactured goods, although exports continue to be dominated by fuels and raw materials. In 1975 the Soviets experienced trade deficits with the West, despite the earlier increases in world fuel and materials prices due to widespread recession and inflation in the West and large imports from the West. These developments and a low Western demand for Soviet manufactured goods may limit short-run growth in trade.

---

[29]Clarke and Avery, *op. cit.*, p. 531.
[30]Jack Brougher, *op cit.*, p. 678.

Any analysis of East-West prospects must consider assumptions regarding political policy as well as economic analysis. Recently the hazards of political forecasting regarding East-West relations have become apparent. Trade between the Eastern and Western countries has shifted; trade between the USSR and China or between the U.S. and China provides evidence of this. Economic analysis of trade and growth rates for Eastern countries is further impeded by incomplete and non-comparable data. Nevertheless the logic of trade interaction and economic growth appear to make autarky a less feasible future alternative for both the East and West.

QUESTIONS

1. Trace the major developments affecting East-West trade since World War II.
2. What factors account for the recent growth of U.S. exports to the socialist countries?
3. How important is the role of U.S. trade with centrally planned economies relative to trade among these countries? How do you account for this relationship?
4. How did U.S. trade in the most recent year for which information is available compare with the estimates for 1980 prepared by the U.S. Department of Commerce?
5. Why is the trade fair useful to American manufacturers first presenting their products to the USSR or the PRC?
6. How does Soviet advertising differ from that in the U.S.?
7. Of what significance is the statement that "both Russians and Chinese adhere strictly to the written contract"?
8. How significant are the activities of Soviet Foreign Trade Organizations (FTO) for American exporters to the USSR?
9. What product groups are major U.S. imports from the USSR and PRC?
10. What "special problems" of market development does the American marketer face in selling to the USSR or the PRC?

SUPPLEMENTARY READINGS

Business International. *Doing Business with the People's Republic of China*. Hong Kong: Business International, 1973.

Business International. *Doing Business with Eastern Europe*. Geneva: Business International S.A., 1972.

Business International. *Doing Business with the USSR*. Geneva: Business International S.A., 1971.

Goldman, Marshall I. *Detente and Dollars*. New York: Basic Books, Inc., Publishers, 1975.

Joint Economic Committee, Congress of the United States. *China: A Reassessment of the Economy*. Washington, D.C., U.S. Government Printing Office, July 10, 1975.

Joint Economic Committee, Congress of the United States. *Soviet Economy in a New Perspective*. Washington, D.C. U.S. Government Printing Office, October 14, 1976.

Mah, Feng-hwa. *The Foreign Trade of Mainland China*. Chicago: Aldine Atherton, Inc., 1971.

Starr, Robert. *East-West Business Transactions*. New York: Praeger Publishers, 1974.

Weigand, Robert E. "Selling Soviet Buyers," *Business Topics*. East Lansing, Michigan: Graduate School of Business Administration, Michigan State University, Spring, 1976.

Index

92; foreign licensing, 86; foreign operations, 84; joint venture, 90; management contracts, 92; other strategies, 91; ownership strategy, 88; into world market, 79

Europe: distribution trends for retailers in, 184; as representative market grouping, 140; Western, factors affecting market structure in, 183

European Coal and Steel Community, 141

European Economic Community, 27, 129; antitrust policy of, 387; effect on market structure of Western Europe, 183; as representative market grouping, 141

European Free Trade Association, 129, 142

European Investment Bank, 299

European Parliament, of European Economic Community, 142

evolving structure, 150

ex (point of origin) price, 285

exchange rate fluctuations: agree-upon exchange rate, 62; international trade profits, 61; effects on price quotations, 61; exporter's protection against, 61; hedging, 62; importer's protection against, 63; indirect risks of, 63; price levels, 64

exchange rates: depreciation of, 64; by country, 58

exchange restriction plan, 66

exchange restrictions: administration of, 67; effects of, 68; systems of, 68

Eximbank, see Bank, Export-Import

Export Administration Act, 398

export barriers, 83; boycotts, 84; exchange barriers, 84; import quota, 83; nontariff barriers, 83; tariffs, 83

export commission houses, 172

Export Control Act of 1949, 398

export cooperation, 380

export credit insurance, see insurance

export department, built-in, 152; separate, 154

Export-Import Bank (U.S.), 296; financing fields of, 296; role in trade promotion, 373

exporting: active, 82; casual, 82; as entry strategy, 80

export manager, duties of, 154

Export Management Company, 151

export merchants, 172

export organization: built-in export departments, 152; Export Management Company, 151; separate export departments, 154

export pricing, see price

exports: country shares of, 15, 17; as share of domestic production, 41; value of U.S., 39

exports, U.S., to socialist countries (1968–1975), 401

Export Trade Act, see Webb-Pomerene Act

Export Trade Associations, 384

F

factors, 317; credit guarantees of, 317; as international marketing intermediaries, 174

FAS (Free Alongside) prices, 287

financial agencies, U.S. government, function of, 295

financial and development policy, U.S. Department of State, 364

firm: ethnocentric, 126; individual, 33, 34; geocentric, 126; polycentric, 126

floating exchange rates, 54, 69

floating exchange system, 56

FOB (Free on Board) prices, 286

foreign collections, see collections

foreign credit, see credit

foreign credit insurance, see insurance

Foreign Credit Insurance Association, 297, 318; types of policies, 318

Foreign Credit Interchange Bureau, 312

foreign exchange, 9; administration of exchange restrictions, 67; control of, 65; direct government intervention, 66; objective of restriction plan for, 66

foreign operations, 84; establishing, 85

Foreign Service: and trade promotion, 365; and trade protection, 365; see also U.S. Department of State

Foreign Trade Arbitration Commission, PRC, 411

Foreign Trade Corporations, PRC, 409

Foreign Traders Index, 368

Foreign Trade Statistics, Guide to, 104

foreign-trade zones: advantages for U.S. importers, 357; significance to international marketer, 355

franchising, 87, 88

free exchange market, see multiple exchange rates

free of damage insurance, see insurance

free of particular average insurance, see insurance

free trade area, 131

free trade association, 131, 132

freight forwarder, 199, 200

freight rate quotations, 199

freight rates: commodity, 199; general cargo, 199

funds, international marketing, sources of, 290

future exchange, 59

G

General Agreement of Tariffs and Trade (GATT), 83

general average damage, 212

General Inter-American Convention for Trademark and Commercial Names Protection 331

gold standard, international, 54

government: influences of packaging and labelling, 236; influences on pricing, 282; influences on product standardization, 226

grid structure, 164

gross national product, U.S., 40

guarantees, for financing by Export-Import Bank, 296

guarantees, credit, 301, 316, 317

H

hedging, 62
hybrid structures, 164
hypermarket, 185, 266

I

import commission houses, 172
import department, built-in, 153
import entry, 201
importers: government agencies as, 349; types of, 347
import facilitating agencies, types of, 350
importing, 344; determining market demand for, 345; determining purchase motivation for, 345; documentation and, 347; locating and negotiating with sources of supply, 346; physical distribution, 346; process of, 345
import merchants, 172
import quotas: absolute, 354; tariff-rate, 354; types of, 354
imports: appraisal of merchandise, 352; dutiable status of, 352; as percentage of new supply, 41; U.S. dependence on, 37; value of U.S., 39; value to consumers and industry, 42
imports, U.S., from socialist countries (1968–1975), 401
indents, 172
indicators, general economic and market, 98
indices, multiple factor and single factor, 98
Indus Water Treaty, 129
insurance: all risk, 211; export credit, 318; for financing by Export-Import Bank, 296; free of damage, 211; free of particular average, 211; marine, 210–212; named perils, 211; self-, 317
insurance agents, see agents
insurance coverage charges, 211
insurance policies, special, 213
integration, economic, 129
Inter-American Convention for the Protection of Inventions, Patents, Designs, and Industrial Models, 332
Interamerican Development Bank, loan activities, 299
interchange or ledger experience, as credit information source, 312
Interministerial Price Commission, 283
International Advertising Association, 245
International Bank for Reconstruction and Development, 298
International Bureau of the World Intellectual Property Organization, 332
International Chamber of Commerce, 339
International Coffee Agreement, as example of cartel action, 392
International Development Association, 299
international division: geographical organization of, 158; influence on corporate policy, 158; international headquarters company, 160; product organization, 157; regional management centers, 158–161; structure of, 156–158
International Finance Corporation, 298
international headquarters company, 160
international market, see world market
international marketing information systems, see market information
international marketing intermediaries, 171; brokers, 174; characteristics of operation, 171; export commission houses, 172; export merchants, 172; factors, 174; import commission houses, 172; import merchants, 172; manufacturer's export agent, 173; trading companies, 175; use of confirming house, 174
international marketing organization, 166
International Monetary Fund, 55, 65
international monetary system, see monetary system
international product life cycle, theory of, 24–26
international purchasing power parity, 64
International Sugar Agreement, cartel action, 393
International Tin Council, cartel action, 393
international trade, see trade
international trade channels, see marketing channels
international trade policies, U.S. Department of State, 364
International Union for the Protection of Industrial Property, provisions of, 331
investments, direct foreign, 18; book value of, 19; importance for individual companies, 20; locations of, 47; theory of, 24; by U.S., 46
investments, international national gains from, 32
investments, portfolio, see portfolio investments
issuer, of letter of credit, 303

J

Jackson-Vanik Amendment, 399
joint venture, 90, 91
Journal of Consumer Research, 6
Journal of International Business Studies, 6
Journal of Marketing, 6
Journal of Marketing Research, 6

K

Kama Purchasing Commission, 408

L

labelling: cultural considerations, 236; design, 235; governmental influences on, 236

landbridges, 196
Latin American Free Trade Area, 129; as representative market grouping, 143
law, antidumping, 274
law, code, 329
law, commerical: business organization recognized by, 334; codification of, 329; use of commercial register, 333
law, commercial and corporation, 333; bankruptcy under, 336; examples concerning influence on packaging and labelling, 237; taxation under, 336; use of power of attorney under, 335
law, common, 329
law, patent, 332
law, trademark, 329
laws: affecting U.S. importers, 353; effect of variation on marketing, 8; influence of ecological concerns of packaging, 237
leasing, 275, 276
letters of credit, 210, 303; advantages to buyers, 307; advice to, 325; confirmed, 306; essential parties to, 303; export, 307; foreign currency, 306; irrevocable, 306; local currency, 306; operation of transaction of, 323; revocable, 306; revolving, 306; unconfirmed, 306
licensing, foreign, 86, 87
lighter aboard vessel, 193
limited liability companies, 334, 335
limited partnerships, 334
liquidation, 353
litigation, 316
loans: Cooley, 297; direct, as financing field of Export-Import Bank, 296; discount, as financing field of Export-Import Bank, 297; soft, 299
London Court of Arbitration, 339

M

Madrid Agreement Concerning the International Registration of Trademarks, 331
Major Projects Program, 372
management contracts, 92
manufacturer-distributor relationship, 179
manufacturer's export agent, 173
marine insurance, see insurance
market analysis: development of marketing plan, 100; screening, 97, 99; sources of information, 104; two-phase approach to, 95
market analysis, comparative, 107
market demand: determining for importing, 345; effect on product standardization 223
market entry, 94
market entry strategies, see entry strategies
market grouping, representative, 140–144
market information: development of systems to monitor, 107; list of periodicals, 110; sources of, 105
market indicators, see indicators
marketing, comparative, 7
marketing, implications for nation-state, 8–10

marketing, international, multinational, 4, 6; differences in domestic marketing, 5; and individual firm, 33; reasons for increased U.S. interests in, 48
marketing channel, 166; in developing countries, 181; effects of industrialization on, 182; factors affecting choice of, 168, 170; variations, 168
marketing combinations: characteristics, 390; types abroad, 387, 389
marketing environment analysis, 103
marketing plan, 100; formulation and implementation, 101; informational base, 102; for resale and use of products in importing, 347
marketing standardization, see standardization
marketing strategy, 100
market integration, regional see regional market integration
mass retailing, 184
master policy, 318
media, advertising: selection of, 253; in Western Europe, 254
mediation, see conciliation
medium-term policy, 319
Ministry of Foreign Trade, Soviet, 408
missionary selling, 263
mixed enterprises, 90
multinational agencies, see agencies
multinational company: 3, 149, 108
multinational enterprise, 27
multinational marketing, see marketing, international, multinational
multiple exchange rates, 67
monetary system, international: 54; effects of 1930s worldwide depression on, 54; post-World War II development of, 56; pre-World War II developments of, 54; recent developments of, 56
monopoly, see cartel

N

named perils insurance, see insurance
National Association of Credit Management, 312, 316
National Council of Physical Distribution Management, 188
National Foreign Trade Council, Inc., 375
nation-state: evolution of multinational firm, 10; implications for marketing, 8; monetary systems, 9; nationalism and business policy, 9; national security policies, 9; variable internal standards, 9; variations in laws and policies, 8
natural factor endowments, 23
New York Foreign Exchange Market, 57
New York State Arbitration Act of 1920, provisions of, 341
nontariff barriers, 138, 139

O

ocean bill of lading, see bill of lading
Office of Field Operations, U.S., 368

open account, as method of payment for export shipments, 301
opener, of letter of credit, 303
organizational adaptation, 150
Organization for Economic Cooperation and Development, 106, 377
Organization for European Cooperation, 141
Organization for Petroleum Exporting Countries, as example of cartel action, 391
ownership, percentage of, 89
ownership strategies, as entry strategies, 88

P

packaging: considerations for international company, 233; economic concerns, 237; effects of climate, 234; effects of family brand, 235; effects of income variations, 235; effects on package size, 235; effects of recycling, 237; effects of retailing and wholesaling systems, 234; effects of traditions, myths, taboos, 236; governmental influences, 236; in promotional mix, 243
packing: climatic considerations, 205; considerations for overseas shipments, 204; containerization, 208; customs duties, 206; customers requirements, 206; effects on freight rates, 205; expense of, 206; objectives of, 203, 204; palletizing, 208; pilfering as a factor, 205; reconciling safety and economy factors, 207; unitization, 207
palletizing, 208
Paris Union, 332
particular average loss, 212
patent filing, alternative international, 333
patents, 332
payee, 302
paying bank, see bank
penetration pricing policy, 270
People's Republic of China: recent trends in trade between U.S. and, 409; trade organizations of, 409
personal selling, see selling
physical distribution, see distribution
piggybacking, see allied company arrangement
pilfering, as packing factor, 205
policies: brand, 228; effect of variations on marketing, 8; international advertising, 246; service, 238
portfolio investment, 88
power of attorney, 335
price: demand-based, 274; domestic, 273; export base, 273; worldwide base, 273
price administration, Export Trade Associations, 384
price controls: direct, 282; effects on food and drug prices, 284
price levels: effects of inflation on, 65; influence on exchange rates, 64
price policy, 266; in basic marketing strategy, 269; objectives of, 268

price quotations: common, 285–289; elements of, 280; foreign currency, 279; other components, 281
price strategy, 269; variations in individual markets, 271
price-support programs, 283
pricing: difficulties for world markets, 266; governmental influence on, 282; involvement of marketing manager in 267; transfer, 277; worldwide system of, 273
private warehousing, 215, 315
produce, 219, 220; adaptation in world market, 78; culture-bound, 258; culture-free, 258
product design, see product standardization
production, domestic, exports as share of, 41
product life cycle, theory of, 271
product line: decision to market abroad, 222; factors affecting branding policy, 228
product standardization: compatibility with company resources and policy, 226; direct influence of government, 226; effect of market demand on, 223; effects on economics of plant and marketing operations, 225; environmental factors on product design, 227; indirect influence of government, 226
promotion, sales, 242; devices used in, 259; effectiveness of devices, 261; in-channel, 260; trade fairs, 260
promotional strategy, 241, 243
purchase motivation, determining for importing, 345

Q

quota, import, 83

R

Radiation Control for Health and Safety Act, 353
reexport, 356, 402
regional development banks, 299
regional management centers, 158
regional market integration: effects of economic growth on, 135; forms of, 130–133; political and social factors of, 136, 137; potential effects of, 133–137
registration, international, 332; trademark in code law countries, 329, 330
reserve currency, U.S. dollar as, 56
resident buyers, function in home market, 170
retailers: major European distribution trends for, 184; role in lesser developed countries, 182
retailing, international, price policies and, 272
retailing systems: effects on package design, 234; see distribution systems; see also marketing channels

roll on/roll off vessel, 193
royalty payments, and foreign licensing, 87

S

sales agents, credit guarantees of, 317
sales engineer, 263
sales missions, types of, 262
screening, in market analysis, 97
selling, missionary, 263
selling, personal, 242; importance of promotional mix, 264; as method of sales promotion, 261; role of distributor in, 262; sales functions in, 262
service: importance to value of product, 220; provisions of, 239
service policies, see policies
Shanghai Communique, 399
Sherman Antitrust Act, 382
shipper's export declaration, 200
Shipping Act of 1916, 198
shipping companies, 197
shipping conferences, 197
shipping documents, commercial and, government, 200
short-term policy, 319
sight draft, 302
skimming policy, 270
Smithsonian Agreement, 56
socialist economies, see centrally planned economies
soft loans, see loans
Soviet Foreign Trade Bank, 408
special customs invoice, 203
special tariffs, see tariffs
standardization: advertising, 257, 258; marketing, 125–126
State Committee for Science and Technology, Soviet, 408
subcultures, 114
subsidiaries, wholly-owned, 89
supertanker, see crude carrier
supply sources: locating and negotiating with, 346; U.S., 44

T

tariffs, 83; ad valorem, 83; specific, 83
taxation, under commercial law, 336
tenor, in payment of a draft, 302
total product concept, 220
trade, international, 7; among developed nations, 17, 18; among lesser developed nations, 17, 18; country shares of world exports, 17; direct foreign investment, 18; export/import data for, 15; growth of, 15; importance of U.S., 39; international product life cycle, 24; gains for individual firm, 33; multinational enterprise, 18; national gains from, 32; reasons for, 20; theory of comparative advantage, 22; theory of direct investment, 24; theory of natural factor endowments, 23

Trade Agreements Extension Act of 1951, 398
trade bills, see bill of exchange; see also drafts
trade centers, 371
trade channels, international, see marketing channels
trade disputes, 327; avoidance of litigation in settlement of, 342; commercial arbitration in settlement of, 338; conciliation and mediation, 337
trade fair: responsibilities of Department of Commerce, 371; role in centrally planned economies, 411; as type of sales promotion, 260
trademark, 229, 330; piracy, 330
trademark law, see law
trademark registration, see registration
Trade Opportunities Program, 368
trade organizations, People's Republic of China, 409
trade organizations, Soviet: major trade plans of, 406; organizational structure of, 407; primary functions of, 406; U.S. contact with, 408
trade promotion: in centrally planned economies, 411; evaluation by government, 377; influence on international marketing environment, 361; by private agencies, 375; by state and local units, 373; by supranational organizations, 376; U.S. government agencies involved in, 362
trader, 333; private, 347
trading company, function as international marketing intermediary, 175
transfer pricing, see pricing
transportation: air, 194; criteria for choosing for physical distribution, 189; intermodal developments for physical distribution, 196; land, 195; modern developments in, 191; sea, 192
Treaty of Rome, basis for antitrust policy of EEC, 387
trust fund, special progress, 299
trust receipt, 325
turnkey operation, international, 91

U

umbrella companies, 164
UN Conference on Trade and Development, 376
Uniform Commercial Code, 329
UN International Trade Center, 377
United Africa Company, 175
United Bureaux for the Protection of Intellectual property, 332
United Nations, and international trade and investment, 376
United Nations Documents Index, 106
United States: contact with Soviet foreign trade organizations, 408; customs values of merchandise, 353; dependence on foreign markets and resources, 37; direct foreign investment, 46; estimated trade potential with centrally planned

economies for 1980, 404; evolution of export credit insurance in, 318; foreign exchange in, 60; gross national product, 40; importance of international trade, 39; increased interests in international marketing, 48; as major exporter and direct investor, 49; markets for products of, 44; merchandise exports and imports of, 40; recent trade trends between PRC and, 409; sources of supply, 44; trade barriers between centrally planned economies and, 402

United States Arbitration Act of 1925, 342

United States Customs Service, 350; appraisal of merchandise by, 352; entry of goods through, 351; organization of, 350

unitization, in packing, 207

unit of quantity, in pricing, 282

United States Department of Agriculture, role in trade promotion, 373

United States Department of Commerce: organizational structure, 367; trade information and promotion services, 368

United States Department of State: economic activities of, 364; organizational structure of, 363

United States Department of Treasury, role in trade promotion, 373

United States Tariff Commission, 354; role in trade promotion, 373

USSR Chamber of Commerce and Industry, 408

USSR Ministry of Foreign Trade, 349

U.S.-USSR Trade Agreement, 399

W

warehouse entry, 351

warehouses: customs bonded, 350; public, 216

Webb-Pomerene Act, 380; basis for establishing, 381; geographical restrictions of, 382; limitations of, 386; problems of, 385; provision and interpretation of, 381, 382

Webb-Pomerene Associations, 383, 385

Western Hemisphere Trade Corporation, 161

West Indian Federation, 130

wholesalers, in developing countries, 182

wholesaling systems: effects on package design, 234; see distributions systems; see also marketing channels

World Bank, 298

world market: contact with, 79; factors of potential profit, 74; major entry strategies of, 74; need for executive interest in, 76; a philosophy for entering, 75; product adaptation, 78; staffing overseas operations, 77; stimuli for entering, 74; see also trade (international)

World Trader Data Reports, 315

worldwide geographic structures, 163

worldwide organization models, 161–164

worldwide product structures, 161, 162

Columbo Part   4/27

EMC

Matrix